OXFORD EARLY CHRISTIAN STUDIES

General Editors

Henry Chadwick   Andrew Louth

THE OXFORD EARLY CHRISTIAN STUDIES series includes scholarly volumes on the thought and history of the early Christian centuries. Covering a wide range of Greek, Latin, and Oriental sources, the books are of interest to theologians, ancient historians, and specialists in the classical and Jewish worlds.

Titles in the series include:

Origen and the Life of the Stars
A History of an Idea
A. Scott (1991)

Regnum Caelorum
Patterns of Future Hope in Early Christianity
Charles E. Hill (1992)

Pelagius' Commentary on St Paul's Epistle to the Romans
Translated with introduction and commentary by
T. S. de Bruyn (1993)

The Desert Fathers on Monastic Community
Graham Gould (1993)

Arator on the Acts of the Apostles
A Baptismal Commentary
Richard Hillier (1993)

Eunomius and the Later Arians
R. P. Vaggione (*forthcoming*)

The Christology of Theodoret of Cyrus
P. B. Clayton (*forthcoming*)

Arnobius of Sicca
Concepts of Deity in the Contemporary
Pagan–Christian Debate
M. B. Simmons (*forthcoming*)

Ascetics and Ambassadors of Christ

The Monasteries of Palestine
314–631

JOHN BINNS

CLARENDON PRESS · OXFORD
1994

Oxford University Press, Walton Street, Oxford OX2 6DP
Oxford New York
Athens Auckland Bangkok Bombay
Calcutta Cape Town Dar es Salaam Delhi
Florence Hong Kong Istanbul Karachi
Kuala Lumpur Madras Madrid Melbourne
Mexico City Nairobi Paris Singapore
Taipei Tokyo Toronto
and associated companies in
Berlin Ibadan

Oxford is a trade mark of Oxford University Press

Published in the United States
by Oxford University Press Inc., New York

British Library Cataloguing in Publication Data
Data available

Library of Congress Cataloging in Publication Data
Ascetics and ambassadors of Christ : the monasteries
of Palestine, 314–631 / John Binns.
Includes bibliographical references and index.
1. Monasticism and religious orders—Palestine—History.
2. Monasticism and religious orders—Jordan—History.
3. Monasticism and religious orders—History—Early church, ca.
30–600.   I. Title.
BR185.B56 1994   271'.0095694—dc20   93–48972
ISBN 0–19–826465–8

1 3 5 7 9 10 8 6 4 2

Typeset by Selwood Systems, Midsomer Norton
Printed in Great Britain on acid-free paper by
Bookcraft (Bath) Ltd.,
Midsomer Norton, Avon

PREFACE AND
ACKNOWLEDGEMENTS

Egypt, Palestine, and Syria were centres of church life during the Byzantine Empire. They were presided over by Archbishops who attained Patriarchal status, at Antioch, Jerusalem, and Alexandria. They each contained a vigorous monastic life.

The monastic life of Egypt is well known. The succinct wisdom of the *Apophthegmata Patrum* and the serene, ascetic *Life of Antony* have become widely read. And since the work published by Peter Brown, especially the 'Rise and Function of the Holy Man in Late Antiquity', the way of life of the monks of Syria has been carefully studied. In comparison, the monasteries of Jerusalem have been neglected.

This study is devoted to Palestinian monasticism. It has three parts. The first considers the main sources for our knowledge of the monasteries, the Lives of the saints, especially the series of seven *Lives* by Cyril of Scythopolis. The second part describes the environment in which the monasteries grew and which led to their distinctive characteristics. The third explores the activities and the achievements of the monks themselves. The whole provides a portrait of a society which was fully integrated into the life of the Church and Empire, using the testimony of the men who participated in the events.

The title shows one of the distinctive features of these monasteries. The monks were people who withdrew from the secular world of the city but also were conscious of belonging to it. This double vocation is shown most clearly in the contrast between the two best-known monks, Euthymius, who consistently sought the seclusion and silence of the desert, and Sabas, who, although a renowned ascetic, was involved in the life of the Church in Jerusalem to the extent of travelling to the imperial capital on two occasions to represent its interests. I have used the terms 'ascetic' and 'ambassador', with the qualification that this latter task was undertaken for the sake of Christ, to refer to these two aspects of the vocation. It is a theme which appears in several contexts; in the monks' awareness of history (Chapter 3), in the presence of monks in both city and desert environments (Chapters 4, 5, and 6), in their involvement in doctrinal dispute (Chapter 8), as well as in their approach to the monastic life (Chapter 7). A modern reader might note that this involvement in the society of the time was appropriate for monks who settled in the places where the Son of God was discovered fully involved in the life of first-century villages and city, even though the monks themselves would not have spoken of their monastic commitment in these incarnational terms.

The dates which form the temporal boundaries of the study are dictated by the primary sources here considered. The year 314 is the earliest date in which the first monastic church in the Jerusalem desert— at the laura of Pharan—could have been consecrated, and 631 is the year in which the last of the Lives of the saints, that of George of Choziba, was written. The first date nearly corresponds with the toleration of Christianity proclaimed by the so-called Edict of Milan in 313, and the second is also the year in which the True Cross was restored to Jerusalem by the Emperor Honorius. It is the Byzantine period of the history of the Palestinian Church.

I have referred to the area in question as Palestine throughout. In doing so, I have in mind the Roman provinces of Palastina Prima, Secunda, and Tertia, rather than any subsequent political entity.

Many people have helped me to understand the world of the monks. Stuart Hall supervised my research at King's College, London, research from which this book eventually emerged. John Peterson, Dean of St George's College, Jerusalem, invited me to spend some time as Visiting Lecturer, enabling me to visit a number of the sites. Yizhar Hirschfeld was generous in sharing his unique knowledge of the desert with me, both through lengthy conversation and some memorable visits, including an unforgettable Good Friday spent at the magnificent site of Khirbet ed Deir during the last weekend of his excavations there. Averil Cameron and John Wilkinson made many helpful suggestions. Yoram Tsafrir kindly provided me with material on the excavations he is conducting at Beth Shan which were unavailable in this country.

I carried out this study project while working as a priest in a London parish. I have received encouragement and support from the congregation of Holy Trinity Parish, Upper Tooting, my fellow clergy, and the church authorities. My wife Sue and son William have tolerated a ten-year obsession with remarkable patience and cheerfulness.

CONTENTS

LIST OF MAPS

ABBREVIATIONS

ACO	*Acta Conciliorum Oecumenicorum*
An. Boll.	*Analecta Bollandiana*
Annales esc.	*Annales, économies, sociétés, civilisations*
Apoph. Patr.	*Apophthegmata Patrum*
BASOR	*Bulletin of the American Schools of Oriental Research*
Bess.	*Bessarione*
BIHBR	*Bulletin de l'institut historique belge de Rome*
BJRL	*Bulletin of the John Rylands Library*
By. Z.	*Byzantinische Zeitschrift*
Byz.	*Byzantion*
CCL	Corpus Christianorum, serie Latina
Chron.	*Chronicle*
CS	Cistercian Studies (Kalamazoo, Michigan)
CSCO	Corpus Scriptorum Christianorum Orientalium
CSCO.S	Scriptores Syrii
CSCO.Ib.	Scriptores Iberii
CSEL	Corpus Scriptorum Ecclesiasticorum Latinorum
E. Or.	*Echos d'Orient*
ET	English translation
FT	French translation
GCS	Die griechischen Schriftsteller der ersten drei Jahrhunderte
GOTR	*Greek Orthodox Theological Review*
GRBS	*Greek, Roman, and Byzantine Studies*
HE	*Historia Ecclesiastica (Ecclesiastical History)*
H. Laus.	*Historia Lausiaca (Lausiac History)*
H. Rel.	Theodoret, *Historia Religiosa (Religious History)*
IEJ	*Israel Exploration Journal*
ILS	*Inscriptiones Latinae Selectae*
Irén.	*Irénikon*
Itin. Aeth.	*Itinerarium Aetheriae (Egeria's Travels)*
JRS	*Journal of Roman Studies*
J. Th. S.	*Journal of Theological Studies*
Kyrillos	E. Schwartz, *Kyrillos von Skythopolis*
LCL	Loeb Classical Library (London)
Mansi	J. D. Mansi (ed.), Sacrorum Conciliorum nova et amplissima collectio
Mart. P.	Eusebius of Caesarea, *Martyrs of Palestine*

MH	B. Flusin, *Miracle et Histoire dans l'œuvre de Cyrille de Scythopolis*
MO	A. J. Festugière, *Les Moines d'Orient*
MSR	*Mélanges de science religieuse*
MUSJ	*Mélanges de l'Université Saint Joseph*
NAWG	*Nachrichten der Akademie der Wissenschaften in Göttingen*
OLZ	*Orientalische Literaturzeitung*
Or. Chr. A.	*Orientalia Christiana Analecta*
Or. Chr. P.	*Orientalia Christiana Periodica*
Ovadiah	A. Ovadiah, *A Corpus of the Byzantine Churches in the Holy Land* (followed by either *no.* to indicate the number of the site, or *p.* to indicate the page in the summary and conclusions)
PEFQ St.	*Palestine Exploration Quarterly*
PG	Patrologiae cursus completus, Serie Graeca
PL	Patrologiae cursus completus, Serie Latina
PO	Patrologia Orientalis
POC	*Proche Orient Chrétien*
Prat.	John Moschus, *Pratum Spirituale (Spiritual Meadow)*
PTS	Patristische Texte und Studien
QDAP	*Quarterly for the Department of Antiquities in Palestine*
RAM	*Revue d'Ascétique et Mystique*
RB	*Revue Biblique*
RE Byz.	*Revue des études Byzantines*
REJ	*Revue des études juives*
RHE	*Revue d'histoire écclésiastique*
RHR	*Revue de l'histoire des religions*
ROC	*Revue de l'Orient chrétien*
RQ	*Römische Quartalschrift für christliche Altertumskunde und für Kirchengeschichte*
SBFLA	*Studii biblici Fransciscani liber annuus*
SC	Sources Chrétiennes
SCH	Studies in Church History
SEG	*Supplementum Epigraphicum Graecum*
SHG	Subsidia Hagiographica, Société des Bollandistes
St. Ans.	*Studia Anselmiana*
TS (I)	*Terra Santa, pubblicazione mensile della custodia franscescana*
TU	Teste und Untersuchungen zur Geschichte der altchristlichen Literatur
Vailhé	S. Vailhé, 'Répertoire alphabétique des monastères de Palestine' (followed by sect. no.)
V. Anton.	Athanasius, *Vita Antonii (Life of Antony)*
V. Char.	*Vita Charitonis (Life of Chariton)*

V. Geor. Choz.	Antony of Choziba, *Vita Georgii Chozibitae (Life of George of Choziba)*
V. Pach. Bo.	*Vita Pachomii (Bohairic Life of Pachomius)*
V. Pach. G1	*Vita Pachomii (First Greek Life of Pachomius)*
V. Porph.	*Vita Porpyrii (Life of Porphyry)*
V. Thds.	*Vita Theodosii (Life of Theodosius)*
V. Thecl.	*Vita Theclae (Life of Thecla)*
V. Thg.	*Vita Theognii (Life of Theognius)*
ZKG	*Zeitschrift für Kirchengeschichte*

I

Introduction: Ascetics and Ambassadors

DESERT AND EMPIRE

In the month of August in the year 377 a child was born to Paul and Dionysia, citizens of Melitene the capital of Roman Armenia. He was given the name Euthymius, derived from the word εὐθυμία, confidence. His parents selected this name because his conception, like that of the prophet Samuel, had taken place in response to prayer and was accompanied by divine visions. The voice in the visions said that the child 'will bear the name of confidence since at his birth he who grants him to you will give confidence to his churches'.[1]

Within a few months of the birth of this child the Arian Emperor Valens was killed at the Battle of Adrianople in 378, and was succeeded by Theodosius I (379–95).[2] This event brought to an end a period in which the church had suffered several vicissitudes. The Emperor Constantine had died in 337 and had been succeeded by, first, Constantius II (337–61) who had encouraged Arianism; then by Julian (361–3) under whom paganism had undergone a short-lived but powerful revival; then by Valens (364–78), another Arian. The new Emperor Theodosius was soon baptized, shared in the eucharistic life of the Church, and sought to promote its welfare. Cyril of Scythopolis begins his literary output with this sigh of relief at the arrival of the Christian Emperor.

The coincidence of these two events—the birth of a baby in Armenia and a battle in Thrace—is no chance but is ordained by divine providence. At the start of his work, Cyril presents his fundamental conviction that the ascetics of the tiny area of desert land to the east of Jerusalem are as essential to the welfare of Christendom as the Emperor

---

[1] *Kyrillos*, 9. 7–9.
[2] Ibid. 9. 15–10. 4.

in Constantinople or the Patriarchs of the great urban centres. Both have a part to play in the evolution of a unified, harmonious, orthodox Christian society. The Emperor fights the battles and promulgates pious laws while the saint struggles against evil. Without either of these actors the divine drama would falter.

For the monks, the little world of the monastic community and the universal dimensions of the Christian Empire interlock. They are aware of the potential impact on their lives of events which take place in the far-off imperial capital which can favour heresies or depose patriarchs. But they are also convinced that their work and witness sustains the Empire. The confused history of the fifth and sixth centuries is more than the backdrop to the actions of the monks on the narrow stage of the Judaean desert. It was a part of their life and demanded their concern. The history of the monasteries of Jerusalem and the history of the Church and Empire proceed together.

THE COUNCIL OF CHALCEDON

In early November two anxious men hurried from the capital to a small monastic community a few miles east of Jerusalem. Although Stephen and John were both bishops they were also monks and disciples of Euthymius, the abbot of a monastery a few miles east of Jerusalem. They had left the church of St Euphemia at Chalcedon, just across the water from Constantinople, where with over 350 other bishops—'almost all the bishops in the world' as Cyril slightly inaccurately claims—they had subscribed to the famous and controversial Definition. Earlier in the Council they had followed their archbishop Juvenal when he had made his dramatic change of sides, rising from his seat near to Dioscorus the Alexandrian patriarch and crossing over to sit on the other side of the church with the Antiochenes and the Constantinopolitans.[3] In the company of the rest of the bishops they had scrutinized the Tome of Leo and acclaimed, 'This we all believe. Peter has spoken through Leo; thus Cyril taught; Leo and Cyril teach the same.'[4] But they were also aware that the language of the Tome, and of the Definition of Chalcedon,

---

[3] For the change of sides by Juvenal, see *ACO* 2. 1. 1, p. 115; and for the number of bishops at Chalcedon, rather less in fact than the traditional number of 600, see M. Goeman, 'Chalkedon als "Allgemeines Konzil" ', in *Das Konzil von Chalkedon*, ed. A. Grillmeier and H. Bacht (Würzburg, 1951), 251–89, 261.

[4] *ACO* 2. 1. 1, p. 81. Cf. *ACO* 2. 1. 2, pp. 82–3, 102–3.

of which they carried a copy, was unfamiliar to members of the eastern churches and might not seem so convincing in the different atmosphere of the monastery. They remembered that only two years previously Bishop Auxolaus of the Encampments, John's predecessor, had been strongly censured by Euthymius for his behaviour at the 449 Council of Ephesus, and had died in disgrace soon afterwards. The announcement of the news of the Council's decisions to their community was a task which filled them with apprehension.[5]

Their anxiety was justified. Although Euthymius accepted the Definition as orthodox, the majority of the Church at Jerusalem did not. The words used to define the existence of the divine and the human in Christ led on this occasion to disagreement, conflict, violence, and death. This explosive potential of Christological discussion had overshadowed the history of the Church, and consequently the Empire, for the previous two decades and would continue to absorb the energies of emperor and episcopate for centuries to come. The sense that issues central to the faith and to eternal life are being discussed; the uncertainty, confusion, and hesitation over how to conduct the task of articulating them; and the speed with which these two emotions could break into open battle— these are presented in this incident of the two bishops and lie behind the history of this period.

Amidst the multiplicity of expression and experience which contributed to the Christian Church, two alternative approaches to Christology had emerged and engaged with each other.[6] The first was associated with Alexandria, and its Patriarch Cyril, who presided over the Church for thirty-two years, from 412–44, and from whose pen a mass of letters, sermons, and biblical commentary proceeded. It begins from the standpoint of the creed of Nicaea which defines belief concerning the second person of the Trinity in almost historical terms, beginning with pre-existence and consubstantiality with the Father, continuing through the stages of the Incarnation, and leading to glorification and final judgement. The continuity of experience of the second person of the Trinity who is the subject of the experiences of the life of Christ is the essential fact which lies behind the salvation of the world and which has to be maintained.

---

[5] *Kyrillos*, 41. 10–23.
[6] For summaries of the Alexandrian and Antiochene traditions of Christology, see A. Grillmeier, *Christ in Christian Tradition* (London, 1965), i. 414–520; J. Meyendorff, *Christ in Eastern Christian Thought* (New York, 1975), 13–28; R. V. Sellers, *The Council of Chalcedon* (London, 1961), 132–81.

The second approach was associated with the theological traditions of Antioch and was presented with clarity and a certain lack of sensitivity to popular piety by Nestorius, who was Patriarch of Constantinople for three years from 428 to 431. It was based on exegesis of the scriptures, especially the Gospel narratives with their blend of the sayings and actions of Christ, some of which describe human weaknesses—such as anger, hunger, ignorance, fear, pain, and death—and some of which describe divine power—such as healings, authoritative teaching, and the triumph of the Resurrection. Allied to this was a philosophical awareness that the categories of the divine and the human are necessarily distinct and cannot be blended into a single reality, as it was feared that Arius had done. It was—for them—of central importance to maintain the duality of Christ's natures. This approach could be combined fruitfully with western theology which, although using a different language and an alternative, more forensic view of salvation, was able to describe the duality and the unity of the experience of Christ in a confident and convincing fashion.

These two views had clashed twice at Ephesus, once in 431, when Nestorius was condemned, and more violently in 449. This Council, branded the 'Robber Council', or Latrocinium, by Pope Leo, had been dominated by Dioscorus of Alexandria, and had rehabilitated the notorious Eutyches; deposed the Patriarchs Flavian of Constantinople (who subsequently died of the injuries he received at the Council) and Domnus of Antioch, another disciple of Euthymius; and ignored the views of Pope Leo by refusing to read his Letter, or 'Tome', to Flavian. The result was 'a sort of Alexandrian dictatorship over the entire east', and action was demanded by Leo of Rome and the new Patriarch of Constantinople, Anatolius.[7] It left an impossible situation, and the new Emperor Marcian, an elderly Thracian senator who had found himself chosen as consort by the powerful Empress Pulcheria, sister of the former Emperor Theodosius II who had died in 450, summoned the bishops to Constantinople to resolve it. They finally met at Chalcedon, across the water from Constantinople, and held fifteen sessions from 8 October to 10 November 451.

The events at Chalcedon have often been described.[8] The Council was presided over by eighteen lay imperial commissioners, with personal intervention from the Emperor himself at the controversial sixth session

---

[7] J. Meyendorff, *Imperial Unity and Christian Divisions* (New York, 1989), 167.

[8] For one account of the events of the Council, see Sellers, *Council of Chalcedon*, 103–29.

at which the Definition was signed. These ensured formal procedure, orderly conduct, fair decisions, and also pressure to adopt a new definition of faith, which most of the delegates, committed to the maintenance of Nicaea, were reluctant to do.

The bishops gathered at Chalcedon were as successful as they could have been in the highly charged and controversial atmosphere left by previous councils. They affirmed that the Tome of Leo was in accordance with the teaching of Cyril of Alexandria, and 454 of them signed a Definition of Faith setting out an understanding of the person of Christ. The ability of the Council to formulate a definition shows that the fundamental unity of faith could be discerned and affirmed when the conditions were favourable. But the potential for division was a constant factor. At two points, especially, this disharmony was shown, and the sources of subsequent conflict were revealed.

The first came in the fifth session when a group of the bishops considered a statement of belief, probably composed by Anatolius of Constantinople. This contained the statement that Christ was a union 'of two natures', a phrase which, the lay presidents decided, would require the approval of the Pope himself. In order to avoid lengthy delay, another was produced in its place which stated that Christ's being was known 'in two natures'. Had the bishops been strenuous in their support for the traditional eastern formula of 'from two natures' later anxieties over the language of Chalcedon might have been allayed.

The second, and more ominous, sign of trouble to come was the refusal of monks led by Barsaumas to anathematize Dioscorus or even Eutyches. So here, in the atmosphere of Chalcedon with imperial encouragement in the direction of unity, the monks gave warning that they had no intention of compromising. This determination was the root from which would emerge the strain of Christian faith which, later, would resolutely refuse to compromise and would resist the efforts of successive emperors to bring unity either through patronage or persecution.

However, for the moment the imperial aim of a doctrinal consensus shared by Constantinople and Rome was achieved, and the bishops returned home uneasy but united. Opposition in Palestine and Egypt was overcome. In Palestine, the monks were mostly unconvinced by the explanation offered by Stephen, John, and others and elected a rival Patriarch, Theodosius, who opposed the Council and presided until 453 when Juvenal was restored by imperial troops. In Egypt, Marcian's authority ensured that Dioscorus' successor was the compliant Proterius, who accepted Chalcedon and was, as a result, unpopular with many Egyptians.[9]

But the Emperor Marcian died on 26 January 457: on 16 March Timothy Aelurus, that is 'the Weasel'—a nickname given to him because he was thin—was consecrated Patriarch of Alexandria: on 28 March the Chalcedonian Proterius was killed by the mob in his baptistery.[10] The new Emperor, Leo I, was, like Marcian, a Thracian officer. He decided to discover the feelings of the east before responding to this prompt exhibition of Egyptian public feeling. In late 457 he canvassed the opinions of all the eastern bishops, and some of the leading monks, over whether Timothy's consecration was valid and Chalcedon legitimate. The responses showed overwhelming support for Chalcedon and rejection of Timothy. So in 458 imperial troops moved into Egypt, ejected Timothy and installed another Timothy whose Greek surname, Salofaciol, is variously translated as 'White Turban' or 'Wobble Cap'. Ten thousand Egyptians lost their lives in the operation. So, for the quarter-century after Chalcedon, a blend of respectful handling of the bishops and the ruthless exercise of force enabled the emperors to maintain the unity of the Church in the east and the acceptance of Chalcedon.

THE FORGETTING OF CHALCEDON

In the year 516 the largest known gathering of monks in the city of Jerusalem took place. The occasion was the election of a new Patriarch, John. The word went round the desert that, as the price of his election, he had promised the imperial authorities that he would enter into communion with Severus, the Monophysite Patriarch of Antioch, and would anathematize the Council of Chalcedon. This was to take place at the Basilica of St Stephen, the largest church in Jerusalem, which had been built to the north of the city by the Empress Eudokia to house the relics of the first martyr.

A huge multitude gathered. There was the nephew of the Emperor, Hypatius; the dux Anastasius; the consul Zacharias. There were citizens of Jerusalem waiting to see which side the new Patriarch would support. Then there were monks. According to Cyril who claims to have checked

---

[9] W. H. C. Frend, *Rise of the Monophysite Movement* (Cambridge, 1972), 148–56.

[10] For Timothy's nickname being 'Weasel' rather than the widely held 'Cat', see R. Y. Ebied and L. R. Wickham, 'Timothy Aelurus, Against the Definition of the Council of Chalcedon', in *After Chalcedon* (Louvain, 1985), 115–66, 115.

the figures with eyewitnesses, 10,000 came together from the Holy City and the monasteries in the surrounding countryside. The imperial authorities waited for the Emperor's wishes to be carried out and for Chalcedon to be anathematized. The new Patriarch ascended the ambo with the two monastic leaders, Sabas and Theodosius, on either side. But then the proceedings started to diverge from the imperial plans. The crowd began to shout out again and again. 'Anathematize the heretics and confirm the council.' When the shouting died down the three rejected a list of heretics including all who did not accept the Council of Chalcedon. And Theodosius added for good measure. 'If anyone does not accept the four councils like the four gospels, let him be anathema!' In some surprise and confusion the dux Anastasius quickly left for the safer haven of Caesarea and the Emperor's nephew wisely opened his purse and gave generous presents to the Church of the Resurrection and the monasteries of the region.[11]

Even though the gathering led to the affirming of Chalcedon, the circumstances in which it took place were very different from those which prevailed at the death of the Emperor Leo forty-one years earlier. It happened in reaction to the policy of the emperors between Leo and Justin I, which was based on the view that the best way to solve the offence caused to many easterners by the Council of Chalcedon was to ignore it.

After Leo died, his brother-in-law Basiliscus and son-in-law Zeno both claimed the throne. In order to gain general support through the east, Basiliscus issued an Encyclical stating that the things transacted at Chalcedon were a novelty and that nobody should advance this faith. Nicaea was sufficient. But as a result of protest from Rome and Constantinople he changed his mind and quickly issued the Anti-Encyclical, contradicting the Encyclical. But, with the exception of Acacius, Patriarch of Constantinople, all the bishops of the east, who fifteen years earlier had affirmed Chalcedon at the request of Leo, subscribed to the first document, the Encyclical. Everybody was in agreement that Nicaea had affirmed the orthodox faith, but Chalcedon was of value only in so far as it confirmed the decisions of Nicaea. This 'optional' character of Chalcedon—in the minds of most of the easterners—suggested an alternative strategy in the pursuit of church unity. This was to forget that Chalcedon ever happened and go back to the situation which prevailed in 433 when the Formula of Reunion showed the possibility of agreement.

This was the approach adopted by Zeno who came to power in 476. He circulated a document called the Henoticon. This latter, originally addressed to the church in Egypt in 482, affirmed the Councils of Nicaea, Constantinople, and Ephesus (431). It went on: 'Anyone who thought or thinks otherwise, either in Chalcedon or at any other Council, we anathematize.' So while Chalcedon was not condemned, it was only referred to in a derogatory context as a place of potential error.[12] The resulting situation was summarized by the historian Evagrius: 'In those days the Council of Chalcedon was neither openly proclaimed in the most holy churches, nor was it rejected by all; each bishop acted according to his conviction.'[13] The policy of overlooking doctrinal difference bore fruit. It enabled enemies to become friends, as happened, for example, in Jerusalem when Marcianus and his supporters, who had been opponents of the Council of Chalcedon, re-entered into communion with Patriarch Martyrius in scenes of great jubilation.[14] But the tolerance, which was its strength, was also its undoing. It could survive only as long as the desire for unity prevailed over the desire for doctrinal rigour and accuracy.

The disruption of this uneasy truce came from the opponents of Chalcedon. These based their theological position on the more uncompromising elements of Cyril's theology and rejected the Council of Chalcedon as incompatible with this. By the mid-sixth century these various strands of opposition had hardened and united to form a distinguishable group with its own theological literature, a rootedness in local culture, and the beginnings of an ecclesiastical hierarchy, existing alongside that which was already established. This development came as part of a long-drawn-out process of theological reflection and historical development. The different aspects of this growing separatism can be conveniently understood through noting the different contributions of three men who were active in the period between 500 and 550.

Severus of Antioch was a theologian. He was born about 465 in

---

[12] The text of the Henoticon is in E. Schwartz, *Codex Vaticanus*, GR 1431 (Munich, 1927), 52–4, with an English version in Frend, *Rise*, 360–1. The suggestion made by the Henoticon that some of the bishops at Chalcedon might have been in error was, in fact, similar to the approach of the Council of Constantinople of 553.

[13] Evagrius, *HE* 3. 30, ed. Bidez and Parmentier, 125. 32–127. 4.

[14] *Kyrillos*, 66. 21–67. 20. This event has been incorrectly and unnecessarily dissociated from the Henoticon as a result of being dated too early. See below, Ch. 8.

Pisidia, the son of a landowner and grandson of a bishop who had spoken against Nestorius in 431. He had a good education and became a monk at Maiuma in Palestine. He resided at Constantinople from 508 to 511 and gained the Emperor's support. In a series of controversial works, sermons, and many letters he developed a rigorous yet sensitive exposition of Cyrillian Christology. He was careful to avoid the teaching of Eutyches which made the flesh of Christ different from that of the rest of humanity, and so emphasized the human nature of Christ in his theology. He became Patriarch of Antioch in 512 but fled to Egypt after the accession of Justin I in 518.[15]

Philoxenus was a Syriac speaker who knew no Greek, and became Metropolitan of Mabbug in 485. His theological writing was more dependent on scriptural citation than that of Severus and was characterized by an uncompromising hardness, a hatred of Chalcedon, and a passion for Syriac culture and language. He helped to forge the connection between Syriac culture, language, national identity, and the Monophysite faith that was to make a significant section of Monophysites so resistant to influence from Constantinople. He entered into a long struggle with Flavian of Antioch and was finally successful in deposing him in 511.[16]

Jacob bar Addai was a missionary. His work of setting up a Mono-physite hierarchy did not start until 542, by which time earlier Monophysite ordinations of priests had already been performed in east Syria by John of Tella between 530 and 537. Jacob was appointed Bishop of Edessa by Justinian in response to a request from his Arab Ghassanid allies. For 35 years he travelled through Asia Minor, Syria, Armenia, and Egypt ordaining bishops and priests. John of Ephesus reports that the result of his labours was a network of two patriarchs, twenty-seven bishops, and more than 100,000 priests.[17] While it is hard to identify the precise time when the Monophysites developed from being a movement within the church to becoming a separate institution, the ordinations of Jacob bar Addai played an essential part in this process. The basis of a new and independent church with its own

---

[15] For the theology of Severus and Philoxenus, see R. Chesnut, *Three Monophysite Christologies* (Oxford, 1976); J. Lebon, 'La Christologie du monophysisme syrien', in A. Grillmeier and H. Bacht (eds.), *Das Konzil von Chalkedon* (Würzburg, 1951), i. 425–580; Meyendorff, *Christ in Eastern Christian Thought*, 37–46.

[16] A. de Halleux, *Philoxène de Mabbog* (Louvain, 1963), 117–25.

[17] The ordinations are referred to in John of Ephesus, *Lives of the Eastern Saints*, ed. Brooks, PO 18 (1924), 690–7. See also S. Harvey, *Asceticism and Society in Crisis* (Berkeley, Calif., 1990), 100–8.

hierarchy was in place by 550 as a consequence of his enormous missionary enterprise.

The work of these three great men show different aspects of a movement which was becoming increasingly self-conscious in culture, was firmly rooted in the rural economy of certain areas, especially Egypt and parts of Syria, but extending to many parts of the Empire, and hostile to any intervention from Constantinople. While such a varied movement cannot be easily summarized, something of its deeply rooted independence is captured by the reaction of a group of Syrian women who were asked, in the reign of Tiberius II, to give up the form of the liturgical hymn, the Trisagion, introduced by Peter the Fuller in Antioch and used in Monophysite circles. 'We are but women,' they said, 'we know nothing about controversy, but from the tradition of the eastern fathers we will not depart as long as we live.'[18]

This vital and resilient movement had one weakness. The rigour which brought it into being also inclined it to fragmentation. It has been calculated that in Egypt alone there were, by the end of the sixth century, twenty Monophysite groups each claiming to be the pure and true form of the Christian faith.[19] This enabled overtures to be made to more moderate groups.

The incident in St Stephen's in Jerusalem, described at the start of this section, took place when the Monophysite movement was growing in self-consciousness and self-confidence. By this time, it had gained the support of the Emperor Anastasius, a pragmatic and devout emperor who was inclined to sympathize with Monophysitism. The Emperor had deposed Patriarch Elias and was wishing to appoint a candidate sympathetic to the Monophysite cause. This sign of the growth in confidence and influence of the Monophysites led to reaction from the Palestinian supporters of Chalcedon. It shows some of the features of this uncertain period between the accession of Zeno in 474 and the death of Anastasius in 518—an inconsistent and uncertain intervention by the Emperor; a decisive reaction from the monks; and an uneasy and

---

[18] Peter the Fuller, Patriarch of Antioch, introduced an interpolated form of the Trisagion, 'Holy God, Holy Mighty, Holy Immortal, who was crucified for us, have mercy on us.' This drew on Egyptian sources, and, in this form, was a hymn addressed to the second person of the Trinity, affirming him to be the subject of Christ's sufferings. It caused offence in Chalcedonian circles where the hymn was addressed to the Trinity, and came to be used as a declaration of anti-Chalcedonian feeling. See S. Brock, 'The Thrice-Holy Hymn in the Liturgy', *Sobornost* 7/2 (1985), 24–34. For the Syrian women, see John of Ephesus, *HE* 3. 3. 19, ed. Brooks, 108.

[19] Meyendorff, *Imperial Unity*, 254–5.

malleable episcopate. The formula was repeated on many occasions with the different participants supporting either side.

THE REINTERPRETATION OF CHALCEDON

A ragged but jubilant procession wound its way along the track that leads from Thekoa to the scattered network of cells high on the hills overlooking the Wadi el Jihar. There were over 100 monks, conspicuous in their black pallia and koukoulia against the grey rock of the harsh desert landscape.[20] It was a moment for which these monks had long been waiting. It was not long since they had been afraid to leave their monasteries. Those who had ventured to the Holy City had been jeered at, abused, and forced out of the gates with the cat-calls and stones of the townspeople flying around their ears. Now the bitter conflict with the Origenists was over. The decisive action of the Emperor in far-off Constantinople had brought to a close a dark chapter in the history of the monasteries, and troops had arrived to cleanse the headquarters of the heretics. The New Laura was theirs. Heretics had received their deserved punishment. Orthodoxy was triumphant. Victory had been won.[21]

These monks of Palestine were in the course of occupying a monastery which had been known for its advocacy of Origenism rather than for any distinctive Christological views. But the Council of Constantinople of 553 which had led to this outcome was the result of the new, and more decisive, religious policy of the Emperor Justinian (527–65).

This policy had begun to be applied at the accession of Justin I (518–27), Justinian's uncle. Both uncle and nephew were Latin speakers, Justin from Dardania and Justinian from Illyria, and shared the same outlook and ambitions. In their view, the Roman Empire consisted of the west as well as the east, and the Emperor was responsible, under God, for the harmony and unity of this divinely ordained and ordered society. The policy which they developed had two elements.

The first was the implementation of Chalcedon. This was enforced both because of the conviction of the emperors and also because it was essential for papal support. Within a week of Justin's accession, the

---

[20] The pallion is a black monastic cloak and the koukoulion is a hood. See Y. Hirschfeld, *Judaean Desert Monasteries in the Byzantine Period* (New Haven, Conn., 1992), 91–3.

[21] *Kyrillos*, 199. 1–200. 4.

names of the Chalcedonian Patriarchs of Constantinople, Euphemius and Macedonius, and even Pope Leo, had been added to the diptychs, and an annual celebration of the Council of Chalcedon was instituted. From that moment Chalcedon became part of the faith of the Byzantine Empire; future emperors did not alter this basic commitment. Neo-Chalcedonianism is one of the titles given in modern research to this new determination to regard Chalcedon as the basis for doctrinal unity.[22]

The second was loyalty to the teaching of Cyril of Alexandria. While the acceptance of Chalcedon enabled union with Rome, it also guaranteed the opposition of those who considered that the Council adhered to the heresy of Nestorius, later to be referred to as Monophysites, who formed, it is estimated, half the population of the eastern half of the Empire.[23] The affirmation of the theological views of Cyril of Alexandria should have appealed to Monophysites. The Emperor tried to encourage as many as possible into unity with the Church through a blend of patronage, theological persuasion, and brute force.

Friendship and patronage were offered by the Empress Theodora. She came from a humble background in Alexandria where, we are told by Procopius in a passage which raises the suspicion of an element of exaggeration, she was the daughter of a circus performer and had earned a living from prostitution.[24] This early life in Egypt, it can be presumed, had left her with a sensitivity to the popular Monophysitism of the area. Among her strategies to strengthen, and so gain the allegiance of, Monophysites, was to arrange the appointment of Theodosius, a friend of Severus, to the Patriarchate of Alexandria and Anthimus to Constantinople, both in 535. Later, after Theodosius had been deposed and Chalcedon was being imposed in Egypt, Theodora provided him with a home in the capital from where he was able to direct the growth of a separate Monophysite Church. Even the Imperial Palace housed a group of anti-Chalcedonian monks and ascetics.[25]

Her personal support of Monophysites, which was continued even

---

[22] For these events see A. Vasiliev, *Justin I* (Cambridge, Mass., 1950), 136–44. Neo-Chalcedonianism is described in P. T. R. Gray, *The Defense of Chalcedon in the East* (Leiden, 1979), and in C. Moeller, 'Le Chalcédonisme et le néo-Chalcédonisme en orient de 451 à la fin du VIe siècle', in Grillmeier and Bach (eds.), *Das Konzil von Chalkedon*, i. 637–720. Grillmeier prefers the term 'neo-Cyrillianism', see *Christ in Christian Tradition*, vol. ii. pt. 1 (London, 1987).

[23] Meyendorff, *Imperial Unity*, 17.

[24] The imperial couple are described in R. Browning, *Justinian and Theodora* (New York, 1981), 63–9, also A. Cameron, *Procopius and the Sixth Century* (London, 1985), esp. 67–73.

[25] See Frend, *Rise*, 270–4; Meyendorff, *Imperial Unity*, 224–5.

alongside official persecution, had the support of Justinian and became a feature of the attempts of later emperors to include Monophysites in the ecclesiastical fabric of the Empire.

Theological persuasion was consistently carried out. Justinian was an enthusiastic theologian, who wrote extensively and was eager to enter into debate, on one occasion with a group of Monophysite shipmasters from Alexandria who cautiously declined his invitation.[26] He, like the bishops at Chalcedon so many years before, sought to demonstrate that, far from being incompatible, the theological approaches of Chalcedon and Cyril were consistent and complementary. Various strategies were adopted. There was the support for the Theopaschite formula that 'one of the Holy Trinity suffered in the flesh', which Chalcedonians were asked to affirm. There was the series of conferences between Chalcedonian and Monophysite leaders held under imperial auspices in Constantinople in 532.

Most important was the Council of the Three Chapters, or Fifth Ecumenical Council, of 553. The Three Chapters were originally sections of dyophysite theological works but the phrase was extended to refer to the persons of the authors, Theodore of Mopsuestia, Theodoret of Cyrrhus, and Ibas of Edessa. Western sources claim that a beleaguered Origenist, Theodore Ascidas, suggested a condemnation of these texts in order to deflect criticism from his own party and on to somebody else, but the three writers were generally treated with suspicion in the east and their condemnation would have met with approval from many.[27] The attack on these writers clearly ruled out a Nestorian dyophysite interpretation of Chalcedon and so affirmed the convergence of the earlier Council and Cyrillian theology. This would, it was hoped, reassure easterners that Chalcedon was in conformity with doctrinal tradition. The Council was welcomed by eastern Chalcedonians like Cyril of Scythopolis, especially as it also condemned in passing the hated Origenists.[28]

The west did not, however, share this enthusiasm since it anathematized respected theologians, two of whom had been rehabilitated at Chalcedon, as well as exercising a considerable level of coercion on Pope Vigilius of Rome who had found himself summoned to Constantinople. Nor did it receive the support of most Monophysites, since it failed to condemn Chalcedon.

---

[26] Michael the Syrian, *Chronicle*, 9. 23, ed. Chabot, ii. 205.
[27] Liberatus, *Breviarium Causarum Nestorianorum et Eutychianorum*, 24.
[28] See below, Ch. 9.

The occupation of the New Laura by Sabaite monks, described at the start of this section, was a consequence of the decisions of the Council, which seemed to vindicate the orthodox Chalcedonians of Palestine. In fact it took place at the expense of the supporters of the Origenist heresy condemned at the Council who were ejected from their stronghold in the New Laura. But it indicates the mood of some sections of the church who felt that their viewpoint had triumphed at the Council of Constantinople.

Justinian's attempts to cajole and persuade Monophysites into union was accompanied by occasional recourse to violence and coercion. This was applied when Monophysite leaders refused to co-operate. When Theodosius of Alexandria would not accept Chalcedon in 537, he was replaced by Paul the Tabennesiote. Paul initiated a brutal policy of repression of Monophysites before being deposed three years later after being charged with murder. The use of force had the effect of strengthening resistance by furnishing the Monophysite Church with martyrs.

Justinian's approach to the religious problems of the Empire was followed by his successors, Justin II (565–78), Tiberius (578–82), Maurice (582–602), and Heraclius (610–41). All were Chalcedonians and all sought to encourage moderate Monophysites into unity.

Justin II, for example, was held in high regard by Monophysites and, in 566–7 held successful discussions in Constantinople with Monophysite leaders including the now aged Jacob bar Addai. The proposals for union were taken to Callinicum, on the border with Persia and deep in Monophysite territory, by the ambassador John Commentiolus. They impressed the bishops and archimandrites but hopes for union foundered on the fanaticism of the monks. The document was ripped up and the ambassador left as a riot threatened, without even waiting for lunch, as Michael the Syrian relates.[29] Justin maintained his attempts to achieve union on the basis of the affirmation of the Council of Chalcedon, and, after 572, the persuasion of Monophysites was reinforced with persecution. One of the victims of this less tolerant policy was John of Ephesus, who was imprisoned until 577 and graphically describes the sufferings of Monophysite martyrs.[30] The pattern continued in the reign

---

[29] For an assessment of the policy of Justin II, correcting the view that he was a secret Monophysite who established religious toleration for all, see A. Cameron, 'Early Religious Policies of Justin II'; in *The Orthodox Churches and the West*, SCH 13 (London, 1976), 51–67. For the events at Callinicum, Michael the Syrian, *Chron*. 10. 2, ed. Chabot, ii. 287.

[30] The persecutions are described by John of Ephesus, *HE* and *Lives of the Eastern Saints*.

of Heraclius with new attempts to find union in the debates over Monoenergism and Monotheletism.[31]

Failure was inevitable. No formula which did not affirm Chalcedon could satisfy Rome. At a geographical and cultural distance from the eastern Christological debates, the popes could maintain the Christology affirmed by the Tome of Leo with unswerving and uncostly determination. And at the other end of the Empire, the Monophysites would not be content with a formula which did not condemn Chalcedon. The standpoint of the Monophysite laity was expressed with clarity by the citizens of Amida: 'We will never accept the synod [of Chalcedon] or the Tome [of Leo].'[32]

The solution to the religious problems of the Empire came from an unexpected quarter. Arab armies attacked from the east and removed the most troublesome of the Monophysite provinces from the Empire and so allowed Chalcedonian unity to be maintained in the provinces which remained with reduced opposition from Monophysites.

The Victory and Defeat of Chalcedon

The contrast between the rugged natural beauty of the valley of the Kelt with its balanced harmony of plants, animals, and men, and the violence, brutality, and noise imported by the Persian army could hardly have been more devastating. Faced with invasion of the desert by the Persian soldiers, the monks, as desert dwellers had done for generations, retired to the deep caves of the surrounding valleys. But they were discovered. The Persian soldiers rounded them up and took them into another, more convenient, cave. Some were killed immediately; some were roped together to be led into captivity; one old man was set free. Given a basket of crusts and a flask of water he was pushed into the hot desert sun and told to wander where he wished.[33]

In this account, from the pen of Antony of Choziba, the Persians have become the enemy, and the anxiety of the monks was aroused by

---

[31] Monoenergism and Monotheletism were attempts made during the reign of the Emperor Heraclius (610–41), through the work of the Patriarch Sergius, to locate the hypostatic unity in Christ first in the energy or activity, and then in the will. Both proved unsuccessful, since Chalcedonians like Sophronius and Maximus the Confessor pointed to the same drawbacks as in Monophysitism.

[32] Michael the Syrian, *Chron.* 9. 26, ed. Chabot, ii. 222.

[33] *V. Geor. Choz.* 31, *An. Boll.* (1888), 129. 14–130. 11.

the threat posed by foreign armies instead of rival groups within the Church. Peace had prevailed between Persia and Constantinople during the reign of Maurice (582–602) but disintegrated after his death. The Persians made conquests in Syria and Egypt, and from 614 until 631 held Jerusalem. Although no permanent damage was done to the monasteries, the report of Antony shows the impact of military campaigning on the lives of the monks.

The adoption in 518 by Justin I and his nephew Justinian of the Council of Chalcedon, with its reliance on the western terminology of the Tome of Leo, heralded a new concern for the western provinces. In 535, Justinian embarked on a lengthy series of military campaigns in the west, conducted by his general Belisarius. The success of these was mixed. North Africa was invaded in 533, captured a year later, and held until 698. The Italian campaign was less successful. After early advances when Belisarius entered Rome in 536 the campaign ran into difficulties. Italy was not conquered until 554, and by 568 the Lombards had launched a new invasion. Elsewhere the Slavs infiltrated across the Danube into Pannonia and Illyricum, which divided the two halves of the Empire.[34]

At the other end of the Empire, border security depended on relations with Arab tribes, who occupied the desert areas between the Byzantine and Persian Empires. Justinian continued the alliance with the Ghassanid Arab tribal federation to the east of the provinces of Arabia and Palestine. This agreement resulted in the dispatch of the two Monophysite bishops, Jacob bar Addai and Theodore, requested by King al-Harith in 541, which had the unforeseen result of the establishment of the separate Monophysite hierarchy. Al-Harith was Monophysite and provided a refuge for Monophysite leaders in difficulties in the Empire. He developed the shrine and pilgrimage centre of St Sergius at Resapha.[35]

This alliance came to an end in 580. Maurice, the general appointed by Emperor Tiberius II, decided on a strike against the Persians. As he advanced he found that the strategic bridge at Circesium had been destroyed. Nobody ever discovered who was really responsible for this act of sabotage but Maurice suspected al-Mundhir, the successor of al-Harith. He persuaded Tiberius to arrest him. The result of this episode was the end of the alliance between the Emperor and the Ghassanid

---

[34] For the military history of the reign of Justinian, see Cameron, *Procopius*, 137–45, 190–206.

[35] For Resapha see J. Sauvaget, 'Les Ghassanides et Sergiopolis', *By. Z.* 14 (1939), 11–130. Also P. Maraval, *Lieux saints et pèlerinages d'orient* (Paris, 1985), 349–50.

Arabs who had played an important part in securing the Eastern frontier. The Ghassanids also suffered and their federation disintegrated. The result was distrust of Christians among the Arabs and lack of security on the eastern frontier which allowed hostile Arabs and Persians to attack the monasteries with impunity.[36]

The weakness of the frontier reduced the resistance which could be offered to the Arab forces which advanced against the Byzantine Empire from 634. The army of Heraclius was defeated at the river Yarmuk in 636 and Jerusalem fell in 638. With the exception of the Latin Kingdom established in Jerusalem by the Crusaders between 1099 and 1187, Jerusalem was never again to be under Christian rule.

[36] The contribution of Maurice is assessed by M. Whitby, *The Emperor Maurice and his Historian* (Oxford, 1988). See also for this event Frend, *Rise*, 329–31.

PART I

Sources

INTRODUCTION

The monks of Palestine fascinated many of their contemporaries in the Byzantine world. There were about three thousand of them occupying over sixty monasteries in a stretch of open country about ten miles square.[1] They gave a warm welcome to visitors and displayed a formidable determination in fighting for their convictions in the ecclesiastical and political arenas. Those who encountered them have left a generous variety of written material in the form of history, reminiscence, and anecdote.

These include passages in the *Ecclesiastical Histories*. Of the historians, Eusebius was a native of Palestine, as were Sozomen and Socrates. Evagrius came from nearby Antioch and Zachariah of Mitylene knew the provinces of Palestine well. They refer both to the involvement of the monks in the life of the Church and Empire, and to the quality of the lives of some of the saints of the desert. Then there are the accounts of visits to the monasteries made by pilgrims to the Holy Land. Egeria, who visited between 381 and 384, is the best known, but many others have left records of their travels. Especially vivid are the descriptions of a pilgrim from Piacenza, often named Antoninus, who visited Palestine shortly after 560.[2]

An unusual and moving document is the testimony to a dark moment in monastic history. Strategius, a monk of the monastery of Mar Saba, or the Great Laura as it was known in the earliest years of its existence, wrote an account of the capture of Jerusalem by the Persians. In a flat and prosaic style, reminiscent of the black-and-white tones of a modern documentary film, he describes the destruction of the achievement of the founders. He includes a grim catalogue of the number of corpses in

---

[1] The number of monks is calculated by Y. Hirschfeld on the basis of the size of the excavated buildings and the number of cells discovered. See Y. Hirschfeld, *The Judaean Desert Monasteries in the Byzantine Period* (New Haven, Conn., 1992), 78–90. Contemporary sources would suggest a higher figure, but these may be exaggerated. For example Cyril tells us that 10,000 monks gathered at a church in Jerusalem for an anti-government demonstration (*Kyrillos*, 151. 10).

[2] The Piacenza Pilgrim's travel diary is in *Itineraria et Alia Geographica*, ed. P. Geyer, CCL 175 (Turnhout, 1965).

the different buildings of Jerusalem found by the monk Thomas who had the sad task of burying the dead.[3]

A little distant from the city of Jerusalem were the Monophysite communities of the coastal regions of Palestine. The acceptance of the Council of Chalcedon by the bulk of the local Church excluded Monophysites from the mainstream of Palestinian Christianity. But a lively community in Gaza, Ptolemais, and elsewhere produced an extensive literature, much of which survives only in Syriac. John Rufus from Maiuma wrote a *Life of Peter the Iberian*, a collection of polemical anecdotes supporting the Monophysite position called the *Plerophoriai*, or Assurances, and an account of the holy deaths of Theodosius, the Monophysite Patriarch of Jerusalem for a few short months after Chalcedon, and Romanus the Monk.[4]

Not all the monks of the Gaza region were Monophysite. A number of important works emerged from this area in the sixth century. Barsanuphius, a monk originally from Egypt, and John provided answers to a variety of questions put to them, and these have been recorded. Another monk, Dorotheus, also developed into a spiritual writer of depth.[5]

The monasteries of the Judaean desert also produced writers. These described the monasteries to which they belonged, the people they knew, and the events they took part in. Their works have a pre-eminent place among the many sources for the monasticism of Palestine. They are the subject of the first part of this study.

---

[3] A Georgian version of Strategius' *Capture of Jerusalem* has been edited and translated into Latin by Gerard Garitte, *La Prise de Jerusalem par les Perses en 615*, CSCO.Ib. 11–12 (1960).

[4] The Life of Peter the Iberian is in R. Raabe, *Petrus der Iberer* (Leipzig, 1895), Syriac text with German translation; The *Plerophoriai*, ed. F. Nau, PO 8 (1911); *de Obitu Theodosii*, ed. E. W. Brooks, CSCO.S 3/25 (1907), 18–27.

[5] These writings come from the 6th c. The *Questions and Answers of Varsanuphius and John* were edited by S. Schoinas (Volos, 1960), and translated by L. Regnault et al. (Solesme, 1972). The works of Dorotheus of Gaza are in *Dorothee de Gaza; Œuvres Spirituelles*, ed. L. Regnault and J. Preville, SC 92 (Paris, 1963).

I

Cyril of Scythopolis

CYRIL THE AUTHOR

The main source for the history of the monasteries of Palestine is a series of Lives of seven of the great monks of the desert. The first of this group, chronologically, was Euthymius, who arrived in Jerusalem in 405 and died in 473. He was the founder and superior of a monastery on a plain a few miles east of the city. The second was a monk named Sabas, a disciple of Euthymius who arrived at Jerusalem in 457 and entered the neighbouring coenobium of Theoctistus. He went on to found several important monasteries and became an influential figure in the Church in Palestine. He died in 532. The other five monks who are the subject of these Lives were John the Hesychast and Cyriac, both younger contemporaries of Sabas; Theognius and Theodosius, founders of monasteries; and Abraamius. This corpus of hagiographical writing provides a comprehensive account of the development of Palestinian monasticism in the century and a half from 400 to 550, a period which included the Council of Chalcedon and its bitter aftermath, and the conflict over Origenism which issued in the Council of Constantinople in 553.

The author was a monk called Cyril, who was born in the city of Scythopolis. He is not only the author of the Lives but a participant in them. He appears as a boy when Sabas made one of his visits to Scythopolis; as a teenager entering the monastic life in the desert east of Jerusalem; as a monk witnessing miracles, debating doctrine, and sharing in the victory over Origenism.[1] Cyril's autobiographical passages have often been conflated to present a historical outline of the course of Cyril's life but the purpose here is different.[2] Cyril's references to his

---

[1] *Kyrillos*, 71. 10–72. 7; 83. 10–84. 21; 180. 2–181. 18; 216. 8–217. 24; 229. 7–31.
[2] The fullest accounts are in *Kyrillos*, 408–15; MH 11–17, 29–32. Errors about the life of Cyril are often made. These include the statement that Cyril was one of John Maxentius' Scythian monks made by R. Sellers, *Council of Chalcedon* (London 1961), 305; and the few lines in A. Grillmeier, *Christ in Christian Tradition*, vol. ii. pt. 1 (London, 1987), 43,

own life furnish insights into his motives in writing and they enable the reader to gain a clearer appreciation of his distinctive qualities as an author. This line of enquiry is not only possible but also especially fruitful in the case of Cyril. He has a close personal involvement in the events described which distinguishes him from other monastic authors of his time.

The early monastic literature was almost invariably the product of those who stood outside the events they described. Some of these works are travel diaries. An example of this form is the *Historia Monachorum in Aegypto*, which was written by one of a group of seven monks from the Mount of Olives who visited Egypt in 394–5. The author describes the journey they took and the old men they visited. The impact of the experience on the writer is apparent from the tone of amazement and admiration which runs through the work. He writes to share the lessons he learned and the inspiration he received with a wider audience. Other examples of this approach are the *Lausiac History* of Palladius, a native of Galatia who spent several years in Egypt before becoming Bishop of Helenopolis in Bithynia; the *Institutes* and *Conferences* of John Cassian, a monk from Bethlehem who also visited Egypt before settling in Gaul; and the *Spiritual Meadow* of John Moschus, which records his travels in Palestine, Egypt, Sinai, Antioch, Cyprus, and Rome.[3]

Further contributions to monastic literature come from the pens of sympathetic bishops. The most famous of these is Athanasius' *Life of Antony*. Athanasius led a controversial and active life as Patriarch of Alexandria, present at the Council of Nicaea and exiled on three occasions. In the *Life of Antony*, the bishop writes with a wistful admiration for the holy monk who lived a life of ascetical seclusion in the desert. The viewpoint of Theodoret is similar. In the *Religious History* the embattled theologian, caught up in Christological controversy, tells the stories of the ascetics of the Syrian mountains with whom he had had close contacts but from whom the demands of his position in the Church had distanced him.

Cyril, in contrast to these writers, describes the land which was his home and the institution in which he spent his whole life. He has a personal knowledge and intimacy with his subject rare in monastic literature.

in which he makes several incorrect remarks, that Cyril was born in 523, that he entered the monastery of Euphemius (it was Euthymius) in 544, and then spent the rest of his life after 555 in the New Laura (when he moved to the Great Laura in 557).

[3] For details of these works, see the Bibliography.

CYRIL THE CHILD

The boy who was to grow up to become our principal source for the
history of the monasticism of Palestine was born in the year 525.[4]
Unfortunately this is not one of the dates recorded by Cyril, but it can
be deduced from several clues given in the text.

When Sabas visited Scythopolis in 518 and met Cyril's parents, there
is no mention of the young Cyril, but in 531, when the saint came to
the city for the second time, Cyril plays a part in the story as a young
boy.[5] This locates his date of birth some time between 518 and 531.

More precise indications are given in the account of a later event—
Cyril's renunciation of the world and acceptance of the monastic life.
Shortly after his entry into the monastic life he went up to Jerusalem
to be present at the consecration of Justinian's 'Nea' Church of the
Mother of God. We know that this event took place in November 543,
so his entry into the monastic life can be dated to the early part of that
year.[6] Cyril does not tell us how old he was at this stage of his life but
he does refer to the moment of entering the monastery in the Lives of
Sabas, John the Hesychast, and Cyriac. These three saints all made
their renunciation of the world when they were 18 years old, a
coincidence which is most plausibly explained by assuming that Cyril
is drawing on his own experience.[7] So, if Cyril was 18 in 543, then it
follows that he was 6 in 531 and born in 525.

His parents were pious. Cyril's mother was described by Sabas as a
'slave of God'. This title was used as a compliment to her piety and
should not be understood to imply that she was a member of a religious
community.[8]

His father, as well as being an admirer of holy men, held some kind
of position in the Bishop's household. Cyril describes his father's
occupation in two passages. As well as a direct reference to John, there
is a parallel passage concerning Euthymius' uncle, Eudoxius. Since

---

[4] Since the name of Palestine was used to refer to the area we are concerned with
during the Byzantine period it will be used throughout this study. Byzantine Palestine
consisted of three Roman provinces and covered what is today Israel, the Occupied
Territories of the West Bank and Gaza strip, parts of Syria, and parts of Jordan.

[5] *Kyrillos*, 164. 20–4. 7. ἐμὲ δὲ παῖδα ὄντα, 180. 9.

[6] Ibid. 71. 1–20. See also, for a description of the Nea, Procopius, *Buildings*, 5. 6. 1–2,
LCL 8 (London, 1914), 342–8.

[7] *Kyrillos*, 90. 17 for Sabas's journey to Jerusalem at the age of 18; 202. 1 for John the
Hesychast becoming a monk at the age of 18; 224. 9 for Cyriac.

[8] Ibid. 180. 21. For the suggestion that δούλη θέου is a title rather than a description,
see *Kyrillos*, 409, and *MO* pt. 2, iii. 109 n. 251.

Euthymius was born about 150 years before Cyril, and Cyril is unlikely to have had access to information about the saint's childhood, it seems that Cyril has drawn on his own family background in constructing a suitable upbrining for the earlier saint. The passages are as follows:

John: ὁ ἐμὸς πατὴρ τοῦ ἐπισκοπείου κρατῶν τὸ τηνικαῦτα καὶ τῷ μητροπολίτῃ συνεδρεύων (180.4–6)

Eudoxius: λογιώτατον εὐδόξιον μὲν καλούμενον, τοῦ δὲ αὐτόθι ἐπισκοπείου κρατοῦντα καὶ τῷ ἐπισκοπειῷ συνεδρεύοντα ... (10.6–8)
παρὰ τοῦ σχολαστικοῦ εὐδοξίου (10.15)

The phrase τοῦ ἐπισκοπείου ... κρατῶν is most likely to mean that John held a responsible post within the episcopal administration. E. Schwartz suggests an alternative reading, in both passages preferring the accusative form of τον ἐπισκοπεῖον to the genetive του ἐπισκοπείου, which he translates as 'inhabit'. He explains: 'I do not see how a married lay person could govern or occupy the Bishop's Palace.'[9] So he proposes the alternative explanation that John had taken up residence in, or inhabited, the Bishop's House. But this cannot be accepted. Not only do the majority of manuscripts read τοῦ ἐπισκοπείου but the use of κράτειν to mean 'inhabit' is rare. Of the fifty-five times Cyril uses the verb, it has this meaning on only once occasion.[10] The more usual meaning of κράτειν is correct, telling us that John was an important official within the episcopal household.

John was a λογιώτατος and σχολαστικός, assuming that these titles really belong to him rather than to the shadowy Eudoxius. A σχολαστικός was a person who had achieved a high level of education. He often came from an exalted level of society and many opportunities for social advancement, both in civil and ecclesiastical life, were open to him. In his study of the term, A. Claus gives several examples of a σχολαστικός enjoying high office in the Church. One σχολαστικός became Patriarch of Constantinople.[11] These passages show that Cyril came from a family which was respected and influential within the Christian community.

So when the great Sabas came to Scythopolis, John was present. Holding his senior position, he would have made the arrangements for

---

[9] Kyrillos, 409 n. 1.
[10] The accusative form appears in only one out of four manuscripts—the 9th- or 10th-c. Ottobonianus 373. For a discussion of these readings, see P. Thomsen, 'Kyrillos von Skythopolis', OLZ 43 (1940), 457–63, at col. 461. For the meaning of the verb, see MH 14.
[11] A. Claus, 'ὁ σχολαστικός', dissertation (Cologne, 1965), 162–4.

receiving the saint and ensured that the visit went well. He was present with him at an exorcism performed at the monastery of Enthemenaith and assisted with it in some way which is not made clear.[12] John not surprisingly cultivated the old man's company and invited Sabas to visit his home. He became a regular visitor and friend of the family.[13] The friendship between the two men was continued during Sabas' second visit. John was his inseparable companion (ἀναπόσπαστον), and the saint paid a farewell visit to his house to bless the family.[14] The family kept in touch with Sabas' monasteries after the founder's death and monks visiting Scythopolis used the family home as a guest house.[15]

A gesture of affection by the great Sabas during his second visit to Scythopolis had lasting consequences for the 6-year-old Cyril. It is not hard to imagine the impression which the venerable and awe-inspiring visitor would have made on the boy for whom the Church was already a second home, nor the warmth with which the old monk would favour a young admirer. These emotions lay behind the moment when the old man gathered Cyril up in his arms, solemnly proclaiming: 'From this moment this child is my disciple and the son of the fathers of the desert.' Then he turned to the Bishop. 'Great Lord, I entrust this boy to you. Take care of him for I have need of him.' The gesture was to be repeated when Sabas made his farewell visit to the family. The boy came out to welcome him and Sabas said: 'Behold, my disciple Cyril.' This time Cyril's father, John, was given instructions about his education. 'Teach him the psalter, for I need him. From now on he is my disciple.'[16]

In later life, as he looked back on these events, Cyril was clear that this was the moment of his 'call' to the monastic life. It colours his understanding of the nature of vocation and influences the way he presents the early lives of his subjects, who are always pious boys set apart from their earliest youth for a life of ascetic struggle.[17]

Cyril did not have to go far to find his education. In spite of the distrust expressed about learning in the early monastic sources, we have plentiful evidence for the educational work of the monasteries. John Cassian describes young boys being received and educated by the fathers

---

[12] *Kyrillos*, 164. 11–12. Cyril describes his father as αὐτόπτης καὶ ὑπηρέτης τὸν θαύματος.

[13] Ibid. 164. 21–4.

[14] Ibid. 180. 8; 181. 1.

[15] Ibid. 217. 14–15.

[16] Ibid. 180. 11–24.

[17] By contrast, Pachomius was converted as an adult. *V. Pach. G1* 5.

of the desert.[18] Antony, who fled to the desert as an illiterate Coptic speaker, is later presented as an educated man capable of holding disputations with visiting philosophers.[19] The monks of the Pachomian monasteries received a sufficient education to ensure that they were literate and familiar with the Bible.[20] In addition to the monastery, the bishop's house was also a place where an education could be obtained. H.-I. Marrou writes of 'la troupe des jeunes enfants qui revêtus des fonctions de lecteurs, s'initiaient à la vie cléricale'.[21] A natural setting in which the young Cyril could apply himself to fulfilling the saint's instruction to study lay close at hand in the bishop's residence.

Cyril's father, the *logiotatos* (λογιώτατος) and *scholastikos* (σχολαστικός), was well qualified to carry out the saint's instructions, and the Bishop retained an interest in how the study progressed. He would enquire, 'How is it with the disciple of Abba Sabas?'[22] And so the boy learned what was necessary for the prospective monk. This is described as learning 'the Psalter and the Apostle' although its scope was somewhat wider as Cyril shows later that he has a detailed knowledge of the Bible, which he refers to naturally and continually throughout his writings.[23] He must also have read the Lives of the saints, which were popular in the Palestine of his day. He seems, too, to have acquired some knowledge of rhetoric, and later showed himself capable of the elegant ekphrasis on the beauties of the site of Euthymius' monastery.[24] But his work reveals no knowledge of classical non-Christian writers. His father took care that the disciple of Sabas should be introduced to only the safest of works.

The transition from pupil to monk was accomplished smoothly. The Bishop tonsured him and admitted him into the first order of the clergy, that of reader.[25] This tonsuring took place sometime before Cyril's eighteenth birthday and is to be distinguished from the next significant step in his career, that of making his monastic renunciation and receiving the habit. In his translation of the Lives, Festugière distinguishes the two events by translating the phrase which introduces the description

[18] John Cassian, *Institutes*, 5. 40. 1, SC 109 (Paris, 1965), 254–6.
[19] *V. Anton.* 72, 73, PG 26. 944C, 954A.
[20] e.g. *V. Pach. G1* 24, 28, trans. Athanassakis, 30. 1–18, 38. 35.
[21] H.-I. Marrou, *Histoire de l'éducation dans l'antiquite*, 2nd edn. (Paris, 1948), 438. For education in the Greek monasteries, see pp. 433–8.
[22] *Kyrillos*, 181. 15.
[23] Ibid. 16.
[24] Ibid. 64. 21–65. 8.
[25] Ibid. 181. 17–18.

of his entering the monastery, ἐν κλήρῳ ἐκκλησιαστικῷ καταλεγόμενος, by 'alors que j'avais été dejà inscrit dans l'ordre du clergé'. He is right to distinguish the two events, even though his translation may have overemphasized the point.[26]

CYRIL THE DISCIPLE

Cyril was encouraged in his vocation by one who was to become a lifelong friend and guide, George of Beella. George received him into the monastic life and clothed him in the monastic schema. This enabled him to make his Great Journey to Jerusalem, the Holy City, as a monk. Cyril was to dedicate his two major works to George, describing him as 'the most honourable and truly virtuous spiritual father George the priest and superior living the life of silence pleasing to God (θεαρέστως ἡσυχάζοντι) at the place near Scythopolis called Beella'.[27] A sixth-century inscription at the monastery named, by its modern excavator, after its benefactor the Lady Mary refers to τοῦ πρεσβυτέρου Γεωργίου καὶ ἡμουμένον καὶ δευτεραρίου.[28] This monastery is located in modern Beth Shan, a few hundred yards outside the old city, and so could well be the home of George and the place where Cyril received the schema.[29] Cyril remained in contact with George throughout his life and often turned to him for advice. He tells us that it was George who advised him to move from the New Laura to the Great Laura in 557.[30] George also encouraged Cyril in his writing. He supplied him with information about the actions of Sabas in Scythopolis which had taken place in Cyril's boyhood or before he was born and, when he discovered that Cyril had been collecting material about the lives of Euthymius and

---

[26] *MO* pt. 2, iii. 126–7.

[27] *Kyrillos*, 5. 1–3; cf. 85. 5–10.

[28] G. M. Fitzgerald, *A Sixth-Century Monastery in Beth-shan (Scythopolis)* (Philadelphia, 1939), 13.

[29] An alternative, but unconvincing, suggested location for Beella is the settlement east of Beth Shan known today as Giv'at Hagamadim where there are extensive Byzantine remains. However the only reason for the identification is its location at a convenient distance outside Scythopolis and the existence of Byzantine remains. See V. Tzaferis, *The Synagogue at Ma'oz Hayim*, in L. Levine (ed.), *Ancient Synagogues Revealed* (Jerusalem, 1982), 86–9.

[30] *Kyrillos*, 181. 7–8. For the date, see E. Stein, 'Cyrille de Scythopolis, à propos de la nouvelle édition de ses œuvres', *An. Boll.* 62 (1944), 169–86, 180. He corrects Schwartz who dates this event in 556.

Sabas, instructed Cyril to put them together in a coherent order.[31]

It is at this period of Cyril's life that we encounter his other great adviser. This was John the Hesychast, a bishop who had anonymously entered the Great Laura and who was to be the subject of one of Cyril's shorter Lives. In his maturity, as he wrote the *Life*, Cyril speaks respectfully of John as the great spiritual director. He tells how he sought the great man's advice over the two important decisions of whether he should move to the New Laura and later to the Great Laura.[32] He was a regular visitor to John's cell. 'I visited him continually, laying before him everything in my mind.'[33] This phrase—πάντα τα κατ᾽ ἐμὲ αὐτῷ ἀνατιθέμενος—or phrases equivalent to it, occur regularly with reference to John but are not used in connection with Cyril's other subjects.[34] For Cyril, John was the spiritual guide *par excellence*.

But this discovery of John as a spiritual guide was not made without cost. It was achieved through the experience of disobedience, punishment, and restoration. When Cyril made his journey to Jerusalem, his mother—his father is not mentioned and so perhaps has died—was anxious about her enthusiastic and impressionable son. She issued a firm instruction to him to rely totally on the unquestioned orthodoxy of John, following his advice in all things concerning the spiritual life.[35] So, after he had participated in the festivities at the dedication of the wonderful new Church of the Mother of God, had visited the Holy Places, and had venerated the life-giving cross, the young Cyril set off to visit John at the Great Laura.[36] But he met an unexpected set-back. Instead of being welcomed into the monastery to live the prestigious life of a hermit, John's counsel followed the principles laid down by Sabas and Euthymius before him, namely that young monks should begin by living in the coenobium before venturing on the more testing way of silence and solitude. 'If you want to be saved', he directed, 'enter the monastery of the great Euthymius.'[37]

This meant leaving the magnificent rocky canyon of the Kidron in the depth of the desert and travelling north-west to the coenobium on the plain of the Sahel not far south of the main Jerusalem to Jericho

[31] *Kyrillos*, 83. 18–20; 164. 25–8.
[32] Ibid. 119. 23–4; 217. 22–3.
[33] Ibid. 217. 12–13.
[34] e.g. ibid 216. 19; 217. 25.
[35] Ibid. 216. 11–13.
[36] Ibid. 72. 2–4.
[37] Ibid. 3–4.

highway.[38] This course of action did not attract the aspiring hermit. So Cyril decided on an alternative plan. He went instead in the opposite direction eastwards across the desert to the celebrated monasteries of the Jordan valley. He chose the most famous of all, Calamon, a settlement of hermits at an oasis where a fertile and beautiful plantation of palm trees grows in the middle of the hot Jericho plain. Perhaps he felt he was obeying the spirit, if not the letter, of John's injunction since the place was a few hundred yards from the coenobium of Gerasimus and the hermits lived in close contact with the coenobium.[39]

This act of insubordination led to a salutary lesson. Cyril immediately fell ill and was sick for six months, grieving that he could not join in the life of the monastery but was forced to be waited on like a guest. John appeared to him in a dream and repeated his instructions. 'You have disobeyed my order and have been suitably chastised. But now rise up and go to Jericho and you will find a certain monk called Gerontius in the guest house of the monastery of Abba Euthymius. Follow him to the monastery and you will be saved.'[40] Cyril rose up, restored to health, and entered the monastery of Euthymius.

These early experiences left Cyril with a deep respect for the authority of his teachers and seniors. Their influence on his understanding of the monastic life and of his own vocation is made clear at several points in his writing. Obedience and humility are the two virtues which he regards as the foundation of the monastic life. 'Those who renounce this life must not have a wish of their own but in the first place acquire humility and obedience.'[41]

Cyril's authorship is properly understood within the context of monastic obedience. The task of collecting information about the lives of the saints was undertaken with the care and precision of the faithful disciple, scrupulous in fulfilling tasks laid upon him by his spiritual father. Further, the editing of his evidence into an orderly account was in response to a command delivered in a vision by Euthymius and Sabas

[38] In his account of the founding of the monastery, Cyril explains that the place which the saint had chosen was not much frequented then, so clearly implying that at the time of writing there *was* much coming and going, *Kyrillos*, 24. 3–4.

[39] Ibid. 216. 21–4. For an account of this laura and the way that the coenobitic and eremetical lives were combined in it, see S. Vailhé, 'Les Laures de Saint Gerasime et de Calamon', *E. Or.* 2 (1899), 106–19; and *MH* 228–9.

[40] *Kyrillos*, 217. 4–7.

[41] Ibid. 17. 13. Cf. for humility, 13. 5; 34. 18; 58. 8; 89. 14; and for obedience, 29. 2; 89. 14; 92. 3, among many references.

themselves.[42] This vision, in particular, shows that he regarded his authorship as an aspect of discipleship, carried out in obedience to the memory of the saints.

CYRIL THE MONK

Obedience was not the only lesson which Cyril learned from his teacher and guide, John. He was also helped to place his trust in the orthodox faith proclaimed at Chalcedon. It had been his mother's hope that John would ensure that her son remained safely in the orthodox church. When Cyril had arrived in Jerusalem he had found himself in a hotbed of controversy. The Origenist party had become a powerful force in the desert. Although in temporary disarray following the 543 Edict of the Emperor Justinian against Origen, they were soon to re-establish their power in Jerusalem to such an extent that a Sabaite monk could not walk the streets without the risk of being insulted, beaten, and thrown out of the city.[43] The power of the Origenists was not overcome until 553.[44]

Cyril experienced at first hand the violence and bitterness of doctrinal controversy. Although the initial time which he spent in the city could not have been more than a few weeks, Cyril then spent nine years in the monastery of Euthymius, six miles or so from the city and close to a main road, in close proximity to the capital and participating in its life. Cyril was well educated, and so belongs among the monks who were λογιώτεροι, or more rational, upon whom he was later to pour such scorn in the *Life of Sabas*.[45] He was stimulated by the debate and at one point describes a discussion he had with the monk Cyriac. At its start, Cyril refers, clearly with some sympathy, to the apparent licence to indulge in theological speculation about matters not essential to the faith which is given in a well-known passage of Gregory of Nazianzus' *Theological Orations*.[46] This comment evoked a long attack by Cyriac on the errors of Origenism.[47] The passage shows Cyril's interest in doctrinal debate and also the process of discussion and debate among the monks.

---

[42] *Kyrillos*, 84. 1–21.
[43] Ibid. 192. 12–17; 193. 21–4.
[44] See Ch. 8.
[45] *MO* pt. 1, iii. 43.
[46] Gregory Nazianzus, *Second Theological Oration*, 27. 10, PG 36. 25A.
[47] *Kyrillos*, 229. 24–231. 19.

Gradually he changed from a sympathetic observer into a committed opponent of Origenism. Again the example of an older monk encouraged him in his discovery of his faith.

In February 555 he was among those chosen to form the vanguard of orthodoxy and to reclaim the New Laura for orthodoxy after the expulsion of the Origenists.[48] It was shortly after this, while he was in the New Laura enjoying the victory over heresy, that he began his task of writing. As he triumphantly occupied this former bastion of heresy, he started to record the events by which the true faith triumphed, presenting the conflict between orthodoxy and heresy as a theme running through his Lives.

Cyril's life as a monk was spent in four monasteries. First, there was his six-month stay at the laura of Calamon. Then he lived at the monastery of Euthymius from July 544 until February 555. From there, he went as one of the group of orthodox monks who reclaimed the New Laura from the Origenists in the aftermath of the defeat of Origenism at the Council of Constantinople in 553. Here he remained from February 555 until early in 557. In 557 he moved to the Great Laura.[49]

When Cyril entered the Monastery of Euthymius, the founder had been long dead.[50] But in spite of the lapse of 71 years the presence of Euthymius still pervaded the monastery. Just to the north of the two-storey building which housed the church and refectory was the chapel in which the founder was buried. Today his tomb can be clearly seen, surrounded by graves of other, now unknown, superiors of the monastery.[51] Then, one would presume, it stood alone, a stone inscribed with the saint's name adorning it, an oil lamp burning continuously, and perhaps gifts of food and money laid around it by petitioners hoping for help from the saint.[52] From it grace radiated over the many who came trusting in the power of the saint's intercession. It was a reassuring and ever-present source of healing and forgiveness, quietly penetrating the life of the monastery. We hear how when the monks—with Cyril

[48] Ibid. 119. 21–200. 3.
[49] Ibid. 72. 5–7; 216. 24; 217. 7–12; 217. 21–4; 199. 21–2.
[50] Euthymius died in 473 and Cyril entered the monastery in 544.
[51] For a description of the buildings of Euthymius' monastery, see Y. Hirschfeld, *List of the Byzantine Monasteries in the Judaean Desert*, in G. C. Bottini et al. (eds.), *Christian Archeology in the Holy Land: New Discoveries* (Jerusalem, 1990), 15–18. For an account of a visit in the 12th c. to the tomb of Euthymius by the Russian Abbot Daniel who saw the bodies 'as if still alive', see J. Wilkinson, *Jerusalem Pilgrimage, 1099–1185* (London, 1988), 141.
[52] For a description of the holy sanctuaries, see P. Maraval, *Lieux saints et pèlerinages d'orient* (Paris, 1985), 183–97. For discussion of healing miracles see Ch. 9.

among them—were collecting mannouthia in the desert, the talk turned to the healing power of the saint's grave and a monk Paul testified to his experience of healing: of how the monks were sitting resting in front of the gate, and a couple of Bedouin arrived bringing a friend tormented by a demon; or how they were washing the leaves of the maloas plant, and a foreigner came rushing up shouting abuse until the monks overpowered him and he spent the night sleeping on top of the tomb of Euthymius to find himself cured in the morning.[53]

These miracle stories were not included to encourage the veneration of the relics of Euthymius and Sabas. As well as stories describing healings received at the tomb, Cyril also recounts miracles performed far away from the monastery as a result of prayers addressed to the saint. A typical example is the prayer of Romanus who lived in a village called Betakabeis near Gaza. Euthymius appeared to him in a dream and granted healing.[54] Most of the posthumous miracles worked by Sabas were performed at a distance through the appearance of the saint in a dream or vision to the petitioner.

Cyril's purpose in telling these stories is to show that the power which the saint exercised during his lifetime continued to be efficacious after his death. They are a posthumous confirmation by God of the virtue exhibited by the saint and show that the protection given by the saint is still available.[55] The story which forms the basis for understanding the others is the dream of the silversmith Romulus, protodeacon of the church of Gethsemane, who prays to Theodore the martyr. Theodore comes to his help only after a delay of five days, and explains that he could not come earlier because he was occupied in leading the soul of Sabas to its place of rest.[56] This makes clear the essential connection between the miracles after the death and the glorification of the saint, who is welcomed into the courts of heaven.[57] The primary emphasis is always on the power of the living saint rather than on any magical properties of his dead body.

Cyril experienced the monasteries in which he lived as places not only founded by great men but also protected by them. They were places in which the memory of the saints was preserved and from which the power of the saints went out. The inclusion of the posthumous

[53] *Kyrillos* 72. 18–74. 27; 75. 11–28; 77. 14–78. 2.
[54] Ibid. 184. 22–185. 16.
[55] Ibid. 82. 19–23.
[56] Ibid. 184. 22–185. 16.
[57] For *parresia* see Ch. 9.

miracles commend the monasteries to the reader as places of significance within the life of the church. Cyril was still alive in 558. This is the last date mentioned in the Greek manuscripts of his writings. In this year, John the Hesychast was 104, and Cyril completed his *Life of John* by recording this fact and praying that he may 'complete his course in peace'.[58] A Georgian manuscript of the Life of John the Hesychast, copied in the eleventh century at the Monastery of the Holy Cross in Jerusalem and preserved today in the British Museum, continues the story a little further by providing a short account of John's death which, it says, took place on Wednesday, 8 January. This combination of date and day of the week occurred in 559. There are strong reasons for accepting that this text preserves an addition made by Cyril, which was not included in the texts used by later Greek copyists. There is, firstly, the ease with which the addition flows from what went before, suggesting that it is the work of the same author. Then, secondly, this text was copied in Jerusalem while most of the Greek manuscripts originated in Italy or Syria. This raises the possibility that the copyist used a supplemented version which was preserved in Cyril's homeland.[59] It is probable that this Georgian text has preserved a final addition which Cyril made to this Life when he heard of John's death. The postscript is especially valuable because they were the last sentences which Cyril wrote which have survived.

So Cyril's literary career ended in 559. He was a conscientious and prolific writer. The most likely explanation for the breaking off of his career is his death.

All that we know about Cyril and his life comes from his own writing. He is a character in the drama as well as the author. His appearances in the works are not simply coincidental—a reference to his having happened to be in the right place at the right time to be an eyewitness. They testify to his deep concern for what he writes about. The lessons he had learnt from his own experience help to shape his writings. He emphasizes the need for obedience and respect for superiors; the monastic vocation to struggle against heresy; the protection given by the saints to those who trust in them. These convictions arose out of his deep involvement in the life of the Palestinian monasteries. The conflict, suffering, and fulfilment of his subjects becomes part of his own experience.

[58] *Kyrillos* 222. 10–14.
[59] G. Garitte, 'Le Mort de S. Jean Hesychaste d'après un texte georgien inédit', *An. Boll.* 72 (1954), 75–84.

CYRIL AND THE CHRISTIAN HISTORICAL TRADITION

The monk from Palestine who never travelled outside his native land and who had little contact with the cultural and academic life of his time has received enthusiastic appreciation from his readers. A historian of this century has contrasted Cyril's writing with that of his contemporaries.

Le terme d'hagiographie désigne aujourd'hui à la fois une branche florissante de la science historique, et une espèce de littérature dont la plupart des produits correspondent à un niveau intellectuel très bas: la seconde a pour but d'édifier des lecteurs naïfs et crédules en leur racontant les vies des saints personnages où censés tels avec force détails miraculeux et sans trop de souçier de la verité; la première consiste à détruire le fatras d'absurdités accumulées par l'autre en établissant l'histoire réelle des mêmes personnages. [Of the first type] nous ne croyons pas diminuer le mérite éclatant des Pères Jesuites qui forment la Société des Bollandistes, en disant qu'ils ont eu un modeste précurseur en la personne de Cyrille de Scythopolis.[60]

This historical perspective in Cyril led, in the view of another historian, to a new literary form: 'Thus he gave a new form to the Lives of the Saints.'[61] Yet this innovation which has been discerned in the literary production of Cyril was the development of an established tradition of Christian historical writing. The appreciation of his originality rests on the recognition of his dependence on his predecessors.

The founding father of Christian history was Eusebius of Caesarea. He recognized the newness of the task he was undertaking in writing a history of the Church. 'I am the first to venture on such a project and to set out on what is indeed a lonely and untrodden path . . . as far as I am aware, no previous church historian has been interested in records of this kind.'[62] Later historians were conscious of continuing the work begun by Eusebius. Theodore Lector saw his task as providing a completeness to what had gone before. He wanted to 'put together those who have set forth the Ecclesiastical Histories and to synthesise them into a single and orderly account'.[63] There was one single historical enterprise to which different authors contributed. 'Ecclesiastical historians saw themselves almost as members of a kind of diachronic

---

[60] E. Stein, *Histoire du Bas-Empire* (Paris, 1949, 1959), ii. 699.
[61] *Kyrillos*, 355.
[62] Eusebius, *HE* I. 1, SC 31 (Paris, 1952), 4.
[63] Theodore Lector, *HE* I. 1, GCS (1971), 1.

syndicate responsible for the instalments which would add up to make a single cumulative "ecclesiastical history".[64]

The list of subjects with which this one great historical enterprise was concerned grew as the circumstances of the Church changed. In the days of Eusebius, the topics to be covered were the preoccupations of a minority Church, at odds with the prevailing classical culture. So Eusebius listed the lines of succession of bishops of the illustrious sees from the times of the Apostles. Then he was concerned with the emerging identity of the Church, its relationships with Jews and pagans and above all with the overcoming of heretics. He promised to record the names of those who 'through a passion for innovation have wandered as far as possible from the truth, proclaiming themselves the founts of knowledge falsely so-called while mercilessly, like savage wolves, making havoc of Christ's flock'.[65] This theme of orthodoxy and heresy runs through all Church histories. Socrates brought his history to an end in 439, hoping that division in the Church had ended as a consequence of the condemnation of Nestorius. 'In such flourishing condition were the affairs of the church at this time. But we shall here close our history praying that the churches everywhere, with the cities and the nations, may live in peace; for as long as peace continues, those who desire to write histories will find no materials for their purpose.'[66]

This concern of the historians was shared by Cyril. He wrote to describe the conflicts in the Church and their resolution. The Lives of Euthymius and Sabas end not, as might be predicted, with their deaths, but with the overcoming of heretics whom they struggled against.[67]

New perspectives were introduced into church history with the accession of Constantine. Slowly the Church moved from being persecuted to being dominant. It assumed a central part in the life of the Empire. So church historians began to include accounts of secular events in their histories. Socrates explained this development to his readers by claiming an organic connection between Church and State. When the life of the State is disordered then 'as if by a kind of sympathy the affairs of the church are disordered too'. The common cause is human wickedness. 'I am persuaded that it [disturbance] proceeds from our

[64] R. A. Markus, 'Church History and the Church Historians', in D. Baker (ed.), *The Materials, Sources and Methods of Ecclesiastical History*, SCH 11 (London, 1975), 8.

[65] Eusebius, *HE* 1. 1, SC 31 (Paris, 1952), 3. For the sociology of the church's self-understanding, see H. Remus, *Pagan–Christian Conflict over Miracles in the Second Century* (Cambridge, Mass., 1983), 73–93.

[66] Socrates, *HE* 7. 48, PG 67. 841A.

[67] *Kyrillos*, 66. 18–67. 20; 198. 7–200. 16. These conflicts are discussed in Ch. 8.

iniquities; and that these evils are inflicted upon us as merited chastisement.'[68] This development can be seen in the different writings of Eusebius, who saw this change taking place and tried to adjust his thinking accordingly.

Eusebius was ... forced to 're-think history' simply because in his scheme of things history had changed with the coming to power of Constantine. The establishment of Christianity as an approved religion and the rule of a Christian Emperor implied a reconsideration of all past history and a developed theory which could provide an explanation in terms of the linear progression of God's promise and its fulfilment.[69]

This approach lies behind Cyril's understanding, and that of other contemporaries, of the role of the monks. From the early pages, when he points to the significance of Euthymius' birth taking place near the beginning of the reign of Theodosius II in 379, to the confident co-operation of Sabas with the Emperor Justinian, he shows how the monks of the desert have an essential place in the life of the Christian Empire and, as a result, in the purposes of God for His world.[70]

After Constantine, monks began to make their appearance in the pages of the histories. They took the place which the martyrs had had in the writing of Eusebius as witnesses to the truth of the Gospel. Sozomen felt he had to recognize their arrival: 'Nor is it foreign to ecclesiastical history to introduce in this work an account of those who were the fathers and originators of what is denominated monachism.'[71]

As monks became popular, so the genre of saints' lives emerged. Athanasius, in the *Life of Antony*, introduced the notion of the saint as the type of the perfect man. So hagiography 'outclassed all other types of biography because all the other types of men became inferior to the saint. In comparison the ordinary biography of kings and politicians became insignificant.'[72] Some of the themes of the Lives of the saints had occurred earlier in Eusebius' *Life of Constantine*. In this work, Eusebius said that he did not intend to discuss the military exploits of Constantine nor his secular legislation but instead would 'concentrate

---

[68] Socrates, *HE* 5 intro., PG 67. 565A.

[69] A. Cameron, 'Eusebius of Caesarea and the Rethinking of History', in *Tria corda: Scritti in onore di Arnaldo Momigliano* (Como, 1983), 71–88, 87.

[70] See above, Part I, Introduction.

[71] Sozomen, *HE* 1. 1, GCS (1960) 4.

[72] A. Momigliano, 'Pagan and Christian Historiography in the Fourth Century AD', in Momigliano (ed.), *Paganism and Christianity in the Fourth Century* (Oxford 1963), 98. See also P. Cox, *Biography in Late Antiquity: The Quest for the Holy Man* (Berkeley, Calif., 1983).

on those circumstances which have reference to his religious character'.[73] In support of his contention that Constantine's life revealed the plan and purpose of God, Eusebius recorded signs and miracles which demonstrated this to be the case. 'He was claiming a status for Constantine which could only be demonstrated by a narrative filled with "proofs".'[74]

Once history is perceived to be guided by God, then the actions of God become its proper subject matter. Religious as well as secular criteria determine the content of the history. Wherever God's guidance is discerned, there is history. The actions of the monks, with their claim to be chosen and appointed by God, cannot be pushed to the periphery of history but have a rightful place in the centre. So, in the work of Cyril, the Lives of monks of Palestine are treated in a consistent historical framework in which the ascetic achievements and their miraculous healings are described alongside the councils of the Church and the succession of bishops with no hint of uneasiness.

These developments in the perception of the nature of history have been described by Evelyne Patlagean as a change of 'space'. She argues that classical historiography

était bornée par la perception exclusives des faits qui pouvaient trouver place précisement dans l'éspace traditionnel de la cité, en conformité avec le système de valeurs et le classement social assortis à cet éspace ... ces limites urbaines et civiques de l'éspace éclatent dès le 4e siècle et surtout à partir du 5e, l'épanouissement de la littérature hagiographique se fait hors les murs materiallement et mentalement . . . Le déperissement de la cité, et la christianisation de la société et de l'Empire sont les deux facteurs d'une evolution.[75]

History has moved from the city to the country. The actors have become holy men as well as bishops and generals.

So a popular element is introduced into historical writing. Patlagean attributes this change to the rise of the form of literature which she calls hagiography, which transformed the rigid and settled categories of historiography.[76] But a sharp contrast between historiography and hagiography is unhelpful. The forces in society which produced hagiography also transformed history. The two developments were part of the same change in popular perceptions. While it is possible to distinguish at opposite ends of a literary spectrum the 'pure' history of, say, Procopius' history of the wars of Justinian, and the 'pure' hagiography of some of the saints' lives, it is more helpful to identify a new form of writing in which classical history and hagiography contribute.

This appeared in the sixth century and was concerned not only with the welfare and history of the Empire but also with events in the lives of lowlier members of society. It was classical in the sense of being the 'highly wrought products of the educated minority' yet popular in the concern to appeal to a broad spectrum of society with an acceptance of the miraculous as an ordinary part of everyday experience.[77] This literature includes the *Chronographia* of John Malalas, the *Topography* of Cosmas Indicopleustes, and the oddly assorted works of Procopius. Averil Cameron describes this style of writing in her comments on Procopius, who has 'an acceptance of the miraculous and supernatural as an adequate replacement for historical analysis, an acceptance which he shared with other writers of late antiquity both ecclesiastical and secular. Thus the supposedly rational Procopius differs little from the authors of "hagiography" and "popular" literature.'[78]

Cyril of Scythopolis is a historian of the sixth century. He stands within a clear tradition of historical writing to which he is an heir. He is also a man of his age, showing the preoccupations and perceptions of people of his time. His writings are both the product of late antique society and a witness to its nature.

[77] A phrase of A. Cameron, *Procopius and the Sixth Century* (London, 1985), 24.
[78] Cameron, *Procopius*, 31.

2

The Other Sources

INTRODUCTION

Cyril was not the only monk of the deserts of Palestine to have written about the holy men. Other works have emerged from the monasteries which add to our knowledge and which are written from different perspectives from that of Cyril.

This material is presented here in three sections. The first considers the Lives of four saints—Theognius, Theodosius, Chariton, and Gerasimus—all of which are related in some way to Cyril's work. The second concerns the *Spiritual Meadow* of John Moschus, a collection of anecdotes and reminiscences which were written after Cyril's Lives and supplement his account. The third discusses a further saint's Life which comes from the time of the Persian conquest of Jerusalem and which is especially concerned with the spirituality of the desert—the *Life of George of Choziba*. These works have not received the attention they deserve.[1]

THE LIVES OF THEOGNIUS, THEODOSIUS, CHARITON, AND GERASIMUS

The Lives of Theognius, Theodosius, Chariton, and Gerasimus were written at about the same time, in about the same place, and with similar concerns to the Lives by Cyril. Two of them were in existence when Cyril wrote and were known to him. One was inspired by him. One might have been written by him.

The first, chronologically, was that of Theognius. Although the author does not name himself in his text, he is elsewhere given the name of Paul, from Elousa. Cyril, in his short *Life of Theognius*, excuses himself

---

[1] French translations have been made of the *Life of Theodosius* and the *Spiritual Meadow*. See bibliography for details.

from writing in more detail since the reader can refer to the fuller Life written by 'Paul the Hesychast of Elousa, shining in monastic virtues and orthodox doctrines'.[2] In later manuscripts, for example Coislin 303 in the Bibliothèque Nationale in Paris, the two Lives are preserved alongside one another.[3] This association in literary tradition combined with the statement of Cyril convinces us of Paul's authorship.

Paul tells us a little about himself. He was a native of Greece and came to Palestine, presumably on pilgrimage. He attached himself to a certain Aemilianus, before entering Theognius' monastery. He took this step on the advice of 'Alexander, a pearl of our generation and a scholastic of Ascalon'.[4] From this piece of name-dropping he makes it clear that he has mixed in educated circles and considers himself to be gifted with rhetorical skills. So it is not surprising to find that he adopts a rhetorical and long-winded style of writing. But while the beginning and end of the work suffer from considerable prolixity, the central narrative sections are more concise and vivid.

While in the monastery, he became acquainted with Theognius. He was an eyewitness of many of the events described and was sufficiently well respected by the community to be selected to write the official biography of the founder.[5] At some stage after Theognius' death, he moved to Elousa, a town near Beersheba in the south of Palestine. There was a laura at Elousa and Paul lived as a hermit.[6] Van den Gheyn has suggested that Paul the author of Theognius' life should be identified with two Pauls mentioned by John Moschus: Paul, the superior of the monastery of Theognius, and Paul Helladicus, or 'the Greek'.[7] Both these identifications are improbable. If Cyril, writing in the 550s, could describe Paul as a solitary of Elousa, it is hardly possible that he would have returned to the monastery of Theognius and become superior by the time that John Moschus began his monastic career sometime after 560.[8] The anecdote told by John which involves Paul Helladicus originates from the laura of Calamon during the second half of the sixth

[2] *Kyrillos*, 234. 8–10.

[3] J. van den Gheyn, 'St Théognius, Évêque de Bételie en Palestine', *RQH* 50 (1891), 559–76, 562–4.

[4] *V. Thg.* 17, *An. Boll.* (1891) 98. 18–98. 10.

[5] Note, e.g., the use of 'us' in '[Theognius] wanted to visit us and make his advice known to those of us who remained.' (*V. Thg.* 15, *An. Boll.* (1891) 95. 11–12).

[6] For the anecdote about Victor from the laura of Elousa, see *Prat.* 164, PG 87. 3. 3031A.

[7] For the relevant passages, see van den Gheyn, 'Théognius', 560; *Prat.* 163 and 160; PG 87 3. 3030 and 3027.

[8] For John Moschus' biography, see below.

century, and so is also unlikely to refer to Paul the author. John's anecdotes come from a later period than the writings of Paul of Elousa and cannot be used as evidence for the lives of these personalities.

The Life is an encomium, proclaimed in Theognius' monastery on the anniversary of the death of the founder. The date of its delivery and composition was probably 526, four years after Paul's death, since the Life refers to drought, famine, and earthquake, all of which afflicted the Empire in 525–6.[9]

Theognius was one of the great monks of the desert. He was born in 425 in Cappadocia. He may have known Theodosius, whose monastery he later lived in, in his youth, since both came from the same region.[10] In 454 he travelled to Jerusalem and after spending some months in Flavia's monastery on the Mount of Olives he moved to the monastery of Theodosius in 456.[11] While there, his finger became ulcerated and, we are told, was prevented from healing because the mountainous region was 'very cold.' (ψυχρότατος)—a complaint which strikes those who have tramped through the hot and arid desert east of Bethlehem as surprising. In order to be rid of this affliction, he went to the Jordan and lived at Calamon, where the temperature was more to his liking.[12] In 470 he returned to found his own monastery in the hills to the south of Theodosius' monastery. Patriarch Elias, himself a former monk, nominated him as Bishop of Betelia, a seaside town north of Gaza, in 494 or 495 and he retained this office until his death in 522.[13]

Paul tells how, even after he became a bishop, Theognius retained a close connection with his monastery, travelling regularly to visit the monks and to spend time in his cell, which was the smallest in the monastery.[14] During the final months of his life, he visited Constantinople to present a petition to the Emperor Justin, where he impressed all in the capital, but then he spent time at his beloved monastery before returning, reluctantly but dutifully, to his episcopal see where he died.[15] The juxtaposition of such different environments as desert monastery,

---

[9] Van den Gheyn, 'Théognius', 564.

[10] According to Cyril, Theognius was born at 'Arartheias' which could be the 'Ariarthia' of the Piacenza Pilgrim. Theodosius was born in 'Mogarissos' which could be the same as the 'Megalossus' mentioned by Ptolemy. See van den Gheyn, 'Théognius', 566. In any case, the shared homeland of both men suggests a background similar enough to attract Theognius to his compatriot's monastery.

[11] *V. Thg.*, *An. Boll.* (1891), 83. 1–9; 85. 1–3.

[12] Ibid. 85. 6–10.

[13] Ibid. 88. 11–89. 2. Also *Kyrillos*, 242. 21–4; 243. 15–16.

[14] *V. Thg.*, *An. Boll.* (1891), 89. 7–8.

[15] *V. Thg.* 21; 104.

city church, and imperial court in the ministry of one man shows the close integration of the monasteries into the life and society of Palestine. It is a main theme of the *Life of Sabas*.

The second of these four Lives, that of Theodosius, was composed in 530, on the first anniversary of the death of the saint. Since the monastery of Theodosius is less than three miles distant from that of Theognius and the Life was composed four years later, it can be assumed that the writer of Theodosius' Life was aware of the earlier work. Cyril also knew the Life. As in the case of Theognius, he excuses himself from writing a full account of the career of Theodosius since the reader can find that in the already existing *Life of Theodosius*.[16]

The author, Theodore, was a monk at Theodosius' monastery whose career overlapped with that of the saint. Throughout the Life, he demonstrates first-hand knowledge not only of some of the events but, more importantly, of the character of the institution. He became Bishop of Petra, the capital of the province of Arabia.[17] Considering the large number of monks in Theodosius' monastery, his selection to write the life of the saint, combined with his appointment as bishop of a major see, it seems that he was a man of learning and influence. His prose style is even more rhetorical and flowery than that of Paul.

The Life has not met with approval from modern editors. A.-J. Festugière precedes his translation of the Life with these words: 'Trois raisons m'ont conduit à joindre au texte de Cyrille cet insipide morceau de rhétorique ... [one of which is that] Il m'a semblé utile de donner un exemple d'un sorte de littérature qui encombre l'hagiographie ancienne et qui fait mieux apprécier, par contraste, la candeur et la précision du récit de Cyrille.'[18]

Its subject matter, in contrast to its style, is of unquestioned importance. Theodosius was one of the great saints of the Judaean desert. He founded a large coenobium in the hills east of Bethlehem in 479, four years before Sabas founded the Great Laura. It became the largest monastery of the desert, with over 400 monks resident at the time of Theodosius' death. There were four churches; the liturgy was celebrated in three languages; and such was its reputation for hospitality that tradition began to place there the Feeding of the Five Thousand.[19]

---

[16] *Kyrillos*, 239. 13–20.   [17] Ibid. 17–18.

[18] *MO* pt. 3, iii. 83. The other reasons for its inclusion are its value as a supplement to Cyril and the additional historical facts.

[19] For the location of the Feeding of the Five Thousand at the Monastery of Theodosius, see Theodore of Petra, *V. Thds.* 39. 20.

Theodosius presided over the monks of the coenobia as archimandrite while Sabas was archimandrite of the monks of the laurae. Theodore of Petra's *Life* gives a fascinating picture of life in this important monastery. Theodosius was from Cappadocia, and, alone of the monks of Palestine, showed himself to have been influenced by the Cappadocian father, Basil. Theodore of Petra describes him teaching his monks using a long section of Basil's *Regulae Fusius Tractatae*.[20] The connection with Cappadocia was shared with Theognius and was a reason for Theognius' joining Theodosius' community. It indicates that Basil's understanding of the coenobitic life influenced both monasteries, and shaped the Palestinian coenobitic tradition. The two traditions of the coenobitic life drawing inspiration from Cappadocia and the laurite life with its connections with Egypt coexisted harmoniously. Monks moved from one way of life to the other as their spiritual maturity developed.[21]

The *Life of Theodosius* gives an alternative account of the conflict between the Chalceonian monks of the desert and the Monophysite Emperor Anastasius to that of Cyril. Theodore's version concentrates exclusively on the part played by Theodosius and makes no mention of Sabas. Both writers describe Theodosius ascending the ambo to solemnly proclaim that whoever did not accept the four Councils as the Four Gospels should be anathematized. Theodore places this event in the Church of the Anastasis on an unspecified occasion while, in Cyril's account, the words are spoken at the dramatic moment when the new Patriarch John announced his acceptance of the Council of Chalcedon before 10,000 monks in the Church of St Stephen, with both Sabas and Theodosius offering firm persuasion. If these two statements refer to the same event, they demonstrate clearly both Theodore's exclusive interest in the contribution of Theodosius and his lack of concern for historical accuracy.[22] The discrepancy shows clearly the different purposes of the two authors. Theodore seeks to praise the memory of Theodosius in a speech on the anniversary of his death while Cyril tries to write a historical account.

The third of the group of four Lives is that of Chariton. It seems

---

[20] Ibid. 50. 13–51. 22; 53. 1–12. For the passage in Basil, *Regulae Fusius Tractatae*, PG 31. 889B–C.

[21] For the peaceful coexistence of the laurite and coenobitic life in Palestine, see K. Holl, *Enthusiasmus und Bussgewalt beim griechischen Mönchtums* (Leipzig, 1898; edn. Hildesheim, 1969) 172–8.

[22] *Kyrillos*, 151. 17–152. 15, cf. Theodore of Petra, *V. Thds.* 61. 26–62. 20.

that a monk of one of the monasteries founded by Chariton was goaded
into writing the Life as a result of reading Cyril's Lives and being
determined that his own founder should not be neglected in this process
of literary production. He refers to the writing of Lives of the great
monks shortly after their deaths or even in one case, during the lifetime
of the saint.[23] This is best understood as a reference to the activity of
Cyril, since the *Life of John the Hesychast* was originally written while
he was still alive.[24] The anonymous author admits that a long time has
passed since the death of Chariton and that he has had to rely on the
oral traditions of the monastery.[25] One manuscript of the Life contains
a lemma which names the author as 'John the son of Xenophon and
brother of Arcadius'.[26] This John is the subject of a fictional work
describing the adventures of a father, Xenophon, and two sons, John
and Arcadius, who are separated in a shipwreck, become monks in
Palestine independently and are finally reunited on Calvary. There is no
reason to suppose that the reference to John's authorship of the *Life of
Chariton* has any more foundation in fact than the improving fable in
which he makes his appearance.[27]

The figure of Chariton takes us back to the origins of the monasticism
of Palestine. His Life tells us that when Chariton started living the
monastic life, there were few other monks, except in the caves of
Calamon near the Dead Sea.[28] The two chronological references in the
Life contradict one another. The first is the statement that Chariton
left his home in Iconium following the persecution under Aurelian, who
died in 275, and the second is that the church of the monastery, which
he founded on his arrival in Palestine, was dedicated by Macarius, who
was bishop of Jerusalem between about 314 and 333, at least thirty-five
years after he was supposed to have left Iconium.[29] The date of the
consecration of the church is more likely to be accurate since it would
be remembered within the monastery. If the church was consecrated
during the two decades after 314 then Chariton would have been more

---

[23] *V. Char.* 42; ed. Garitte, 44. 27–45. 4.

[24] If this passage is to be referred to Cyril, then obviously the author of the *Life of
Chariton* was not using the version of John's Life which included the account of his death.
See Ch. 1.

[25] *V. Char.* 42; ed. Garitte, 44.23 to 45.

[26] The MS is Ottobaniansus graecus, 373.

[27] See F. Halkin, *Bibliotheca Hagiographica Graeca* (Brussels, 1952), 1877, u–y. The
text is in PG 114. 1014–43.

[28] *V. Char.* 13; ed. Garitte, 26. 1–4.

[29] *V. Char.* 8 and 13; ed. Garitte, 22. 4 and 28.8.

likely to have been arrested during the persecution under Galerius
(d.311), Maximin Daia (d.313) or Licinius (d.324), rather than that of
Aurelian.

The life of Chariton describes the foundation of three of the oldest
monasteries of the desert, Pharan, Douka, and Souka or the Old Laura.
The oral traditions used by the author of the Life are supplemented by
references in other literary works which testify to the existence of all
three monasteries in the fourth century.[30]

The Life devotes a surprisingly large amount of space to Chariton's
sufferings under the persecutions in Iconium and emphasizes the continuity between the two halves of his career, as martyr and monk.
Following his unexpected release from prison as he awaited his death,
Chariton decided that, since he had already given up his life to Christ
as a potential martyr, he should go to Jerusalem. On the way he was
captured by robbers and imprisoned in their hide-out in a cave. Being
miraculously released, he remained in the cave, and was joined by others
who formed a monastic community.[31] The remainder of his life is
presented as a struggle to retain his silence and solitude in the face of
the disciples who were continually attracted to him by his reputation
for holiness. No other monastic source presents so clearly the inner
identity of the vocation of the martyr and the monk.

The fourth life is briefer and more fragmentary, but, although short,
it has attracted the attention of historians and a plausible case has been
made for attributing at least a part of it to Cyril.

The *Life of Gerasimus* was discovered in a manuscript on Patmos by
A. Papadopoulos-Kerameus, who attributed it to Cyril on grounds of
style.[32] This attribution was accepted by others, including F. Diekamp.[33]
In a more detailed analysis, H. Grégoire suggested that the Life is a
compilation of various short pieces of writing about Gerasimus made
by a monk of his monastery in the sixth century.[34] A section of the Life,
consisting of the end of chapter 2 and chapters 3 and 4 in the Patmos

---

[30] See D. J. Chitty, *Desert a City* (Oxford, 1966), 15. He refers the reader to the *Lausiac History*, 48, for Douka; John Cassian's *Conferences*, 6. 1, for Souka; and *Kyrillos*, 14. 9 for Euthymius arriving at the monastery of Pharan in 406, by which time it was clearly well established. See also beginning of Ch. 7.

[31] *V. Char.* 2–11; ed. Garitte, 17. 10–25. 9. Over a third of the Life describes the period before Chariton became a monk. In the Lives of Cyril, the period before the entry into the monastery is described with brevity.

[32] *MH* 226–9.

[33] See F. Diekamp, *Die Origenistischen Streitigkeiten im sechsten Jahrhundert* (Münster, 1899), 6.

[34] H. Grégoire, 'La Vie anonyme de S. Gérasime', *By. Z.* 13 (1904), 114–35.

manuscript, also appears in a version of Cyril's *Life of Euthymius* and in the Metaphrastic version of the Life.[35] This passage, he suggested, is the work of Cyril.

B. Flusin raised objections to this conclusion. He pointed out that it is unlikely that Cyril would include a section describing the virtues of Gerasimus in a work commending Euthymius. He also notes that the passage contains a description of the way of life followed by Gerasimus' monastery and that such descriptions are unusual in Cyril's work.[36] He concluded that the *Life of Gerasimus* was written by a monk of his monastery.

These objections become less persuasive when the course of Cyril's life is taken into account. The inauspicious beginning of his monastic career took place at the laura of Calamon, which was closely related to the monastery of Gerasimus. The two monasteries share the aetiological tradition that the Virgin Mary, Joseph, and the child Jesus rested at the site during their flight to Egypt. They are only a mile distant from each other and it has been suggested that they were originally one community which became divided as a result of the conflict following the Council of Chalcedon.[37] Cyril's interest in Gerasimus is accounted for by his residence at Calamon. He would probably have had material about Gerasimus noted down in his collection of sheets of paper.[38]

It would have been natural to include this material in the *Life of Euthymius*. Gerasimus came to Jerusalem from Lycia in 451 and his friendship with Euthymius was soon forged as they united in support of the Chalcedonian faith.[39] The two men, along with other hardened ascetics, later spent several Lenten fasts together in the inhospitable part of the desert near the Dead Sea, called Rouba.[40] After the death of Theoctistus, Euthymius sent younger monks to spend time with Gerasimus in order to prepare themselves for the laurite way of life. Among these was Cyriac.[41] Gerasimus was informed of the death of Euthymius

---

[35] The manuscript of Cyril is Codex Sinaiticus graecus 524, used by the monk Augoustinos for his edition of the *Life of Euthymius* in *Nea Sion*, 11–12 (Jerusalem, 1911–12). The text of the section concerning Gerasimus is reprinted in *MH* 226–9.

[36] See *MH* 35–40.

[37] For the history of the monasteries, see D. J. Chitty, 'Two Monasteries in the Wilderness of Judaea', *PEFQ St.* (1928), 134–52; O. Meinardus, 'Notes on the Laurae and Monasteries of the Wilderness of Judaea', *SBFLA* 16 (1965–6), 328–56, 332–7); S. Vailhé, 'Les Laures de saint Gérasime et de Calamon', *E. Or.* 2 (1899), 106–19.

[38] *Kyrillos*, 83. 6–7.

[39] Ibid. 44. 19–24.

[40] Ibid. 56. 25–9; 225. 10–13.

[41] Ibid. 224. 24–6.

through a vision, attended his funeral, and then died two years later, in March 475.[42] A later superior of Gerasimus' monastery, Eugenius, who presided over the community from 481 to 526, assisted Sabas in his responsibilities as archimandrite of the laurites.[43]

These circumstances form the historical background to the interest of Cyril in the life of Gerasimus and account for the inclusion of material about Gerasimus in the *Life of Euthymius*. Although the section concerned was written by Cyril, the inclusion in some of the versions of the *Life of Euthymius* was probably the work of a later redactor, just as another redactor included it in his *Life of Gerasimus*.

JOHN MOSCHUS

The works so far considered tell the story of desert life in the first half of the sixth century. The continuation is found in the work of John Moschus called the *Leimonarion*, or, to use the Latin title, *Pratum Spirituale*, that is, *Spiritual Meadow*. Moschus was a traveller. Like Palladius, like the monks from the Mount of Olives who wrote the *Historia Monachorum*, and like John Cassian, he travelled widely around the monastic east accumulating a compendium of anecdotal material from a wide variety of sources. From this material, he wrote his *Spiritual Meadow*. His companion in his travels was his friend Sophronius, who is often referred to in the text and later became Patriarch of Jerusalem.

The chronology of John's life and travels is built up from two sources. First, there are autobiographical notes scattered through the *Spiritual Meadow*. These references are not connected and are difficult to harmonize. Second, there is a biographical prologue attached to some manuscripts of the *Spiritual Meadow*.[44] The information gathered from these two sources enable a fragmentary biography of John to be pieced together.

John, like Sophronius, was a Cilician. This is implied by the comment that both men enjoyed a good relationship with Zoilus, a reader of Alexandria, who shared 'the same country and the same education'. One version adds that Zoilus was ὁ αἰγεότης, from a region of Cilicia. John

---

[42] Ibid. 225. 13–17.
[43] Ibid. 239. 11–12. Eugenius is not mentioned in the equivalent passage in the *Life of Sabas*, 115. 24–6.
[44] For the text of the prologue, see H. Usener, *Der heilige Tychon* (Leipzig, 1907) 91–3.

seems to have enjoyed meeting monks from his homeland, since he makes a point of noting which monks come from Cilicia, while generally he shows little interest in such details.[45] John, like many young monks, began his monastic career in a coenobium, in his case that of Theodosius, and then progressed to the laura of Pharan, where he spent the ten years or so between about 568 and 578.[46]

At the start of the reign of the Emperor Tiberius II (578–82) he visited Egypt.[47] This was followed by a stay of ten years or so—all Moschus' monastic sojourns are said to have lasted ten years, which suggests that the figure is, to say the least, approximate—at the laura of the Aeliotes. Some have thought that this laura was on Mount Sinai, but it seems more likely to have been near Jericho. The reason for this confusion is that Moschus tells us that while he was there a monk was working on a reservoir being constructed by the Patriarch of Jerusalem, either 'on Sinai' (according to the Greek text) or 'in [the shape of] Sigma' (according to the Latin).[48] Of the two readings the Latin is to be preferred. It is improbable that a Patriarch of Jerusalem should construct a reservoir in Sinai which was far outside his area of jurisdiction, and very plausible that the semi-circular shape of a sigma, as it was then written, would have become the distinguishing feature of a new reservoir.[49] So it should be concluded that both the monastery and the reservoir were near the Jordan. His visit to Sinai, during which he

---

[45] *Prat.* 171, PG 87/3. 303 C. For the addition found in the F group of manuscripts, see P. Pattenden, 'The Text of the Pratum Spirituale', *J. Th. S.* NS 26 (1975), 38–54, 41 n. 1. For the references to Cilicia as the place of origin of monks, 'the reflection of a regional patriotism' see H. Chadwick, 'John Moschus and his Friend Sophronius the Sophist', *J. Th. S.* NS 25 (1974), 41–74, 56. Earlier S. Vailhé, in 'Jean Mosch', *E. Or.* 5 (1902), 108, had suggested Damascus as John's place of origin.

[46] This date is arrived at from John's account of meeting Cosmas the Eunuch and Auxanon the Syncellus, both of whom served with Gregory who was Patriarch of Antioch, 570–93. Our knowledge of their careers enables us to date John's stay at the monastery. See Chadwick, 'John Moschus', 55–6.

[47] *Prat.* 112, PG 87/3. 2975C–2977B.

[48] *Prat.* 66, PG 87/3. 29/7A. The Latin text is a translation by Ambrogio Traversari of a text sent to him in the 1430s. However this Greek text was from the F group which claims to have been copied in the 9th c., while the Greek texts on which Migne based his version are probably later. The Latin text may preserve an older tradition. See Pattenden, 'Text of the Pratum Spirituale', 38–41.

[49] Federlin suggests that the remains which he discovered north of the aquaduct leading to the monastery of St John the Baptist mark the site of the monastery of the Aeliotes. See J. L. Federlin, 'Recherches sur les laures et monastères de la plaine du Jourdain et du désert de Jérusalem', *La Terre Sainte*, 20 (1903), 329–30. Among those who have considered that the monastery of the Aeliotes is on Sinai are Chitty, *Desert*, 149; Chadwick, 'John Moschus', 57.

collected several anecdotes which were included in the *Spiritual Meadow*, would have been of shorter duration. According to the biographical prologue, Moschus also stayed at the New Laura at some stage in this period.[50]

After 604 conditions in Palestine became increasingly unstable as the threat from the Persians grew, and Moschus left on his travels. He went first to Antioch, then to Egypt, then to some islands including Cyprus and Samos, and finally to Rome, where he died.[51] His death took place in the eighth indiction, which fell in both 619 and 634. Of these two possible dates, there are fewer historical and literary difficulties involved in selecting the latter.[52] His friend Sophronius brought his body back to Palestine and buried him in the cave of the Magi in the monastery of Theodosius, where he had begun his long and mobile career.[53]

A full analysis of the *Spiritual Meadow* is outside the scope of this study but a few points arising out of this brief biography should be noticed.

First, John's career lasted a long time. If he was present at Pharan between 568 and 578, then he lived at the monastery of Theodosius in the 560s, only a few years after Cyril was producing his literary output. When John entered the monastic life, monks who are mentioned by Cyril were still alive. Conon, for example, was elected superior of the Great Laura in 548, and so was Cyril's abbot. He was also known to John Moschus who includes reference to him in the *Spiritual Meadow*.[54] We also meet a certain Leontius, who, at the time of John, presided over the Monastery of Theodosius. This same Leontius had, earlier in his career, been one of the party of Chalcedonian monks who occupied the New Laura in 555, among whom was also Cyril of Scythopolis.[55] His stories follow on where Cyril's Lives leave off. While lacking the thoroughness and unity of Cyril's writing, the *Spiritual Meadow* gives vivid glimpses of life in the monasteries in the later part of the sixth century, the period which follows directly after that described by Cyril, and into the early years of the seventh.

Second, he knew the monasteries of the Jordan. As well as writing about monasteries known to us from the writing of Cyril, his stay at

[50] See Usener, *Der heilige Tychon*, 91.
[51] Usener, *Der heilige Tychon*, 91–2, 19–37.
[52] Chadwick, 'John Moschus', 50–3.
[53] Usener, *Der heilige Tychon*, 92–3, 38–70.
[54] *Kyrillos*, 196. 20; 198. 2; 198. 7. *Prat.* 42, PG 87/3. 2986B–C.
[55] *Kyrillos*, 200. 0. *Prat.* 4, PG 87/3. 2856C.

the Jordan provided him with a mass of stories from monasteries in this area. For many of these, the *Spiritual Meadow* is the only literary source. He tells of the monastery of the Towers which had been founded by Jacob, a disciple of Sabas, and probably received its name from the shape of the cells of the monks.[56] In addition there were Penthucla, also called the monastery of the Baptism and so situated close to the Jordan; the monastery of Petrus, also 'near the Jordan'; Chorembe; and two monasteries called Soubiba, possibly a popular Syrian name for a monastery, of the Syrians and the Bessans; and, on the east bank of the river, Sapsas.[57]

The impression of a connected network of monasteries clustered close to the river is confirmed by the survey of the area conducted by Federlin in the early years of this century.[58] In an area of perhaps four square miles to the south-east of Jericho, he discovered the remains of thirteen monasteries. His evidence is of particular value since building and agricultural development has now removed many of the traces which he observed. It confirms John Moschus' picture of thriving settlements of monks near the Jordan. In the absence of earlier evidence for the existence of these monasteries and the absence of any new foundations in the central desert area around the Great Laura, we can presume that in the late sixth century the focus of monastic life was moving east to the Jordan valley.

The third point of interest arises out of the second. A consequence of this new vitality of the communities of the Jordan was a loosening of the links with Jerusalem. As the focus of monastic life shifted, the monks became increasingly detached from the ecclesiastical and political life of the province. This helps to account for the difference in the literary forms chosen by Cyril and John. While Cyril wrote history, describing how the monks helped to shape the church of the Empire, John Moschus tells stories. This anecdotal style is a result of a change in the self-awareness of the monks. Their horizon has shrunk and their world is smaller. For him, monks belong in the monasteries, not in the cities. It is hard to imagine one of Moschus' monks setting out for Constantinople to bargain for a tax rebate or an increase in the number

---

[56] *Kyrillos*, 99. 21. *Prat.* 9; 10, PG 87/3. 2860A; 2860B. For the shape of the Towers, see A. Augustinovic, *Gerico e dintorni* (Jerusalem, 1951), 100.

[57] *Prat.* 3, PG 87/3. 2853C, for Penthucla; 16. 2864.A, for Petrus; 157. 3025B, for Chorembe; 157. 3025B, for Soubiba; 1. 2853B, for Sapsas.

[58] Federlin, 'Recherches', *Terre Sainte*, 19–21 (1902–4), *passim*.

of troops stationed in the province. Moschus' monasteries are self-contained and inward-looking.

But although the monks do not seem to be involved in the rough and tumble of ecclesiastical politics, Moschus is a convinced supporter of Chalcedon. Many of his anecdotes demonstrate the truth of the Chalcedonian faith and the errors of the Monophysites. He gives several examples of a form of miracle absent from Cyril's writings, in which a miraculous sign confounds the heretics. One of these describes two stylites who challenge each other to a test of faith. Each proffers a piece of their host. That of the Monophysite dissolves in hot water while that of the Chalcedonian not only does not dissolve but also reduces the water to coldness, such is the power enclosed within it.[59] John's companion, Sophronius, witnessed to this orthodox Christology in a more sustained and theological manner. After he buried John's body, he was chosen to be Patriarch of Jerusalem, some time before the end of 634. His Synodical Letter, sent out as soon as he became Patriarch, expounded the doctrine of the two energies of Christ and was to be a document of central importance in the debate over Monoenergism.[60] The allegiance of the Palestinian monks to the Council of Chalcedon was expressed in different ways but with equal conviction both in Cyril's *Lives* and in John's *Spiritual Meadow*.

CHOZIBA

The last work to be considered here presents a different face of monastic Palestine. The *Life of George of Choziba* describes events which took place in a monastery near Jericho. Choziba, hugging its cliff on the north side of the Wadi Kelt only a few miles from Jericho, is today the most visited of all the monasteries, with a tradition of hospitality that goes back to Byzantine times.

George and Antony, the writer of the Life, were master and disciple. George came from Cyprus after the death of his parents to avoid entanglement in marriage and property ownership and, after a time spent in the coenobium of Choziba on account of his youth, joined his natural brother Heraclides at Calamon. When his brother died, he returned to Choziba where he remained until his death. He lived first

---

[59] *Prat.* 29, PG 87/3. 2876C–2877A.
[60] Sophronius' Synodical Letter is in *ACO* 2nd ser. 2. 1, pp. 410–94.

in the Cells of Choziba, a group of cells a mile or so east of the monastery, and then, after the Persian invasion, in the monastery itself.[61]

Antony, arriving later with a companion, intended to go on to Rhaithou on Sinai but political instability in the region forced them to stay at Choziba. The companion continued his journey secretly but Antony stayed with George.[62] He wrote George's Life in 631. This precise date can be arrived at because he refers in passing to Modestus as the present Patriarch of Jerusalem. Modestus was Patriarch for only a few months, in the year 631.[63] To the Life is appended a series of miracles which took place at Choziba through the power of the Mother of God.[64]

There is a certain triumphalism in Cyril born out of his experience that, however great the tribulations of the saints, their cause in fact finally prevailed. In contrast to this, the Life of George describes a society under threat. The attacks of the Persians form the background to large parts of the Life. Antony decided to stay for a while at Choziba because it was dangerous to travel on to Sinai. As the Persians came close to Jerusalem, some monks fled to Arabia, some to Calamon by the Jordan, and some into hiding in the caves around the monastery. George was discovered in his cave but was spared captivity because of his venerable appearance.[65] Antony saw Jerusalem fall and was part of a monastic community struggling to survive a series of hostile attacks.

The silence of Choziba was also threatened by invaders of a different and more friendly kind. The monastery lay within sight of the highway between Jerusalem and Jericho and, because of this closeness, received many visitors. Dorotheus, the superior for much of Antony's time at the monastery, offered a warm welcome to visitors. We read of him pressing guests to stay at the monastery. These included Antony himself and a certain Cilician 'lucator'[66]. One of the tasks of the monks, shared by George, was to wait on the road to offer refreshment to travellers.[67] An example of the quality of hospitality for which Choziba became famous is the story told by John Moschus of a monk who used to wait at the roadside for travellers so that he could carry their luggage or even

---

[61] The *Life of George of Choziba* is in *An. Boll.* 7 (1888), 97–144, 336–59.

[62] *V. Geor. Choz.* 32–4, *An. Boll.* 130. 12–134. 7.

[63] *V. Geor. Choz.* 16, *An. Boll.* 115. 6–7.

[64] *The Miracles of the Blessed Virgin Mary in Choziba* are in *An. Boll.* 7 (1888), 360–70.

[65] *V. Geor. Choz.* 31, *An. Boll.* 129. 14–130. 11.

[66] *V. Geor. Choz.* 16; 32, *An. Boll.* 115. 5; 131. 7.

[67] *V. Geor. Choz.* 23, *An. Boll.* 122. 10–11.

their children up the long road to Jerusalem.[68] The presence of visitors and travellers was a fact of life for the monks and influenced the development of the spiritual traditions of the monastery. Antony's stories are set against the backdrop of the simple domesticity of the monastery. He describes the baking of bread; the cutting of mannouthia, the desert thistles used for food, and fuel; the collection of the capparis berries.[69] As these events take place, George gives his teaching. His words are suffused with a warmth and compassion which are deeply attractive. On his arrival at Choziba he was entrusted to the care of a hardened ascetic. While he was collecting water, his master hid his clothes and so George had to return to the monastery late and semi-naked, an offence for which he was hit by his master. As he administered the punishment the master's hand was withered and was only healed after the young George prayed for him.[70] This story sets out a theme to be often repeated. The monastery is a place ruled by the love of God. Harshness is out of place.

George lived a life of asceticism and prayer. His diet of sun-hardened kitchen scraps rolled into little balls and the small dimensions of his cell are carefully described, as are the ecstasies of his prayer.[71] Yet he showed no desire to leave the monastery to search out the solitude of the eremetical life. He preferred to carry out his ascetic struggles within the context of a community. The spirituality presented in Antony's *Life of George of Choziba* is based on the love of God, discovered through community life and ascetic practice, and available to all who come.

This Life was written in the twilight of the Byzantine period in Palestine. The True Cross was restored to Jerusalem by the Emperor Heraclius in the year in which the Life was written, but only seven years later the city was to be surrendered to the Caliph Omar and the Arabs. As the forces of invasion gathered, this Life of a simple monk stands as a final testimony to the true vitality of the monasteries of Palestine. A story of a man who lived a life of asceticism and of love for all sums up the true achievement of the monk.

---

[68] *Prat.* 24, PG 87/3. 2869B.
[69] *V. Geor. Choz.* 23; 14 and 42, *An. Boll.* 122. 16–17; 110. 1–5 and 143. 7–8.
[70] *V. Geor. Choz.* 4–5, *An. Boll.* 99. 6–101. 2.
[71] *V. Geor. Choz.* 12; 13 and 36, *An. Boll.* 108. 7–12; 109. 4–5 and 135. 6–136. 7.

3

Monastic Culture

MONASTIC CULTURE

The literature of the desert describes the 'outer world' of the monks. This is the catalogue of ascetic achievement, the instruction given by the saints, the foundation of monasteries, the involvement in church life, and the other actions which the monks performed. It is a story which the writers take delight in telling. They present it in a robust and sometimes racy fashion. Behind the series of stories lies another, 'inner' world. The chapters which make up the Lives were composed by men who thought, and communicated their thoughts to each other. They conversed together, they told each other stories, they had favourite books, they kept records of events they felt to be important. This inner world of thought and conversation, of self-consciousness and self-understanding, can be called the culture of the monasteries.

The writing of Cyril provides a rare opportunity to enter into this inner world of culture. The route to its discovery lies through the analysis of the material which Cyril used in the construction of his Lives. Researchers have examined Cyril's work with the aim of discovering what source material he used. But the scope of their enquiries has been limited to specific types of source material and a limited range of evidence.[1]

This chapter seeks to add to these studies by providing a more comprehensive and inclusive presentation of the variety of Cyril's sources than has yet appeared. From this, we can glimpse the interior world of monastic culture in which Cyril moved. The material which Cyril drew on in the construction of the Lives was that which was available to him in the monasteries. Insights into the nature of this culture can only be partial and fragmentary since they are presented through the medium of one writer. None the less, the conclusions which can be drawn from

---

[1] The fullest discussion of the written sources is in *MH* 43–86 and the oral sources are discussed in *MO* pt. 2, iii. 9–16.

the study of Cyril also have a general reference, since Cyril is an accurate and faithful witness to what he sees and hears.

CYRIL'S LIBRARY

In his brief yet perceptive comments about Cyril in *The Desert a City*, Derwas Chitty wrote: '[Cyril's] works have yet to be fully explored as a mine of quotations from earlier works—the Vita Antonii, the Vita Pachomii, the Apophthegmata Patrum, etc.'[2] This fruitful and fascinating exploration was in fact well under way when Chitty wrote and, as he predicted, was to continue. It has revealed a detailed network of literary dependence by Cyril on earlier works. It tells us which books he enjoyed reading and the kinds of material within them which impressed him sufficiently for him to note down and reproduce in his own writing.

Before describing how Cyril used his sources, we should note the large amount of careful literary analysis which has been carried out.[3] These separate researches have been gathered together and considerably expanded by B. Flusin. He states his aim as 'reprendre et compléter cette recherche avec un double but: montrer que les emprunts, chez Cyrille, sont plus étendus qu'on ne le suppose généralement: nous servir des résultats de cette analyse pour mieux situer l'œuvre de Cyrille.'[4] Flusin lists over 120 places where it is likely that Cyril has copied from or been directly influenced by the work of an earlier author. His work

---

[2] See D. J. Chitty, *The Desert a City* (Oxford, 1966), 131.

[3] These studies have explored areas of literary dependence: W. Bousset, *Apophthegmata: Textüberlieferung und Charakter der Apophthegmata Patrum* (Tübingen, 1923), 67–8 (for the sayings of the Desert Fathers). P. Devos, 'Cyrille de Scythopolis: Influences littéraires, vêtement de l'évêque de Jérusalem, Passarion et Pierre l'Ibère', *An. Boll.* 98 (1980), 25–38 (for Theodoret, Gregory of Nazianzus, and a miracle of Menas). R. Draguet, 'Réminiscences de Pallade chez Cyrille de Scythopolis', *RAM* 98–100 (1948), 213–18 (for Palladius' *Lausiac History*). A.-J. Festugière, *Collections grêques de miracles: Sainte Thècle, saints Côme et Damien, saint Georges* (Paris, 1971), 79–81 (for the life and miracles of Thecla). G. Garitte, 'Réminiscences de la Vie d'Antoine dans Cyrille de Scythopolis', in *Silloge bizantina in onore di Silvio Giuseppe Mercati* (Rome, 1957), 117–22 (for the life of Antony). G. C. Hansen, *Theodoros Anagnostes, Kirchengeschichte*, GCS (Berlin, 1971), pp. x–xxi (for Theodore Lector). A. Guillaumont, *Les 'Kephalaia gnostica' d'Évagre le Pontique et l'histoire de l'Origénisme chez les Grecs et les Syriens*, Patristica Sorbonensia, 5 (Paris, 1962), 124–70 (for Origenist texts). E. Schwartz, *Kyrillos von Skythopolis* (Leipzig, 1939), 362 (for Justinian's theological writings).

[4] *MH* 43.

contains some mistakes of detail and omission, but nevertheless provides a comprehensive collection of evidence.[5] Four comments should be made on this currently definitive catalogue. First, it is incomplete. Flusin of course recognizes this when he writes: 'Le dossier que nous avons réuni est sans doute incomplet.'[6] The comparison of texts with the purpose of demonstrating borrowings is bound to involve an individual judgement which will leave the list unfinished and the selection random. Here are a few passages which should, in my opinion, be added to the list as a reminder that many more are still awaiting discovery.

1. James of Nisibis becomes a bishop.

Ἀναλλάξας δὲ τὴν ὄρειον ἐκείνην διατριβήν ... οὔτε τὴν τρ φην ὄντε τὴν ἀμπεχόνην ἐνήλλαξεν ... ἡ δε πολιτεία μεταβολὴν οὐκ ἐδέχετο (Theodoret, H. Rel. 1. 7. 4–7)

John the Hesychast.

καὶ οὕτως τὴν ἀρχιερωσύνην ἀκουσίως δεξάμενος τὸν κανόνα τῆς μοναχικῆς πολιτείας οὐκ ἐνήλλαξεν (Kyrillos, 202. 22–4)

2. ἐξηγωνίζετο τα πάντα ἐν ἑαυτῷ κατέχειν ταπεινοφροσύνῃ καὶ πρᾳΰτητι καὶ ἀληθείᾳ, ὡς λόγος ὁ κυρίος, Μάθετε ἀπ᾽ ἐμοῦ ὅτι πρᾶός εἰμι καὶ ταπεινὸς τῇ καρδίᾳ (V. Pach. G1 14. 16)

εἶχεν γὰρ πραότητα πολλὴν καὶ ταπεινοφροσύνην ἀληθίνην μιμούμενος ἐν τουτῷ χριστὸν ... φήσαντα, Μάθετε ἀπ᾽ ἐμοῦ ὅτι πρᾶός εἰμι κὰι ταπεινὸς τῇ καρδίᾳ (Kyrillos, 100. 15–19)

3. οὕτως ἀρχὴ λογισμοῦ φιλαρχίας ἡ κλῆρος (V. Pach. G1 34. 7)

τῆς φιλαρχίας ἀρχὴ καὶ ῥίζα ἐστιν τῶν λογισμῶν ἡ τοῦ κληρωθῆναι ἐπιθυμία (Kyrillos, 102. 20–1)

4. εὐλαβούμενος ἀποδύσασθαι, ἵνα μὴ γυμνὸν αὐτὸν ἴδῃ (H. Laus. Butler, 29. 102)

εὐλαβούμενος ... μὴ ἑαυτὸν γυμνὸν θεωρεῖν (Kyrillos, 202. 26–7)

5. A list of nine Pachomian foundations (V. Pach. G1 112)

The list of seven Sabaite foundations has the monasteries of Euthymius and Theoktistos added to bring the total number to nine (Kyrillos, 158. 20–159. 2)

Second, the discussion on the relationship between Cyril and one of

---

[5] e.g. he claims to add two references to Garitte's list of parallels with the *Life of Antony*, one of which is in fact included by Garitte (cf. the reference to 53. 11–15 at *MH* 45 with Garitte, 'Réminiscences', 119). He points correctly to Cyril's dependence in *Kyrillos*, 6. 4–8 on *Miracles of Thecla* 4. 4–11, ed. Dagron, 404, but neglects to mention the use of the same passage in 86. 1–4.

[6] *MH* 83.

his sources, the *Lausiac History* of Palladius, has not been satisfactorily assessed. It might seem surprising that Cyril should have known and used the writing of Palladius, a self-confessed admirer of the Origenist theologian Evagrius Ponticus, but there are several passages which reveal that Cyril has read and drawn ideas and phrases from Palladius.[7] The article of R. Draguet on the relationship of Cyril and Palladius listed nine of these parallel passages 'attestant une dépendance de Cyrille vis-à-vis de Pallade'.[8] Flusin is rightly critical of this list and is prepared to accept three as established, one as doubtful, and five as insufficiently close to be used as evidence of dependence.[9] He went on to note that, of the three convincing references, two come from Palladius' chapter about Macarius the Egyptian, and these both occur in the same couple of pages of Cyril's writing.[10] So he suggests that Cyril in fact knew only a short section of the Lausiac History and that Palladius can no longer be considered as a significant source.

But the list of parallel passages can be extended. The following four passages should be added to the list showing that Palladius' influence on Cyril was greater than has been previously thought. They show that the *Lausiac History* was known to Cyril and impressed him sufficiently for him to borrow from the earlier work.

1. Elias' vision of the death of the Emperor Anastasius, emphasizing that the vision occurred at the same time as the event.
   ταύτῃ τῇ ὥρᾳ ἐτελεύτησεν Ἀναστάσιος (*Kyrillos*, 161. 18)

   Didymus' vision of the Emperor Julian's death.
   σήμερον ἑβδόμην ἐτελεύτησεν Ἰουλιανος (*H. Laus.*, Butler, 20. 19)

2. Sabas discovers the dead body of Anthimus, over which angels have sung (*Kyrillos*, 133. 10–134. 6)

   Palladius and others discover the dead body of Alexandra, with similar signs of divine approval of the departed (*H. Laus.*, Butler, 21)

3. Paul the superior of the New Laura is described as ἁπλουστατον on two occasions (*Kyrillos*, 124. 13 and 23)

   Paul the disciple of Antony is ἄκακος καὶ ἁπλοῦς ... λίαν ἁπλοῦς (*H. Laus.*, Butler, 69; 73. 5; 74. 15 and 19)

4. Elias builds a monastery for scattered monks.

   Ἡλίας ᾠκοδόμησε μέγα μοναστήριον καὶ συνήγαγε πάσας τας ἀλωμένας

---

[7] For the Evagrian influence on Palladius, see R. Draguet, 'L'Histoire lausïaque, une œuvre écrite dans l'esprit d'Évagre'. *RHE* 41 (1946), 321–64.

[8] R. Draguet, 'Réminiscences de Pallade', 217.

[9] *MH* 43–4.

[10] *Kyrillos*, 78. 12–13; 79. 6–8.

Ἠλίας ῳκοδόμησεν μοναστήριον ... ἐντὸς ἀκολούθως αὐτῶν φροντίζων,
καὶ ἐν αὐτῷ περισυνήγαγεν τοὺς τῆς ποιήσας αὐταῖς ἀνάπαυσιν πασαν καὶ
ἁγίας Ἀναστοεως σπουδαίους ... κήπους καὶ χρηστήρια ... συνήγαγε
κελλία ἑκάστῳ αὐτῶν διανείμας γάρ ὡς τριακοσίος (H. Laus., Butler,
πᾶσαν σωματικὴν ἀνάπαυσιν ἔχοντα 84)
παραδεισίων (Kyrillos, 116. 4–8 and
25)

The third observation on this dossier of literary dependence is that
there are some works which Cyril does *not* seem to have used. For
example, the *Life of Porphyry* attributed to Mark the Deacon, probably
written in the early fifth century in Gaza, and Gerontius' *Life of Melania*,
written at the same time in Jerusalem, were saints' Lives with a
Palestinian provenance. Yet there is no sign that they influenced Cyril's
thinking or vocabulary.

In addition, on some occasions a surprising lack of literary dependence
can be clearly demonstrated. Compare, for example, Cyril's expression,
ὁ δὲ λέων ὑπὸ τῆς εὐχῆς τοῦ γέροντος ὡς ὑπὸ μάστιγος διωκόμενος with
that of Athanasius' *Life of Antony*: ἔφυγον ἐκεῖναι ὡς ὑπὸ μάστιγος τοῦ
λόγου διωκόμεναι. In contrast, the *Historia Monachorum* describes the
prayers of Abba Bes putting a hippopotamus to flight, ὡς ὑπὸ ἀγγέλου
ἐλασθείς.[11] Cyril's choice of phrase suggests not only that he knew the
Life of Antony but also that he did not know the *Historia Monachorum*.

Fourth, Flusin's list of sources does not include that which is the
most important by far, the Bible. The Bible is used consistently and
frequently in all parts of his Lives. He quotes freely from both the Old
and the New Testaments, and from all parts of both. In his edition
Schwartz notes the points at which Cyril has used the Bible and these
are reproduced in Price's English translation. Any assessment of literary
influence on Cyril must begin with the book which dominated the life
of the monasteries and shaped the devotion and thought of the monks.

After the Bible, saints' Lives were the form of literature which was
most valued by the monks. The list of Cyril's borrowings shows that a
wide selection was available and that they were read with enthusiasm.
Their popularity is shown by their rapid circulation around the Mediterranean world. The speed of transmission is shown by the case of the
Life of Martin. Martin died in 393, and within only four years, in 397,
Paulinus of Nola was writing to thank Sulpicius Severus, the author of

---

[11] *Kyrillos*, 107. 14–15; cf. 119. 27–8; *V. Anton.* 52, PG 26. 920A: *H. Mon. Bes.* 1. 14,
cf. Epilogue 13, SH 53, 138.

the Life, for sending him a copy. Six years after that, in 403, Melania the Elder visited Paulinus and he read extracts from the Life to her. A year after that, Sulpicius claims, with obvious satisfaction, that the Life is being read at Carthage, Cyrene, Alexandria, Nitria, the Thebaid, and Memphis. Since Melania knew the book, he could have added Jerusalem.[12] A simple process of copies being sent from one friend to another and personal recommendations ensured that this saint's Life became known across a wide area in a small number of years.

Although books circulated quickly, they were expensive and difficult to obtain. A hermit in one of John Moschus' anecdotes worked as a building labourer for several months in order to save the three gold coins necessary to purchase a New Testament.[13] Usually books were held in libraries and we read of monks borrowing books, either from the library or from each other.[14] A book was a scarce and much-valued item.

The list of books which Cyril used as sources shows the titles which were available in the monastic libraries of the Judaean desert. These were the books which were seen as essential texts for monastic instruction and formation, and the selection of works implies that a monastic library consisted almost exclusively of these Lives of the saints and did not include theological or philosophical works. In his study of Palestinian monasticism, Chitty comments: 'By the end of the fourth century the library of the monks was growing. By Cyril's time it had reached considerable proportions—a corpus of "case-law" of the desert which, because it dealt with the world the monks knew, might often seem a safer guide than Holy Scripture itself, subject as that is to such a variety of personal interpretations.'[15]

The study of Cyril and his literary sources does not only tell us the books which could be expected to be found in a reasonably well-stocked monastic library in sixth-century Palestine. It also shows the purposes to which the books were put.

Continually present in Cyril's mind as he writes is the importance of demonstrating that the lives of the saints conform to biblical models.[16]

---

[12] Paulinus of Nola, *Epistolae*, 2. 11; 29. 14. Sulpicius Severus, *Dialogues*, 1. 26. 178–9, PL 20. 200B–D. Also J. M. Petersen, *The Dialogues of Gregory the Great in their Late Antique Cultural Background* (Toronto, 1984), 103.

[13] *Prat.* 134, PG 87/3. 2997B.

[14] *Prat.* 55, PG 87/3. 2909A, for a monk borrowing a copy of the *Apophthegmata Patrum* from his superior; *Life of Stephen the Sabaite*, 10. 6, *An. Boll.* (1959), 355, for the reference to the library at the Great Laura.   [15] Chitty, *Desert a City*, 131.

[16] See *Kyrillos*, and *Cyril of Scythopolis*, ed. Price, *passim*.

Verses from the Bible are quoted with persistent regularity to show that the actions of the saint reproduce the kinds of events described in the Bible and that the teaching of the saint conforms with the Bible. Within the first five lines of the Prologue of the first of the Lives, Cyril refers to the passage in the Epistle to the Hebrews describing faith as that which 'gives substance to things hoped for'.[17] This is the first of countless references.

Sometimes a passage of the Bible has given shape to Cyril's narrative. When Sabas was locked in conflict with the devils of Castellion, the only witnesses to his struggle were shepherds. As he describes this event, another occasion when shepherds witnessed a remarkable event was in Cyril's mind. The parallel passages show the extent of the influence on Cyril's imagination of this famous story of the nativity as told by Luke:

καὶ ποιμένες ἦσαν ἀγραυλῶντες καὶ φυλάσσοντες ... ἐπὶ τὴν ποιμνην αὐτῶν ἐφοβήθησαν φόβον μέγαν ... οἱ ποιμένες ἐλάλουν πρὸς ἀλλήλους, Διέλθωμεν δὴ ἕως Βηθλεεμ καὶ ἴδωμεν τὸ ῥῆμα τοῦτο τὸ γεγονὸς ... (Luke 2: 8–15)	καὶ ποιμένες ἦσαν αγραυλοῦντες καὶ φυλάσσοντες τὴν ἑαυτῶν ποίμνην ... ... λίαν φοβηθέντες ... ἔλεγον πρὸς ἀλλήλους ... ἀλλὰ διέλθωμεν δὴ ἕως τοῦ βουνοῦ καὶ ἴδωμεν τί τὸ γεγονός (Kyrillos, 111. 5–12)

Here Cyril's familiarity with the Bible has influenced his style and shaped his narrative. There are other passages which resonate with biblical associations and vocabulary. These include the healing by Sabas of a woman with a haemorrhage and the miraculous feeding of a crowd of 4,000 Armenians.[18]

After the Bible, Cyril's writing is influenced by Egyptian monastic literature. He is conscious of the dependence of Palestinian tradition on that of Egypt, explaining that 'old men from Egypt' (τινὲς γέροντες Αἰγύπτιοι) have passed stories on to Euthymius who then used them in his own teaching.[19]

The extent to which Egyptian traditions penetrated the Judaean

---

[17] *Kyrillos*, 5. 5, cf. Hebrews 11: 1.

[18] *Kyrillos*, 163. 23–164. 10, cf. Acts 3: 6 and Matt. 9: 22; *Kyrillos*, 27. 5–28. 8, cf. 2 Kgs. 4: 44; 7: 14; Matt. 15: 37; 2 Cor. 9: 6; Heb. 13: 2, the last two of which refs. are quoted directly. A further example of the effect of the Bible on hagiographical narrative is a healing in the *Life of Theodore of Sykeon*, 96, ed. A.-J. Festugière, SHG 48/1 (Brussels, 1970), 78. 16–79. 3. Here a woman who has suffered from an issue of blood for ten years mingles with the crowd in order to come close enough to Theodore to pour myrrh on his feet.

[19] *Kyrillos*, 36. 31, cf. 30. 28–9.

desert can scarcely be overemphasized. L. Regnault has shown that the *Apophthegmata Patrum* were being read in Palestine in the fourth and fifth centuries. He argued that, while the shorter collections of *Apophthegmata* on specific subjects contain only sayings attributed to Egyptian monks, the systematic and alphabetical collections contain, in addition, stories of the Palestinian monks. The presence of this material leads him to suggest that the first collections of the alphabetical version of the *Apophthegmata Patrum* originate from Palestine rather than Egypt.[20]

Cyril's borrowings from these sources are diverse. They include cases where a similar phrase is reproduced, like the statement that the monks have 'made the desert into a city' (ἡ ἔρημος ἐπολίσθη ὑπὸ μοναχῶν).[21] Then there are occasions when a story is used to teach an aspect of monastic observance, as when Cyril uses a tale from the *Apophthegmata* to illustrate the charismatic gift of the discernment of spirits.[22] In describing the ascetic virtues of the saint, models from the Egyptian desert are drawn on, especially in the comparison of Arsenius and Euthymius.[23] Then, sometimes, Cyril has modelled a complete section on an Egyptian source, as when the Prologue of the *Life of Euthymius* follows a section of the *Life of Pachomius* describing how ascetics are faithful to the tradition of Christian witness descending through the apostles and martyrs.[24] These very different kinds of use being made of the Egyptian texts shows the regard in which they were held and their application to many purposes.

Another work which was not from Egypt but had a special place in Cyril's estimation was the *Religious History* of Theodoret. The large number of parallel passages include cases where Cyril has copied directly but also passages where his understanding of the monastic life has been shaped by that of Theodoret.[25] In particular, the concept of *parresia* as

[20] L. Regnault, 'Les Apotegmes des pères en Palestine aux Ve–VIe siècles', *Iren.* 54 (1981), 320–30, 328. Note also Chitty's remark in *Desert a City*, 131, that Cyril's writing is 'roughly contemporary with the early Latin versions of the *Apophthegmata Patrum*, while the earliest Syriac MS of a collection of these comes from the year of St Sabas' death'.

[21] *Kyrillos*, 126. 15; 158. 17–18, cf. *V. Anton.* 14, PG 26. 865B.

[22] *Kyrillos* 37. 1–20, cf. a story from the *Apoph. Patr.* in Nau, 'Anonymous Collection', *ROC* 13 (1908), 266–97, 279.

[23] *Kyrillos*, 34. 17–24, cf. the phrases from the *Apophthegmata* collected in *MH* 56. For the influence of Arsenius, see I. Hausherr, *Penthos* (Kalamazoo, Mich., 1982), 33.

[24] *Kyrillos*, 6–8, cf. *V. Pach. G1* 1–2, Athanassakis, 2–4.

[25] Flusin finds nineteen cases of direct copying. For an example cf. 39. 20–30 and Theodoret, *H. Rel.* 3. 16. 1–9, SC 234 (Paris, 1977), 276–8.

the goal of the ascetic path was learned from Theodoret.[26] The respect that Cyril had for Theodoret is shown by the careful omission of Theodoret's name from the list of the theologians anathematized at the 553 Council of Constantinople.[27]

The other books he used had less influence on him. These are books which he has read and from which he has extracted short passages. The passages concerned seem to be those which have either stuck in his memory, or which he jotted down on one of his little bits of paper, or which he happened to have been reading at the point at which he came to a certain stage in his own writing and so copied directly into his text. For example, there are only two quotations from Gregory of Nazianzus' *Elogium on Basil*, both of which occur in the description of Euthymius' youth in Melitene. Another example is the *De Monastica Exercitatione* of Nilus of Ancyra, which Cyril borrows from on four occasions. Two of these are found in the Prologue to the *Life of Euthymius* and two in a chapter describing the virtues of Sabas as a superior.[28] These works are examples of writing which was available in the desert and read by monks but which did not have the profound influence of the classics from Egypt, perhaps because they were not representative of the familiar genre of monastic lives.

These source books provide an indication of the material which could be found in a typical, well-stocked monastic library. They were available to the monks who were able and willing to read and to study.

An examination of the passages where Cyril has borrowed from earlier authors also shows how the books were used and the lessons which the monks learned from them. The places where Cyril is clearly dependent on his sources are unevenly distributed through his works and occur in three distinct types of material.

The first of these are the Prologues. In the introductions to the Lives of the saints, Cyril is careful to follow the example set by those who have gone before him. The Prologue to the *Life of Euthymius*, for example, is modelled on that of the *Life of Pachomius*, as well as quoting twice from Nilus of Ancyra, once from the *Miracles of Thecla*, and

---

[26] *Kyrillos*, 15. 8–9, cf. Theodoret, *H. Rel.* 1. 3. 78, SC 234 (Paris, 1977), 164. Other passages of *H. Rel.* which have contributed to Cyril's understanding of *parresia* not mentioned by Flusin are 1. 14. 2; 3. 9. 2; 7. 3. 23; 9. 7. 7; 13. 5. 10; 13. 8. 8; 18. 4. 13: 18. 15. 11–13. For a fuller discussion of *parresia*, see Ch. 9.

[27] *Kyrillos*, 199. 3–6.

[28] Ibid. 7. 21–4; 99. 13–17; 129. 18–21. Cf. Nilus of Ancyra, PG 79. 721C–D, 760C–D.

drawing extensively on sections of Justinian's dogmatic writing.[29] Here, Cyril takes care to follow the traditional literary forms.

The second type of material is ascetic teaching. This is found mainly in the *Life of Euthymius*, and in it Cyril makes extensive use of his sources. One short section of ascetic discourse contains two references to the *Life of Pachomius*, two to the *Life of Antony*, and two to the *Religious History*.[30] Another piece of teaching is given on the occasion when two monks, Maron and Clematius, decided to leave the monastery. The instruction reported to have been given by Euthymius is composed largely out of borrowed material. There are five occasions in this brief section when he has used the *Apophthegmata Patrum* as a source and single references to the *Lausiac History*, the *Religious History*, and Paul of Elousa's *Life of Theognius*.[31] Altogether more than half of all borrowings by Cyril from earlier literary works occur in the relatively few passages which contain ascetic teaching or the description of ascetic teaching.[32]

This use of source material in these contexts suggests that written material was used especially in the instruction of the monks and in ascetic formation. P. Rousseau has argued that the committing of the teaching of the monks to writing was a phenomenon of the second generation of monastic life, when the freshness and vigour of the early days had become institutionalized and codified.[33] Cyril's excessive dependence on books in these passages confirms Rousseau's argument that books became an essential part of monastic nurture after the original example of pioneers like Euthymius had been removed by the passage of time.

The third type of material is dogmatic. In Cyril's mind ascetic achievement is inseparable from doctrinal purity. Theodosius, we are told, was conspicuous for three virtues. One of these was 'a very rigorous (ἀκριβεστάτην) ascesis with a true and orthodox faith which remained from youth until old age'.[34] There is as little originality in the dogmatic aspect of virtue as there is in the ascetic. Approved dogmatic texts are

[29] *Kyrillos*, 6–8. Parallels listed in *MH* 48, 54, 70–1, 74–6. Cf. the Prologue to the *Life of Sabas*, 85. 12–86. 26, with parallels in *MH* 70–1.

[30] *MH* 44–7, 68–9. Also Garitte, 'Réminiscences', 118–19.

[31] *Kyrillos*, 29. 27–32. 5. *MH* 44. 56–9, 68–70.

[32] For further examples of ascetic teaching, *Kyrillos*, 34. 1–30, cf. *MH* 56; *Kyrillos*, 36. 13–37. 29, cf. *MH* 59; Garitte, 'Réminiscences', 119; *Kyrillos*, 99. 5–101. 5, cf. *MH* 46, 68, 71; *Kyrillos*, 107. 23–109. 2, cf. *MH* 57; *Kyrillos*, 110. 1–111. 5, cf. Garitte, 'Réminiscences', 119–20.

[33] P. Rousseau, *Ascetics, Authority, and the Church* (Oxford, 1978), 68–76.

[34] *Kyrillos*, 238. 25–6. The other virtues are hospitality and ceaseless prayer in the liturgy.

mined for suitable material which is then reproduced. Favoured sources are the Acts of the relevant Councils and the writings of the Emperor Justinian.[35]

In his writing Cyril made considerable use of literary sources. He was only able to use books in the manner in which he had been instructed, and their availability was, of course, limited, so the reconstruction of his careful use of sources provides insights into the books which the monks of his day enjoyed reading.

One final qualification needs to be made. Cyril lived in orthodox Chalcedonian circles. A Monophysite or Origenist library would have displayed their particular interests and a different set of saints who were revered.

THE CONVERSATION OF THE MONKS

Literary sources have been considered first because these examples of dependence can be more clearly demonstrated. But books were not the most usual means of communication. The spoken word was far more important than the written word. The day-to-day conversation of the monks was the means by which the collective memory of the monastery was accumulated and communicated.

The largest part of Cyril's writing consists of the stories told to him by older monks. He describes the process of collecting information which resulted in his writing: 'I made assiduous enquiry among the most ancient of the inspired fathers of the desert, who had acquired by oral transmission an accurate knowledge of the facts about the great Euthymius and had been contemporaries and fellow-combatants with the all-praiseworthy Sabas.'[36]

He describes an occasion when he visited the old monk Cyriac in his hermitage at Sousakim, and tells how Cyriac gave him information. 'After telling me many things about Saint Euthymius and the other fathers of the desert, he invited me to eat with him . . . After I had spent one day there and enjoyed his reaching to the full, on the following day he gave me a gift and adding his blessing sent me on my way in peace.'[37] His other main oral source was his friend and mentor, John

---

[35] *Kyrillos, 362.*
[36] Ibid. 82. 20–83. 2.
[37] Ibid. 232. 14–22.

the Hesychast. John had entered the Great Laura in 491, forty years before the death of Sabas. To his personal knowledge of the events of Sabas' life he could add the stories about Euthymius which he had heard from Sabas. The long visits which John made to the Extreme Desert in the company of Sabas during Lent and at other times had provided an opportunity for John and another monk called Thallelaius to hear about the exploits of Euthymius and the monks of this earlier generation, information which John passed on to Cyril.[38]

Festugière describes the information given about Euthymius by Cyriac and John as 'presque directe'. Cyriac, entering the monastery soon after Euthymius' death, found that 'le souvenir était alors tout vivant, et nous croyons que, jusque dans son extrême vieillesse, Kyriakos a reçu de ce souvenir ... comme il s'était longtemps entretenu avec les successeurs d'Euthyme et qu'il avait appris ainsi toute sa manière de vivre, Kyriakos pût-il transmettre exactement à Cyrille la tradition le plus fraîche sur le fondateur'.[39] The series of conversations which Cyril had with Cyriac, John, and others enabled him to capture the quality of life of previous generations of monks. His writing witnesses to the oral tradition which handed down a tradition of spirituality.

The monastic communities developed formal and regular ways of remembering the events in their history. The lives and exploits of the founders of the monasteries played an important part in the memory of the community, and was carefully passed to successive generations. The anniversaries of the deaths of the saints were times when their lives were remembered by the community. The Lives of Theognius and Theodosius were composed as panegyrics for delivery on the saints' feasts.[40] Sometimes these spoken memories were then committed to paper for public reading. In his study of the Lives of Stylite saints, Delehaye claims: 'Il ne faut pas oublier que ces vies étaient composées avant tout pour la lecture publique soit à l'office soit au moins durant le repas des moines ou à la collation, et la jour de la fête du saint où on lisait au moins due partie.'[41] Sabas used to postpone his departure into the desert until after the memorial of Euthymius on 20 January, because this was an important day in the monastic year in which the community shared together in remembering a pioneer of monastic living.[42]

---

[38] Ibid. 56. 19–21.
[39] *MO* pt. 1, iii. 10–11.
[40] See Ch. 2.
[41] See H. Delehaye, *Les Saints Stylites*, SHG 14 (Brussels, 1923), 94.
[42] *Kyrillos*, 106. 13.

The remembering of the events of the saints' lives included the placing of them into a simple chronological framework. Cyril gives many examples of dates transmitted in this way. The stages of the ascetic's career were remembered by his age at certain key moments. Cyriac, for example, was able to tell Cyril that he had been 'canonarch and ceimiliarch' for thirty-one years during which time he had not eaten during the hours of daylight.[43] Cyril concludes the Lives with a summary of the important moments of the ascetic's career—such as his birth, entering the monastery, becoming a solitary—and his age at each of them.[44] Many similar examples can be found in ascetic literature of the intervals of time in the monk's career being noted.[45]

The written Lives which are available to us preserve just a part of a large and compendious memory. Far more material than has survived would have existed. At least one other *Life of Euthymius* was in circulation in the desert, of which a fragment is preserved in a sermon by John of Damascus on the Dormition of the Blessed Virgin Mary.[46] The remark in the *Life of John the Hesychast* that there is an obligation on others to describe his 'combats, persecutions and perils ... after his death' points to the importance attached to remembering the lives of the saints.[47] The fascination evoked in our own day by the few saints' Lives which have survived points to the universal appeal of the stories. The oral tradition which framed and preserved them was rich in vitality and creativity. It was the mediator of a monastic culture.

HISTORICAL AWARENESS

Cyril has most often received praise from modern critics for his skills as a historian. This quality of his work arises from his perception that the monks contributed not just to the growth of monasticism in Palestine but also to the welfare of the whole Church. This was true even of those who had little contact with the world outside the monastery. For

[43] *Kyrillos*, 227. 2–3.

[44] Ibid. 60. 8–14; 183. 14–184. 0; 222. 3–12; 234. 31–235. 12.

[45] Schwartz, ibid. 350–1, lists references in the works of Palladius, Jerome, and Gerontius.

[46] John of Damascus, *Homilia II in Dormitionem bv Mariae*, ed. B. Kotter, *Die Schriften des Johannes von Damaskos V* (Berlin, 1988), 536 with discussion at p. 504. The interpolation is introduced with the words: ἐν τῇ εὐθυμιακῇ ἱστορίᾳ τρίτῳ λόγῳ κεφαλαίῳ τεσσαρακοστῷ οὕτως αὐτολεξεὶ γέγραπται.

[47] *Kyrillos*, 221. 25.

example, Euthymius, once he had completed his journey from Melitene to Jerusalem and then settled at Pharan, seems never to have left the Judaean desert, yet his life and ministry is still presented as having a significance within the context of the whole of Christendom.[48]

Sabas was more actively involved in political and ecclesiastical life. He travelled to Constantinople twice, and, while there, showed concern for the expansion of the Empire and the overthrowing of heresy.[49] This political involvement enabled Cyril to show his own interest in the affairs of the Empire. He sets the scene for Sabas' first embassy to the imperial capital by giving an extended summary of contemporary political conditions, a type of material unusual in hagiography.[50]

The detail given in some sections of the Lives suggests that Cyril had access to official documents held, we can suppose, in archives either at the Great Laura or at Jerusalem. Evidence from Egypt and Syria shows that monastery archives existed and it is probable that large communities, such as the Great Laura, would keep copies of important documents.[51]

Of the documents included in Cyril's Lives, the longest is the official letter of Sabas, Theodosius, and the monks of the desert to the Emperor Anastasius. This is reproduced in full in the *Life of Sabas*.[52] Other official letters are quoted at other points in the text and reference is made to written records.[53] As well as specific quotations, there are detailed accounts of historical events which are clearly based on archival material. For example, there is a full account of the orders of Justinian given in response to Sabas' requests, which provided for a remission of taxes and the rebuilding of churches destroyed by the Samaritans.[54] These are presented with precision and detail, suggesting access to official documents. Schwartz comments that they 'are presented in such a specialized and detailed fashion, that Cyril must have had a copy of the Imperial proclamation in front of him; it would not have been hard for him to have obtained this from the Patriarchate'.[55]

These official documents included doctrinal material, which formed

[48] Ibid. 14. 3–11; 9. 7–9.
[49] Ibid. 175. 19–176. 20.
[50] Ibid. 139. 29–141. 23.
[51] For evidence of archives in the monasteries of Tabennisi and of St Simeon Stylites, see A.-J. Festugière, *Antioche Païenne et Chrétienne* (Paris, 1959), 353–7.
[52] *Kyrillos*, 152. 21–157. 23.
[53] Ibid. 112. 1–11; 141. 8–11; 143. 25–8; 193. 1–6.
[54] Ibid. 176. 21–178. 13.
[55] Ibid. 345.

an important part of Cyril's source material. The passages in which
Monophysitism is attacked are based at many points on the Acts of the
Councils and the dogmatic treatises of the Emperor Justinian. Extracts
are taken from these documents and placed in the mouths of the saints
to ensure that their words conform with the orthodox faith. For example,
Euthymius' defence of the Council of Chalcedon is taken in part from
the Acts of the Council.[56] Other passages depend on the theological
writing of Justinian, the troparion, ὁ μονογενής, the *Contra Monophysitas*,
the *Confessio Fidei*, and the *Edict against Origen*.[57] Cyril wisely ensures
that he propounds a doctrinal stance which has the support of the
Emperor.

In the case of the arguments against Origenism, it is harder to identify
the material which Cyril has drawn on. Cyriac's refutation of Origenist
teaching has close verbal parallels with the Fifteen Anathematisms issued
by the 553 Council of Constantinople, but Cyril, through Cyriac, gives
the extra detail, not contained in the Anathematisms, that Origenists
believe that in the apocatastasis souls will have the power to create
worlds.[58] This divergence requires us to look for another document
which could lie behind Cyriac's statement. In the course of his narrative,
Cyril refers to three other polemical writings which are possible candidates. First, Sophronius and Gelasius, successors to Theodosius and
Sabas respectively, composed a *libellus* against the Origenists, which
Peter Archbishop of Jerusalem sent to Constantinople.[59] Then, some of
Cyril's companions wrote a refutation of the errors of the Origenist
sects of the Isochrists and Tetradites.[60] Third, Conon, the superior of
the Great Laura, addressed a *libellus* to the Emperor Justinian.[61] These
three documents were all written between 543 and 553 and show that
there were various attacks on Origenism circulating in Palestine. Of
these three possible prototypes for Cyriac's refutation it is most probable
that Cyril used the second document mentioned above, since both share
the purpose of revealing the errors of the Origenist sects.[62]

---

[56] *Kyrillos*, 43. 10; 43. 25; 44. 1–4; cf. *ACO* 2. 1, p. 320. 30–2.
[57] *MH* 74–6. For the authorship of the troparion, see V. Grumel, 'L'Auteur et la date
de composition du Tropaire o monogenes', *E. Or.* 22 (1923), 398–418.
[58] *Kyrillos*, 230. 6. Festugière here translates δημιουργεῖν as 'créer', but as 'gouverner'
at 230. 7 (*MO* pt. 3, iii. 47). For these anathematisms, see F. Diekamp, *Die Origenistischen
Streitigkeiten im sechsten Jahrhundert* (Münster, 1899), 88–97.
[59] *Kyrillos*, 189. 13–190. 14.
[60] Ibid. 197. 10–11.
[61] Ibid. 198. 14–17.
[62] Cf. ibid. 197. 10–12 and 230. 2–3. See *MH* 83.

The existence of these, and the awareness of their importance in monastic society, shows that monastic society was fully integrated into the political and ecclesiastical world. The monks were well aware of the events taking place in the capital and elsewhere and the importance of these to the welfare of their communities. They kept records of events and composed their own contributions to debates. 'L'œuvre de Cyrille ... suppose, dans les monastères de Palestine, toute une élaboration de documents. L'œuvre hagiographique ... prend le rélai de cette activité pour fixer sous une forme durable l'essentiel de ces documents et l'image de lui-même que le monasticisme Palestinien a voulu connaître et conserver.'[63]

Perhaps the most surprising feature of Cyril's interest in history is his concern to provide precise chronological information for the events he describes. This unusual feature is deliberate. To the words he quotes from the Prologue to the *Miracles of Thecla* promising to commemorate 'places, facts and names', he adds that he intends to remember 'times' as well, and he puts this first on the list.[64] He is faithful to this commitment and sprinkles his work liberally with chronological information which has been invaluable in reconstructing the history of the period.

Dates are given in a variety of forms—the indiction year, the year of the Emperor's reign, the year of the consulate, the year of the ascetic's life, the 'world-year' and the lapse of time since the Incarnation.[65]

Comparable monastic texts show no interest in events outside the direct experience of the subject. This characteristic of Cyril's writing raises the question of the source of his information and, more generally, of the extent of historical awareness and interest within the monasteries.

Recent research has concentrated on the task of working out a consistent and full chronological framework for the events Cyril describes and of relating this to information from other sources.[66] The problem which has confronted those who have undertaken this task is that Cyril is not always consistent. The most notorious error concerns the date of the death of Sabas. The importance of this event resulted in its being used as a reference point by which later events were dated. Altogether there are nine chronological references to the event. Of these, three

[63] *MH* 66–7.
[64] *Kyrillos*, 86. 22–4, cf. *V. Thecl.* 9. 21, SHG 62 (Brussels, 1978), 284.
[65] See *Kyrillos*, 340–55.
[66] e.g. T. Hermann, 'Zur Chronologie des Kyrill von Scythopolis', *ZKG* 45 (1926), 318–39; F. Dolger, 'E. Schwartz: Kyrillos von Scythopolis' *By. Z.* 40 (1940), 474–84.

indicate a date in December 531 and six a date in December 532. Of the two, the correct date has been shown to be 532. But, although this date is to be preferred, when Cyril dates subsequent events according to the lapse of time since Sabas' death he mistakenly uses the wrong date of 531. This uncharacteristic mistake by Cyril requires that all dates after 531 in the *Life of Sabas* have to be adjusted by one year to produce the correct date.[67]

This attempt to harmonize the information has resulted in the reduction of all Cyril's dates to one chronological system, which has helped in the task of historical reconstruction but does not assist us to appreciate the different ways in which dates were remembered. Such variety shows how the monks remembered events and the purpose behind this historical awareness. To this end, we need to distinguish the three different categories of dates, which are drawn from different sources.

The first has already been discussed in the preceding section. It is the years of the life of the saint, which was a part of the memory of the life preserved in the monastery.

The second derives from the Christian chronographical tradition. The deaths of Euthymius and Sabas are dated with particular care. That of Euthymius took place 'on the twentieth of the month of January of the 11th indiction, from the creation of the world, when time started to be measured by the revolution of the sun, 5965 years, from the incarnation of God the Word from the Virgin and his birth in the flesh 465 years'.[68] The sources which Cyril gives for this long-term time-scheme are the *Chronographies* of Hippolytus the Old, Epiphanius of Cyprus, and Heron the ascetic and confessor.[69]

Christian chronography originated in the second and third centuries with the work of Hippolytus (who was one of the three mentioned by Cyril), Clement of Alexandria, and Julius Africanus. It was developed and corrected by Eusebius of Caesarea. The intention of the chronographers was to show, first, that Christianity was not a novelty but had its roots in the past and was a fulfilment of the past; and, secondly,

---

[67] This solution to a complex problem was proposed by Diekamp, *Die Origenistischen Streitigkeiten*, 11–15. Schwartz, in *Kyrillos*, 341–6, argued that, while 532 was the date of Sabas' death, the indiction dates referring to events after 531 were given correctly. E. Stein, in 'Cyrille de Scythopolis, à propos de la nouvelle édition de ses œuvres', *An. Boll.* 62 (1944), 169–86 at 171–80, reaffirmed Diekamp's solution, and subsequent critics have agreed, see *MO* pt. 3, iii. 113 and *MH* 11–12.

[68] *Kyrillos*, 59. 23–60. 5; cf. 183. 5–10.

[69] Ibid. 60. 6–7; 183. 11–13.

that history had a purpose and pattern behind it. Momigliano wrote of the chronologies: 'Christian chronology was also a philosophy of history ... it showed concern with the pattern of history rather than the detail.'[70]

Since both the half millennium after the birth of Christ and also the sixth millennium after the creation of the world fell in the same year in the reign of Anastasius, there was an interest in chronography and a sense of living in critical times. The apocalyptic awareness is especially strong in Monophysite works, such as the *Oracle of Baalbek* written in 510 which expected the reign of Anastasius to be followed by the end-time.[71] While such climactic importance is not attached to the deaths of Euthymius and Sabas, the insertion of these events into the chrono-graphical time-scheme is a statement about the significance of the two men for the history of the world.

The third category of dates are the occasions when Cyril refers to the date, the month, and the year in which an event took place. He tells us, for example, that Eudocia died on '20 October in the 14th Indic-tion'.[72] The works contain a total of twenty-seven examples of this form of dating. On some occasions, Cyril gives the year of the Emperor's reign or the Patriarch's tenure of office in addition to the indiction year.[73]

The majority of events dated in this way are the deaths of bishops, monks, or other persons. These account for fourteen of the indiction dates.[74] A further seven refer to the founding of a monastery or the

[70] A. Momigliano, 'Pagan and Christian Historiography in the Fourth Century AD', in Momigliano (ed.), *Paganism and Christianity in the Fourth Century* (Oxford, 1963), 79–99, 83, 85. See also R. M. Grant, *Eusebius as Church Historian* (Oxford, 1980), 3; A. Mosshammer, *The Chronicle of Eusebius and Greek Chronographic Tradition* (Lewisburg, NJ, 1979), 85.

[71] Further examples of eschatological themes in Monophysite literature in John of Maiuma, *Plerophoriai*, 7, 12, 13, 19, 26, 89. See S. Harvey, 'Remembering Pain; Syriac Historiography and the Separation of the Churches', *Byz.* 58 (1988), 295–308, at p. 289; and, for the passages in the Oracle of Baalbek, P. J. Alexander, *The Oracle of Baalbek, the Tiburtine Sibyl in Greek Dress* (Washington, 1967), 17, 19–20, 136–7.

[72] *Kyrillos*, 54. 10. The indictions were counted in cycles of fifteen years, so that another 'first indiction' follows after the 'fifteenth indiction'. A system for the calculation of tax payment, the use of the indiction originated in 312–13, but it was not in general use until the time of Justinian. See *Kyrillos*, 341–2.

[73] For the year of the reigns, ibid. 71. 12; 140. 1. For the year of the Patriarch's office, ibid. 52. 1; 98. 14; 103. 10.

[74] Ibid. 54. 10; 54. 13; 70. 22; 93. 13; 103. 10; 112. 15; 116. 1; 161. 5; 170. 1; 171. 27; 195. 7; 196. 18; 225. 22; 239. 27.

consecration of a church.[75] The remaining few examples date either important events in the life of the church or significant moments in Cyril's personal life.[76]

The events that are remembered by the use of the indiction date suggest the source of the information. Deaths and consecrations were often commemorated in inscriptions, and many inscriptions have survived which use the indiction year as a method of dating. It is this epigraphical evidence that provides the closest parallel to Cyril's extensive reference to the indiction year.

Among many examples from Palestine, there is an inscription found in Jericho which dates from 566: 'The grave of Cyriac the most blessed priest and superior who founded the (ἐναγές εὐκτήριον) of the most holy and glorious martyr George ... He died in the month of December in the 15th indiction in the second year of our Emperor Flavius Justinian'.[77] Other memorial inscriptions include twenty-nine found at Sobota in Arabia, almost all of which include the month, the indiction year, and the age at death. From the monasteries of Palestine, the monastic cemetery at Choziba contains many more examples.[78]

Then there are the inscriptions which commemorate the dedication of a church. This example comes from Khorsia on the eastern shore of the Sea of Galilee. 'Under the God-loving Stephen priest and superior took place the building of the baptistery in the month of December in the 4th indiction under our most pious and Christ-loving Emperor Maurice in the first consulate.'[79]

The monasteries in which Cyril lived and the buildings of Jerusalem contained many similar inscriptions. They were a source of chronological information available to Cyril. As well as providing this information they testify to the custom of remembering the date of these significant events, which received an expression in the writing of Cyril.

Most saints' Lives show little interest in historical information. This was a result of literary convention rather than any lack of evidence. Cyril's writing shows that there was no lack of archival and inscriptional

[75] *Kyrillos*, 26. 21; 104. 25; 110. 1; 117. 17; 195. 20. 150. 10 and 195. 20 refer to the consecration of a Patriarch and the installation of a superior.

[76] Ibid. 173. 10 and 179. 12 date Sabas' departure to and return from Constantinople. 192. 12 dates the publication of the edict against Origen. 220. 2 and 216. 9 refer to events in Cyril's Lives.

[77] *SEG* viii. 315.

[78] *SEG* xxxi. 1981 and 1425–54; A.-M. Schneider, 'Das Kloster des Theotokos zu Choziba im Wadi-el-Kelt', *RQ* 39 (1931), 197–232.

[79] *SEG* xxvi. 1976–7. 1677; see also *SEG* xxx. 1697.

material which could be drawn on in the course of composition. The combination of the historical awareness of the monks and the careful collation of information by Cyril ensured a full and accurate historical record of the monasteries which is a testimony to the lively interest of the monks in events going on around them.

AUTOBIOGRAPHY

The other source on which Cyril drew for his writing was his own experience. Similarities between his own childhood and his account of that of Euthymius have already been noted.[80] Since Cyril's informants were not able to tell him about this distant part of his subject's life, Cyril devised a suitably edifying childhood, drawing on his own experience. The slow nurturing in monastic living following an early sign of vocation and the absence of any sudden conversion experience in maturity was how his own life developed. It was an understanding of vocation which he applied to his other subjects as well as to Euthymius.[81] The only deviation from this pattern is the description of the young Cyriac being seized by a desire to live in the desert after a Gospel reading had pierced his heart.[82]

It is common to find an author transferring his own experiences to his subject. Jerome, for example, tells us that Hilarion was 'committed to the charge of grammarian at Alexandria, where, so far as his age allowed, he gave remarkable proofs of ability and character; and in a short time endeared himself to all and became an accomplished speaker'.[83] Just as Jerome's saints were brilliant scholars, Cyril's were precociously pious youths.

The intermingling of biography and autobiography is harder to discern in later parts of the Lives, since the other sources provide more abundant material. But his own experience of monastic living has coloured his presentation of the lives of the saints.

---

[80] See Ch. 1.
[81] *Kyrillos*, 10. 5–13. 8; 86. 27–88. 17; 223. 1–12.
[82] Ibid. 224. 1–2. Cf. *V. Anton.* 2, 3, PG 26. 841C.
[83] Jerome, *Vita Hilarionis*, 2, in W. A. Oldfather, *Studies in the Text Tradition of St Jerome's Vitae Patrum* (Urbana, Ill., 1943), 313. Perhaps the description of the saint 'endearing himself to all' is wishful thinking on Jerome's part.

CONCLUSION

By the time that Cyril wrote, the monasteries were large and were integrated in the life of the capital. This involvement in society ensured that a rich culture developed. Cyril was a conscientious and attentive witness to the events in the lives of the monasteries. His Lives give many insights into the preoccupations and interests of monastic society, as well as to the events which are described. They show that monastic communities were no longer small groups of ascetics who sought to withdraw from the world, but a part of the society of the time, lively and concerned about the world around them.

PART II

Environment

INTRODUCTION

The home of the monk is the desert.

The monk renounces the world and flees from human company. He—for most of the early monks were men—goes into the desert. There he engages the devils in combat, deprives himself of food and sleep, and learns to live at peace with the animals.

This simplified picture does not fit the monks of Palestine. For them the City was as important as the Desert. The City was Jerusalem, where Jesus Christ died and rose again and where, as a result, the Holy Places contained the power of God in a tangible form. The intractable centrality of the Holy City forced a paradox on the monks. The City was both to be avoided and to be welcomed. It was a place where monastic vocation was both threatened and nurtured.

Although Jerusalem was unique, other cities shared in some of its qualities. Holy Places abounded in the Holy Land. Every city could find a biblical event to which it had been host or the body of a saint which had been buried in it. The monks, like everybody else, revered these places and they became intimately concerned for the welfare of the Church. The presence of the cities, and the growing churches within them, was a call to expand and to extend the blessings of the monastic life.

But Desert is never far away. A short walk over the ridge of the Mount of Olives to the east of Jerusalem leads into the emptiness and silence of the desert. For inhabitants of Jerusalem, Bethlehem, and Scythopolis the desert is very close. It is a desert which offers many opportunities for the establishment of growing communities.

The monk lived between Desert and City.

4

Jerusalem: Resurrection of a City

A Monastic Suburb of Jerusalem

The hills, ravines, and little plains of the barren landscape which lies
between the Judaean hills and the Dead Sea would not have become
the home of thousands of monks except for one simple fact—Jerusalem.
All the monastic sites are within easy travelling distance of the city
of Jerusalem. The site which was chosen by Euthymius for his laura,
Khan el Ahmar, is on a level plain, the beauties of which were extolled
by Cyril, and by other, later visitors.[1] But this was not all that
commended it. It was also a few hundred yards from the main highway
which runs from Jerusalem to Jericho, only about seven miles distant
from the centre of the city. Cyril is a little embarrassed that the great
lover of solitude should have chosen to settle so near a busy road. He
explains that although it is now a 'place of passage' ($\delta\iota\delta\delta os$), when
Euthymius settled there it was 'impassable' ($\dot{a}\delta\iota\delta\delta\epsilon v\tau os$).[2] But here Cyril
is being somewhat disingenuous. The road is built in the drainage basin
of the Wadi Kelt, which crosses the northern section of the desert, and
is the only natural route across an uneven and precipitous terrain of
numerous hills and deep wadis. It had been used by traffic since time
immemorial. Euthymius had tramped through the desert from Pharan
in the north-west to Masada in south-east, and had an intimate knowledge of the area. His choice of the site was deliberate. He wanted to
be near Jerusalem.[3]

The Great Laura of Sabas is further from the city—about twelve
miles as the crow flies. But its position in the Wadi Qidron ensured that

---

[1] *Kyrillos*, 23. 24–24. 1; 64. 21–65. 2. For a contemporary admirer of the location, see
J. Murphy-O'Connor, *The Holy Land* (Oxford, 1980), 216.

[2] *Kyrillos*, 24. 2–3.

[3] The site also attracted him because it was near the first monastery which he had
founded, at that time presided over by his friend Theoctistus, ibid. 23. 20–1.

the journey to Jerusalem would not be difficult. On foot it takes a few hours and was, in Cyril's time, made sufficiently often for the track below the south-east wall of the city to be known as the 'road to the Great Laura' (τὴν ὁδὸν τῆς Μεγίστης λαύρας).[4] Most other monasteries of the Judaean desert could be reached in a comfortable day's journey from Jerusalem.

Not only were the monasteries near to Jerusalem, they were also near to each other. The most recent list of the monasteries of the desert catalogues sixty-four monasteries.[5] Since the southern and eastern parts of the desert are too inhospitable to maintain the life of a community, the monasteries are concentrated into limited areas, especially the central plateau in which there were forty monasteries, and the plain to the south-east of Jericho where twenty monasteries have been identified. In the desert plateau the average distance between monasteries is between three and four miles, and those near Jericho are even closer, sometimes separated by less than a mile. These small distances shrink further when it is taken into account that many monasteries were laurae. The cells of laurite monks were scattered around the core buildings, sometimes at a distance of a mile, with the result that a laura covered a wide area. The outlying cells of the Great Laura were closer to the Coenobium to the North than to the centre of their laura.[6]

The monasteries were connected by a network of paths. These were carefully constructed with retaining walls where necessary, in order to make the path broader and more secure, and with bridges over precipitous parts of the wadi. A researcher comments: 'Between the various monasteries ... an extensive network of trails was laid, a network which changed the face of the desert during the Byzantine period. The trails to and from the monasteries made the desert into part of the inhabited areas near them.'[7] The texts often describe monks travelling from one monastery to another. One example is a monk on his way to the monastery of Chorembe who is led the path by the dog belonging to the superior of another monastery, Soubiba of the Syrians.[8]

The interlocking network of monasteries could be described as the

---

[4] Ibid. 168. 8.

[5] See Y. Hirschfeld, 'List of the Byzantine Desert Monasteries in the Holy Land', in *Christian Archeology in the Holy Land*, ed. G. Bottini *et al.* (Jerusalem, 1990), 1–90, 81–2.

[6] See Y. Hirschfeld, *The Judaean Desert Monasteries of the Byzantine Period* (New Haven, Conn., 1992), 12; and 'List', 33.

[7] Hirschfeld, *Judaean Desert Monasteries*, 208. The paths are described at 205–12.

[8] *Prat.* 157, PG 87/3. 3025B.

monastic suburb of the city. As a part of Jerusalem their history is connected inextricably with its history.

RESURRECTION OF A CITY

'Jerusalem effectively no longer existed.' P. W. L. Walker's comment in his study of the development of the Holy Places refers to the end of the second century.[9] The Emperor Hadrian had destroyed the Jewish Temple and expelled the Jews with an edict which included the Apostolic Jewish-Christian Church. The population of the city was reduced by half and a legion was installed at the highest point of the city. Roads were laid out according to the standard plan of a Roman military camp. Where Jewish Jerusalem had been, Hadrian created the military town of Aelia populated by Gentile colonists. These new inhabitants included some Christians, but their church was small and lacking in power.[10] They looked to the provincial capital of Caesarea for leadership.

With the reign of Constantine and the new status of Christianity as the state religion, the fortunes of Jerusalem rapidly improved. The Emperor's mother, Helena, arrived in Palestine, finding, according to the historian Socrates, 'that which was once Jerusalem desolate as a preserve for autumn fruits'.[11] This situation did not last long. The True Cross was discovered and a huge building programme initiated.[12] From this moment on, more and more holy places came to light and the pilgrimage movement was under way. Maraval makes this comment about the increasing number of rediscovered holy places: 'Les lieux saints sortent de terre comme des champignons.'[13]

Not everybody welcomed the rebirth of Jerusalem. In his study, Peter Walker traces the conflict between the conservative, intellectual theology represented by Eusebius of Caesarea and the emerging, popular, incarnational theology developed by Cyril of Jerusalem. He shows that the new enthusiasm for Jerusalem represented a threat to Caesarea, challenging its position of pre-eminence within the Palestinian Church and threatening the authority of the metropolitan bishop. These ecclesiastical anxieties

[9] P. W. L. Walker, *Holy City, Holy Places?* (Oxford, 1990), 5.
[10] Ibid. 5–8.
[11] Socrates Scholasticus, *HE* 1. 17, PG 67. 117B.
[12] Ibid. PG 67. 121A; Sozomen, *HE* 2. 1. 4–8; 2. 26. 1–4, GCS (1960) 48. 4–49. 15; 87. 15–88. 3.
[13] P. Maraval, *Lieux saints et pélerinage d'orient* (Paris, 1985), 63.

were reinforced by Eusebius' theological convictions, according to which the earthly Jerusalem of the Jews had been destroyed by an act of divine judgement, and had been replaced by the new heavenly Jerusalem, a spiritual reality which encouraged all Christians to set their sights on the things above. Interestingly, Eusebius refers to the earthly city either as 'Aelia' or 'Ierosoluma', but never as 'Ierosalem' which is reserved for the heavenly city. Jerusalem in Judaea was neither 'new Jerusalem' nor 'true Jerusalem'.[14]

Eusebius was also wary of encouraging pilgrimage. The only holy places he would recognize were the Constantinian Triad of Holy Caves.[15] These were the sites of some of the earliest building projects of Christian Palestine and, at each of them, basilicas were built over caves. They consisted of the caves of the Nativity at Bethlehem, the burial at Jerusalem, and the Ascension on the Mount of Olives. The three caves had a clear value in expounding the articles of the creed, and possibly took some of the emphasis away from Jerusalem by including the Mount of Olives, outside the city, and Bethlehem. He showed no interest in the multiplicity of holy places which were being discovered and was clearly worried that Jerusalem was becoming the most popular tourist attraction of the time. Both his ecclesiastical status and his theological convictions were threatened by Jerusalem.

Cyril of Jerusalem, who gave his Catachetical Lectures while still a presbyter in 348 and who was Bishop from about 351 until 386, presented his hearers with a new and attractive approach to their faith— soteriological, incarnational, and personal. Within his understanding, the city of Jerusalem was all-important. It was the centre of the Christian faith for many reasons. It was, of course, the place of Crucifixion and Resurrection. But also it was the place where the sacraments were instituted—and, should an objector point out that the Baptism took place at the Jordan, he would remind them of the words of Scripture that 'all Jerusalem' went to the Jordan. It was the city where the Spirit descended at Pentecost. It was the diocese of James, the Lord's brother. He pointed out that 'others merely hear, but we see and touch'.[16] 'An aspiring bishop in the church at Jerusalem was asserting the pre-eminence of Jerusalem in every department of the Christian life— personal, local, ecclesiastical and even global.'[17]

[14] Walker, *Holy City, Holy Places?* 376–80.
[15] Ibid. 171–98.
[16] Cyril of Jerusalem, *Catachetical Lectures*, 13. 22.
[17] Walker, *Holy City, Holy Places?* 345–6.

With the Emperor Constantine ordering the building of basilicas at the holy places and the Bishop Cyril encouraging devotion at them, the scene was set for the huge movement of people and resources into Jerusalem which we call pilgrimage. It happened quickly. In 324 Constantine defeated Licinius and became the ruler of the east. In 325 the Council of Nicaea took place. In 326 building work began at Golgotha. In 333 the author of the first main surviving pilgrim text, an anonymous visitor from Bordeaux, made his journey. He describes a tour which included a comprehensive itinerary of well-established sites.[18] At about the same time monasteries appeared in the desert.[19] From this moment, pilgrims and monks entered into Jerusalem society, although it was not until the next century that rapid growth in the size of the monastic communities took place. Jerusalem became a city of pilgrims and monks. Many visitors, like Euthymius and Sabas, came to worship the holy places *and* to lead a life a silence. The two vocations of pilgrim and monk intermingled and combined.

The nature of monastic vocation underwent a strange transformation in the case of the monks of Palestine. It is shown by a surprising phrase used by Cyril. He speaks of Cyriac resolving 'to withdraw to the Holy City' (ἐπι τὴν ἀγίαν πόλιν ἀναχωρῆσαι).[20] This withdrawal is not to the solitude of the desert but to the communal life of the city. In the case of Euthymius and other monks, the process of withdrawal was from a rural monastery to a city—a reversal of the usual progression from city to desert.

Both Euthymius and Sabas were monks before they travelled to Jerusalem. Cyril himself felt it right to follow their example, and did not undertake his own journey to Jerusalem until he had first made his monastic renunciation before George of Beella.[21] He travelled to the city as a monk, showing that the call to live in silence at Jerusalem is a stage within the monastic vocation.

Jerusalem itself was a city of monks. The monastic communities presided over by Maelania and Gerontius on the Mount of Olives were well known in the early fifth century, providing support for the Origenists of Egypt in the controversy which developed after 400. Later the area around the Tower of David on Mount Sion became a monastic colony

[18] *Itinerarium Burdigalense*, ed. P. Geyer and O. Cuntz, CCL 175 (Turnhout, 1965). The date of the journey is calculated from the names of the consuls.
[19] See beginning of Ch. 7.
[20] *Kyrillos*, 224. 2; cf. 204 3–4.
[21] Ibid. 71. 11–20.

and gained a reputation for disorderliness. Immediately he acceded to the Patriarchal throne, Elias built a monastery near the episcopal palace and gathered together the 'ascetics of the Holy Church of the Resurrection who had been scattered in the district around the Tower of David' and assigned to each of them a comfortable cell.[22] Other monasteries are known to have existed within the city. The convent of women presided over by Bassa in the fifth century, for example, has left its remains within the present-day Armenian Cathedral of St James.[23]

The City was as essential as the Desert to the vocation of the monks. Its importance is clearly expressed in the letter written by Sabas and Theodosius to the Emperor Anastasius.

In the Mother of Churches, Sion, the great mystery of piety for the salvation of the world was manifested and accomplished, and then, beginning from Jerusalem, through the divine and evangelical preaching, the light of truth was raised to the ends of the world. Through the victorious and venerable cross and life-giving resurrection, we, the inhabitants of the Holy Land have all received the true and not illusory confession and faith . . . the Holy City of God, Jerusalem, [is] the eye and luminary of the whole world whose inhabitants touch, as it were with their own hands, the truth each day through the venerable places in which were wrought the mystery of the Incarnation.[24]

The monks, inhabiting the City of Jerusalem, live within touching distance of God.

MONEY

Jerusalem attracted men and women from all parts of the Empire and from all social classes. Studies of pilgrimage, such as that of E. D. Hunt and J. N. D. Kelly, have concentrated on pilgrims who were wealthy and western.[25] These included Jerome's circle of noble Roman ladies, such as Paula and Eustochium, or Egeria from Galicia in north-west Spain who travelled around Egypt and Palestine some time between 381 and 384.[26] Their journeys were often carried out in extravagant style.

---

[22] Ibid. 116. 4–8.
[23] Ibid. 49. 19–22; Murphy-O'Connor, *The Holy Land*, 49.
[24] *Kyrillos*, 152. 21–157. 23.
[25] E. D. Hunt, *Holy Land Pilgrimage in the Later Roman Empire AD 312–460* (Oxford, 1984), and J. N. D. Kelly, *Jerome* (London, 1975).
[26] Hunt, *Holy Land Pilgrimage*, 136–46.

Another noble lady, Poememia, in her visit to Egypt, travelled down the Nile to see the famous ascetic John and used a fleet of boats for transport.[27] The arrival of these aristocratic entourages caused quite a stir and often the bishop came to greet the visitor personally. Egeria reports how she was welcomed by the bishops in Arabia, Edessa, and Carrhae.[28] But the wealthiest and most impressive of all the pilgrims was the Empress Eudocia whose lavish expenditure caused such an impression that 900 years later the chronicler Nicephorus Callistus reported that she spent 20,480 lb. of gold while she was in Jerusalem. This is equivalent to 1,500,000 gold pieces, when two gold pieces were sufficient to keep a person for a year.[29]

The arrival of these rich ladies was encouraged by political developments. Barbarian tribes were advancing on the western Empire. Faced with the prospect of invasion, Melania sold her estates in Spain, a sale which raised, according to her biographer, only a small amount of money 'snatched from the jaws of the lion'.[30] The number of refugees increased after the Fall of Rome to Alaric in 410, leading to Jerome's complaint about the arrival of people once rich but now reduced to poverty relying on establishments such as his monastery for maintenance.[31] The political uncertainty in the west led to a growing number of these pilgrim refugees transferring themselves and their resources eastwards to the safer environment of Jerusalem.

The arrival of pilgrims led to generous donations to the Church. Some of these donations were direct gifts from grateful pilgrims to the land they felt privileged to see. Others were indirectly the result of pilgrimage since the arrival of greater numbers of visitors increased the fame and prestige of the city, and so led to an influx of revenue from those who were not able to make their own personal visit but valued what it represented.

The most substantial of these payments came from the imperial authorities. On his official visits to Constantinople, Sabas was given substantial sums by the Emperors Anastasius and, later, Justinian. Although Anastasius sympathized with Monophysitism, he gave the

---

[27] Hunt, *Holy Land Pilgrimage*, 76–7.

[28] *Itin. Aeth.* 8. 1; 9. 1; 19. 5; 20. 2. SC 296 (1982), 160, 162, 204, 214.

[29] Nicephorus Callistus, *HE* 14. 50, PG 146. 124D. Cf. Evagrius, *HE* 1. 22, ed. Bidez and Parmentier, 29. 18–25. See also M. Avi-Yonah, 'Economics of Byzantine Palestine', *IEJ* 8 (1953), 39–51, 41–4; and Hunt, *Holy Land Pilgrimage*, 239.

[30] *Vita Melaniae*, 37, SC 90 (Paris, 1962), 196.

[31] Jerome, *Commentaries on Ezekiel*, 3, prologue; 7, prologue. CCL 75 (Turnhout, 1964), 91, 277–8. See also Kelly, *Jerome*, 305–6.

Chalcedonian Sabas a total of 2,000 pieces of gold.[32] This money was distributed by Sabas among his monasteries.[33] Another report, which could refer to the same event, since the sums of money involved are similar, is told by Theodore of Petra about Theodosius who received 30 lb. of gold from Anastasius—although here Theodore distrusts the Emperor's motives and considers the money to be a bribe.[34] A similar gift of Justinian was distributed around the desert.[35] In addition, legislative changes during the reign of Justinian encouraged gifts to monasteries, so increasing the wealth and revenue of those in Palestine.[36]

As well as these large government grants, there were smaller-scale gifts from visitors and residents alike. These included systematic and regular distributions by wealthy citizens, like those described by Theodore of Petra who 'made of their riches a means of saving their soul' and 'distributed to all who followed a life of poverty up to a maximum of a third of a piece of gold to each individual'.[37] Local people sometimes felt a responsibility to support the local monastery. The villagers of Lazarion, or Bethany, took care that Euthymius and Domitian did not go short of what they needed.[38]

Other offerings were occasional and unexpected. These gifts prompted many lively anecdotes. One Easter John the Hesychast and his disciple were in the desert. They had insufficient food and the disciple lost heart and left John. Shortly afterwards a man arrived with a mule-load of gifts—bread, wine, oil, cheese, and honey. By a happy chance the disciple lost his way and returned. He was able to enjoy the gifts and find his faith strengthened.[39] Another story is told by the pilgrim from Piacenza, whose party travelled around the country in about 560. They arrived at a monastery which boasted the interesting tourist attraction of a tame lion. 'One traveller gave the nuns large amounts of food, in the hope that they would sell him the (tame) lion and ass—thirty cassocks, vegetables, oil, dates, baskets of roast chickpeas. He did not

---

[32] *Kyrillos*, 143. 8–9; 146. 21.

[33] Ibid. 147. 25–7.

[34] Theodore of Petra, *V. Thds.* 55. 2–15.

[35] *Kyrillos*, 179. 13–14.

[36] For legislative changes, see E. Patlagean, 'La pauvreté à Byzance au temps de Justinien', in *Études sur l'histoire de la pauvreté*, ed. M. Mollat (Paris, 1974), 59–81, 72–4.

[37] Theodore of Petra, *V. Thds.* 27. 10–15. Unfortunately they neglected, on this occasion, to include Theodosius in this liberality, but a timely miracle ensured that his community did not suffer.

[38] *Kyrillos*, 16. 7–8.

[39] Ibid. 210. 15–211. 14; and, for similar stories, see 160. 5 and Theodore of Petra, *V. Thds.* 26. 18–22.

get the animals and we were quite unable to soothe his disappointment and grief. All he could say was—devil take it, what's the use of being a Christian!'[40]

By far the largest amounts of money were spent on building. To build was considered to be a sign of 'greatness of soul' and it added glory to the reputation of the benefactor. Procopius, for example, set out to praise the Emperor Justinian and did so by writing a book describing the buildings he was responsible for.[41] Among the powerful and influential members of society who adorned Jerusalem with their monuments was the Empress Eudocia. She arrived for her second visit to Jerusalem in 441 or 442 after she had fallen into disgrace in Constantinople, and never returned to the capital. The reasons for this dissension in the imperial family are not clear. Sexual infidelities with Paulinus, the *magister officiorum*, were always strenuously denied by Eudocia, but intrigues and the shifting balance of power at court led to her years in Jerusalem having the character of an exile. She had been responsible for the building of churches at Constantinople but the speed and scale of her building programme accelerated on her arrival at Jerusalem.[42] Cyril refers to this activity: 'The blessed Eudocia built a huge number of churches for Christ, of monasteries, hospices and hospitals, which it is not in my power to number.'[43] The origin of this frantic and ambitious construction lies in her exclusion from the court. She wanted her new home of Jerusalem to rival Constantinople in the grandeur of its monuments, and for her prestige to grow in spite of her political misfortunes.

Another reason for imperial support of building in Palestine was its closeness to the unstable eastern frontier. The prosperity of Palestine, at the eastern edge of the Empire, was preserved by a vigilant watch on the border areas. In the fourth century, Ammianus Marcellinus described Palestine: 'Ultima Syriarum est Palaestina per intervalla magna protenta, cultis abundans terris et nitidis et civitates habentes quasdam egregias, nullam nulli cedentem sed sibi vicissim velut ad perpendiculum aemulas.'[44] Fortified synagogues have been excavated at Beth-Yarah in the Jordan valley and at Ma'on in the southern Negev. These were occupied

---

[40] Antoninus Placentinus, *Itinerarium*, 34, CCL 175 (Turnhout, 1965), 146.
[41] See A. Cameron, *Procopius and the Sixth Century* (London, 1985), 89.
[42] Hunt, *Holy Land Pilgrimage*, 237; see also J. Tsatsos, *The Empress Athenais: Eduokia* (Brookline, Mass., 1977), 79–92, for Eudocia's disgrace at court.
[43] *Kyrillos*, 53. 5–7.
[44] Ammianus Marcellinus, 14. 8. 11–13, LCL 1 (London, 1952), 70–1.

from the fourth century and show that Jews were encouraged to settle in border areas and to provide fortified strongholds to protect both themselves and the frontier.[45] Churches were also constructed in vulnerable areas, adding a divine protection to that provided by the military. 'A church, as often as not dedicated to the Virgin Mary, was essential for the defence of the Empire against the barbarians, for sacraments and relics represented a power greater than human armies.'[46] The building of churches and monasteries in frontier areas was seen as providing a population both human and divine which would deter barbarian advance.

The buildings of the Holy Land are a monument to the piety, the wealth, and the needs of the pilgrims. There were churches to adorn the sites which attracted visitors; there were hostels and hospitals to house and care for visitors; and there were the monasteries. Within the programme of building which was continued throughout the Byzantine period, three phases can be discerned. The first was at the time of Constantine, when the three large basilicas of the Anastasis, Eleona, and Nativity at Bethlehem were among the churches built.[47] The second period, up to the death of Eudocia in 460, was characterized by private initiatives rather than imperial programmes.[48] But by far the most productive period was the third—the extensive construction programme during the reign of the Emperor Justinian. Armstrong states: 'The age of Justinian was the greatest single period of building activity in Palestine.'[49] These phases illustrate the initial encouragement given to the pilgrims by Constantine which led to a growth in the investment made by individuals which in turn led to a further period of strong imperial encouragement.

Fuller evidence is provided by A. Ovadiah. His analysis of the remains of Byzantine churches according to the date of foundation shows the acceleration in the rate of building. The distribution of excavated churches in the Byzantine period is as follows:[50]

---

[45] P. Bar-Adon, 'A Possible Fortified Synagogue at Beth-Yarah', and S. Levy, 'The Ancient Synagogue at Ma'on', both in *Roman Frontier Studies, 1967*, Proceedings of the 7th International Congress held at Tel Aviv (Tel Aviv, 1971), 185.

[46] G. Armstrong, 'Fifth and Sixth Century Church Building in the Holy Land', *GOTR* 14 (1969), 17–30, 23.

[47] Sozomen, *HE* 2. 2. 1; 2. 24. 1, GCS (1960) 50. 10–15; 87. 15–88. 3; Socrates, *HE* 3. 5. 1, PG 67. 120B–121A.

[48] Avi-Yonah, 'Economics', 41–4.

[49] Armstrong, 'Fifth and Sixth Century Church Building', 27; also J. W. Crowfoot, *Early Churches in Palestine* (London, 1941), 139–48.

[50] See A. Ovadiah, *A Corpus of Byzantine Churches in the Holy Land* (Bonn, 1970), 193.

Century	4th	4–5th	5th	5–6th	6th	7th	8th	undated
No. of churches	9	3	45	14	56	15	3	52

Many of these churches were built in monasteries. The dates of the monastic foundations in the Judaean desert are as follows:[51]

Century	4th	early 5th	late 5th	early 6th	late 6th	7th	8th
No. of foundations	3	3	13	12	10	0	1

This table shows the growth in the number of monastic foundations as a result of the work and example of Euthymius, who lived in the fifth century, and Sabas, who was active in the early sixth century. It shows the high number of foundations made in those periods. Often churches in monasteries were built after they were founded, as the community grew in size or wealth and the old church, often a cave, became inadequate for their needs.[52]

These figures confirm the development pointed to by Avi-Yonah, and show that the sixth century was the period of greatest building activity, and also of greatest prosperity: 'The building expansion in the sixth century is a facet of the flourishing economic position and the relatively stable political situation of the Byzantine Empire under the long rule of Justinian I, who gave both political and financial support to the construction of churches in Palestine.'[53]

The lavish decoration and ornamentation of the churches also points to the prosperity of the country. The magnificent mosaics, such as those at Beth-Alpha and the Monastery of the Lady Mary at Beth Shan, come from this period.[54] Avi-Yonah contrasts Palestine, with its mosaic pavements of the fifth and sixth century, with Africa and Gaul, where the majority of these pavements were produced earlier—in the second

---

[51] The best summary of the foundation dates of the monasteries is in Hirschfeld, 'List', 81–2.

[52] At Ruhama the church was the ancient refectory and at Sede Nahum it was built over another structure with a mosaic floor, presumably an earlier church. Ovadiah, *Corpus*, nos. 157, 160.

[53] Ovadiah, *Corpus*, 193.

[54] See G. Fitzgerald, *A Sixth-Century Monastery in Beth Shan (Scythopolis)* (Philadelphia, 1939), 5–10.

and third centuries. He finds in this phenomenon a further indication that Palestine was at its most prosperous during these later centuries.[55]

This prosperity was based on public investment and led to an increase in population which in turn stimulated demand for agricultural and other goods. But it was short-lived. Once the resources stopped entering the country and the building programme drew to a close, then economic decline set in.[56]

The arrival of pilgrims, whether they settled in the country or returned home after a brief visit, was a cause of this prosperity. Not only did they spend their own money through the giving of gifts or the financing of building, but they also contributed by their visits to the growing reputation of Palestine. The monasteries benefited from the prosperity of the province. Their growth took place because the money became available to finance it.

PEOPLE

The phenomenon of pilgrimage led to an influx of population as well as resources. The attention of modern critics has often been directed towards pilgrims from the west, but by far the greater number of pilgrims came from the eastern parts of the Empire.

The eastern pilgrims came from a different social background from those from the west. A visitor who caused a stir was the monk Barsaumas, born near Samosata, who made several visits to Jerusalem accompanied by parties of monks, between forty and a hundred in number. Accounts of these visits convey the fear which these wild men of the mountains evoked in the local townspeople. Barsaumas and his companions passed through the land destroying temples and synagogues. At Petra, the gates were closed against the visitors who then threatened to burn down the town if they were not admitted. Barsaumas entered and prophesied the end of a four-year drought, and before long his prophecy was fulfilled so dramatically that the force of the rain broke the city walls. On another occasion 15,000 armed Jews confronted Barsaumas but his 'iron tunic (presumably the heavy metal weights which he carried as an ascetic

---

[55] M. Avi-Yonah, 'Mosaic Pavements in Palestine', *QDAP* 2 (1932), 79.

[56] The population of the country in the Byzantine period is estimated to be four times that of the Israelite period. See Avi-Yonah, 'Economics', 39–40. For agricultural expansion, see D. Sperber, *Roman Palestine, 200–400: The Land* (Ramat-Gan, 1978), 64–8.

discipline) and hair which fell to the ground terrified them and he pursued them and burned their temples.'[57]

The story of Barsaumas provides the likely context for an event in the Life of Euthymius. A group of four hundred Armenians arrived at the monastery on their way from Jerusalem to the Jordan. Euthymius told Domitian, the steward, to give them something to eat but Domitian reported that there was only enough food for ten people in the storehouse. Euthymius told him to look again and when he tried the storehouse door he found that the room was so full with grain that there was no space to open it.[58] Schwartz entitles the chapter, 'Wunderbare Speisung einer Karawane' but, in the light of the stories of Barsaumas, the miracle might be more aptly described as a miracle of preservation of the monastery from a hungry and unruly gang rather than the multiplication of loaves.

The presence of the poor in Palestine, suggested by these stories, is confirmed by literary and epigraphical evidence. Cyril of Scythopolis notes the nationalities of many of the monks, including the first twelve companions of Euthymius. Of these, three came from Cappadocia, three from Armenia, three from Rhaithou in the Sinai, one from Antioch, and one from Scythopolis—none from the west and only one native of Palestine.[59] References to the places of origin of the monks are more frequent in the *Life of Sabas*, and the concluding shorter Lives. In these, the nationalities of forty-three monks are included. Only one, Paul, who became superior of the New Laura, was from the west, from Rome, and a mere seven came from within Palestine.[60]

Another valuable piece of evidence comes from the monastic cemetery at Choziba. A.-M. Schneider discovered 213 funerary inscriptions in these burial caves. They date from the fifth to the tenth centuries but the majority come from the sixth and seventh.[61] Of these inscriptions seventy-three give the place of origin of the monk. Of the monks whose birthplace is recorded, the largest group, of thirty names, came from Northern Syria and Asia Minor, including twelve from Cilicia, nine from Cappadocia, four from Isauria, and three from Antioch. The next

---

[57] F. Nau, 'Deux épisodes de l'histoire juive sous Théodose II', *REJ* 83–4 (1927), 184–206, 188.

[58] *Kyrillos*, 27. 5–28. 7.

[59] Ibid. 25. 17–26. 14.

[60] A list of all the nationalities of the monks mentioned by Cyril is given by Schwartz, *Kyrillos*, 359–60.

[61] A.-M. Schneider, 'Das Kloster des Theotokos zu Choziba im Wadi el Kelt', *RQ* 39 (1931), 297–332, 317–29.

largest group came from the south-west of Palestine. There are seventeen names in this group, with thirteen from Ascalon, two from Gaza, and one from Maiuma. Smaller numbers come from Greece and Cyprus (nine, including one from Thrace) and from the regions immediately to the north of Palestine (six from southern Syria). Other areas represented on the list are Mesopotamia, Georgia, Persia, India, Rome, and Arabia. From this list, it is clearly shown that the monks tended to come from the north and the east. Few were from Palestine and hardly any from the western part of the Empire.

Before their arrival in Palestine these visitors from the east would have enjoyed a very different life-style from that of the noble Roman ladies to whom Jerome ministered. In her comments on the inscriptions of Choziba, Evelyne Patlagean comments: 'On reconnait à Choziba le recrutement des montagnes peuplés et pauvres, dont les hommes ont été attirés par la Terre Sainte en dépit de la distance.'[62] She also suggests that, since it was customary in Syrian inscriptions for the town of origin to be mentioned as well as the region, the absence of this information in the Choziba inscriptions implies that these were nomadic wanderers with no settled home.[63]

The pious longing to worship at the Holy Places was reinforced by economic necessity. Numerous studies have analysed the growing pressure on the poor in the fifth and sixth centuries.[64] They describe the causes of deterioration in the living conditions of the poor and its results. An important factor was the pressure of taxation which could force peasants to abandon their lands and to seek employment with a neighbouring landowner.

This abandonment of land and flight from the tax collector was known as *anachoresis*—a term long used of the flight of villagers in Egypt who had opted out in moments of distress or oppression. Economic deprivation led to displacement.[65] The use of the same term both for this flight caused by economic pressure and for the entering of a monastery implies that many were forced into the monasteries because of the lack of a livelihood outside. John Cassian describes three kinds

[62] E. Patlagean, *Pauvreté économique et pauvreté sociale* (Paris, 1977), 336.

[63] Patlagean, *Pauvreté*, 338.

[64] G. E. B. de Sainte-Croix, *The Class Struggle in the Ancient World* (London, 1981), 453–61; A. H. M. Jones, *The Later Roman Empire* (Oxford 1964), iii. 810–11; Patlagean, *Pauvreté, passim*.

[65] P. Brown, *The World of Late Antiquity* (London, 1971), 98. But P. Rousseau, *Pachomius* (Berkeley, Calif., 1985), 9–12, argues that the need to escape the burden of taxation has been exaggerated and that small-scale farming was still profitable.

of monastic vocation—that from God, through a dream or vision; that from man, through the example of a holy man; and that through necessity, when circumstances such as the death of loved ones or loss of property led to compunction.[66] The last of the three was an important cause of the rapid growth of Palestinian monasticism in the economic and social conditions of hardship in the provinces of the eastern Empire. Many came to Palestine to find work. The building programme required a huge labour force. It was calculated by Tchalenko that the construction of the large monastery at Qal'at Siman, in Syria, would have given employment to several thousand labourers.[67] The construction of so many churches and monasteries in Palestine would not have been accomplished using only local labour. The construction sites recruited from the huge numbers of itinerant landless labourers travelling around the Mediterranean world.[68] 'The lowest stratum of the urban population was formed by the casual labourers, who were particularly numerous in the building industry.'[69]

Building labourers often found their way to the monasteries. They went primarily to work. When the deacon Fidus set out to extend the monastery of Euthymius, he collected an 'engineer and a crowd of workmen' (ἕνα μηχανικὸν καὶ πλῆθος τεχνιτῶν) in Jerusalem before going to the laura to start the work.[70] The same noun (τεχνίτας) is used of the labourers which Sabas took with him from the Great Laura when he went to assist the rebellious monks at the New Laura by building a church and bakery. These men were probably recruited in Jerusalem, since Sabas had gone there to obtain the money to finance the work from the Patriarch.[71] During the time taken to complete the work, the labourers lived in the monastery. There they shared the life of the monks and were cared for by them. Preparing food for the workmen was a regular duty in many monasteries.[72]

As well as labourers living with the monks, we hear of monks becoming labourers on building projects outside the monastery. Ephraem, the *comes orientis*, employed a bishop, who preferred manual labour to the

---

[66] Cassian, *Conferences*, 3. 4, SC 42 (Paris, 1955), 141–3. Cf. A. Vööbus, *A History of Asceticism in the Syrian Orient*, ii (Louvain, 1960), 120, for economic pressures on labourers to become monks.

[67] G. Tchalenko, *Villages antiques de la Syrie du Nord*, i (Paris, 1953), 229.

[68] Patlagean, *Pauvreté*, 166.

[69] Jones, *Later Roman Empire*, iii. 858.

[70] *Kyrillos*, 64. 16.

[71] Ibid. 123. 25–124. 1.

[72] Ibid. 138. 11–12.

cares of office, on the work of rebuilding Antioch after the earthquake. Another monk worked on the construction of a reservoir near the Jordan, which was organized by the Patriarch John of Jerusalem.[73] In the informality of living conditions in the desert, the demarcation between professed monks, building labourers, and visitors was not clearcut. Visitors might prolong their stay and attach themselves to the community. Labourers might stay on after the initial work was completed and find themselves absorbed into the community. Monks might leave to work on secular projects. The simplicity and poverty of monastic living conditions was not only a sign of ascetic virtue but was also the normal way of life for the class from which many of the monks originated.[74] For some, more wealthy, monks the act of entering a monastery was a true act of renunciation leading to a new and harsher way of life. For others, the monastery was a natural part of the society to which they belonged, and they moved with a natural ease from building site to monastery to farm at harvest time to the open road, as they sought to earn a living.

MINISTRY

The monasteries benefited from the wealth attracted into Palestine by the pilgrims, and were enabled to minister to others in their turn. The care of pilgrims became a function of the monasteries and their reputation for hospitality grew. This concern of the monks was expressed by their leaders Sabas and Theodosius in a letter to the Emperor Anastasius. They wrote to him of their desire that visitors should be edified and consoled and not scandalized by the presence of Jews, Samaritans, and others.[75] But their interest extended to more practical measures. Theodosius' first act in establishing his monastery was to build a hostel (ξενοδοχεῖον) and to receive anyone who came to him.[76] As his monastery grew, so did its ability to serve visitors. Eventually, there were a variety of buildings available so that everyone who came could receive what he needed. There were separate houses for monks from abroad, wealthy visitors, poor visitors, and the mentally ill.[77]

---

[73] *Prat.* 37; 134. PG 87/3. 2855D–2888C; 2997A–D.
[74] The social background of the monks is explored in Patlagean, *Pauvreté*, 49–53.
[75] *Kyrillos* 154. 9–10.
[76] Ibid. 238. 16–17.
[77] Theodore of Petra, *V. Thds.* 34. 15–16.

Remains of a large hostel can be seen at the monastery of Martyrius at Ma'ale Adummim. It was built outside the gate. The dimensions are about 40m. in length and 25m. in width, and in this space are found six or seven sleeping halls, a church, and stables. It could accommodate 60–70 people.[78] It is not possible to identify the hostels at other monasteries but clearly all would have provided some form of accommodation for guests, and the larger monasteries would have had buildings set aside exclusively for this purpose.[79]

In addition to hostels for guests in the monastery itself, the larger communities maintained premises in the cities of Jerusalem and Jericho. As soon as money became available to Sabas, he bought houses in both cities in order to welcome and to minister to guests.[80] The Jerusalem guest houses of the Great Laura and Castellion were near the Tower of David, which has been described as 'un centre de tout de quartier monastique avec des cellules, couvents et hôtelleries des grands monastères du desert de Jérusalem'.[81]

Particular attention was given to caring for the sick. Theodosius' monastery had a special house for the sick, and it can be assumed that Sabas' monastery provided similar facilities since monks are described as receiving medical attention.[82] The monks were also concerned for the provision of hospitals in Jerusalem. Sabas asked the Emperor Justinian to provide a hospital. He agreed, granting a revenue of 1,850 *nomismata* to pay for a hospital with 100 beds, which was later extended to offer a further 100 beds.[83] This hospital is mentioned by Procopius and should be identified with the Royal Hospital attached to the Nea Church which is also mentioned by Strategius.[84] An even larger hospital was the

---

[78] For a description of the site, see Hirschfeld, *Judaean Desert Monasteries*, 197.

[79] For reference to the location of the hostel at the Great Laura being clearly visible from Sabas' tower, see *Kyrillos*, 130. 31–131. 4.

[80] Ibid. 109. 13–17; 116. 8–25.

[81] J. T. Milik, 'La Topographie de Jérusalem vers la fin de l'époque byzantine', *MUSJ* 37 (1960–1), 127–89, 187.

[82] *Kyrillos*, 131. 26. A description of medical care in a monastery is preserved in the *Life of Theodore of Sykeon*, 'If any required medical treatment for certain illnesses or surgery of a purging draught or hot springs, this God-inspired man would prescribe the best thing for each, for even in technical matters he had become an experienced doctor. He might recommend one to have recourse to surgery and he would always state clearly which doctor they ought to employ,' 145. 29–45, ed. Festugière, 114. See also H. J. Magoulias, 'The Lives of the Saints as Sources of Data for the History of Byzantine Medicine in the sixth and seventh centuries', *By. Z.* 57 (1964), 127–50.

[83] *Kyrillos*, 177. 9–14.

[84] Procopius, *Buildings*, 5. 6. 25, LCL 8 (London, 1914), 348. Milik, 'Topographie', 152.

Patriarchal Hospital attached to the monastery of St George, two miles south of Jerusalem. This could cater for 400 people and received all kinds of visitors, among whom was John the Hesychast who stayed there on his arrival in Jerusalem.[85]

The provision of services and care of the poor played an important part in Byzantine society which, as R. Browning has commented, was 'organised for the transmission of wealth rather than the creation of wealth'.[86] The traditional mechanisms by which wealth had been used for the common good had been concentrated in the cities. Leading citizens accepted obligations to provide for the welfare of others through the services paid for by the curial classes. There is evidence from the fifth and sixth centuries that eligible citizens were declining to enter the curia and so evading the charges necessary to maintain the services.[87] New agencies were entering this vacuum and were encouraged to provide the necessary support for the poor. Among these were the churches and monasteries.

Jerusalem, the Holy City, attracted people from many parts of the Empire and from all social classes. Not only did this volume of visitors provide a pool of personnel who could be recruited to join the growing number of monastic communities but it also provided the economic conditions in which monastic growth became possible.

The monasteries provided an environment in which the monk could continue his work and receive in return what he need to live. This suggests that they were responding to a need in the changing social circumstances of the late Roman Empire. They cared for the poor, not only by providing food and lodging, but also a permanent home and employment for those who were able. 'S'il est vrai que les rôles sociaux sont transposés et non effacés lors de l'entrée au cloître, la société monastique doit logiquement recevoir en plus grand nombre des pauvres, vêtus en quête de travail s'ils le peuvent, ou d'assistance s'ils sont invalides . . . La monastère a-t-il été le terme des itinéraires spirituels ou le havre des déracinements sociaux.'[88]

Jerusalem was more than a centre for pilgrimage. It became a place of employment, of shelter, of refuge for many thousands of inhabitants

---

[85] *Kyrillos*, 204. 7–9, 16. See Milik, 'Topographie', 142–4. These hospitals had the capacity to minister to many different groups of people.

[86] R. Browning, 'The Low-Level Saint's Life in the Early Byzantine Period', in S. Hackel (ed.), *The Byzantine Saint* (London, 1981), 117–27, 121.

[87] See Jones, *Later Roman Empire*, iii, 740–8; de Ste-Croix, *Class Struggle in the Ancient World*, 471–2.

[88] Patlagean, *Pauvreté*, 33.

of a changing and uncertain international society. The growth of the monasteries took place in response to economic pressures as much as to spiritual revival.

5

This Desert

GEOGRAPHY

When Cyril describes Euthymius' longing to inhabit the desert, he is remembering the feelings which inflamed his own heart when he undertook the same journey. 'The glory-hating and God-loving Euthymius, considering that this care [in Euthymius' case the care of the monasteries of Melitene] stood in the way of virtue, left the city and took flight to Jerusalem, desiring to live in this desert.'[1] The monasticism of Palestine grew up in *this* desert. It was a unique environment and its qualities determined the way of life of the monks.

Its uniqueness becomes apparent when it is compared with two other desert areas inhabited by monks, those of Egypt and Syria. In Egypt there is an extreme and defined contrast between the desert and cultivated land. The average annual rainfall is minimal, a little under an inch (or 20mm.), and the peasants depend now, as they did in Byzantine times, almost exclusively on the waters of the Nile for both drinking and irrigation. The monk, like the rest of the population was drawn towards the river, or the few oases of the desert. Even a short distance away from the waters of the Nile, the aridity of the desert imposed on monastic life the character of a struggle for survival. 'To survive at all in the hostile environment of such a desert, the Egyptian had to transplant into it the tenacious and all-absorbing routines of the villages of the oikoumene. To live at all, a man had to remain in one place, earning his living from manual labour, from pottery and reed weaving. Groups had to reproduce exactly on the fringe of the desert, the closed-in, embattled aspects of the fortified villages of Upper Egypt.'[2]

The Syrian desert was different. Here, wild mountains and farming land intermingled. A monk who wished to withdraw into the desert

---

[1] *Kyrillos*, 13. 27–14. 2. For similar passages in other Lives, see ibid. 90. 8–9; 204. 3–4; 224. 16; 236. 10–11; 242. 6.

[2] P. R. L. Brown, 'The Rise and Function of the Holy Man in Late Antiquity', *JRS* 61 (1971), 80–101, 83.

would make the short journey into the unproductive mountainous regions around his home. A sometimes erratic but usually plentiful supply of rain ensured that the hermit could support himself from the pools of water which collected in the rocks and the plants which grew naturally. The monastic life was informal and unsettled. If he became disillusioned with the ascetic life or if employment prospects in the villages improved, the monk could always rejoin the ranks of landless labourers seeking work.[3]

The distinctiveness of the Palestinian desert is a consequence of two basic geographical facts. The first, which has been discussed in the previous chapter, is that it is close to Jerusalem. The second is that it is very varied. This variety conditioned the style of life which was developed. It is the variety of terrain and its effect on the monasteries which is the theme of this chapter.

The unusual qualities of the landscape impress themselves on the many visitors to the land who undertake the popular journey, rich with Biblical association, from Jerusalem to Jericho. The distance is about fifteen miles and the time required, using modern means of transport, less than thirty minutes. But during that short journey, the traveller descends from the high ridge of the Mount of Olives, 800 feet above sea level, down to the lowest point on the earth's surface, the flat plain surrounding the Dead Sea. The landscape quickly empties, with the olive trees of the Judaean hills thinning out and then disappearing to give place to a grey expanse of bare rounded hills until the road drops through the rocky mountain scenery to the hazy flatness of the plain. A simplified but accurate explanation for the rapidly changing landscape is that in this narrow stretch of land three continents meet, each with its distinct soil structures and vegetation. The Judaean hills are Mediterranean, with the characteristic red soil in which vines and olives grow. The valley of the Dead Sea is an extension of the African Great Rift Valley, with plants and animals native to East Africa. In between is Asian steppe country, dry but not waterless, a land of nomadic shepherds. These three 'continents' are arranged in roughly parallel bands running north-east to south-west (see Map 1).

Corresponding to the change in soil structure is a change in climate. In the Judaean hills the rainfall is as high as 700mm. per annum, similar

---

[3] For a description of the characteristics of Syrian monasticism, see A. Vööbus, *A History of Asceticism in the Syrian Orient*, ii (Louvain, 1960), 292–315. The terrain of one area of Syria is described by G. Tchalenko, *Villages antiques de la Syrie du Nord*, 3 vols. (Paris, 1953–8), i. 61–8. He points out that the rainfall in this desert is 500mm. p.a.

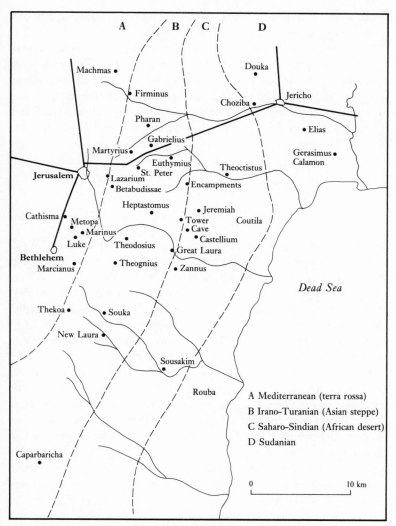

1. Soil variation in the Palestinian desert

to that in most of Europe, but with the difference that all the rain falls in the winter months. It declines to less than 100mm. on the shores of the Dead Sea. Meanwhile the mean temperature rises from 17.7 °C around Jerusalem to 25.4 °C at Jericho. The south is drier and warmer than the north, so the most arid and inhospitable region is the south-eastern part of the desert, called Rouba by the monks.[4]

It is often and correctly noted that most of this region is not a 'real' desert, like the deserts of North Africa or Saudi Arabia. When the word is applied to this region it describes the comparative emptiness of the landscape. It was through taking advantage of the opportunities provided by the different environments fortuitously coexisting within a small area that the monks developed a style of monastic living which was different from the monastic life of Egypt or Syria, or indeed anywhere else.

THE NECESSITIES OF LIFE

The first requirement for those living in the desert is water. Water could come from two sources: springs and rain. There are several springs in the Judaean desert. The largest is the spring Ein Kelt which produces a plentiful supply of water which is carried by an aqueduct to the plain of Jericho where it is used by local residents. Other springs are smaller and are to be found mainly, but by no means exclusively, in the desert margin area at the foot of the Judaean hills or in the cliffs overlooking the Dead Sea. The monasteries made use of available springs. For example the monastery of Choziba in the Wadi Kelt uses the water of the spring to irrigate the extensive and fertile gardens below the monastic buildings. In the Great Laura a spring was discovered at an early stage in the life of the community. Sabas was shown the location of an underground spring by a donkey digging a hole in the ground and drinking the water which it uncovered. This spring gave a much needed supply of water to the fathers who had previously had to travel fifteen *stades* to collect water from a cistern. The importance of this discovery for the life of the community is shown by the observations of the Russian abbot Daniel, who visited the monastery in the twelfth century: 'I saw the well of St Saba, which a wild ass showed him one night, and from this well I drank water which was sweet and very cold. In that place there is no river nor stream nor spring, but only the well of St Saba for it is a waterless place in rocky mountains and the whole of

---

[4] The geographical details are set out in the introduction to Y. Hirschfeld, *The Judaean Desert Monasteries in the Byzantine Period* (New Haven, Conn., 1992). This study presents the results of extensive archeological research on the monasteries.

that wilderness is dry and waterless, and the fathers who dwelt in that wilderness lived by rainwater alone.'[5]

The winter rains provided a more widespread source of water (see Map 2). The monastic desert was full of cisterns. Sometimes these were natural holes in the rock but more often were artificially and laboriously constructed. Each monastery had a system of canals, cisterns, and reservoirs to collect and preserve all the rain-water possible. Topography influenced the design of the water collection system but the basic principle was constant. The hard soil of the desert absorbed little water, and the rain which fell flowed over the surface down into the deep wadis. This 'run-off' could be diverted into channels which fed the water conservation system.

An elaborate and extensive arrangement of channels and cisterns was a feature of all desert monasteries. Water was collected as it ran off the natural slope or the roofs and paved courtyards of the monastery, and was then carried in channels or ceramic pipes into cisterns. Often two or three sedimentary pools would filter stones and loose earth from the water before it overflowed into the cistern itself. The cisterns were lined with successive layers of dressed building stones, pebbles in greyish cement and waterproof cistern plaster to prevent water seeping into the ground. They were usually dug into the ground and often arches were constructed to strengthen the roofs. Larger reservoirs might be covered by a network of ropes over which mats were laid to protect the water from evaporation in the hot sun.

An example of a complex water system was found in the monastery of Martyrius. Here water was collected from the drainage of the roofs and courtyards and from a channel bringing water from a ridge to the west of the monastery. The water drained into three large cisterns, the total capacity of which is estimated by the excavators at 20,000–30,000 cu.m. of water.[6]

The growth of the monasteries described by Cyril took place in a period which was wetter than usual. The years between 250 and 330 were dry, and during this period there was a decline in agricultural production throughout the provinces of Palestine. Then the average rainfall increased and remained at a high level until about 500.[7] There-

---

[5] *Kyrillos*, 101. 6–19; 98. 19–20. For Abbot Daniel's account, see J. Wilkinson, *Jerusalem Pilgrimage, 1099–1185* (London, 1988), 140.

[6] See Hirschfeld, *Judaean Desert Monasteries*, 156–7.

[7] See D. Sperber, *Roman Palestine, 200–400: The Land* (Ramat-Gan, 1978), 70–2; C. E. P. Brooks, *Climate through the Ages*, 2nd edn. (London, 1949), 305–15.

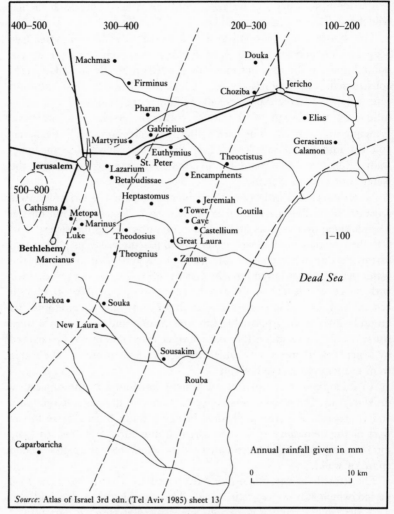

400–500   300–400   200–300   100–200

Machmas •

Douka •

• Firminus

Choziba • Jericho

Pharan

• Elias

Gabrielius

Martyrius •

Gerasimus •
Calamon

• Euthymius
St. Peter   Theoctistus

Jerusalem

• Lazarium
• Betabudissae   • Encampments

500–800

Heptastomus

Cathisma

• Jeremiah

Metopa   • Tower   Coutila
• Marinus   • Cave
Luke   • Castellium

1–100

• Theodosius   Great Laura

Bethlehem
Marcianus   • Theognius   • Zannus

Dead Sea

Thekoa •   • Souka

New Laura •

Sousakim •

Rouba

Caparbaricha
•

Annual rainfall given in mm

0   10 km

Source: Atlas of Israel 3rd edn. (Tel Aviv 1985) sheet 13

2. Rainfall in the Palestinian desert

after the level of rainfall declined. A sign of this drier weather after 500 is the five-year famine and drought which, Cyril tells us, was ended as a result of the prayers of Sabas.[8]

[8] *Kyrillos*, 167. 25–169. 24.

The impact of even a small variation in rainfall could be considerable. 'A slight increase in the average winter's rainfall and a greater proportion of good years to bad years would have its greatest effort in marginal lands, and make a settled habit of life possible where now it seems impossible.'[9] The years in which the monasteries grew coincide exactly with this wet period of Mediterranean history. Climactic conditions favoured the monks and allowed them to settle even in dry and remote areas of the desert.

In Palestine rain is expected between November and March. From this weather pattern developed the distinctively Palestinian monastic custom of hardened ascetics leaving the monastery to spend Lent wandering in the more remote parts of the desert. The practice may have originated in Asia Minor, as we read that Euthymius used to retire to a local mountain top during Lent when he was a youth in Melitene.[10] The rainfall pattern resulted in another fortunate climactic coincidence in that the period of Lent fell during the wettest time of the year when the desert was at its most fertile and productive. The desert is more hospitable in this season than at any other time of the year. Both Euthymius and Sabas used to set off towards the end of January, when the rain was at its height, the streams were at their fullest, and the vegetation at its most abundant. For most of the year the need for water concentrated the monastic settlements in places where water was available from springs or cisterns, but when more water was available the area of occupation widened and monks were released to wander over a wider area.

The monks had to eat as well as drink. Three main sources of food should be distinguished. First, food could be grown. In some areas monasteries developed into major agricultural enterprises. Agriculture is associated with the Pachomian coenobia of Southern Egypt. Here, as a consequence of the hard work of the monks and the gifts of benefactors, the monasteries developed to the extent that Theodore remarked that 'owing to the excuse of needing food and other bodily needs, the monasteries had acquired numerous fields, animals and boats'.[11] Similarly in the mountains of Syria, 'chaque monastère constitute une enterprise agricole autonome, très vaste et très bien organisée'.[12]

---

[9] G. F. Kirk, 'The Negev or Southern Desert of Palestine; *PEFQ St.* (1941), 57–71, 68. These remarks were made of the Negev but apply equally to the Judaean desert.
[10] *Kyrillos*, 13. 20–6.
[11] *V. Pach. Bo.* 197.
[12] Tchalenko, *Villages antiques*, i. 20.

The fertile hillsides around Bethlehem and Jerusalem were suited to the cultivation of olives and other crops. Here agriculture was a natural occupation for the monks, and monasteries developed into major producers. The monastery at Siyar el Ghanam, at Beit Sahur not far from Bethlehem, consisted of an extensive network of buildings. These included several olive- and winepresses, grain silos, and stables, as well as the more familiar water cisterns and bakery. As well as providing for the needs of the monks, produce was sold to increase revenue. This is shown by the size of the oil-presses which are larger than would be required for the needs of the monastery.[13]

This monastery can be dated to the sixth century.[14] It should be identified with the monastery of Marcianus which, according to Cyril, was 'near Bethlehem', and was large enough to provide donkeys and provisions for the building of Castellion and comfortable enough for Marcianus to feel he was living a life of ease.[15] Theodore of Petra tells how Theodosius visited Marcianus on his way from Jerusalem back to his own monastery, and a natural route of this journey would pass through Khirbet Siyar el Ghanam.[16] The excavation of these remains show the kind of establishment which could develop in the agricultural regions at the western end of the desert. Several monasteries of the period followed this agricultural way of life.

The monasteries described by Cyril lay further to the east, in the grazing steppe country. He makes no reference to the cultivation of crops, but archaeological excavation has shown that the monastic buildings were surrounded by extensive gardens. The skill of the monks in the preservation of water allowed vegetables to be grown even in more arid parts of the desert. An example is the garden at the site of Khirbet ed Deir, several miles east of Thekoa, where the monks built huge retaining walls to protect the garden from the winter flood water and created many stepped terraces. The area cultivated was at least 33,000 sq.m. and, since the excavators calculate that the number of monks would not have exceeded fifty, this indicates that there was over 600 sq.m. for each

---

[13] G. Corbo, *Gli scavi di Kh. Siyar el-Ghanam (Campo dei Pastori) e i monasteri dei dintorni* (Jerusalem, 1955), 254–5.

[14] Corbo, *Gli scavi*, 19–88; Corbo, 'L'ambiente materiale della vita dei monaci di Palestina nel periodo Bizantino', *Or. Chr. A.* 153 (1958), 235–57. This monastery is built on a possible site of the Shepherds' Fields.

[15] *Kyrillos*, 49. 12; 66. 25; 112. 2–9; 237 15–16.

[16] Theodore of Petra, *V. Thds.* 73. 22. Corbo, in *Gli scavi*, 162–3, suggests that Khirbet Giohdham is the site of this monastery, but the remains are too small and the distance from Bethlehem too great for this identification to be convincing.

monk. The excavators conducted the experiment of planting figs, pomegranates, and vines in the garden and, so effective is even what remains of the monks' irrigation system, that the plants have flourished. Another interesting discovery, showing the monks' agricultural skill, was the remains of a Byzantine vineyard in the grounds of the New Laura, deep in the desert.[17]

The plants most frequently grown by the monks were vegetables (λαχάνα) and pulse (ὅσπρια), although we also read of the lupine (θερμός), a plant which produces edible seeds eaten by the very poor; a dish made probably of peas (πισάριον); pumpkins (κολοκύνθια); carobs (κεράτια); dates (φοινικία); and figs (σῦχη). This list, drawn from contemporary sources, indicates the extent of the monks' horticultural skills which enabled the production of such a variety of crops in such a difficult terrain.[18]

The second source of food was the local plant life. The desert plateau contains several plants which could be eaten not only by the sheep and goats of the herdsmen, but by humans as well. The sources refer to several plants which the monks used to collect on a systematic basis.

The plant most frequently mentioned is mannouthia. This was collected in bundles on foraging expeditions and each monk would expect to return with one or more loads daily.[19] It was prickly, and Anthony of Choziba tells of a monk collecting mannouthia who was cut by the leaves of the plant until he bled. It was possibly used for fuel as well as for food, since we are told that the monks of Choziba used to keep it by the bread oven.[20] Mannouthia has been identified with the thistle, named *gundelia tournefortii* in Latin and known as *aqub* in Arabic. It grows on the edge of the desert, and so, for monks in many monasteries, required a journey to reach suitable areas. When it first sprouts in February and March all parts of the plant—leaves, roots, flowers, and seeds—are edible, but as the year progresses the leaves become yellow and spiky, and suitable only for fuel.[21]

Another plant collected was melagria. This was a root dug up by monks especially during their Lenten wanderings into the Extreme

---

[17] Hirschfeld, *Judaean Desert Monasteries*, 204.
[18] Ibid. 86–8.
[19] A sign of Sabas' virtue was his capacity for work in collecting three loads, *Kyrillos*, 92. 8.
[20] *V. Geor. Choz.* 14; 24, *An. Boll.* (1888), 110. 2; 123. 14.
[21] Hirschfeld, *Judaean Desert Monasteries*, 89; Hirschfeld, 'Edible Wild Plants: The Secret Diet of the Monks in the Judaean Desert', *Israel: Land and Nature* 16 (1990), 25–8.

Desert, on which journeys the little trowel for digging was an essential piece of equipment.[22] It is identified with the *Asphodelus microcarpus*, a common plant with edible roots.[23] An earlier user of this plant was John the Baptist, the archetypal desert dweller, who lived, according to Matthew, on μέλι ἄγριον, misleadingly rendered into English as 'wild honey'.[24]

The monks also collected the salt bush, or maloah, known to the Old Testament as mallow, and the seeds of capers or κόκκια κάππαρεως.[25] Squills, or σκίλλαι, were too bitter and required a miracle to make them edible.[26]

The eating of wild plants collected in the surrounding countryside appears to have been a distinctive practice of the Palestinian monks. Evagrius Scholasticus, the church historian, writes of ascetics who he describes as 'grazers' (βόσκοι). In his account, these men practise the extreme and unusual form of asceticism of living off plants like animals.[27] A way of life strange and exotic to Evagrius, who reflects a Syrian outlook, was commonplace to a Palestinian. John Moschus met several 'grazers' and, although he can identify them by this title, he does not seem to regard their way of life as unusual or worthy of special comment.[28] The way of life of the *boskos* was the individual form of the widespread monastic practice of living off the land in a grazing area. While these plants would not be considered as suitable for human consumption today, they were a natural source of nourishment in a region in which survival was difficult. They became a staple of the monks' diet.

The third source of food was outside the country, through import. Food which could not be grown locally was bought or given. The most essential import was the grain needed for baking bread. Chariton's instructions to his monks to eat only bread, salt, and water show that bread was basic to the monastic diet; and monks who set out into the desert would take with them a bag of bread.[29] Storerooms for grain and

---

[22] *Kyrillos*, 209. 19; 96. 15; 288. 19. Price wrongly translates mannouthia as 'faggots' at these points.

[23] See Hirschfeld, *Judaean Desert Monasteries*, 89. Du Buit wrongly suggests that these are wild mushrooms, in *MO* pt. i, iii. 48.

[24] Matt. 3: 14.

[25] Job 30: 14. For capers, see *V. Geor. Choz.* 42, *An. Boll.* (1888), 143. 8–12.

[26] *Kyrillos*, 227. 9–17.

[27] Evagrius, *HE* i. 20, ed. Bidez and Parmentier, 30.

[28] *Prat.* 19; 21; 86; 92; 129; 154; 159; 167, PG 87/3. 2865B; 2868B; 2944B; 2949B; 2993C; 3021C; 3028A; 3033C.

[29] *V. Char.* 16. 28 and 17. *Kyrillos*, 107. 25; 228. 3; 232. 17.

bakeries are found in every monastery in the desert.[30] The land in Palestine is better suited to the growing of fruit and vegetables than it is to grain, which was imported into the country from across the Jordan valley. Cyril tells us of grain bought at Machairous, on the eastern shore of the Dead Sea, carried across the water, presumably by boats such as those depicted on the Madaba Mosaic Map, and then transported by camel to the Great Laura.[31] The monastery of Choziba maintained a buyer (προαγοραστής) in Jordan to arrange the purchase of grain.[32]

Occasionally the monks enjoyed luxuries such as wine, oil, honey, and cheese. These were brought as gifts from well-wishers. A mouth-watering selection of goods was brought by a visitor to John the Hesychast—hot, fresh white bread, wine, oil, fresh cheese and eggs, and a jar of honey.[33] A monastic storehouse would often contain a wide selection of foodstuffs to provide entertainment for visiting dignitaries.

The monks of the monasteries described by Cyril lived in the central section of the desert. Since the land was unsuitable for large-scale agriculture, food was obtained from a variety of sources—from gardens, from wild plants, from the markets, and from charitable donation.

In the eastern section, called the Extreme Desert or πανερήμος by the monks, there was little water and few plants. It could not sustain even the simplest or smallest of communities. It was a place which beckoned the hardiest of the ascetics who often journeyed in this area during Lent when scarce winter rains had fallen. One of them, Cyriac, even established a hermitage in which he managed to live all the year round. But this is the only known monastic settlement. The Extreme Desert can be considered as empty and unoccupied land.

LIVELIHOOD

The high central plateau was the desert in which the form of settlement known as the 'laura' developed. The monastic use of the word 'laura' does not occur in fourth-century Egyptian sources and seems to have originated in Palestine. The word, in secular use, can refer to a ravine, but more usually describes a lane or alleyway in a town, where small

---

[30] *Kyrillos*, 123. 27. Theodore of Petra, *V. Thds.* 37. 20–2. Hirschfeld, *Judaean Desert Monasteries*, 84–5.

[31] *Kyrillos*, 186. 17.

[32] *V. Geor. Choz.* 25, *An. Boll.* (1888), 125. 4.

[33] *Kyrillos*, 210. 5–211. 14.

houses would be located on either side. It was consequently applied to
the settlements of monks in the ravines of the desert. Here a path led
along the side of the ravine with caves or huts leading off it. The
surprising use of the same word to describe both an alleyway in a town
and a path in a monastery comes about because there is a similarity in
the way of life in both places in spite of the very different physical
environments.

One of the earliest known monastic settlements, which was founded
in the fourth century, was the Old Laura or Souka, in the Wadi
Khareitun, south of Bethlehem. D. J. Chitty suggests that the name
Souka is equivalent to the Syriac *Shouga* or Arabic *Suq*, which would
be a suitable translation of the Greek *laura*.[34] The narrow *suq*, with
jostling crowds, noise, and numerous little workshops, is a familiar sight
in a Middle Eastern town. Its use in the monastic context suggests a
way of life modelled on that of the inhabitants of the poorer areas of
the town.

Leading off the pathway, or *laura*, were the dwellings of the monks.
These were called cells, or κελλία. The word κελλίον described the
simple lodging of the poor man, where he worked, lived, and slept.[35]
The monastic κελλίον was also arranged to provide a place where the
monk could live his life. Although small, it would usually include two
rooms, with a cistern and probably a garden. The distance between the
cells, on average about 35m., is a further indication that the occupants
led independent lives.[36] Both the usage of the word in secular life and
the arrangement of the cells confirm the impression that they were seen
as workplaces as much as living-quarters.

The work done in the cells of laurae is often referred to in the Lives.
In Gerasimus' monastery, for example, the monks 'came to the church
on Saturdays and Sundays and partook of the divine mysteries, then
they went into the coenobium [equivalent in this monastery to the
buildings at the centre of the laura] to eat cooked food ... Each of them
carried to the coenobium on Saturday the work he had done in the
week, and on Sunday evening he took provisions for the week, bread,
dates, water, and palms, and went back to his cell.'[37] In the course of

[34] D. J. Chitty, *The Desert a City* (Oxford, 1966), 15–16.
[35] E. Patlagean, *Pauvreté économique et pauvreté sociale à Byzance, 4e–7e siècles* (Paris,
1965), 58.
[36] For a description of the cells discovered in the Judaean desert, see Hirschfeld,
Judaean Desert Monasteries, 176–90.
[37] In *MH* 228. A similar regime is followed by Sabas in his cave near the monastery
of Theoctistus, *Kyrillos*, 94. 7–12.

the week a variety of hand-crafted goods were produced, using the palms mentioned in this passage as raw materials. These goods included ropes and baskets.[38] The laura owned mules which were used to transport finished goods to the market and then to bring back necessary provisions purchased with the proceeds.[39]

Patlagean describes the economic basis of the laura as 'la communauté d'artisans'. 'Derrière les commentaires spirituels se dessinent les faits économiques, la multiplication de petits artisans libres, dispersés et sans famille, rattachés cependant à d'autres hommes seuls par des solidarités religieuses, à un marché par le necessité des échanger'.[40]

The words used to describe the basic living units of the monks have an economic origin. They show that there are parallels between the monastic economy and sections of the urban economy. There is a similarity between the way of life of the inhabitant of the busy and noisy markets of the city and the monk in his empty and silent wadi.

INHABITANTS

This desert was not an empty landscape. It was land used for grazing and the main indigenous population consisted of Arab shepherds. Relationships between the monks and the local people were usually good. Sabas, on an early expedition in the desert, came upon four Arabs, called Saracens by Cyril, who were faint with hunger. He shared his meagre rations with them and, later, they sought him out, bringing in their turn bread, dates, and cheese as a gift.[41] This paradigm tale of mutual support points to a basic harmony between Greek monk and Arab shepherd. Only once are we told of conflict. The monks of the monastery of the Cave complained to Sabas that they had no peace because shepherds were pasturing their flocks on monastery property and were continually begging. The monks' problem was resolved when the ewes ceased to give milk and the lambs began to die. Wisely, the shepherds withdrew.[42]

The normally friendly relationships were an opportunity for evangelism by the monks. Arab villagers were among those who came to the

---

[38] *Kyrillos*, 14. 12–13; 94. 10–12.
[39] Ibid. 28. 13–17.
[40] Patlagean, *Pauvreté*, 316.
[41] *Kyrillos*, 96. 12–18.
[42] Ibid. 160. 14–18.

tombs of the holy men seeking a miracle. In the posthumous miracle stories several of the petitioners have Arab names—Thalabas, Argob, and the woman from the Arab village of Betaboudissae.[43] One of these, Thalabas, was baptized after he received healing.[44]

An Arab name is a surer guide to ethnic origin than a national title. For example, the lists of the bishops present at the Council of Ephesus in 431 shows three names which are clearly Arabic. Abdelas, or Abdullah, of Elousa; Saidas, or Said, of Phaeno; and Natiras, or Nadir, of Gaza. These are all from Palestinian sees, and are clear evidence for the existence of an Arab presence in the Palestinian church. By contrast two 'false' Arabs are Stephanus and Elias. Stephanus, who was superior of Euthymius' monastery from 514 to 535, was described as ἄραψ, but his Greek name suggests that he might have been a Roman citizen from the province of Arabia. Elias, who became Patriarch, was also described as an Arabian. He could have been either from the province of Arabia or, since he had been a monk at Nitria, from the area in Egypt known by the Ptolemaic name of Arabia.[45]

An important event in the history of Arab Christianity took place when an Arab chieftain, Aspebetus, led his tribe from Arabia to the monastery of Euthymius to seek healing for his son, Terebon, who was paralysed. After the miracle, the Arabs were baptized and settled near to Euthymius' monastery, establishing a tent-village so that they could continue to benefit from the saint's wisdom. Their leader Aspebetus was renamed Peter and consecrated Bishop of the Paremboles or Encampments by Patriarch Juvenal. Peter and his successors were prominent within the Church in Palestine, being present at the Councils of Ephesus in 431 and 448 and the Council of Chalcedon.[46] The bishops of the Paremboles continued missionary work among the Arabs of the Jordan valley.

As time went on, the harmony was lost. The monasteries grew in number, size, and wealth, and became more integrated into the life of the province. They became less dependent on the countryside in which they were set and looked instead towards the cities of Jerusalem and Jericho. The monks became less able to live peaceably with successive

---

[43] *Kyrillos*, 75. 13; 76. 6; 76. 13. See also I. Shahid, *Byzantium and the Arabs in the Fifth Century* (Washington, DC, 1989), 198–202.

[44] *Kyrillos*, 75. 25–8.

[45] Shahid, *Byzantium and the Arabs*, 225, 192.

[46] The passages in the *Life of Euthymius* which describe his ministry to the Arabs are *Kyrillos*, 18. 12–21. 19; 24. 11–25. 12; 33. 1–3; 41. 11–12.

waves of advancing invaders. The village of the Encampments was destroyed and the inhabitants moved to a new site a couple of miles to the west, close to the large coenobium of Martyrius, and then were more thoroughly dispersed into the surrounding villages. This focus of Arab Chalcedonianism disintegrated although the succession of bishops continued.[47]

The weakening of the mission of the monks to the Arabs took place against the background of the deteriorating security situation on the frontier. Successive waves of hostile tribes threatened the monasteries in their exposed situation at the eastern fringe of the Empire. From 475 Skenite nomads mounted raids in Syria and Palestine, one of which was responsible for the destruction of the settlement of the Encampments.[48] These continued intermittently until a treaty was signed in 502 between the Emperor Anastasius and the King of the Kinda, Harith ibn 'Amir ibn Hujr. But peace was short-lived. The independent Arab kingdom of the Lakhmids was becoming increasingly powerful. Although Simeon Stylites had been an influence on these Arabs, especially through his conversion of their king, al-Noman, who died in 418, the centre of the kingdom was in the city of Hirah on the lower Euphrates. This was within the Persian Empire and under the influence of the Nestorian catholicosate of Seleucia-Ctesiphon. Although Christian, the Lakhmids did not have associations with either the Council of Chalcedon or the Byzantine Empire.[49] Their growing power threatened the frontier and struck terror into the monks. The effect of the invasion by al-Mundhir is described in the Life of John the Hesychast: 'At the same time, Alamandurus the son of Sikka ... invaded Arabia and Palestine in great fury ... carrying off everything as plunder, taking countless thousands of Romans into captivity ... with a multitude of barbarians swarming over the desert.'[50]

In response, Justinian gave his support to the Ghassanid tribes in 528. Their leader al-Harith ibn Jabala defeated al-Mundhir in 554. Twelve years previously, Theodore had been consecrated Metropolitan of Bostra to minister to the Arabs and, although he did not conduct numerous ordinations and consecrations like his contemporary Jacob

[47] Ibid. 67. 21–5.
[48] Shahid, *Byzantium and the Arabs*, 203; and J. S. Trimingham, *Christianity among the Arabs in Pre-Islamic Times* (London, 1979), 114.
[49] See J. Meyendorff, *Imperial Unity and Christian Divisions* (New York, 1989), 111.
[50] *Kyrillos*, 211. 15–20.

Bar Addai, he presided over an Arab Monophysite church menacingly close to the Palestinian monasteries.[51]

The relationship between the monks and the Arabs raises the question of the language used. The monks spoke Greek, and, while they also used their native languages of Armenian, Bessan, or some other language, they were not reputed for their linguistic ability. The achievement of the monk Gabrielius in knowing Latin, Greek, and Syriac is sufficiently rare to be especially noted.[52] Arab nomads did not speak Greek, according to information provided by Theodoret: 'As to our neighbours, the nomads, I mean the Ishmaelites who live in the desert and have not the least conception of Greek letters ...'[53] This lack of a common language must have complicated the catachetical process.

No information is given about how they overcame the language barrier. We can assume that an interpreter was used, as was the case when John of Jerusalem preached in Greek and an interpreter translated his words into Syriac and Latin for those who did not understand Greek.[54] We can also assume that the practice of allowing ethnic groups to use their own language for worship which took place in the monasteries of Sabas and Theodosius was also permitted in the settlement of the Paremboles.[55] Here Arabic liturgy would have evolved. At a later date the biographer of Theodosius, Theodore from the Arab city of Petra, spoke approvingly of the effect caused by hearing God praised in many languages in the monastery.[56]

These are early indications that Arabic was current in the monasteries. Its use was to develop and grow. In later centuries sophisticated Arabic theological works were produced in the desert communities. An example of these is a *Summa Theologiae Arabica* produced in the monastery of Chariton in 877. Eulogius of Toleda tells of a monk, George of Bethlehem from the Great Laura, now called Mar Saba, who arrived in Cordoba in 852. He spoke Greek, Latin, and Arabic and said that there were 500 monks in his monastery.[57] The foundations of an Arab Christianity in

---

[51] See Shahid, *Byzantium and the Arabs*, 205; Trimingham, *Christianity among the Arabs*, 115. Also John Malalas, *HE* 18. 199–204.

[52] *Kyrillos*, 56. 15–16.

[53] Theodoret, *Graecarum Affectionum Curatio*, ed. P. Canivet (*Thérapeutique des Maladies Helléniques*), SC 57 (Paris, 1958), i. 250. 6–11.

[54] *Itin. Aeth.* 47. 1–4; SC 296 (Paris, 1982), 314.

[55] Theodore of Petra, *V. Thds.* 45. 6–12.

[56] Ibid. 44. 15–23.

[57] See Sidney Griffith, 'Greek into Arabic, Life and Letters in the Monasteries of Palestine in the Ninth Century, the example of the *Summa Theologiae Arabica*', *Byz.* 56 (1986), 119–38, 119, 133.

Palestine were laid by the mission of Euthymius and others and were to have a rich development.

These comments on how the monks adapted to life in the desert have emphasized their close relationship with the environment. This showed itself in their skilful exploitation of scarce water resources, mastery of traditional agricultural techniques, and the discovery of the nomadic custom of plant gathering. Perhaps these skills were learned as a result of the most important relationship of all, their sharing of the desert with the indigenous nomadic Arab population.

MAP

The map of the monastic desert illustrates the location of the monasteries in the different parts of the desert and the spread of monasticism. The monasteries have left many traces of their existence. There are historical and topographical references in contemporary sources, such as the work of Cyril and John Moschus. These are conveniently collected in S. Vailhé's alphabetical list of the monasteries.[58] Then there are Arabic place-names which often preserve the memory of the old Byzantine monastery many centuries after it has ceased to exist. Sometimes the Arabic name makes direct reference to the Byzantine monastery, such as Khirbet Luqa, or the ruin of Luke, which leaves little doubt that this was the site of Luke's monastery. Sometimes the name is descriptive, such as Khan Saliba, or Inn of the Christians, which marks the site of St Adam, a Byzantine memorial church with accommodation attached. And, most importantly, there are archaeological remains. Because of the emptiness of the terrain, many sites are well preserved and have yielded much information in the course of excavation.

An archaeological survey of the monasteries in the Judaean desert was carried out between 1981 and 1990 by a team led by Yizhar Hirschfeld on behalf of the Archaeological Survey of Israel and the Hebrew University of Jerusalem. This has built on the work of earlier archaeologists, correcting some of their findings. It has examined the whole area and the researchers are confident that no significant monastic remains have been overlooked. The work has been concluded, in part as a consequence of the deteriorating political situation in the occupied

[58] S. Vailhé, 'Répertoire alphabétique des monastères de Palestine', *ROC* 4 (1899), 512–42, 5 (1900), 19–48, 272–92.

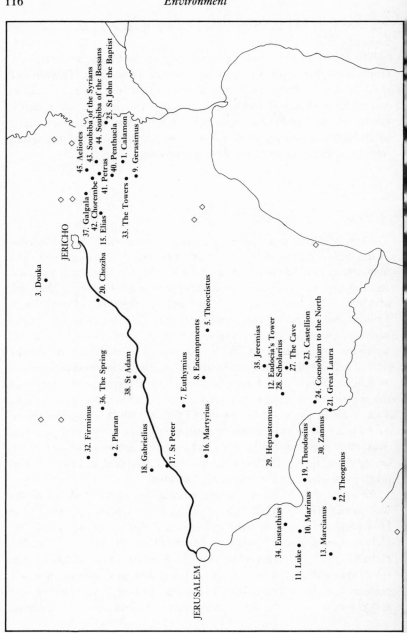

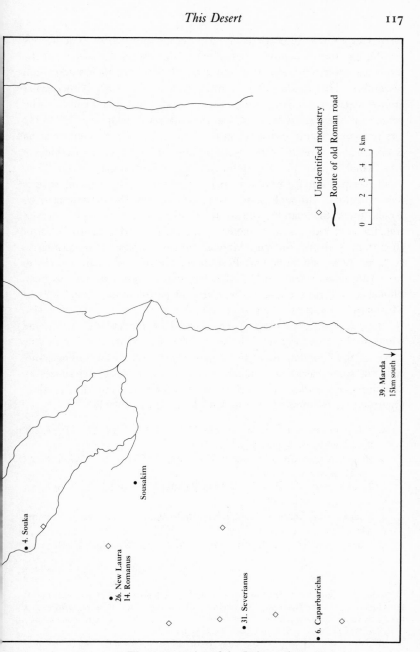

3. The monasteries of the Judaean desert

territories of the West Bank as the decade proceeded. The team's
conclusions form a definitive statement of the present knowledge of the
monastic desert and give full information about previous studies and
researches. This needs to be supplemented by the work of the earlier
archaeologists, especially Charles Conder and Jean Louis Federlin, who
visited the sites before building and agricultural development led to the
loss of some remains, especially in the Jericho area. Further information
is provided as a result of the work of Virgilio Corbo in the Bethlehem
area, which lay outside the region covered by Hirschfeld's survey.[59]
    The map produced by the British Ordnance Survey team in 1940 is
recommended. Although more recent surveys have been conducted by
Israeli teams, this map has the advantage of using the Arab place-names
transliterated into Latin characters. This assists in the identification of
sites from Arab place-names. Maps in previous studies of monasticism,
such as those of Chitty and Festugière, are on too small a scale to
record locations accurately.[60] A detailed archaeological survey has been
published in three sections by the Israeli Department of Antiquities and
Museums.[61] These are the sources for Map 3.
    The following chronological list is based on Hirschfeld's work; the
name of the monastery is followed by the date of its foundation, the
name of the founder, the type of monastery, the Arabic place-name,
with, in some cases, an English translation, and select references to
contemporary works, where they exist, which refer to the location.
Query marks indicate where this knowledge is unavailable.

    1. Calamon: 3rd cent.; ?; laura; 'Ein Ḥajla; *V. Char.* ed. G. Garitte, 26.
       1–4; Paul of Elousa, *V. Thg.* 85. 10–11.
    2. Pharan: *c.*330; Chariton; laura; 'Ein Fara; *V. Char.* ed. G. Garitte, 25.
       10–26. 9; *VE* 14. 9; 79. 24.
    3. Douka: *c.*340; Chariton; laura; 'Ein Duyûk; *V. Char.* ed. G. Garitte, 31.
       11–32. 4; *H. Laus.* 48.
    4. Souka: *c.*345; Chariton; laura; Khirbet Khareitûn; *V. Char.* ed. G. Garitte,
       33. 15–16.
    5. Theoctistus: 411; Euthymius; coenobium; Deir Muqallik; *Kyrillos*, 15.
       12–19.

   [59] The best summary of archaeological work, with bibliographical reference, is Y.
Hirschfeld, 'List of the Byzantine Monasteries in the Judaean Desert', in G. Bottini *et al.*
(eds.), *Christian Archaeology in the Holy Land: New Discoveries* (Jerusalem, 1990), 1–90.
   [60] See *MO* pt. 2, iii. 137; Chitty, *Desert a City*, 96.
   [61] Y. Hirschfeld, *Archeological Survey of Israel: Maps of Herodium, Talpiot and Mar
Saba* (Jerusalem, 1985).

6. Caparbaricha: 422; Euthymius; coenobium; Khirbet Umm Rukba; *Kyrillos*, 22. 11–17.
7. Euthymius: 428; Euthymius; laura; Khan el Ahmar; *Kyrillos*, 23. 21–24. 4.
8. Encampments: *c.*430; Euthymius; settlement; *Kyrillos*, 24. 14–20.
9. Gerasimus: 455; Gerasimus; laura; Deir Ḥajla; *V. Gerasimi*, 1–2.
10. Marinus: *c.*455; Marinus, disciple of Euthymius; Khirbet Abu Ghunneim, *Kyrillos*, 16. 12–14; 114. 3–4.
11. Luke: *c.*455; Luke, disciple of Euthymius; Khirbet Luqa; *Kyrillos*, 16. 12–14; 114. 4–5.
12. Eudocia's Tower: *c.*456; Eudocia; tower; Khirbet el-Muntâr ('ruin of the watch-tower'), *Kyrillos*, 48. 6–11.
13. Marcianus: *c.*456; Marcianus; coenobium; Khirbet Siyar el-Ghanam; *Kyrillos*, 49. 12; 66. 25; 111. 25.
14. Romanus: *c.*456; Romanus; coenobium; Bir el-Waʿar; *Kyrillos*, 49. 12.
15. Elias: 458; Elias, disciple of Euthymius; two coenobia; Khirbet Mugheifir ('ruin of the pardoned'); *Kyrillos*, 51. 17–19.
16. Martyrius: 458; Martyrius, disciple of Euthymius; coenobium; Khirbet el-Murassas; *Kyrillos*, 51. 19–21.
17. St Peter: 459; Eudocia; coenobium; Qasr ʿAli; *Kyrillos*, 53. 9.
18. Gabrielius: *c.*460; Gabrielius, disciple of Euthymius; coenobium; Qasr er-Rawabi; *Kyrillos*, 56. 5–9.
19. Theodosius: 479; Theodosius; coenobium; Deir Dosi; Theodore of Petra, *V. Thds.* 15. 4–6; 237. 6–10.
20. Choziba: 480; John of Thebes; coenobium; Deir Mar Jirjis; *V. Geor. Choz.* 66. 3–11.
21. Great Laura: 483; Sabas; laura; Deir Mar Saba; 97. 26–98. 14.
22. Theognius: 490; Theognius; coenobium; Khirbet Makhrûm ('ruin of the mountain peak'); *Kyrillos*, 242. 16–17.
23. Castellion: 492; Sabas; coenobium; Khirbet el-Mird, ('the lofty place'); *Kyrillos*, 110–12.
24. Coenobium to the North: 493; Sabas; coenobium; ?; *Kyrillos*, 113. 5–6; 206. 14–15.
25. St John the Baptist: 500; ?; coenobium; Qasr el-Jahûd; Theodosius, *De Situ Terrae Sanctae*, 20.
26. New Laura: 507; Sabas; laura; Bir el-Waʿar; *Kyrillos*, 123. 1–125. 25 (near Romanus' monastery, no. 14).[62]

---

[62] The site of the New Laura was discovered by Hirschfeld. It is described ibid., *Herodium*, 54–6*, and id., 'List', no. 22. This is a valuable addition to the knowledge of monastic sites, since previous suggestions did not conform to the literary evidence. For the history of the search for the site and earlier incorrect identifications by Marcoff and Chitty, Corbo and Bagatti, see ibid.

27. The Cave: 508; Sabas; coenobium; Bir el-Qattâr ('well of drops') *Kyrillos*, 126. 13–20.
28. Scholarius: 509; Sabas; coenobium; 'Khirbet el-Muntâr ('ruin of the watch-tower'); *Kyrillos*, 127. 15–129. 2 (on site of Eudocia's Tower, no. 12).
29. Heptastomus: 510; Sabas; laura; Khirbet Jinjas; *Kyrillos*, 129. 3–130. 27.
30. Zannus: 511; Sabas; coenobium; El-Burj ('the tower'); *Kyrillos*, 132. 20–133. 7.
31. Severianus: *c.*515; Severianus, disciple of Sabas; coenobium; El-Qasrein ('the two fortresses'); *Kyrillos*, 99. 22–3; 124. 15–18.
32. Firminus: *c.*515; Firminus, disciple of Sabas; ?; Wadi Suweinit; *Kyrillos*, 99. 22–3.
33. The Towers: *c.*515; Jacob, disciple of Sabas; ?; ?; *Kyrillos*, 99. 21; *Prat.* 9 and 10.
34. Eustathius: before 522; ?; coenobium; Khirbet Bereikut; Paul of Elousa, *V. Thg.* 95. 16–17.
35. Jeremias: 531; Sabas; laura; Khirbet ez-Zarâniq ('ruin of the streamlets') *Kyrillos*, 179. 14–25.
36. The Spring: before 552; ?; ?; 'Ein el-Fawwar; *Kyrillos*, 198. 28.
37. Galgala: 6th c.; ?; ?; Tel Ghalghala; Antoninus Placentinus, 13.
38. St Adam: 6th c.; ?; coenobium; Khan Salîba ('the inn of the Christians'); Epiphanius Monachos.
39. Marda: 6th c.; ?; laura; Masada; *Kyrillos*, 22. 2–7; *Prat.* 158.[63]
40. Penthucla: 6th c.; ?; coenobium; ?; *Prat.* 13.
41. Petrus: 6th c.; ?; laura; ?; *Prat.* 16.
42. Chorembe: 6th c.; ?; coenobium; ?; *Prat.* 157.
43. Soubiba of the Syrians: 6th c.; ?; coenobium; ?; *Prat.* 157.
44. Soubiba of the Bessans: 6th c.; ?; coenobium(?); ?; *Prat.* 157; *Kyrillos*, 193. 24–5.
45. Aeliotes: 6th c.; ?; laura; ?; *Prat.* 66 and 68; *Kyrillos*, 134. 20.

A further twenty-three monastic sites have been discovered but cannot be identified from historical sources.

---

[63] Marda is usually identified with el-Mird or Hyrcania, the same site as Castellion. This identification was on the basis of the survival of the name Marda in the Arabic el-Mird and an assumption that the garden of the monastery, mentioned by Moschus, in *Prat.* 158, was at ein Feshka. However Masada was proposed by Lagrange and supported by, among others, Chitty and Hirschfeld. It is the more likely since Euthymius travelled to Marda along the Dead Sea (*Kyrillos* 22. 2–10); since it is hard to imagine the laura of Marda existing in the same place as the coenobium of Castellion; and since remains of a laura exist on Masada. For fuller detail see Hirschfeld, 'List', no. 35.

6

The City of Scythopolis

The monks might have been fired to undertake the great journey to Palestine by the almost magnetic attraction of the Holy Places. They might then have been drawn to the great monasteries of the desert, tantalizingly close to the city and just over the horizon formed by the Mount of Olives. But they did not stay there. A monastic vocation which emerged out of a journey would not stay still. The dynamism inherent in their vocation drew the monks out of the desert back into the cities.

The return to the cities took place in several ways. Some monks were chosen to become bishops, others spent time in the cities through the management of guest-houses, or on monastery business, or in carrying out duties on behalf of the wider Church. All these links are signs of a symbiotic relationship between city and desert which contributed to the vitality of both. Palestinian monasticism was rooted not only in the fascinatingly varied soils of the Judaean desert but also in the blend of faith, race, and culture found in the cities of Palestine.

Cyril himself is the product of the monastic diaspora and demonstrates the influence of the monks on an urban society. He came from the city of Scythopolis, the capital of the province of Palestine II. Here monasticism had penetrated into the fabric of city society so that it was the form of church life which was able to capture the imagination of the young boy and retain it as he grew.

The nature of provincial urban society can be viewed through the example of Scythopolis. Although it was a unique and specific society it also shared in the life of Palestine through links of communication, shared history and common culture. Like many cities of Palestine, it had a long history, reaching back many hundreds of years. Also like many cities of Palestine, it was populated by a cosmopolitan blend of faiths and communities. Among these was a thriving church. Unlike many cities, it has left plentiful evidence of its buildings and life a few

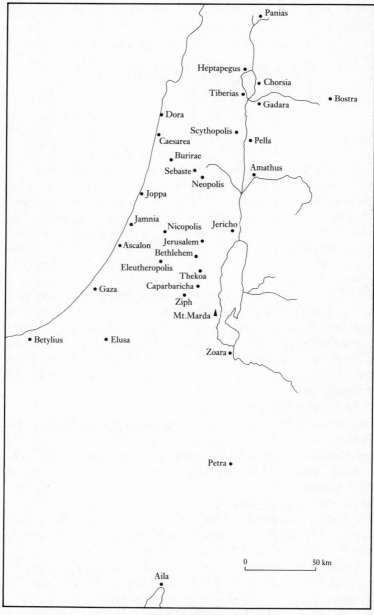

4. The cities of Palestine

feet beneath the scrubby vegetation on the outskirts of the town, which is quickly and dramatically being brought to light at the time of writing. This makes it possible to imagine what the town looked like, which in turn helps the understanding of what its life was like.

The modern visitor to the town of Beth Shan who climbs the steep path leading to the summit of the Tell el Husn, 80m. above the Harod river below, is rewarded by a magnificent view. It is a panorama of river valleys, of green vegetation, of sparkling water. There are two great valleys which meet at Scythopolis. To the east is the wide sweep of the Jordan valley with the hills of the east bank in the far distance. It runs from north to south and the flat and fertile fields, irrigated by the waters of the Jordan, fill the landscape. To the west is the smaller, but still wide, valley of the Harod, which runs from its source in the Hamore hills past the Gilboa range and the Tel el Husn to issue into the Jordan. This valley is an extension of the larger valley of Jezreel which stretches below the Carmel mountain range to Haifa and the Mediterranean. The land around Beth Shan is rich and fertile, with olives and date palms in abundance. There are many pools and fishponds which glitter in the hot sun.

The view presents in clear visual form the reason why this site has been a centre of civilization for 7,000 years.

The river valleys cut through the inhospitable mountainous terrain to provide natural highways along which trading caravans can pass. In this part of the Middle East there were two great trade routes. The first, the Way of the King, ran through the Jordan valley, from the ports of the Red Sea into Asia and Europe. The second, the Way of the Sea, ran along the coast of the Mediterranean Sea, and connected Africa with the lands to the north.[1] Beth Shan stands at the junction between the Way of the King and a branch route connecting it with the Way of the Sea. As far back in history as has been recorded, trade and transport has passed beneath the Tell el Husn.

A clear demonstration of its importance is given by its central position in the network of roads built by the Romans. A plan of the Roman roads of Palestine can be constructed using the evidence of the milestones which have been discovered.[2] Roads led from Scythopolis to Arabia, through Pella and Gerasa; to Damascus in Syria; to the Mediterranean

[1] See F.-M. Abel, *Géographie de la Palestine*, 3rd edn. (Paris, 1967), 103, 217–20, 224.
[2] See ibid. 222–31; M. Avi-Yonah, 'The Development of the Roman Road System in Palestine', *IEJ* 1 (1950–1), 54–60.

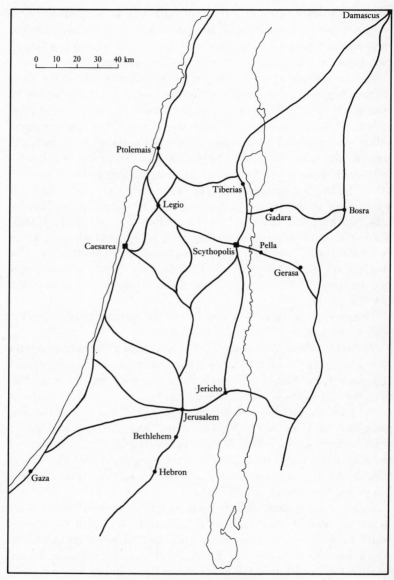

5. The Roman roads of Palestine

port of Ptolemais by way of the garrison town of Legio. At Scythopolis, subsidiary roads connected the two great road systems based on the coastal road, which was extended to Jerusalem, and the Arabian roads.[3] The trading system based on the Jordan valley and the Mediterranean coast is shown by the routes chosen by the Roman road builders.

As well as being located in a strategic position, the Beth Shan valley was fertile. The neighbourhood was known for its agricultural productivity. Polybius, in his account of the campaigns of Antiochus III in 218, says that the two cities of Scythopolis and Philoteria could easily provide everything necessary for the nourishment of the entire army.[4] In the third century AD Rabbi Simeon ben Lakhish was lavish in his praise of the natural richness of the area: 'If Paradise is situated in the land of Israel its entrance is Beth Shan (Scythopolis).'[5] In the valley, dates, rice, olives, corn, flax, sugar cane, and sesame seed were grown.[6]

Since Beth Shan is situated at the edge of the great desert stretching east into Gilead and south into the Negev, rainfall is erratic. Recent records show that the precipitation at Beth Shan can vary from as little as one third to as much as twice the national average. But the uncertainty of the rainfall is compensated for by the profusion of natural spring water. There are over thirty natural springs and these produce over 130 million cu.m. of water each year, which is sufficient for the irrigation of the neighbourhood of Beth Shan.[7]

The city was known as Beth Shan, or Beth Shean, in the Bible and in modern Israel; as Scythopolis by the Greeks; and as Beisan by the Arabs. Information about its long history is gathered from literary and archaeological evidence. The archaeological evidence has been gathered in a series of important excavations. Beth Shan lay in the Sultan's private domain until World War I and so remained conveniently free of recent building. This made the site ideal for the excavations carried out between 1921 and 1933 by the University of Pennsylvania Museum, referred to

---

[3] Avi-Yonah, 'Development of the Roman Road System', 56–9.

[4] Polybius, *Histories*, 5. 70. 4, ed. W. Paton, LCL iii (London, 1923), 172. This is the first occurrence of the name 'Scythopolis' in literary sources.

[5] Babylonian Talmud, Erubin 19a. The rabbi's enthusiasm is partly due to his desire to halt the drift of Jews into the cities.

[6] Sesame seed has been found in levels dating from 1300 BC in the excavation. A. Rowe, *Beth-Shan, Topography and History*, Palestine section of the University Museum (Philadelphia, 1930), 3.

[7] For these figures see the summary of the Proceedings of the 17th Annual Convention of the Israel Exploration Society, *IEJ* 11 (1961), 198–9.

in an encyclopaedia article as 'in scope and conception ... the pioneer excavation in the archeology of Palestine'.[8] This excavation concentrated on the Tell el Husn (or Mound of the Fortress), the site of the ancient city. Further work followed below the tell. The Roman theatre from the Severan period, the best preserved in Israel, was excavated in the 1960s. Now, at the time of writing, a huge archaeological project is in progress.[9] In 1986 this long-term excavation programme was undertaken by the Department of Antiquities of Israel and the Institute of Archeology of the Hebrew University of Jerusalem. The work is in the process of uncovering the civic buildings, streets, and amphitheatre of the Roman and Byzantine cities and will ultimately, it is hoped, turn the site into a major centre for visitors and tourists. The discovery of Byzantine Scythopolis, according to the excavators, is intended to 'bring about a change in the character and structure of Beth Shan, so that it can again take the place it deserves . . . as a national and international tourist attraction'.[10] The ascendancy of Scythopolis was built on economic prosperity and international traffic and so the prospect of the archaeological remains bringing visitors and income to a currently somewhat depressed area provides unexpected historical continuity.

FROM BETH SHAN TO SCYTHOPOLIS

The researchers on the tell have provided information about the ancient city. Stratum 18, the lowest, provides evidence of occupation in the neolithic age, in the 5th millennium BC. The earliest buildings are dated to the 3rd millennium when Beth Shan was a town with multi-roomed structures and intersecting streets.[11]

Beth Shan is mentioned in the Bible. In the 13th century it lay in the area which fell to the tribe of Manasseh, but the Israelites were not strong enough to drive the Canaanites out of it.[12] By the eleventh century it had become a Philistine city and, following the battle on nearby Mount Gilboa, the bodies of Saul and Jonathan were exposed on

---

[8] F. James, Beth-Shean, in M. Avi-Yonah, *Encyclopedia of Archeological Excavations in the Holy Land*, i (London, 1975), 207–25, 209.

[9] For references to the excavation of the theatre, see S. Applebaum's notice in *IEJ* 10 (1960), 126–7, 263–4. The claim for the quality of the theatre is in 'Glorious Beth-Shean'; *Biblical Archeology Review*, 16 (1990), 17–32, 23.

[10] 'The Bet Shean Project' *Excavations and Surveys in Israel*, 6 (1987), 7–45, 7.

[11] See 'Glorious Beth Shean', 18; Rowe, *Beth-Shan*, 5–6.

[12] Josh. 17: 11; Judg. 1: 27.

the city walls. This provoked the valourous expedition of recovery by the men of Jabesh-Gilead.[13] David finally captured the city, and it appears in the list of towns presided over by Solomon's regional governors.[14]

During the third century BC the history of the city entered a new stage. It moved from the summit of the tell to the foot and changed its name to Scythopolis. The evidence from the foundation stage of the Greek city is sparse. A few pottery fragments from the Hellenistic period have been discovered, but future stages of excavation may provide further information as bedrock has been reached in only a few places.[15] The earliest literary references to the new name of Scythopolis are in a passage of Polybius and in the apocryphal book of Judith, which can be dated to the mid-second century BC.[16] Although the Greek name was used in Hellenistic circles the city was still called Beth Shan by the Semitic-speaking people who lived in the rural areas around the Greek city. The continued use of both names is found in an inscription on an ossuary discovered in Jerusalem. Alongside the Judaeo-Aramaic 'Ammyiah no-Beshanit' and 'Henin(?) ha-Beshani' is written the Greek Ἀμμία Σκυθοπολίτισσα and Ἀνιν Σκυθοπολείτης.[17] An inscription dating from the second century AD refers to Scythopolis as 'one of Coele Syria's Greek cities' (τῶν κατὰ κοίλην Συρίαν Ἑλληνίδων πόλεων).[18] The emphasis of the Greek character of Scythopolis in this inscription implies that the authorities were seeking to maintain and promote Greek culture and predominance in a mixed population.

The origin of the name 'Scythopolis', or 'city of the Scythians' has provoked much speculation. This hinges on the reasons for the unlikely association of the Galilean city with the Scythians, who were a group of nomadic tribes who migrated from what is now South Russia to the shores of the Adriatic. It has intrigued writers from Eusebius of Caesarea onwards. A recent study goes so far as to suggest that 'l'explication du nom grec de la ville est sans doute la clé du problème de la date de la fondation'.[19]

---

[13] 1 Sam. 30: 1–12.

[14] 1 Kings 4: 12.

[15] 'Bet Shean Project', 42.

[16] Polybius, *Histories*, 5. 70. 4, LCL iii (London, 1923), 174; Judith 3: 10.

[17] J. B. Frey, *Corpus Inscriptionum Iudaicarum*, ii (Rome, 1952), nos. 1372–3, cited in Avi-Yonah, 'Scythopolis', *IEJ* 12 (1962), 123–34, 123.

[18] G. Foerster and Y. Tsafrir, 'Nysa-Scythopolis: A New Inscription and the Titles of the City on its Coins', *Israel Numismatic Journal*, 9 (1986–7), 53–60, 53.

[19] B. Lifshitz, 'Scythopolis, l'histoire, les institutions et les cultes de la ville à l'époque hellénistique et imperiale', in *Aufstieg und Niedergang der Römischen Welt*, 2/8 (Berlin, 1977), 262–94, 270–1.

There have been a wide variety of explanations offered.[20] The most likely is that of M. Avi-Yonah who points out that the Scythians had a reputation in classical times as horsemen and archers. They served in armies in the Mediterranean area, including that of Ptolemy II. Veterans could have been settled in the fertile area around Beth Shan where there would have been plentiful grazing for their horses.[21] A parallel example comes from nearby Caesarea where the Emperor Vespasian settled former soldiers when he elevated the status of the city to that of a Roman colony.[22]

The name Nysa-Scythopolis is also encountered. Nysa was the nurse of Dionysus who was buried at this site by Dionysus who founded the city and named it after her. This aetiological tradition is related by Pliny in the first century and Solinus in the second.[23] The tradition is also referred to in an inscription on an altar to Dionysus which dates from AD 11/12. It is dedicated to Dionysus the founder ($\kappa\tau\iota\sigma\tau\eta s$) of the city.[24]

After its foundation the city grew in prominence. It gained the juridical status of a city under the Seleucids and was the only city of the Decapolis, a league of cities created after Pompey conquered Palestine in 63 BC, which lay to the west of the Jordan. At the start of the fifth century the Roman province of Palestine was divided into three provinces and Scythopolis became the capital of Palestine II. This tripartite division took place before 409, since it is mentioned in a law of that date which is preserved in the Theodosian code.[25] As a result Scythopolis became a provincial capital alongside Caesarea, the capital of Palestine I.[26]

The layout of the city was dictated by the topography of the site. The presence of the tell and two deep valleys prevented the planners from following the geometrical street plan characteristic of Roman cities,

[20] For summaries of the debate about the origin of the name, see Avi-Yonah, 'Scythopolis' and Lifshitz, 'Scythopolis'.

[21] Avi-Yonah's attempt to date the foundation of the city in autumn, 254 BC, rests on inadequate evidence and is rightly rejected by Lifshitz in 'Scythopolis', 267.

[22] L. Levine, *Caesarea under Roman Rule* (Leiden, 1975), 34–5.

[23] Pliny, *Natural History*, 5. 16. 74; Solinus, 36, ed. Mommsen.

[24] Foerster and Tsafrir, 'Nysa-Scythopolis: A New Inscription', 53.

[25] *Codex Theodosianus*, 7. 4. 30, ed. T. Mommsen and P. Meyer (Berlin, 1905), 322. See also Abel, *Géographie*, 171–8.

[26] Caesarea has been the subject of two recent studies: Levine, *Caesarea*, and J. Ringel, *Césarée de Palestine* (Paris, 1975). These studies depict a city with a history very different from Scythopolis. It was a new city, founded between 22 and 9 BC, which grew to prominence as a result of being a Mediterranean harbour.

with the *cardo* and *decumanus* forming the main axes of building development. In other respects the city was laid out in the best traditions of Roman town planning. The impressive city centre was dominated by a monument of columns and arches. Next to this was a small temple, a large basilica, and a *nymphaeon* or ornamental fountain structure. From the centre, wide and colonnaded thoroughfares led to the theatre in the south-west part of the city, and to the east, and thence to the various gates. Outside the main city, a large oval amphitheatre was constructed, perhaps at the time when the Sixth Roman Legion (*Ferrata*) was stationed in the area. Above the city was the tell, which had in earlier ages been the centre of population, but was now an acropolis surmounted by a temple dedicated to Zeus Akraios. No remains of a Roman city wall have been found, although a wall was built in the Byzantine period. The main construction period of this Roman city was the second and third centuries.[27]

In the Byzantine period the city expanded. Further public buildings were constructed. These included the largest bath-house yet found in Israel, 95m. long and 60m. wide, which was built in stages through the fifth and sixth centuries. The Nymphaeon was extended and beautified by the governor or archon Artemidorus in the late fourth century.[28]

The main contribution of the Byzantines was not in the sphere of public building but of urban expansion. The streets were widened and shops were built. A new street was built, covering over an ornamental pool. In the suburbs new development took place in a haphazard way with little regard for careful planning. The old basilica was covered by new buildings. Residential areas were set up around the amphitheatre, which was falling into disuse, and then in the amphitheatre itself. Other houses were built on the slopes of the tell. The population grew fast to reach a peak of 30,000–40,000, with the result that the demands of the inhabitants for homes took priority over maintaining the elegant splendour of the Roman city.[29]

A portrait of the Byzantine city is given by an inscription from the Byzantine period found in the synagogue at Rehov. It refers to the gates

---

[27] 'Bet Shean Project', 42; 'Glorious Beth-Shean'.
[28] The text of the inscription is in 'Bet Shean Project', 27–8.
[29] 'Bet Shean Project', 43. For other examples of Byzantine cities see D. Claude, *Die Byzantinische Stadt im Sechsten Jahrhundert* (Munich, 1969), 15–106; for population, M. Broshi, 'The Population of Western Palestine in the Roman Byzantine Period', *BASOR*, 236 (1980), 1–10.

at different points in the walls, a watch-tower, an oil press, with fields and villages around.

These are the places which are permitted [for Jews to carry out agriculture without the restraint of legal prohibitions] around Beth Shan: on the south which is the 'campus' gate till the white field; on the west which is the gate of the oil press till the end of the pavement; on the north which is the gate of the watch tower till Kefar Qarnos, and Kefar Qarnos is as Beth Shan; and on the east which is the 'dung gate' till the tomb of . . . and the gate of Kefar Zimrin and the gate of the uncleared field.[30]

The key to the expansion of the city was commerce and industry. Its water supply, grazing land, and good communications made it a natural centre for the textile industry. A fourth-century text puts it first in the list of cities which provide textiles to the entire world: 'In linteamina sunt hae: Scythopolis, Laodicia, Byblus, Tyrus, Berytus, quae linteamen omni urbi terrarum emittunt, et sunt eminentes in omni abundantia.'[31] *Diocletian's Price Edict* lists five brands of linen—Scythopolitan, Tarsian, Byblian, Laodicaean, and Tarsian Alexandrian (fabrics in the Tarsian style produced at Alexandria). Products from Scythopolis include 'tunics without stripes, dalmatics for men and women, short and tight mantles, short cloaks with hoods for women, kerchiefs and sheets'. All these varied products of the classical linen industry are stated to be in the first of the three grades, a standard which none of the other linen-producing cities achieved. A shirt, or 'stiche', of the first grade, for example, would cost 7,000 denarii if produced in Scythopolis but only 4,000 denarii if of the poorer sort from Alexandria.[32] An edict of 374 refers to a state linen mill or *linyphia* which manufactured clothes for the army, and implies a distinction between the *linteones*, or slaves in this state factory, and *linyfos*, or linen workers. Perhaps, as A. H. M. Jones suggests, local guilds of weavers delivered fabrics to the local factory for finishing.[33]

Scythopolis was a commercial centre. Its importance in the economy of the Roman Empire and its strategic location led to its becoming the capital of the province. The city attracted people of different nationalities,

[30] See J. Sussmann, 'The Inscription in the Synagogue at Rehob', in *Ancient Synagogues Revealed*, ed. L. Levine (Jerusalem, 1982), 146–53.

[31] *Expositio Totius Mundi et Gentium*, 31. 5–8, SC 124 (Paris, 1966), 124.

[32] *Diocletian's Price Edict*, 26. 1–28. 30, ed. S. Lauffer, *Diokletian's Preisedikt* (Berlin, 1971), 169–81.

[33] *Codex Theodosianus*, 2. 20, ed. Mommsen and Meyer, 562. See also A. H. M. Jones, *The Later Roman Empire*, 4 vols. (Oxford, 1964), ii. 836–7.

faiths, and social classes. The main influences on its culture came from four sources—pagan, Jewish, Samaritan, and Christian.

FROM PAGANISM TO CHRISTIANITY

The Hellenistic pagan culture, introduced into the city under the Seleucids, influenced all aspects of life. The building programme undertaken in successive centuries below the tell was a sustained and planned creation of a Greek city. Through architecture and art, through the veneration of the gods, through the pastimes enjoyed in theatre and amphitheatre—Greek classical culture shaped the day-to-day life of the citizens.

Pagan religion has left traces of its vitality in the remains found by the excavators. These preserve the names of the gods honoured in Scythopolis.

On the hill above the town stood a temple. It was built in honour of Zeus. Its date of construction cannot be established with certainty, but the discovery of a lamp beneath the reservoir below the temple provides indications. The lamp is of a kind which was in use in the first century AD, which rules out the possibility of an earlier construction date. In the absence of further evidence it can be presumed that this large building on the hill which dominated the town was built about AD 100.[34] An inscription was found on the tell which names two of the priests of Zeus who ministered there, Olympios-Eubolos, son of Epikrates, and Herodiclides, son of Serapian. The second of these names is Egyptian, showing the eclectic religious heritage of the eastern Mediterranean.[35]

The Seleucids promoted the cult of Zeus as a means of cementing the unity of the kingdom, encouraging their subjects to honour the King as a manifestation of the great god Zeus Olympios on earth. This cult is associated with that of Zeus Akraios. An octagonal altar dedicated to Zeus Akraios by Theogene, daughter of Tobios, was found in a building below the tell. The excavators believe that it was originally used in the temple on the tell and was later removed to the place where it was found. A dedicatory inscription was also found erected by a Roman citizen L. Varius Quirina Proclus in AD 159. The lettering is

---

[34] G. M. Fitzgerald, *Beth-Shan Excavations of 1921–1923: The Arab and Byzantine Levels* (Philadelphia, 1931), 33. The earlier view that the lamp was from the 3rd c. BC has been rejected.

[35] The text of the inscription is in Rowe, *Beth Shan*, 45.

defaced but B. Lifshitz suggests a reading of 'Zeus Baka' or 'Bakl', which would imply that the god Zeus has absorbed a Semitic deity of that name.[36] Pagan religion is again shown to have the capacity to blend with local cults and to develop a flexible and eclectic character.

The temple in the city centre was small in comparison. The façade, which is all that has been discovered, is only 16.8m. wide. A hexagonal limestone altar dedicated to Dionysus the founder of the city in AD 12 was discovered in the nearby basilica, to where it is presumed to have been removed from the temple. It is likely that the temple was a memorial temple (*heroon*) commemorating the tradition of the burial of Nysa, Dionysus' nurse, in the city.[37]

Other inscriptions witness to devotion to Demeter, the Dioskouroi, and Ares Hoplophoros.[38]

During the reign of the Emperor Constantine, Christianity received official approval. The traditional faith and culture of paganism began a lengthy and uneven process of decline. The glimpses of life in Scythopolis in the fourth century which are given through the buildings, inscriptions, and episodes reported in literature show a society in which Christianity was slowly growing in prominence but in which classical paganism was resilient and persistent.

Classical culture continued to influence the buildings and inscriptions of the city. A building constructed by the Byzantines over the old Roman Odeon contains a magnificent mosaic floor depicting Tyche, portrayed as the goddess of the city. She wears a turreted crown and holds a cornucopia. The same goddess may be the subject of a statue discovered in the theatre.[39] A similar nostalgic reverence for the old deities is shown in an inscription commissioned by a city official. It records that a statue, which has not survived, is dedicated to the 'queen of all the earth, the glorious, the gilded one, who is seen on all sides'. The closing phrase is taken from the Odyssey, but the governor, aware of the growing influence of the Christian faith in the city, added a

---

[36] Lifshitz suggests this reading, following J. and L. Robert and correcting A. Ovadiah's 'Zeus Bakchos', Lifshitz, 'Scythopolis', 275.

[37] See 'Bet Shean Project', 27, 31. This view replaces that of Rowe, that the temple on the tell was dedicated to Dionysus on the basis of a fragment of a temple frieze and figurines depicting the god, found on the tell, and a dedicatory inscription from the 2nd or 3rd c. When Rowe wrote, there was no knowledge of the temple beneath the tell. Rowe, *Beth-Shan*, 44.

[38] 'Bet Shean Project', 29.

[39] Ibid. 19. 21. This mosaic was stolen but has been laboriously reconstructed in its original position.

carefully carved cross, so diplomatically combining pagan and Christian elements.[40] A further example of the combining of classical and religious elements is seen in the mosaic floor of the synagogue of Kyrios Leontis, which contains the characters of Ulysses and the Sirens.[41] These are all examples from the decorative art of the period, probably of the fourth century, when pagan culture retained its hold on the popular imagination but the new Christian symbols were becoming more frequent and powerful.

Slowly pagan buildings fell into disuse. One of these was the Temple of Dionysus in the city centre. The main part was destroyed and an aqueduct was built over the ruins. Walls from the Byzantine period have been discovered in the open space in front of the Temple. The façade was left standing, so preserving an elegant feature of the city centre, harmless since the sacred interior was no more.[42]

Other buildings which became ruined under the Byzantines were the theatre and amphitheatre. The theatre provided seating for the huge number of 8,000 spectators. Coins found in it show that it was thriving in the second and third centuries, but it quickly became derelict. The seats are surprisingly little worn, a feature which indicates that the theatre was in use only for a short period. By the fourth century homes were being built over the west gate of the theatre.[43] The amphitheatre suffered a similar fate. Built in the second century, it was converted into a housing estate under the Byzantines. This change of use is related to the decline of pagan worship, since the games were associated with religious observance.[44]

The decline of paganism happened earlier in Scythopolis than in neighbouring areas. In Caesarea, for example, the theatre was in use as late as the sixth century, and the school of rhetoric and legal studies flourished.[45] Perhaps the decline of paganism was the reason for the choice of Scythopolis as the location for the infamous trial of those seeking guidance and answers from the pagan god Besa in 359. The written questions were discovered in a temple in Abydos in Egypt and

---

[40] Ibid. 29.

[41] The synagogue is described in N. Zori, 'The House of Kyrios Leontis at Beth Shan', *IEJ* 16 (1966), 123–34.

[42] 'Bet Shean Project', 27.

[43] Applebaum, in *IEJ* 10 (1960), 126–7, 263–4. The theatre in Caesaea was in use until the 6th c. and, since games were connected with religious observance, this implies pagan worship. Levine, *Caesarea*, 57, and Ringel, *Césarée*, 47–51.

[44] 'Bet Shean Project', 35–8.

[45] See Ringel, *Césarée*, 47–51; Levine, *Caesarea*, 58–60.

the persons responsible were tortured or executed, penalties which the historian Ammianus Marcellinus thought were excessive. He tells us that Scythopolis was selected for this stern warning against paganism partly because it was conveniently situated between Antioch and Alexandria, but also because it was more secluded (*secretior*). This presumably means that it was distant from centres of pagan influence.[46]

But pagan feelings could still emerge strongly in this period. The Christian historian Sozomen writes of the resilience of paganism in Scythopolis among other places in the fourth century. He recounts how a pagan demonstration attacked the funeral procession of the Bishop Patrophilus, destroying his coffin.[47]

An important symbolic moment of ascendancy for the new Christian faith came when the temple to Zeus on the summit of the tell was destroyed and replaced by a Christian church. This is the only church to have been discovered within the Byzantine city of Scythopolis. It was an unusual structure, round and roofless. It consisted of two circular walls with an atrium and narthex at the west end and an apse at the east. West to east the church measures 50.4m. A drainage system was provided to evacuate the water which flowed into the interior during winter, the main indication that the temple was unroofed. The two circular walls, one inside the other, were roofed and so formed an ambulatory.[48]

The date of the construction is unclear. Ovadiah notes a similarity between the Corinthian capitals used with those of the church of St Stephen in Jerusalem built by the Empress Eudocia between 431 and 438. The mosaics seem to resemble those in another fifth-century Jerusalem church, the Eleona on the Mount of Olives. Hence a construction date in the early fifth century is suggested.[49]

The reason for the unusual choice of style is also unclear. Another unroofed church was that of the Ascension in Jerusalem. Perhaps, like this, it contained a footprint or other relic associated with the ascension

---

[46] Ammianus Marcellinus, 19. 12. 12–16, ed. R. J. C. Rolf, LCL (London, 1952–6), 534–43. Abel, in *Histoire de la Palestine*, ii (Paris, 1952), 276, has misunderstood the passage. He sees the trial as evidence for the extent of paganism, understanding Ammianus to say that the trial brought to light further oracles being sought at Claros, Dodona, and Delphi. But Ammianus says that the offences are trifling and the punishments excessive 'as if people had been asking advice at these places'.

[47] Sozomen, *HE* 7. 14. 2–3, GCS (1960), 318; *Chronicon Paschale*, PG 92. 740.

[48] Fitzgerald, *Beth Shan Excavations: Arab and Byzantine Levels*, 18–31; Ovadiah, *Corpus of Byzantine Churches in the Holy Land* (Bonn, 1970), no. 24.

[49] Ovadiah, *Corpus*, no. 24.

of some Biblical character, but there is no evidence for such a tradition.

The most illuminating parallel is the church dedicated to the Mother of God built by the Emperor Zeno on Mount Gerizim. Here too was a high place on which a temple to Zeus stood.[50] Its demolition and replacement with a Christian church testified to the triumph of Christianity and the need for the protection offered by the Mother of God. It was a sign of the eclipse of pagan worship.

But although the hill above the town was dominated by a church, the centre of the town contained civic rather than religious buildings. A surprising feature of the recent excavation of the city is that no new churches have been discovered, although there are references to churches in contemporary literature. The round church on the tell and the monastery of the Lady Mary outside the city, both found in the earlier excavations of the 1920s, remain the only Christian monuments of Scythopolis known to us. Like the Jews and the Samaritans, Christians practised their religion in the suburbs and built the churches, yet to be discovered, in the quarters in which they lived. While Jewish and Samaritan quarters have been identified, the Christian quarter awaits discovery.

During the Byzantine period the practice of pagan religion declined and temples fell out of use. Synagogues and churches were built in the suburbs but not in the city centre. While the concept of a secular society is the product of modern post-Enlightenment culture and could not be applied helpfully to a Byzantine city, nevertheless it seems that neither the Christian faith, nor any other faith, played much part in shaping the public buildings of Scythopolis. Religion was practised by the communities located in the suburbs and the legacy of classical culture remained a formative influence in the centre.

THE JEWISH COMMUNITY

In AD 66 Jews vanished from Scythopolis. Josephus recounts how 13,000 Jews were massacred and their possessions divided among their killers.[51] While this high figure is no doubt an exaggeration, the episode testifies

---

[50] Ibid. no. 143.
[51] Josephus, *On the Jewish War*, 2. 466–76, ed. H. St J. Thackeray, LCL ii (London, 1927), 504–9.

both to the existence of a substantial Jewish community in Hellenistic times and also to its removal in the first century. Those remaining after such a massacre would be few and demoralized.

In the years that followed, Jews re-established themselves. Avi-Yonah and Lifshitz disagree about the time-scale of this renaissance of Judaism.[52] The city, referred to as Beth Shan, is mentioned twice in the Mishnah, which was compiled between AD 180 and 220. Both passages concern commerce.[53] One allows Jews to buy goods during pagan festivals but only from shops which have not been decorated for the feast. Avi-Yonah assumes that the non-decorated shops belong to Jews and so takes the passage to be evidence for the existence of a Jewish community in Beth Shan, a city 'where on the days of pagan festivals the garlanded shops of non-Jews jostle the undecorated shops of the Jews'.[54] To this Lifshitz objects that not only is there no suggestion that the undecorated shops were owned by Jews but also that the passage has the context of the avoidance of idolatry by Jews in their commercial relationships with Gentiles. So the sense of the passage requires that both the decorated and undecorated shops are owned by non-Jews.[55] The other Mishnah reference is to wine bought by a Jew from a Gentile.

Avi-Yonah also refers to texts in the Talmud which exempted produce from the valley of Beth Shan from the regulations concerning crops in the Sabbatical year. He suggests that the abolition of the Sabbatical year took place about sixty years earlier than elsewhere in the Beth Shan valley, and considers this to be an indication of the integration of Jews into a Hellenized urban society.[56] But this early abolition could equally well be the result of a small and scattered Jewish community unable to maintain its cultural influence. The evidence of the inscription from the Rehov synagogue is of little use in deciding when Jews returned to the city since, although it clearly refers to the abolition of the regulations, its date is uncertain.[57]

From the third century evidence is clear and unambiguous. A reminiscence of a visit to Scythopolis is preserved: 'R. Samuel b. Nahman said: I was seated on my grandfather's shoulder going up from

[52] Avi-Yonah, 'Scythopolis', 131–2; Lifshitz, 'Schythopolis' 284–5.
[53] Mishnah, Avodah Zarah 1. 11; 4. 12.
[54] Avi-Yonah, 'Scythopolis', 131, with the meaning of shops *used by* Jews, rather than *belonging to* Jews.
[55] Lifshitz, 'Scythopolis', 284–5.
[56] Jerusalem Talmud, Demai 22c; Babylonian Talmud 6b; Avi-Yonah, 'Scythopolis', 132.
[57] For Rehov inscription, see above, n. 30.

my own town to Kefar Hana via Beth Shan, and I heard R. Simon b.
R. Eleazar as he sat and lectured in R. Meir's name.'[58] The synagogue,
presumably that in which R. Simon lectured, was rebuilt in the time of
R. Ammi, at the end of the third century.[59]

Several synagogues have been discovered at Beth Shan. They were
built at times which harmonize with the literary sources. The oldest
was constructed in the third or fourth century with a mosaic pavement
depicting scenes from the Odyssey laid down a century later. Zori, the
original excavator, considered that it was a private house, but subsequent
investigation uncovered inscriptions which leave the identification of the
building in no doubt. One reads: 'Remember for good the members of
this holy congregation who have laboured for the restoration of this
holy place.' Similar dedications have been discovered at synagogues near
Jericho and Tiberias.[60] The presence of classical themes in a synagogue
mosaic is evidence of a similar cultural syncretism to that found in the
pagan inscription adorned by the cross mentioned above. The Jewish
community was well integrated into the city. Other synagogues have
been excavated at Rehov near the city; and at Ma'oz Hayim east of Beth
Shan.[61] These synagogues are located both in the town and in nearby
villages, testifying to a thriving and prosperous Jewish community.

A discovery of the recent excavations was a Jewish bronze lamp
decorated with ceremonial motifs—a menorah, a shofar (or ram's horn),
a *lulav* (or palm branch) and an *ethrog*. It was cast in the Byzantine era
and was found at the site of a shop. Other remains in the same shop
suggest that it belonged to a goldsmith or metal-worker. Perhaps the
owner had brought it in for repair.[62]

Within the city itself, it is suggested that the Synagogue of 'Kyrios
Leontis' formed a focus of a Jewish quarter. But since this area is
covered by modern Beth Shan it will be difficult to gain further
knowledge.

---

[58] H. Freedman and M. Simon (trans.), *Midrash Rabbah, i. Genesis (Bereshith)*, i
(London, 1939), 66.
[59] Jerusalem Talmud, Megillah 738.
[60] N. Zori, 'The House of Kyrios Leontis at Beth-Shean', *IEJ* 16 (1966), 123–34. A
translation of the inscriptions is given by B. Liftshitz, *Donateurs et fondateurs dans les
synagogues juives* (Paris, 1967), no. 77a–c.
[61] V. Tsaferis, 'The Synagogue at Ma'oz Hayim', and F. Vitto, 'The Synagogue at
Rehob', in L. Levine (ed.) *Ancient Synagogues Revealed* (Jerusalem, 1982), 86–9, 90–4.
[62] 'Bet Shean Project', 34.

THE SAMARITAN COMMUNITY

The Samaritan community had spread during the second and third centuries from Samaria to towns as far afield as Jericho, Gaza, and Ptolemais.[63] The main concentration of Samaritans remained in Samaria where there were as many as 300,000.[64] But they formed large communities in other towns as well. The Talmud states that the number of Samaritans in Caesarea was larger than that of the Jews and Gentiles and was only exceeded by the combined numbers of the other two groups.[65]

There were Samaritans in Scythopolis. They lived especially in the northern part of the city. At Tell Mastaba a synagogue has been discovered which was a centre for the community. This conclusion is suggested because of features which would not appear in a Jewish synagogue. There are, in this synagogue, no human figures in the mosaic floor, while the floors of contemporary Jewish synagogues usually contain figures. In addition the synagogue is not oriented towards Jerusalem and the lettering in the inscription reveals Samaritan influence.[66] The inscription shows that the floor was 'the work of Marianos and his son Hanina'.[67] These were the craftsmen responsible for the mosaic at Beth Alfa, which includes another inscription dating the floor to the time of the Emperor Justin, presumably Justin I (518–27). The synagogue, with its fine mosaics, testifies to a wealthy and well-established community.

A leading figure in the Samaritan community was Arsenius. According to Procopius, he had 'acquired great power and a vast amount of money and had achieved the dignity of the senate'.[68] Cyril of Scythopolis adds the information that he had the title of ἰλλούστριος and wielded considerable influence over Justinian and Theodora.[69] The accounts of Procopius and Cyril contain some discrepancies. Cyril says that Arsenius became a Christian, while Procopius, with the relish he customarily

---

[63] For the Samaritans in Jericho, Ovadiah, *Corpus*, 116; in Gaza and Ptolemais, Levine, *Caesarea*, 107–9.

[64] A figure calculated by M. Avi-Yonah on the basis of casualties reported in the Samaritan revolts. English summary of Hebrew article in K. G. Holum, 'Caesarea and the Samaritans', in R. Hohlfelder (ed.), *City, Town and Countryside in the Early Byzantine Era* (New York, 1982), 65–73.

[65] Jerusalem Talmud, Demai II. 1. 22c, a legal passage in which accuracy was of prime importance. Also Levine, *Caesarea*, 107.

[66] 'Glorious Beth-Shean', 31.

[67] Lifshitz, 'Scythopolis', 262.

[68] Procopius, *Secret History*, 27. 6, ed. H. B. Dewing, LCL vi (London, 1935), 318.

[69] *Kyrillos*, 172. 20–173. 3.

exhibits in the *Secret History*, tells of his being impaled after unwisely annoying Theodora.[70] But it is scarcely possible that two Samaritans both with the name of Arsenius could have exercised such power simultaneously.

The Samaritan revolt of 529–30 was a response to imperial legislation which threatened the Samaritans position.[71] It broke out in Neapolis where Bishop Mamonas was murdered, and spread over a wide area. Churches were pillaged and burnt; property was destroyed; Christians were tortured and killed.[72] Arsenius' father Silvanus and his mother used whatever influence they could against the Christians but the mob of Scythopolis exacted a fearful revenge against him by burning him alive in the city centre. The people became anxious lest Arsenius should use his power in the court to punish the city for this lynching. Patriarch Peter of Jerusalem was encouraged to send Sabas on a hasty mission to Constantinople to speak for the Christians.[73]

Scythopolis escaped comparatively lightly in the Samaritan revolt. Justinian allocated twelve *centenaria* for rebuilding churches destroyed in the uprising, of which the bishops decided that only one should be spent in the area around Scythopolis because of the limited devastation. Cyril thought this an ungenerous allocation to his native city and wrote of 'only one centenarion' (ἑνὸς καὶ μόνου κεντηναρίου).[74]

The episode of the Samaritan revolt in Scythopolis confirms the picture of an influential and well-integrated Samaritan community. The lightness of the damage and ability of the Christian mob to take the law into their own hands in lynching Silvanus suggests that it was a minority and did not have the power or size of the community in centres of Samaritan population like Neapolis or Caesarea.

THE CHRISTIAN CHURCH

The early history of the Christian Church in Scythopolis can be divided into three stages.

---

[70] Ibid. 174. 19–22.
[71] The Samaritan revolt was not seeking to re-establish Samaritan customs, already abandoned in most places. See Jerusalem Talmud, Pesahim 1. 1. 276m, cited in Levine, *Caesarea*, 109.
[72] *Kyrillos*, 172. 4–9.
[73] Ibid. 173. 3–9.
[74] Ibid. 181. 22.

The faith first gained a following from among the Aramaic-speaking community. Perhaps the first Christians in the city were workers in the linen trade. The humble origins of the local church are shown by what we know of the early leadership. A certain Procopius was sent from Jerusalem. As well as reading the Scriptures and exorcising demons, he had the task of translating the Scriptures into Aramaic. He became the first to lose his life in the wave of persecutions under Diocletian, refusing to offer libations to the four Emperors and being decapitated on 7 July 303.[75] He showed his education by responding to the command to offer libations with a verse from the *Iliad*: οὐκ ἀγαθὸν πολυκοιρανίη, εἷς κοίρανος ἔστω, or 'It is not good that there should be many masters, but let there be one master, one king.'[76] The other martyr from Scythopolis whose death is recorded by Eusebius was the virgin Ennathas, whipped through the streets of Caesarea and then burnt. Her Aramaic name is further evidence for the Semitic character of the church in Scythopolis.[77]

The memory of the early martyrs was valued and preserved by the Church, which looked back to their sacrifice with reverence. As well as the chapel dedicated to Procopius at Scythopolis, there were also churches sacred to his memory at Caesarea, rebuilt by the Emperor Zeno in 484, and in Constantinople.[78]

From its insignificant beginnings, the Church grew increasingly influential in the ecclesiastical life of the province. Its prestige reflected in the career of the most eminent of its early bishops, Patrophilus, who was bishop in the middle of the fourth century. He was renowned for his learning. His reputation was such that Eusebius of Emesa, having studied the Scriptures as a boy and then decided that he wanted to progress further, travelled to Palestine to study with Eusebius of Caesarea and Patrophilus.[79] These two bishops were conservative in their theology, had little sympathy for the novelties propounded at Nicaea and remained sympathetic to the cause of Arius. Together they dominated the Church in Palestine. A sign of their authority was the ejection of Maximus, Bishop of Jerusalem, and the installation of Cyril in his place.[80] This

---

[75] Eusebius, *Mart. P.* 1. 1–2, SC 73 (Paris, 1960), 122.

[76] Homer, *Iliad*, B204.

[77] Her martyrdom took place in Nov. 308. Eusebius, *Mart. P.* 9. 6–8. SC 73 (Paris, 1960), 149.

[78] *Kyrillos*, 108. 8. See H. Delehaye, *Les Origines du culte des martyrs*, SHG 20, 2nd edn. (Brussels, 1933), 169, 182–3, 237.

[79] Socrates, *HE* 2. 9, PG 67. 197B.

[80] Ibid. 2. 38, PG 67. 324B.

alliance continued after Acacius replaced Eusebius as Metropolitan of Caesarea. They declined to attend a synod of Palestinian bishops which met Athanasius on his return from exile in 346.[81] Later Acacius wrote to Jovian affirming the Nicene faith, but Patrophilus remained firm in his opposition.[82] The Scythopolis of Patrophilus must have been an obvious choice for the Emperor Constantius II when he was seeking a place to banish Eusebius of Vercellae after he refused to take part in the condemnation of Athanasius at the Council of Milan in 355.

Patrophilus was a figure of learning and authority. He demonstrated that the bishop in a prominent city like Scythopolis could take a leading part in the life of the Palestinian Church. This possibility remained even if his successors were lesser figures. Philip and Athanasius, who also sympathized with Arianism, presided over the church until 380. Bishop Saturnius participated in the Council of Constantinople in 381, accepting its Nicene theology. A certain Theodosius was bishop in 404 and Acacius in 431.[83] Severianus was among those bishops who accompanied Archbishop Juvenal to Chalcedon and, like him, ascribed to the Council's Definition of Faith and was killed on his return by the followers of the usurping Patriarch Theodosius.[84]

Some time after 553, a leading apologist for the theology of Chalcedon was a certain John, Bishop of Scythopolis.[85] John is a shadowy figure who is known mainly from second-hand accounts. According to Leontius of Jerusalem, 'John Bishop of Scythopolis ... laboured in writing against the Apollinarians.'[86] Severus of Antioch said that he wrote a 'very long book' in support of the Council of Chalcedon, a work also referred to by Photius, who calls him John the Scholastic.[87] The Acts of the 680 Council of Jerusalem testify to a 'John Bishop of Scythopolis in the saints' who wrote against Severus of Antioch.[88] A possible further work by John is a set of Scholia on pseudo-Dionysius, often considered to be a product of the pen of Maximus the Confessor. The evidence for attributing this work to John of Scythopolis rather than to Maximus is

[81] Ibid. 2. 24, PG 67. 261B. See also Abel, *Histoire*, ii. 290.
[82] Socrates, *HE* 3. 25, PG 67. 543C–545A.
[83] See F.-M. Abel, 'Beisan', *RB* 9 (1912), 409–23, 420.
[84] *ACO* 2/1. 3, pp. 132–3.
[85] See below Excursus 1, for the debate over the date of John's episcopate.
[86] Leontius of Jerusalem, *Against the Monophysites*, PG 86. 2 1865B–C.
[87] Severus, *Liber Contra Impium Grammaticum*, 3. 1, trans. J. Lebon, CSCO 94 (Louvain, 1930), 201–2. Photius, *Bibliotheca*, cod. 231, ed. R. Henry (*Bibliothèque*), v (Paris, 1967), 66.
[88] Mansi, xi, col. 437D; Photius, *Bibliotheca*, ed. Henry, ii (Paris, 1960), 48.

contained in a letter from Anastasius the Librarian to Charles the Bald
and in Phocas bar Sargis' introduction to his translation of pseudo-
Dionysius into Syriac. Although these two pieces of evidence are late,
there is no good reason to doubt their reliability and so John's authorship
of the Scholia.[89] The author of these Scholia had read widely. The list of earlier
authors cited contains seventy-eight names.[90] They include classical
authors like Plato, Aristotle, and Euripides; early Christian writers like
Hermas and Clement of Rome; the historian Eusebius of Caesarea;
heretics like Nestorius, Eutyches, and Apollinarius; contemporaries like
Antipater of Bostra and pseudo-Dionysius; as well as the great Christian
fathers, Origen, Basil of Caesarea, Gregory the Theologian.

Although individual figures such as Patrophilus and John had a
reputation for their learning, the city itself did not develop an intellectual
life comparable to that in, for example, neighbouring Caesarea. Caesarea
was a centre of learning and study. In the third century schools of
rhetorical, legal, literary, and Rabbinic studies flourished as well as the
famous Christian academy founded by Origen.[91] But although no
equivalent institution is known to have existed in Scythopolis, the
presence of such figures as Patrophilus in the fourth century and John
in the sixth testify to the influence of classical learning on the Church.
The authority of these bishops combined with the economic importance
of the city ensured a prominent place for the church of Scythopolis
within Palestine.

The third, and for our purpose most important, influence on the
Church was monasticism.

The first monks to arrive in Scythopolis, as far as we know, were
refugees from Egypt. Theophilus, the Patriarch of Alexandria, con-

---

[89] This question has received special attention because of the implications for the
provenance of the Dionysian corpus. See, for bibliographical references, H. Urs von
Balthasar, 'Das Scholienwerk des Johannes von Scythopolis', *Schol.* 15 (1940), 16–38,
62–3; B. R. Suchla, 'Die sogenannten Maximus-Scholien des Corpus Dionysiacum
Areopagiticum', *NAWG* (1980), 3. Reservations over John's authorship were expressed
by C. Moeller, 'Un représentant de la Christologie Néochalcédonienne au début du
sixième siècle en Orient, Nephalius d'Alexandrie, *RHE* 40 (1944–5), 73–140, 121, but
were withdrawn by the same author in a later article, 'Le Chalcédonisme et le néo-
chalcédonisme en Orient de 451 à la fin du VIe siècle', in *Das Konzil von Chalkedon*, ed.
A. Grillmeier and H. Bacht, i (Würzburg, 1951), 637–720, 675.

[90] *MH* 22–4.

[91] The intellectual history of Caesarea is presented by Levine, *Caesarea*, 58–60. 88–9,
120–3. For Origen's school, see Gregory Thaumaturgus, *Panegyric on Origen*, 7–15, SC
148 (Paris, 1969), 72.

demned Origenism in 400 and many Origenist monks fled from Egypt. Three hundred of them came from the Nitrian desert to Palestine. Most settled in Jerusalem but about eighty, including the famous ascetics Dioscorus and Ammonius—two of the 'Tall Brothers' mentioned in contemporary sources—came to Scythopolis. They were attracted by the plentiful palm trees to be found in the region, the leaves of which served as raw materials for their 'usual trade'.[92] The arrival of these unusual newcomers must have aroused the interest of the Christians of Scythopolis, especially as Palestinians were involved in the debates over Origenism in the early fifth century, but the monks' stay in Scythopolis was probably brief. In 401 some of them continued their wanderings to Constantinople.[93]

Later in the century a monk became bishop. 'Some time after the death of Theoctistus', which took place in 466, Bishop Olympius died and was succeeded by Cosmas.[94] Cosmas was one of the first of Euthymius' disciples, the oldest of three Cappadocian brothers brought up in Syria, a founder member of the laura at Khan el Amar. He became a deacon at the Church of the Resurrection and then was appointed to the important post of Guardian of the Cross, or *staurophylax*, before his consecration as bishop of the provincial capital.[95] He presided over the church for thirty years and made a great impression. Cyril speaks highly of him: οὗτος τοίνυν ὁ μακαρίτης Κοσμᾶς μεγάλως ἐν τῇ δευτέρᾳ τῶν Παλαιστινῶν διέλαμψεν ἐπαρχίᾳ...[96] There is no record of him founding monasteries but he introduced the monastic tradition of the Judaean desert into the urban Church.

Cosmas died some time after 496 and within a few years, between 500 and 507, another monk made his appearance. This was the great Sabas, discouraged by growing opposition to his leadership in the Great Laura and in search of peace.[97] His fame had preceded him and it was not long before curious visitors from Scythopolis and nearby Gadara arrived at his cave.[98] Among them was the wealthy Basileius, who lived

[92] Sozomen, *HE* 8. 13. 1, GCS (1960), 366. 13–16. Also D. J. Chitty, *The Desert a City* (Oxford, 1966), 58.
[93] Sozomen, *HE* 8. 13. 1, GCS (1960), 366. 13–16.
[94] *Kyrillos*, 55. 20.
[95] Ibid. 25. 17–21; 32. 24–5; 33. 31–2.
[96] Ibid. 56. 1–3.
[97] Ibid. 118. 27–32.
[98] Perhaps Sabas had visited Scythopolis in his Lenten travels through the desert, which extended on one occasion through Galilee as far as Panias on the slopes of Mount Hermon. Ibid. 107. 27–108. 15.

the ascetic life under Sabas' guidance. Two robbers came to steal Basileus' goods but were prevented from carrying out this intention by two lions and were only enabled to escape by invoking the name of Sabas. They joined the community growing up around the saint.[99] This informal group of disciples was constituted as a coenobium by an Isaurian named Eumathius who was succeeded by another Isaurian called Tarasius.[100] So a Sabaite monastery was in existence in the region of Scythopolis in the early years of the sixth century.

The descriptions of Sabas' next visits to the city in 518 and 531 show a Church in which monastic life was firmly established. There was a monastery at Enthemenaith, where Sabas visited the anchorite John, and a chapel, or *apostoleion*, which was the home of the Hesychast Procopius.[101] The Bishop, Theodosius, was a patron of monks. On his second visit, Sabas stayed with the Bishop. 'The great old man was brought into the bishop's building (ἐν τῷ ἐπισκοπείῳ) and he stayed in the monastery of the holy martyr Procopius.'[102] It seems from this that there was a monastery attached to the bishop's house. Perhaps scattered monks had been gathered together and provided with a home by the Bishop in his residence, as happened at Jerusalem under Patriarch Elias.[103]

The monasteries were large and prosperous, enjoying the patronage of leading citizens. The most extensive remains are those of the monastery on the north side of the river Harod excavated by G. Fitzgerald in 1930 and called by him the Monastery of the Lady Mary. It consisted of a complex of rooms with a church at the north-east corner. The decoration is magnificent and includes fine mosaic floors with plant and animal motifs. Inscriptions in the entrance hall and elsewhere commemorate the monastery's patrons: 'The offering (προσφορά) for the memory and perfect rest in Christ of Zosimus the Illustrios (ἰλλουστρίου) and for the salvation and acceptance of John the Endoxotatos (ἐνδοξοτάτου) the ex-prefect (ἀπὸ ἐπαρχῶν), and of Peter

---

[99] *Kyrillos*, 119. 20–120. 3.
[100] Ibid. 120. 7–12. See also S. Vailhé, 'Répertoire alphabétique des monastères de la Palestine', *ROC* 4 (1899), 512–42, no. 45, who gives the date of the foundation of the monastery as 503, which is possible but not mentioned by Cyril. It is on the east bank of the Jordan at M'Keiss.
[101] *Kyrillos*, 180. 14–19.
[102] Ibid. 180. 6–8. Cyril uses the word *oikos* to describe this monastery; *oikos* is also used ibid. 151. 12 and 19 to refer to the monastery of St Stephen at Jerusalem, a monastery of which the superior was Gabrielius, the younger brother of Bishop Cosmas.
[103] Ibid. 116. 4–7. See also *MO* pt. 2, iii. 80 n. 165.

and Anastasius the Christ-loving Counts (κομίτων) and of all their blessed house, for the prayers of the saints. Amen.' Another inscription shows that the monastery was founded by the 'Christ-loving Lady (κυρίαν) Mary and her son Maximus'.[104] Other important officials and wealthy citizens have left evidence of their patronage of monasteries in the tessarae of mosaic inscriptions in other places too. There was the nameless *scholastikos* in an inscription dated to 522 and the count and archon (κόμητος καὶ μεγαλοπρεπεστάτου ἄρχοντος) in a building inscription of Eustathius also dated to 522.[105] These are some of the powerful and rich friends who helped the monastic movement to extend its influence in Scythopolis.

The poor people also supported the monasteries. They revered the monks and turned to them in times of trouble. The needs of the poor encouraged the growth of monasticism just as much as the money of the rich. It provided the ascetics with a status and a ministry in the social fabric of the city.

Cyril describes one poor woman. She suffered from a haemorrhage, and her destitution was such that nobody went near her because she smelled so strongly. She lay in the street near the Church of St John, where an ascetic lived who was also called John. As a result of a meeting with Sabas she was healed.[106] This one sick woman who dragged herself to the neighbourhood of a local monastery to lie close to it and who turned in her need to a visiting monk is an example of the devotion of many other poor of the city to the holy men and the churches where they lived.

In this episode both the church and the ascetic had the name John. John the Baptist was the archetypal monk, living in the desert and witnessing to the demands of God in a godless society. His association with the city is shown by several texts and is an indication of the important part played by monasticism in Scythopolis.

John baptized at Aenon near Salim, according to a verse of St John's Gospel.[107] There are two places which claimed to be the site of his baptizing, both near Scythopolis. Egeria recounts a visit she made, when she approached Aenon near Salim (which was eight miles from Scythopolis) through the village of Sedima, and found it set in an

---

[104] The excavations are described in G. M. Fitzgerald, *A Sixth Century Monastery in Beth Shan (Scythopolis)* (Philadelphia, 1939). The texts of the inscriptions are on p. 13.

[105] *SEG* 8. 37; 28. 144–7. See also *SEG* 20. 459.

[106] *Kyrillos*, 163. 23–5.

[107] John 3: 23.

attractive garden. Her skeletal topographical information is confirmed by the Madaba Mosaic Map which shows Aenon near Salim to be at a distance from any town.[108] But the Map also shows Aenon, now Sapsaphas.[109] This was the Aenon visited by the Piacenza pilgrim. He records his pilgrimage: 'In that part of the Jordan is the spring where St John used to baptise, and which is two miles from the Jordan, and Elijah was in that valley when the ravens brought him bread and meat. The whole valley is full of hermits.'[110] John Moschus includes anecdotes about the hermits of Sapsaphas, which he calls Sapsas, including one who lived in a cave and was visited by John the Baptist himself, who gave some timely advice about his vocation.[111] This monastic centre was in the area of Scythopolis and had a sufficient reputation for it to be included on the pilgrim routes.

The memory of John the Baptist extended to the city. The Piacenza pilgrim described it as the place where 'St John performs many miracles'.[112] Several churches and chapels were dedicated to the saint. Among the signatories of the Acts of the Council of Constantinople in 536 was 'a deacon and monk of the monastery of St John' who signed 'on behalf of all the monks of Scythopolis'.[113] This could be the monastery at Enthemenaith, or Enthemane, which was in the place dedicated to St. John. It was approached along a wide street in the middle of the town with colonnades on either side which was near yet another building associated with John, 'the apse of St John'.[114] It has been suggested that this apse was either a circular vaulted building which housed a relic of the saint or a structure housing a fountain or well.[115] The name Enthemane could be a Graecized form of En Temane, which means 'Well of Eight'. If so, it would be a healing well, where,

---

[108] *Itin. Aeth.* 13. 2–4, SC 296 (Paris, 1982), 182–4. The Madaba Mosaic Map is dated to 560–5 by M. Avi-Yonah, in the *Madaba Mosaic Map* (Jerusalem, 1954), 16–18. So it is contemporary with the writings of Cyril. For Aenon, see *Madaba Mosaic Map*, 35.

[109] Avi-Yonah, *Madaba Mosaic Map*, 37.

[110] Antoninus Placentinus, *Itinerarium*, 13, CCL 175 (Turnhout, 1965), 136.

[111] *Prat.* 1–2, PG 87/3. 852C–853C.

[112] 'Ubi sanctus Johannes multas virtutes operatur', Antoninus Placentinus, *Itinerarium*, 8, CCL 175, p. 133.

[113] See Abel, 'Beisan', 420.

[114] *Kyrillos*, 163. 14–15, 21–6; 164. 12. The location is described thus: καὶ διὰ μέσης τῆς πόλεως γενομένος κατὰ τὴν λεγομένην ἀψῖδα τοῦ ἁγίου Ἰωάννου ... ἔκειτο ἐν τῷ δυτικῷ ἐμβόλῳ τῆς αἰτῆς πλατείας.

[115] See *MO* pt. 2, iii. 92 n. 196. Avi-Yonah, in *Madaba Mosaic Map*, 35–7, considers that Cyril is referring in this passage to the sites of Aenon and Sapsaphas, south of the city. This would make nonsense of Cyril's narrative.

perhaps, the miracles referred to by the Piacenza pilgrim were performed. In the twelfth century, the Russian abbot Daniel visited Scythopolis and was shown 'a remarkable cavern which spreads out into a miraculous pool'.[116] While the texts do not give clear topographical information and the recent excavations have not revealed any buildings which conform to these references, they show that John the Baptist was venerated, that healings were performed, and that monks were present. All these are signs of a thriving shrine tended by monks.

A further indication of John's popularity is the fact that three persons who appear in the brief protion of Cyril's narrative which refers to Scythopolis were called John. There was the holy anchorite John in the monastery of Enthemenaith, John the Expulsor, and John the father of Cyril.[117]

The city into which Cyril was born was a large and busy commercial centre. Within its church, monks had established themselves. They were present in monasteries, mostly in the outskirts of the town or in the surrounding country, where there is evidence of several monasteries.[118] They had made an impact on the popular imagination through the visit of well-known characters like Sabas. They lived in some of the churches and shrines of the city. In these ways, the ascetic monastic strain of Christianity had penetrated the church and exercised an influence on the local people. Cyril was one of these.

The inscriptions found in the city and the literary references present a portrait of a growing and developing church. It was established among the poor, Aramaic-speaking population, was led by an educated Greek episcopate, and gradually came to be dominated by the ascetic strain of Christianity popularized by the monks.

---

[116] J. Wilkinson, *Jerusalem Pilgrimage, 1099–1185* (London, 1988), 156. J. T. Milik, in 'Notes d'épigraphie et de topographie Palestiniennes', *RB* 66 (159), 550–75, 563–5, attempts to show that Egeria's description of Aenon refers to this well, En Temane in Scythopolis. He argues that Eusebius has mistranslated En Temane, the Well of Eight, which was the original Aenon in the city, and instead located Aenon at a place *eight* miles south of Scythopolis: 'La source des Huit dans la banlieue de Scythopolis est devenue sous sa plume le lieu à huit milles de la ville' (p. 565). He objects that the site 8 miles to the south, Tell er Ridgah, has insufficient remains for such an important site. But the whole point of Egeria's account is that it is not built up. The tradition placing Aenon south of Scythopolis is too strong to be discounted.

[117] *Kyrillos*, 163. 15; 163. 3–4; 164. 20. Festugière, in *MO* pt. 2, iii. 91 n. 193, identifies John the Expulsor with Cyril's father, but Cyril does not identify the two and so Festugière's suggestion should be rejected.

[118] For the monasteries in the Beth-Shan area, see Ovadiah, *Corpus*, nos. 21, 23, 24, 25.

PART III

Themes

INTRODUCTION

Cyril conceived his two main Lives—of Euthymius and Sabas—as two parts of one project. He says that he began by collecting material about the life of Euthymius but discovered that the monks who were best informed about the traditions concerning Euthymius had also been 'contemporaries of and fellow-strugglers with' Sabas.[1] So he found himself collecting information about Sabas as well. The result was a disordered jumble of notes on little bits of paper.[2] He was at a loss what to do with them, and describes himself sitting in his cell at night hopelessly holding his collection of information. At this point Euthymius and Sabas appeared to him in a dream and gave him miraculous encouragement to proceed to order his notes into coherent accounts.[3] So the two Lives formed one project. He spoke of them as the first and second 'word' respectively.[4] The other five lives were part of a new stage of Cyril's literary career. He speaks of the *Life of John the Hesychast* as a new beginning: πρῶτον προτίθημι τῷ λόγῳ τὸν ἀββᾶν ἰωάννην.[5] This break between the first and second stages of his work encourages us to consider the two longer Lives together.

In writing them he followed a similar structure. This is set out below. It shows not only the many points of similarity between the two Lives, but also significant areas of difference. These differences point to development in the nature of the monasteries between the times of the earlier and later leaders.

The structure of the Lives of Euthymius and Sabas

Refs. are to Kyrillos.	Euthymius	Sabas
1. Prologue	5. 1–8. 20	85. 5–86. 27
2. Birth, with divine election	8. 21–10. 4	86. 28–87. 19

---

[1] *Kyrillos* 82. 30–83. 2
[2] Ibid. 83. 5–7.
[3] Ibid. 83. 25–84. 21.
[4] Ibid. 84. 24; 86. 11.
[5] Ibid. 201. 4. H. Usener, in *Der heilige Theodosius* (Leipzig, 1890), p. xviii, suggests that Cyril intended to write a preface, as he had done in the Lives of Euthymius and Sabas, which would have demonstrated the relationship between the *Life of John* and the two earlier Lives.

The division of the Lives into clearly defined sections shows that Cyril seeks to demonstrate a similarity between the ministries of the two saints, and so a picture of what the ministry of the monk should be. Many of the elements are commonplace. There are, for example, passages which describe the exemplary qualities displayed by the saint in childhood and collections of anecdotes about monastic life, in sections 3, 11, and 14. Sometimes passages come at a different point in the different Lives, as with the lines which describe Cyril's life, in section 23. On rare occasions there are no parallel passages, when he did not have equivalent material about the other saint, and so there is extra information about Sabas, in sections 14 and 17; and an account of Euthymius' early wanderings in the desert, in section 8.

But as well as the commonplace hagiographical material, this shared structure contains sections which demonstrate the main themes of Cyril's work, and so of the lives of the monks of Palestine.

First, within the common structure there are passages which describe the personal achievement of the two saints, in sections 13 and 16. These show a clear distinction. Passages which describe the ascetic virtue of Euthymius (34. 1–39. 17; 45. 4–47. 4) have as a parallel in the *Life of Sabas* passages which describe the founding of monasteries (125. 27–129. 2; 158. 12–162. 19). These sections compare the work of the saints and from this comparison the development of the institution of monasticism can be discerned. I have described this contrasting vocation as that of Ascetic and Ambassador, and present it in more detail in Chapter 7.

Second, both saints were involved in the struggle against heresy and both saints used a similar strategy to defeat it, as Cyril described in sections 12, 15, 18, and 21. They reacted to the outbreak of error by fleeing away from the monastery into remote parts. They returned and then gained the support of the secular authorities. In the case of Euthymius the support came from the Empress Eudocia and in the case of Sabas from a series of interviews with the Emperors Anastasius and Justinian. The conflict continued to torment the saint and apparently ended in defeat as he died without seeing the heretics overcome. It is finally resolved only after his death. Behind this common pattern lies the presentation of the faithful witness of the saint, which is vindicated by the power of God acting after his death and by the temporal power of the imperial authorities. The emergence and decline of the two heresies in Palestine is explored in Chapter 8.

Third, as with all saints' Lives, miracles abound. They occur at every stage of the saint's life and form an integral part of every section of the narrative. This is because God acts through the saint. This simple claim presents the theology of the monastic life in the Byzantine world. Through ascetic discipline the monk draws close to God and becomes a focus of the love and power of God in an insecure world. This place of the monk in the economy of God is the subject of Chapter 9.

7

Ascetics and Ambassadors
of Christ

ORIGINS

Among the claimants to the title of the first monk in Palestine must be included Bishop Narcissus of Jerusalem. He was an energetic and conscientious bishop who antagonized some of the less virtuous members of his church. These promoted intrigues and slanders against him so that he became wearied by the cares of office. Like many before and since, he resolved to escape. 'He had long ago embraced the philosophic life ... [and] turning his back on the church community, he fled into remote and desert areas where he remained in hiding for many years.'[1] His retirement took place in the early third century and is an example of what has been described by A. Guillaumont as 'pre-monasticism'.[2] This refers to the ideals of celibacy, asceticism, and solitude which were inherent within the Christian faith from the beginning—as well as being found within classical and Jewish traditions—and which led to isolated individuals or groups living a way of life similar to that which later developed into the institution of monasticism.[3]

Narcissus' flight was a personal response to a specific circumstance and he did not encourage others to follow his example. There is no evidence for a community growing up around him. The first ascetic communities in Palestine emerged a century later. Jerome claims that the first monastic community was founded by Hilarion, a native of Thavatha near Gaza, who was educated in Alexandria and fell under the influence of Antony. He returned to Gaza in 308, and settled in a

[1] Eusebius, *HE* 6. 9. 8, SC 41 (Paris, 1954), 99. 10–14.
[2] A. Guillaumont, *Aux origines du monachisme chrétien*, Spiritualité orientale, 30 (Begrolle-en-Mauges, 1979), 218.
[3] e.g. K. Heussi, *Der Ursprung des Mönchtums* (Tübingen, 1936); P. Rousseau, *Pachomius* (Berkeley, Calif., 1985); A. Vööbus, *A History of Asceticism in the Syrian Orient*, CSCO 184, subs. 14 and 17 (Louvain, 1958, 1960).

hut by the sea where he lived in solitude for twenty-two years. His lonely example was to encourage many to emulate him and, by 330, monasteries were established. Jerome presents this as the start of the monastic life in Palestine. 'There were no monasteries in Palestine nor did anyone know anything about monks in Syria before the holy Hilarion' and 'by his example numberless monasteries were established in all of Palestine and many monks flocked to him'.[4] Jerome's historical accuracy has often been questioned but there can be no doubt that Hilarion was a historical figure and that Gaza became a centre of monasticism, retaining its links with Egypt.

Monastic communities began to appear in the Judaean desert during the same period. The *Life of Chariton* reports hermits living at the oasis south of Jericho called Calamon before the arrival of Chariton in the early years of the fourth century.[5] Chariton founded his monastery of Pharan at the time when bishops were assembling at Nicaea and went on to establish monasteries in two other parts of the desert. These monasteries quickly grew to prominence in the life of the Church and are mentioned in texts from the fourth century.[6] The triangular area enclosed by Chariton's foundations of Pharan, north-east of Jerusalem, Douka, near Jericho, and Souka, near Thekoa, contains many of the desert monasteries founded in the succeeding three centuries.

These alternative traditions surrounding the origins of monasticism in the fourth century confirm the view that there was no single identifiable source for the monastic life. The foundations of Hilarion and Chariton are examples of a phenomenon which appeared spontaneously in different parts of the Christian world in the same period. Guillaumont's study contains this verdict: 'Le monachisme est apparu en plusieurs points de la Chrétienté de façon indépendante et presque simultanée.'[7]

---

[4] Jerome, *Life of Hilarion*, 14, 24, in W. A. Oldfather, *Studies in the Text Tradition of St Jerome's* Vitae Patrum (Urbana, Ill., 1943), 317.

[5] *V. Char.* ed. Garitte, 13, 26. 3–5.

[6] See above, Ch. 2.

[7] Guillaumont, *Origines*, 217. See also, for this view, P. Canivet, *Le monachisme syrien selon Theodoret de Cyr*, Theólogie Historique, 42 (Paris, 1977), 27; Vööbus, *History of Asceticism*, ii. 111–17.

EUTHYMIUS THE ASCETIC

When Euthymius arrived in Jerusalem in 405, he found monastic life already in existence. He was able to visit monks who were living the ascetic life to learn from them. Cyril recounts how he 'visited the god-bearing fathers in the desert, studying the virtue and way of life of each one and impressing it upon his own soul'.[8]

After this he began to live as a hermit and remained in the desert for the next sixty-eight years. During this period the monasteries became an established part of the life of the Church of the province. Euthymius is presented by Cyril as the foremost monk of his century in Palestine, whose leadership and example shaped the rapidly growing monastic communities of the desert.

He loved solitude and accepted the responsibility for leading a community with the greatest reluctance. After he had left Pharan in search of greater solitude than was possible in the laura, he settled in an inaccessible cave with his friend Theoctistus. The two were discovered by some shepherds who told others about the two holy men living in the wadi Muqallik. Quickly, a community built up around him.[9] Euthymius became profoundly discouraged and, ignoring the pleas of the monks, decided to leave.[10] Later, when he returned, he avoided living in the monastery itself and preferred to stay at a distance, visiting his former colleagues once a week on Sundays. He chose this course of action because of his desire for the silence of his new residence—πόθῳ τῆς ἐν τῷ τόπῳ ἡσυχίας.[11]

The word *hesychia* and its derivatives occur frequently in the *Life of Euthymius*. While he was still living in Melitene, he is described as φιλομόναχος . . . ἐκ παιδόθεν καὶ . . . ἐπιποθῶν τὴν ἡσυχίαν.[12] The longing for silence led him to make his journey to Jerusalem and, once arrived, he chose a hermit's cell at Pharan to live in: φιλήσυχος ὢν ἔμεινεν εἰς ἀναχωρητικὸν κελλίον ἔξω τῆς λαύρας.[13] The Life repeatedly speaks of his yearning for silence.[14] He preferred to avoid contact with church or state officials and even the Empress Eudocia could only

---

[8] *Kyrillos*, 14. 6–8.
[9] Ibid. 16. 7–14.
[10] Ibid. 21. 20–22. 2, with a contrast drawn between his name and his state of mind.
[11] Ibid. 24. 8–10.
[12] Ibid. 13. 17–18.
[13] Ibid. 14. 10–11.
[14] e.g. ibid. 13. 8; 15. 1; 17. 4; 19. 19; 20. 2; 29. 2; 30. 9; 31. 3; 51. 20.

gain an interview after lengthy negotiation.[15] Festugière points to the connection between the term *hesychia* and withdrawal from society: 'L'hesychaste est proprement l'anachorète, celui qui s'est retiré.'[16] His achievement was to take the individualistic and isolated examples of the ascetic life, of which figures like Chariton were pioneers, and to adapt this style of living so that it could be the basis of a settled and stable community. In doing this he did not seek to innovate but to remain faithful to the traditions which he inherited. Cyril emphasizes that the two most famous of his foundations, the monastery in the wadi Muqallik which came to be presided over by Theoctistus, and his own laura at Khan el-Ahmar, were intended to be lauras similar to Pharan (λαύραν κατὰ τὸν τύπον Φαράν).[17] These foundations constitute the second generation of Palestinian monasteries when the movement gathered momentum and, as Cyril puts it with a little exaggeration, 'all the desert was colonised by his [Euthymius'] seed'.[18] Throughout the *Life of Euthymius*, Cyril points to the virtues and qualities which characterized this stage of the evolution of the monasteries.

The dominant influence came from Egypt. It was not difficult to travel to and from the monasteries of Egypt. A road along the coast connected Jerusalem with Alexandria. It was the first road in the area to be completed by the Romans, laid during the First Jewish Revolt, and along which Titus marched with his troops from Alexandria to Caesarea.[19] At first it continued north along the coast to Antioch but later road-building connected it to Jerusalem to the east by way of Antipatris and Gophna.[20] The journey from Alexandria to Jerusalem is about 200 miles, only two-thirds of the distance from Alexandria to the Pachomian foundations of Upper Egypt. Since it was quicker and easier to get to Jerusalem from the capital of Egypt than to many parts of

---

[15] e.g. ibid. 44. 18–45. 5; 51. 22–52. 18; 53. 19–26.

[16] *MO* pt. 1, iii. 55. Festugière notes that Sabas does not seem to share Euthymius' commitment to silence and is a man of action. 'Autant que je sache ils [ἡσυχία and its derivatives] n'apparaissent pas dans la Vie de Sabas, du moins pour Sabas lui-même.' In fact, Cyril shows that, in spite of exertions on behalf of his monks, he retained a love of solitude. The word ἡσυχία is used of him on several occasions, e.g. *Kyrillos*, 93. 24; 94. 5; 95. 15; 120. 25.

[17] *Kyrillos*, 16. 26; 26. 17. Schwartz, ibid. 358–9, incorrectly interprets this statement as showing that Euthymius based his life on Egyptian tradition learnt at Pharan. But Pharan had no special connection with Egypt.

[18] Ibid. 24. 4.

[19] Josephus, *Jewish Wars*, 3. 6. 2, ed. H. St J. Thackeray, ii (London, 1927), LCL 610–15.

[20] M. Avi-Yonah, 'The Development of the Roman Road System in Palestine', *IEJ* 1 (1950), 54–60.

Egypt itself it is not surprising that the highway was well used by monks and pilgrims.

Many stories in the literature of the monasteries demonstrate the close links between Egypt and Palestine. Jerusalem monks were such regular visitors to Antony that he instructed his disciples to ask visitors where they came from. If they said they were from Egypt, then a meal was to be prepared, but if they said Jerusalem, then a spiritual discourse was a more fitting welcome. Whether this was because the Jerusalem monks had their minds on higher things than food or were more in need of basic instruction is not revealed.[21] There are several examples of monks from Palestine who lived for a while in Egypt before returning to their homeland. Abba Silvanus, the subject of twenty-six sayings in the *Apophthegmata Patrum*, was a Palestinian who lived with twelve disciples at Scetis, then led them first to Sinai, then to Gaza, before concluding this peripatetic life by founding a monastery at Gerara.[22] Martyrius and Elias, both Patriarchs of Jerusalem, were natives of Cappadocia and Arabia. They lived as monks at Nitria, but fled to Palestine during the unrest in Egypt following the murder of Proterius by the followers of Timothy the Weasel. They came to Euthymius, who seems already to have been recognized as the unofficial leader of the monks of the desert, and then went on to found their own communities.[23] This procession of travellers between the two centres of monasticism ensured that practice, anecdote, and custom were shared.

So Egyptian tradition helped to nourish the monasteries of Euthymius. 'Honoured fathers often visited him from Egypt,' and the visitors told him about the exploits of Arsenius, who had settled at Scetis in 394 and was still alive when these visits took place, since they occur in Cyril's narrative after the Council of Ephesus of 431 and Arsenius did not die until 440.[24] Euthymius was impressed and, according to Cyril, consciously sought to model his life on that of the famous ascetic in Egypt. Like Arsenius, Euthymius deflected a visit from the Patriarch

[21] See B. Ward, introduction to *Lives of the Desert Fathers* (London, 1980), 4.

[22] For Silvanus, see L. Regnault, 'Les Apotegmes des pères en Palestine', *Iren.* 54 (1981), 320–30.

[23] *Kyrillos*, 50. 20–51. 21. For further references to Egyptian monks in Jerusalem, see John Cassian, *Institutes*, 4. 31. 5–9, SC 109 (Paris, 1965), 170; *Itin. Aeth.* 49. 1, SC 296 (Paris, 1982), 319. For a comment on the name of Timothy Aelurus being translated as Timothy the Weasel, rather than Timothy the Cat, see R. Y. Ebied and L. R. Wickham, 'Timothy Aelurus: Against the Definition of Chalcedon', in *After Chalcedon: Studies in Theology and Church History* (Louvain, 1985), 115 n. 1.

[24] *Kyrillos*, 34. 10–16.

on the grounds that if he received the Patriarch, to be fair he would
have to receive anybody who came to him, and so he would have to
leave the monastery.[25] It is noticeable that when Cyril gives a catalogue
of the virtues for which Euthymius was celebrated, they are similar to
those attributed to Arsenius in the *Apophthegmata Patrum*.[26]
These visiting fathers from Egypt also recounted the anecdotes
popular in their own monasteries. These entered the oral tradition of
the community and were used by Euthymius in his own instruction.
Faced with an act of insubordination from two of his monks, Maron
and Clematius, who planned to abscond from the monastery without
the permission of the superior, Euthymius encouraged them to remain,
completing his exhortation with a story: 'For the confirmation of what
has been said, listen to a story of certain Egyptian fathers which they
described to me.'[27]

Some of the customs followed by the monasteries, which were an
embryonic form of monastic rule, also came from Egypt. Among these
was the firm refusal to allow an unbearded monk to settle in the laura.
When faced with this demand, Euthymius arranged for the youthful
aspirant to spend a probationary period in the neighbouring coenobium.
This was to save the monks from temptation, and implies that the
coenobitic life was seen as providing a greater degree of supervision. He
seems to have made this requirement throughout his ministry. When he
received his first twelve disciples, he insisted that the eldest of three
brothers should be responsible for the youngest and not to allow him
out of his cell. The Egyptian provenance of this response is shown by
a parallel passage in the *Apophthegmata*.[28] The informal arrangement
hardened into an established custom. Sabas was required to live in the
monastery of Theoctistus and to prove his resolution before he was
permitted to live as a solitary. Sabas, in turn, made the same demands
on young monks.[29] A result of this was the association between a laura
and a nearby coenobium. So, the laura of Euthymius was connected
with the coenobia of Theoctistus and Gerasimus, and the Great Laura
of Sabas with the coenobium of Theodosius. The relationship between

---

[25] Ibid. 52. 1–8.
[26] See *MH* 56.
[27] *Kyrillos*, 30. 27–8. Cf. 36. 30–1. These passages contain several parallels with the
Apophthegmata Patrum. The use made by Euthymius of Egyptian teaching material is
evidence for the circulation of the apophthegmata in Palestine before being written down.
See Regnault, 'Apotegmes', 32.
[28] *Kyrillos*, 26. 2–3, with a parallel with *Apoph. Patr.*, Eudaimon, 1, PG 65. 176B.
[29] *Kyrillos*, 50. 5–6; 91. 8–9; 91. 21–6.

the two types of monastery allowed monks to graduate from one to the other and contributed to the peaceful coexistence of the communal and solitary ways of life.[30]

Euthymius was a solitary who loved silence. He shaped his life on the traditions exhibited with greatest clarity in the desert of Egypt. He showed no desire to found his communities. These came into existence as a result of others being attracted by his reputation and settling near to him to learn from him. They grew as more disciples arrived.[31]

The relationship between Euthymius and his monks was that of teacher and disciple. His personal example and authority created and sustained the life of the community. Cyril describes the process by which this informal style of authority was exercised. The fathers were gathered together on a Saturday; a problem was brought to Euthymius; advice and, if necessary, correction was administered to the brother concerned; those present were edified by what had taken place.[32] There was a similar scene when Euthymius realized his death was imminent. He summoned the fathers together into the church at the time of the memorial of St Antony. There he gave a summary of his instruction, arranged for the appointment of a successor, and made plans for the development of the monastery.[33] These events show the personal, charistmatic, catachetical style of leadership which gave coherence and order to the communities of ascetics which developed in the time of Euthymius.

This style of organization is temporary and can only survive as long as there is a leader with sufficient authority to sustain it. The fragility of these communities was demonstrated after the powerful figure of Euthymius was removed. Within ten years of his death, the laura was destroyed and rebuilt as a coenobium.[34] The excessive care taken by Cyril to claim that this was in response to the wish of Euthymius, stated on his death-bed and repeated in an apparition to the deacon Fidus in the course of a shipwreck, suggests that Cyril was embarrassed at the

---

[30] This is in contrast to the tension between the two ideals in Egypt, where the solitary life was valued, and Asia Minor, with its preference for the communal. See K. Holl, *Enthusiasmus und Bussgewalt beim griechischen Mönchtums* (Leipzig, 1898; new edn. Hildesheim, 1969), 172–8.

[31] *Kyrillos*, 25. 13–14.

[32] Ibid. 28. 9–29; 29. 27–32. 5.

[33] Ibid. 57. 23–59. 15, a passage modelled on the death of Antony. See G. Garitte, 'Réminiscences de la Vie d'Antoine dans Cyrille de Scythopolis', in *Silloge bizantina in onore de Silvio Giuseppe Mercati* (Rome, 1957), 117–22, 121.

[34] *Kyrillos*, 66. 15–16.

speedy disintegration of the community and felt that a justification was necessary.[35] The Saracen Camp was destroyed at about the same time.[36]

Euthymius' lasting contribution was not the establishment of a stable institution but the setting of an example which inspired many to live as monks. He took the traditions associated with the figure of Chariton and with Egypt and handed them on to succeeding generations. The desert, we are told, was colonized not by Euthymius himself but by his descendants (ὑπὸ τῶν αὐτοῦ σπερμάτων πολισθείσης ἐρήμου).[37] Cyril describes how the disciples of Euthymius were elevated to prominent positions in the Church. His first followers, Marinus and Luke, founded their own monasteries in the neighbourhood of Bethlehem, where Theodosius, the future archimandrite of the coenobites, stayed to learn monastic living before founding his own monastery.[38] The three Cappadocian brothers, Cosmas, Chrysippus, and Gabrielius, became Bishop of Scythopolis, guardian of the Cross or staurophylax at the Church of the Resurrection, and superior of Eudocia's Convent of St Stephen respectively.[39] Domnus became Patriarch of Antioch.[40] The three Melitenian brothers, Stephen, Andrew, and Gaianus, became Bishop of Jamnia, superior of Bassa's Monastery of Menas, and Bishop of Madaba.[41] And two of his monks, Martyrius and Elias, became patriarchs of Jerusalem.[42] The monastery of Euthymius was a training ground for church leaders. Euthymius provided the example, the teaching, and the ascetic tradition which shaped the Church of Palestine and was later embodied in institutional form in the foundations of Sabas.

SABAS THE BUILDER

Sabas founded the Great Laura in 483, ten years after the death of Euthymius. He was the dominant figure in the life of the desert for the following fifty years until his death in 532. During this period, the third generation of monastic development, the monasteries grew from being communities of ascetics into an ecclesiastical institution. The personality

---

[35] Ibid. 58. 28; 63. 24–7.
[36] Ibid. 67. 21–68. 2.
[37] Ibid. 24. 4.
[38] Ibid. 16. 9–16.
[39] Ibid. 25. 20–6. 5; 33. 30–1; 49. 13–19; 55. 20; 66. 18.
[40] Ibid. 26. 5–7; 33. 22–8.
[41] Ibid. 26. 9–10; 49. 19–23; 53. 2–4.
[42] Ibid. 50. 20–51. 20.

and ministry of Sabas were suited to the enabling of this development.

Sabas' relationship with his monks did not depend on the personal
contact which had been at the heart of Euthymius' style of leadership.
He seems to have shown little interest in the welfare of his monks.
Indeed, with the exception of his first foundation, the Great Laura,
there is no indication in his Life that he ever visited his monasteries
after they were established.[43] The monks do not seem to have depended
on his personal presence to guide them.

Nor did they rely on a tradition of ascetic teaching originating from
him. There is no piece of sustained instruction attributed to Sabas in
the course of Cyril's writing. Teaching comes in the form of remarks
directed to the novices; of a brief explanation as to why he had taken a
certain decision; or of a rebuke given to an offending monk.[44] Nowhere
in the *Life of Sabas* is there the equivalent of the lengthy address of
Antony to his disciples or of the continual questioning of older monks
by enquirers seeking a 'word'.[45] Cyril does not portray Sabas as a
teacher. The monks do not seem to have depended on his guidance in
the leading of the ascetic life.

Nor were they held in subjection under a dominant authority. Sabas
was not a powerful leader. Cyril writes that, although he was pugnacious
towards devils, he was meek in his dealings with men (πραὺς μέν
ὑπάρχων πρὸς ἀνθρώπους μαχητὴς δὲ πρὸς διάμονας).[46] Faced with
opposition from a rebellious faction within the community, he preferred
withdrawal to the challenge of disciplining the offenders.[47] He was also
patient and persistent in exhorting heretics to renounce their errors and
to return to the fold of the Catholic Church.[48] As all monastic leaders,
Sabas could be firm in his treatment of individual monks, as is shown
especially in the cycle of stories about the monk Jacob, but this approach
to individuals should be distinguished from his reluctance to act
authoritatively within the institutional life of the monasteries.[49]

If, then, Sabas was not an ever-present solicitous guide and pastor to

---

[43] Distance was not a reason for this, since all the monasteries were close to the Great
Laura.

[44] *Kyrillos*, 113. 10–15 for remarks addressed to novices; 130. 8–10 for an explanation
of a decision; 131. 10–16 and 138. 3–7 for rebukes to offenders.

[45] *V. Anton.* 16–43. This discourse comprises over a quarter of the total length of the
Life. The asking for a 'word' is a common form of learning in the *Apophthegmata Patrum*.

[46] *Kyrillos*, 118. 28–9.   [47] Ibid. 118. 29–30; 120. 13–27.

[48] Ibid. 128. 11–12.

[49] Ibid. 129. 3–132. 19.

the monks, nor a wise ascetic teacher, nor a formidable authoritarian autocrat—what was he?

The relationship of Sabas with his monks was original and complex. It is encapsulated in a simple form in the titles which Cyril chose to use to refer to his hero. There are several designations given to Sabas through the Life, to which can be added the titles used of Theodosius, who had a jurisdiction over the coenobites similar to that exercised over the laurites by Sabas. Sabas is spoken of as the founder of the monasteries, the πολίστης and ἀρχηγέτης.[50] He is also lawgiver, or νομόθετης.[51] Theodosius is the provider or patron, or προστάτης a function clearly fulfilled for the laurites by Sabas.[52] Both hold the ecclesiastical position of archimandrite, a transliteration of the Greek ἀρχιμανδρίτης.[53] Other titles are less specific. There is leader, which translates both ἄρχων and ἔξαρχος; and guide which translates ὁδηγός.[54]

These titles present a composite and complete picture of the varied responsibilities which were accepted by the two great leaders of this next and third phase of the development of the monasteries, Sabas and Theodosius. They involved themselves in many aspects of the life of their communities.

Both temporally and logically, the first function is that of founder, πολίστης or ἀρχηγέτης.

The comparison of the structure of the Lives of Euthymius and Sabas, made in the Introduction to Part III of this study, shows that the passages in the *Life of Euthymius* which describes ascetic teaching are equivalent to those in the *Life of Sabas* which describe the founding of monasteries. The founding of monasteries is elsewhere seen as the main achievement of Sabas' life: 'Sabas, the wise and knowledgeable teacher, the advocate of orthodoxy and condemner of heresy, the faithful and prudent steward who multiplied talents from God ... has colonised the desert with a multitude of monks and has founded there seven monasteries.'[55] After this summary of the life's work of the saint, Cyril lists the monasteries by name. They consist of three lauras, including the Great Laura and the New Laura which are claimed as the most important among the lauras of Palestine, and four coenobia. One of the

---

[50] Ibid. 91. 23.
[51] Ibid. 116. 14.
[52] Ibid. 166. 24–6.
[53] Ibid. 115. 23.
[54] Ibid. 115. 24; 166. 15.
[55] Ibid. 158. 12–15.

lauras—the Great Laura or, as it was later called, Mar Saba—is still occupied by monks today. This unbroken history makes it the oldest continuously inhabited Christian monastery in the world.[56]

A phrase used repeatedly by Cyril is 'colonise the desert.'[57] One example of its use occurs when Sabas comes to Jerusalem as a young man. He undertook the journey, Cyril says, because 'it was necessary that the desert should be colonised by him' (ἔδει γὰρ δι'αὐτοῦ ταύτην πολισθῆναι).[58] This arresting image originated in the *Life of Antony*: ἡ ἔρημος ἐπολίσθη ὑπὸ μοναχῶν ἐξελθόντων ἀπὸ τῶν ἰδίων καὶ ἀπογρα-ψαμένων τὴν ἐν τοῖς οὐρανοῖς πολιτείαν.[59] Here the description of the monastery as a city is metaphorical. The monk's true citzenship is not of this world. A common title for a monk was ὁ οὐρανοπολίτης, or citizen of heaven.[60] It is in this sense that the phrase was used by Derwas Chitty for the title of his fine study, *The Desert a City*. The monks' sense of belonging to heaven rather than to the earth led them to retire from the urban society of the empire and to live in deserted and isolated places. The point here is precisely that the Desert was not the City.

But for Cyril the City in the Desert was not a metaphor. It was the description of a historical process. Sabas encouraged his monks to build their own cells if they could afford to do so. 'Whoever founds or re-founds a cell in this place; it is as if he is founding the Church of God.'[61] The action of physically building up the monastery was in itself a contribution to the building up of the church. New cells and new monasteries led to a physical extension of the church into places where it had not existed before.

It was inevitable that Cyril should describe this process using language current in the society in which he lived. That society was an urban society. In his magisterial survey of late Roman society, A. H. M. Jones described how the Empire was built up out of a network of cities: 'The Byzantine Empire was an agglomeration of cities, self-governing communities responsible for the administration of the areas which they occupied . . . Constitutionally and administratively the cities were the

---

[56] For the later history of the monastery, see G. Heydock, *Der heilige Sabas und seine Reliquien* (Geisenheim, 1970), and for an account of the life in the monastery in this century, E. Mercenier, 'Le Monastère de Mar Saba', *Iren.* 20 (1947), 283–97.

[57] e.g. 126. 5; 158. 17.

[58] *Kyrillos*, 90. 9.

[59] *V. Anton.* 14, PG 26. 865B.

[60] For examples in *Kyrillos*, 8. 20; 84. 24; 235. 27.

[61] Ibid. 113. 22–4.

cells of which the Empire was composed.'[62] The City was a social entity constructed out of a network of relationships and values: 'On entendra par cité une forme citadine des rapports sociaux, explicitement fondé sur des valeurs civiques, la concorde entre les citoyens, la compétition en generosité des citoyens éminents et sur un classement social tout entier déterminé par les exigences de vie et survie de la forme citadine.'[63]

Since the cities were the units out of which the Empire was built, it follows that the founding of new cities was the means by which Roman civilization was extended. The emperors took pride in the cities which they established, often giving their own name to the newly created polis.[64] The Emperor Diocletian, in granting the rank of city to the village of Tymandus, declared that it lay near to his heart that 'throughout the whole of our dominions the honour and number of the cities should be increased'. Constantine announced that 'the inhabitants of Orcistus, from now on a town and a city, have furnished a welcome opportunity for our munificence. For, to us, whose aim it is to found new cities or to restore the ancient or to re-establish the moribund, their petition was most acceptable'.[65]

There were only small areas of the Empire which did not have the civilizing benefit of being divided into cities. These were found in the Diocese of Oriens and were mainly frontier areas of Arabia, Palestine I, and Palestine II, which were backward and not yet fully developed. These uncivilized parts included the towns of Jericho, Gadara, and Livias, and the desert east of Jersualem.[66] Sabas lived in a society which valued civic culture and inhabited one of the few regions of the Empire in which the civilizing effects of urban administration had not yet been applied. It was an area waiting to be urbanized.

The founding of a city involved two processes. First, there had to be building, for example, 'the fortification of a previously unwalled town or village, or . . . some public buildings'.[67] Second, there had to be people, which could involve a transfer of population. Once founded, the city had a responsibility to provide whatever was necessary for civilized living.

---

[62] A. H. M. Jones, *The Later Roman Empire*, 4 vols. (Oxford, 1964), iii. 712.

[63] E. Patlagean, *Pauvreté économique et pauvreté sociale à Byzance, 4e–7e Siècles* (Paris, 1977) 9.

[64] Jones, *Later Roman Empire*, iii. 719–20.

[65] ILS 6090, 6091.

[66] Jones, *Later Roman Empire*, iii. 713.

[67] Ibid. 720.

It was the duty of the city to preserve law and order, and all must have possessed some kind of police force ... The most onerous responsibility of the city council was to ensure that bread was bought and sold at reasonable prices ... All cities worthy of the name had a drainage system and a public water supply ... Public baths were considered an essential amenity of civilised life, and every self-respecting city retained one or two ... The larger cities had their education and health services ... The heaviest burden which fell on the civil authorities was the maintenance of public works.[68]

The founding of the monasteries followed this pattern. They needed the same facilities as a secular city. The accounts of the establishing of the monasteries in the *Life of Sabas* clearly show the stages by which the community was set up. The fullest and clearest description of the process is given for the Great Laura, the first and largest of Sabas' communities. Cyril describes the progressive development of the site until it becomes a sophisticated unit of urban society, well provided with necessary amenities.

First the site of the monastery-city had to be chosen. This was done by God rather than by the arbitrary will of the founder. Before Sabas had founded any monasteries he was living alone in the desert. 'In prayer to God by night an angelic shape in a shining robe showed itself to him [Sabas] and said, "If you wish this desert to become a city ...".'[69] The angel then revealed to Sabas the location which had been chosen for the monastery. A similar miraculous sign preceded the founding of the monastery of Theodosius. The founder was shown the site for his monastery by the miraculous process of walking through the desert with an unlighted censer. Where the incense ignited, there he began to build.[70] The descriptions of the founding of both monasteries emphasize divine intervention and selection.

The monasteries were built in the desert, which was a hostile area under the control of devils, wild beasts, and Saracen tribes. The selected site had, therefore, first to be cleansed of these occupants and claimed by the founder for its new purpose.[71] The devils were driven out after a titanic spiritual struggle in which they found themselves vanquished by the holy man. The founding of the Great Laura comes after a lengthy process by which Sabas shows his mastery over the threefold enemy of

---

[68] Jones, *Later Roman Empire*, 734–6.

[69] *Kyrillos*, 97. 26–98. 2. Cf. the voice heard by Euthymius, at 25. 25, and the vision seen by Pachomius, *H. Laus.* 32, ed. Butler, 88. 4–9.

[70] Theodore of Petra, *V. Thds.* 28. 23–32. 10.

[71] For the desert as a habitation of devils, see *MO* i. 31.

the devils, the Saracens, and the wild animals.[72] The victory is more succinctly described in the case of Castellion, a later foundation in a place which had a reputation as a place of devils. These devils complained bitterly at being expelled by the prayers of the saint. As they left, they shouted, 'What violence we suffer from you, Sabas, it is not enough that the ravine should be made into a city by you (ὁ χείμμαρος ὁ πολισθεὶς παρὰ σοῦ) but you come up to this place of ours. Behold, we withdraw from what is ours.'[73] Only when the former occupants have left the site empty can the city be built.

The first structure to be erected at the Great Laura was the tower. 'First of all on the hill which is at the southern extremity of the ravine . . . he built a tower, wishing to secure the place which was still unoccupied.'[74] Towers were frequently built as part of the monastery buildings. There has been debate about their purpose. Often they were attached to the church, sometimes at the side of the façade. They served as lodging houses for the pilgrims and as a convenient place from which the summons to prayer, by voice or simandron, could be made.[75] The tower at the Great Laura was one of many used as a residence, in this case for Sabas himself.[76] In spite of their use for residential purposes, the main reason for their existence was to provide security and to act as a defence.[77] They were places from which the impending arrival of enemies could be observed, which could be defended against attack, and which commanded the site of the monastery. They protected the site once it had been claimed. The importance of security is indicated by the request of Sabas to the Emperor Justinian that he should order a camp (κάστρον) to be built in the wilderness as a defence against Saracen attack.[78] A pilgrim contemporary with Cyril described how 800 soldiers were maintained in the desert at public expense to protect the monasteries and hermitages.[79] Often the lauras imitated the layout of coenobia by placing the church, cemetery, water cisterns, and other buidings within a square, walled area.[80] The tower was an essential part of the monastery. It provided a basic level of security against incursion.

---

[72] Sabas' first sojourn in the desert is described in *Kyrillos*, 94. 13–97. 2.
[73] Ibid. 110. 27–111. 2.   [74] Ibid. 100. 7–9.
[75] G. Tchalenko, *Villages antiques de la Syrie du Nord* (Paris, 1953–8), i. 30–3.
[76] *Kyrillos*, 102. 23–6.
[77] Ibid. 122. 26; 133. 10–11; 182. 18–19. See also A.-J. Festugière, 'La Vie de Sabas et les tours de Syrie-Palestine', *RB* 70 (1963), 82–92.
[78] *Kyrillos*, 175. 15–19.
[79] Antoninus Placentinus, *Itinerarium*, 40, CCL 175 (Turnhout, 1965), 150.
[80] V. Corbo, 'L'ambiente materiale della Vita dei Monaci di Palestina nel periodo

Once the site was secure, then the building could continue. The most important edifice was the church. When he had completed the tower, Sabas 'made a beginning of establishing the [Great] laura with the grace and co-operation of the Holy Spirit guiding him'.[81] He built a small oratory but later he was shown in a vision a huge cave shaped like a church and this became the place where the monks assembled for worship.[82] Churches were built at an early stage of the construction of most monasteries. Sometimes the church was built by the monks themselves, as was the case at Castellion where, after the hill had been vacated by the evil spirits, Sabas and some of the monks of the Great Laura began the construction work. Later they received help from Marcianus of Bethlehem.[83] This account is confirmed by the appearance of the site. 'The first structures of the monastery were set up hastily by unskilled hands. It would seem that the remains of the church belong to a slightly later phase.'[84] The presence of monks with skill in building was of great value. Two Isaurian monks, Theodulus and Gelasius, were overseers during a major expansion of the Great Laura, which included the construction of a large new church.[85] On other occasions the building was done by hired labourers, as at the New Laura.[86] The community needed to have the resources to erect the necessary buildings as a priority in the early stages of its existence. Monks were, among other things, builders.

A requirement of all cities was a water supply. This was especially urgent in the arid conditions of the desert. This came next, after the oratory of the Great Laura had been built and the first monks began to arrive. The provision of water became essential and a sign from God showed how this could be provided. Sabas, after he had prayed, was shown a spring, conveniently located in the centre of the laura and sufficient for the needs of the fathers, supplying neither too much water in winter nor too little in summer.[87] As the numbers inhabiting the laura grew, further water was needed and a number of cisterns were

Bizantino', *Or. Chr. A.* 153 (1958), 235–57; Y. Hirschfeld, *The Judaean Desert Monasteries in the Byzantine Period* (New Haven, Conn., 1992), 171–6.

[81] *Kyrillos*, 100. 9–11.

[82] Ibid. 102. 1–6.

[83] Ibid. 111. 19–20; 112. 7–9.

[84] J. T. Milik, 'The Monastery of Castellion', *RB* 42 (1961), 21–7, 22.

[85] *Kyrillos*, 117. 1–12.

[86] Ibid. 123. 22–8.

[87] Ibid. 101. 6–19.

dug.[88] Am elaborate system of conduits, cisterns, and reservoirs was built in all the desert monasteries.

The founder had to arrange for the construction of other necessary buildings. These included a bakery, since a supply of bread was a necessity for the provision of food for the numerous pilgrims and other visitors, as well as for the monks themselves.[89] Medical care was also arranged. Although its building is not mentioned in the account of the founding, there was a hospital (νοσοκομεῖον) among the buildings of the Great Laura, and monks who were injured could be treated by a doctor.[90]

Some facilities which would be expected of the civic authorities were not seen as necessary in the monastery. Although baths have been found at the monastery of Martyrius, they were not generally felt to be appropriate in a society which respected the avoidance of washing rather than cleanliness and hygiene.[91] Educational establishments seem also not to have been provided by Sabas. His lack of concern for learning led to dissatisfaction among the more intellectual monks.[92]

A new city needed people as well as buildings. In addition to providing necessary amenities, the founder sometimes needed to encourage people to settle in the city. In the case of the monastic cities of the desert, this transfer of population had already taken place. Pilgrimage was the result in part of the displacement of persons through economic or political pressure.[93] It produced the human resources from which the city was created. The migration of monks into the area was the reason for the setting up of the cities. The Great Laura came into existence at the point when Sabas decided to accept those who wanted to join him. Very many of the scattered anchorites and 'grazers' (βοσκοί) came and remained with him.[94] When their number reached seventy, Sabas began the process of building the Great Laura.[95] In the case of the New Laura, sixty monks withdrew from the Great Laura and eventually settled near

---

[88] Ibid. 117. 14.

[89] V. Corbo, *Gli scavi di Kh. Siyar el-Ghanam (Campo dei Pastori) e i monasteri dei dintorni* (Jerusalem, 1955), 5–6. At the New Laura the bakery was built at the same time as the church, *Kyrillos*, 123. 27.

[90] *Kyrillos*, 117. 8; 131. 26–7. Cf. Theodore of Petra, *V. Thds.* 35. 9–14. For further detail, see H. J. Magoulias, 'The Lives of the Saints as Sources of Data for the History of Byzantine Medicine in the Sixth and Seventh Centuries', *By. Z.* 57 (1964), 127–50.

[91] Not washing (ἡ ἀλουσία) was one of John the Hesychast's virtues, *Kyrillos*, 203. 1.

[92] Ibid. 103. 25–6; 122. 19–125. 25.

[93] See above, Ch. 4.

[94] *Kyrillos*, 99. 17–18.

[95] Ibid. 100. 5.

the deserted monastery of Romanus.[96] In the absence of the facilities necessary to sustain life, Sabas made arrangements for money and workmen so that the construction work could take place.[97] On other occasions Sabas founded monasteries after unsuccessful attempts by others to establish a community. He used his influence and organizing capabilities to ensure that the necessary resources were available. When he planned a monastery in a deserted place, the monastic body came from the Great Laura. At Castellion, a group from the Great Laura settled first and later a 'numerous community' (συνοδίαν ἱκανὴν) joined them.[98] The surplus population of the original settlement was moved to colonize a new area.

These new settlements were not independent of the Great Laura but retained their relationship with the original foundation. They were connected through the acknowledgement of a common founder, Sabas, and were referred to as 'Sabaites'.[99] Access from one to another was made easy by the elaborate system of interconnected paths which joined the monasteries together.[100] Together the monasteries of Sabas constituted one large city, established on several sites.

Before the lifetime of Sabas, the desert was unclaimed territory, a space at the edge of the Empire where devils, beasts, and barbarians roamed. As a result of Sabas' shrewd opportunism and organizing abilities, the growing stream of pilgrims was diverted into this wasteland and settled in well-equipped and economically viable units. The new monastery-cities were part of the fabric of society, contributed to the economy, and helped to secure the borders. Their political and social role was as significant as their spiritual and religious life. Indeed, in the society of the time, these elements belonged together. It was the achievement of Sabas to establish this extension of the Christian Empire.

LEADERSHIP

Once the city was set up, the founder was expected to administer and preside over it. The process of building up the monastery, described in the last section, invested the founder with a continuing authority. This

---

[96] *Kyrillos*, 122. 20–123. 8.
[97] Ibid. 123. 16–28.
[98] Ibid. 112. 20.
[99] Ibid. 193. 23.
[100] See above, beginning of Ch. 5.

authority is clearly shown by the admonishment of the rebellious intellectuals of the Great Laura by the priest Cyricus. 'If he ... brought you together in this place and colonised this place which was a desert, how could he govern still more both the place which he has colonised and you whom he brought together in union? God, who assisted him in ... founding the place will assist him still more in governing it.'[101]

This government is defined by the next three titles, those of lawgiver, patron, and archimandrite.

'*νομοθέτης*' or lawgiver, and, to a less clear extent, '*ὁδηγός*' or guide, show that the saint exercises his leadership through the maintenance of order and the formulation of rules.

The provision of a set of rules was a part of the process of founding the monastery. In the case of the monastery of Jeremiah, Sabas 'built a small oratory and some cells; he allowed some brothers to live there and, giving Jeremimah the responsibility of presiding over them, he handed over to them the rules of the Great Laura' (*παραδοὺς αὐτοῖς τοὺς τῆς ἑαυτοῦ Μεγίστης Λαύρας κανόνας*).[102] These rules are mentioned again when Sabas was near to death. He committed them to his monks and, by this stage, they had been recorded in writing (*παρραγγείλας αὐτῷ τὰς παραδόσεις τὰς παραδοθείσας ἐν τοῖς ὑπ' αὐτὸν μοναστηρίοις ἀτρώτους δια φυλάξαι δοὺς αὐτῷ ταύτας ἐγγραφως*).[103] This rule was discovered by A. Dmitrijevskij in a twelfth- or thirteenth-century manuscript on Mount Sinai. It is entitled *τύπος καὶ παράδοσις καὶ νόμος τῆς σεβασμίας λαύρας τοῦ ἁγίου Σάββα* and contains a number of regulations which governed life in the monastery.[104]

The text, as it now stands, derives from a period later than the life of Sabas. But many of the rules emerge out of problems and concerns which existed while the saint was still alive. One rule enshrines the old practice of Euthymius that no unbearded person should be admitted to the laura. Another forbids any monk to go into the desert without the permission of the superior. Iberians and Syrians can say the psalms in their own church but must come into the great church for the Eucharistic liturgy. No monk should leave the laura during the vigil on a Saturday or Sunday.

---

[101] *Kyrillos*, 104. 4–12.
[102] Ibid. 179. 20–2.
[103] Ibid. 182. 21–3.
[104] For a summary, see E. Kurtz, 'Review of A. Dmitrijevskij, Die Klosterregeln des hl. Sabas (Kiev 1890)', *By. Z.* 3 (1894), 167–70; S. Vailhé, 'Les écrivains de Mar-Saba', *E. Or.* 2 (1899), 1–11, 33–47, esp. 2–3.

Among later additions is the rule that anybody behaving in an unseemly manner in the woman's monastery was to be expelled immediately. Cyril makes no mention of a woman's monastery under the direction of Sabas, although the saint did assist in the monastic renunciation of his mother, Sophia.[105]

Episodes in the *Life of Sabas* show how these rules were formulated. They arose during the day-to-day life of the monastery when problems needed to be solved. Cyril has collected together a series of anecdotes which deal with disciplinary processes in the section of the Life which describes Sabas' relationships with his monks.[106] A group of these stories describes the errors and eventual correction of the monk Jacob, presented as the archetype of the 'bad' monk. He tries to establish a monastery within the area of the Great Laura without Sabas' permission; he wastes and throws away uneaten food; he even attempts to kill himself in a fit of despair. In each of these situations Sabas intervenes, finally dismissing him from the laura and sending him to live the coenobitic life with Theodosius. In the last of the collection of tales, Jacob reforms and is restored, dying reconciled with Sabas.[107] Other stories describe a monk killing a mule in a fit of anger, or a monk on a journey looking appreciatively at an attractive young woman, or a monk committing fornication while on business in the city.[108] The preponderance of anecdotes on the theme of a fault committed by a monk and the stern discipline and eventual restoration achieved by the superior shows the importance of the role of the leader as judge and lawgiver. Sabas' residence in the Tower overlooking the cells in the ravine was visual reminder that he watched over them and stood in authority over them. From this vantage point he could see what went on.[109] The way in which Sabas responded to difficulties was remembered and formed the basis of the rules when they came to be written down.

The leader was also the προστάτης. This carries the implication that he was provider and protector. As leader he was expected to provide the monks with what they needed. The role of provider was especially important at the foundation of the monastery. When the New Laura was built Sabas bought all the necessary materials as well as finding the

---

[105] *Kyrillos*, 109. 10.
[106] Ibid. 129. 3–139. 19.
[107] Ibid. 129. 3–139. 19.
[108] Ibid. 134. 9–135. 28; 137. 33–138. 10; 139. 9–10. This collection has a parallel with a similar group of stories in the *Life of Euthymius*, 28. 9–32. 5.
[109] Ibid. 122. 26; 133. 10–11; 182. 18–19.

workmen. This ability to produce the materials needed for proper building persuaded the rebels to overcome their fierce hostility and to accept him as their provider.[110] The provision of 'all the necessities' (τὰ ἐπιτήδεια πάντα) is also recorded of his work in the building of a new monastery on the site of Eudocia's Tower. Here he also laboured himself until the monastery was completed.[111]

The word προστάτης was used to describe a leader and protector of a rural community. The figure of the rural patron has been described by P. R. L. Brown in a study which drew on the evidence from the works of Theodoret and Libanius.[112] He demonstrates the important part played by the patron in the village. The patron was a powerful figure who could use his influence to make life run more smoothly. He was expected to intervene in the internal working of the community, settling disputes between villagers, ensuring that all had access to the water supply and defending the interests of the poor. Even more important was his awe-inspiring ability to manage relationships with the world outside, especially in assisting with negotiations with the dreaded figure of tax-collector. Libanius recognized the importance of the patron as somebody who was not only involved in village life but also worked to ensure just dealing and proper care for its inhabitants. He was concerned when this postion was filled by the wrong person, and described how villagers would sometimes bribe the '*dux*' of the province to eject the tax-collector and then protect them by claiming the case for his own court, so taking them under his patronage.[113]

Brown argues from evidence from Syria that the holy man was in a favourable position to take on the patron's role. As he used his power in this way he fulfilled a valuable social function. He gives the example of the ascetic, Abraham. Abraham settled in a large village in the Lebanon with some companions, earning a living by trading in nuts. Their pious practices and celebration of the liturgy aroused the hostility of the villagers who tried to drive them away by burying the hut in earth. In spite of this unfriendly treatment, Abraham negotiated on their behalf with the tax-collectors and arranged a loan through some of his friends in Emesa. Then 'they invited him to be their patron—for the

[110] Ibid. 123. 25–6.
[111] Ibid. 128. 22–5. Similar language is used of the building of the coenobium of Zannus at 133. 1–2.
[112] P. R. L. Brown, 'The Rise and Function of the Holy Man in Late Antiquity', *JRS* 61 (1971), 80–101.
[113] Jones, *Later Roman Empire*, iii. 772–8.

village did not have a master'.[114] Here the position of the holy man as
a figure with both authority and connections, but who had a position
which was outside the immediate community, made him ideally suited
to represent and act on behalf of the village.

The description of Sabas' activities in the monastery shows him in
an equivalent role. He was patron to the monastery, ensuring access to
water, the means of earning a living, and the administration of justice.
He also carried out that other side of the patron's responsibilities by
exercising his power on behalf of the monks in their relationships with
the wider community.

An essential part of the building up of the monastery was the
acquisition of property in the neighbouring centres of population. With
a legacy from his mother he bought a house in Jericho which was used
as a guest-house. This strengthened the position of the monastery.[115]
Before long he had gained a base in Jerusalem too.[116] This was especially
important because Jerusalem was the centre of pilgrimage. Here, money,
materials, and resources were to be gained, as well as new recruits. A
strong connection with the capital ensured an influence in society,
prestige, and wealth.[117]

Sabas' position as patron is shown at its best when he set off to
Constantinople to present the greviances of the inhabitants of the Holy
Land to the Emperor. In his first visit he was granted three interviews
with Emperor Anastasius. In the course of these conversations, he
received gifts of money for the monasteries, an assurance that Jerusalem
and its Patriarch would be allowed to live in peace, and a remission of
the taxation practice known as περισσοπρακτίαν, translated by Festugière
as *superflua descriptio*. This was the compulsory transfer of land to
wealthy landowners in cases where the original owners could not afford
to pay the tax levied. The new owners then became liable for the
taxation. This was of concern to the monasteries since their lands were
vulnerable to this enforced confiscation and they needed protection from
the Emperor.[118]

When he visited Constantinople for the second time, he presented
the Emperor Justinian with a list of five requests. These were a further

---

[114] Theodoret, *H. Rel.* 17. 2–3, SC 257 (Paris, 1979), 36. 7–38. 18.

[115] *Kyrillos*, 102. 12–15.

[116] Ibid. 116. 9–25.

[117] Cf. the desire of national groups to occupy a church in the centre of Constantinople
rather than in the suburbs. See Patlagean, *Pauvreté*, 209.

[118] *Kyrillos*, 143. 8–10; 144. 1–28. See *MO* pt. 2, iii. 72, for Festugière's translation.

petition for relief from taxation, money for the rebuilding of churches destroyed in the Samaritan revolt, money to build a new church to the Mother of God in Jerusalem, money to build a hospital, and a military camp in the desert.[119] During their meeting in his first visit, the Emperor Anastasius recognized Sabas' position and is not surprised by his requests. He asked him: 'As for you, venerable father, if you have no petition, why did you undertake such a troublesome journey?' Then, after he had provided Sabas with money, concluded, 'pray for me, for I have heard that you take care of many monasteries in the desert'.[120] The conversations at the Imperial Court show Sabas acting as the good patron, using his influence on behalf of the monasteries, and the Emperors Anastasius and Justinian recognizing this position and responding to it. It is as ambassador to the capital that Sabas' position in the desert is demonstrated with greatest clarity.

The title which is most strongly emphasized by Cyril is that of ἀρχιμανδρίτης, or archimandrite. This position was bestowed jointly on Sabas and Theodosius by the Patriarch Sallustius while he was on his death-bed.[121]

The title 'archimandrite' can have a general meaning, referring to the superior of a group of monks. It was a common title in the Byzantine Church and could be given to a deacon or layperson as well as to a priest. Often it applied to the superior of a prominent monastery whose authority was recognized by monks in the monastery or in the neighbourhood. So, when Sabas was admitted to the monastery of Flavianae as a young man, it was the archimandrite who admitted him.[122] In a similar way, Cyril wrote of a certain 'Mamas, archimandrite of the Aposchist monks of Eleutheropolis', whose monastery is not named which indicates an authority recognized over the whole area.[123]

The authority of the archimandrite could be extensive. A leading figure in the church of Constantinople was Dalmatius, a monk. Following the deposition of Nestorius in 451, Maximianus was consecrated Patriarch. He was a weak character and could not command the loyalty of the powerful monastic population of the capital. The resulting power vacuum made the influence of the leader of the monks more significant. Dalmatius was recognized as the monks' spokesman and the title of

---

[119] *Kyrillos*, 175. 8–178. 9.
[120] Ibid. 142. 26–143. 10.
[121] Ibid. 114. 23–6.
[122] Ibid. 87. 25.
[123] Ibid. 147. 13–14.

'archimandrite' was used to define this role. At the Council of Ephesus of 431, before the increase in his authority after the deposition of Nestorius, Dalmatius was already being referred to as 'archimandrite and father of monks', and he signed himself as 'priest and archimandrite, father of the monasteries'.[124] Here the archimandrite was a superior who represented the monks of several monasteries and had a status recognized in the church of the capital.

In Jerusalem, the authority of the archimandrite also extended over a wide area. In the case of Passarion, who visited Euthymius' monastery in the company of Patriarch Juvenal, the title of 'archimandrite of monks' was combined with that of *chorepiscop* (χωρεπίσκοπος) or rural bishop. He was τὸ χωρεπίσκοπον καὶ τῶν μοναχῶν ἀρχιμανδρίτην.[125] The *chorepiscop* was a bishop who had, in earlier times, presided in rural areas or villages and who had become an anachronism in a Church increasingly centred on the city. He came to be seen as an assistant to the bishop of the city. It has been suggested that the *chorepiscop* in the Diocese of Jerusalem was not only the assistant but also the designated successor of the Patriarch.[126] Mark the Deacon reports that Porphyry was consecrated by Praylius at a time when John was still Patriarch of Jerusalem.[127] From this reference it seems that Praylius exercised episcopal powers appropriate to the Patriarch when he was *chorepiscop* and so was an inevitable choice to become Patriarch on John's death. In a similar example, Nicephorus Callistus called Anastasius the Bishop of Jersualem in a passage referring to a period before he was consecrated and when, according to Cyril of Scythopolis, he was still *chorepiscop*.[128]

By the time of Passarion the office of *chorepiscop* was dying out in the Church. At Nicaea in 325 there are the signatures of fifteen *chorepiscops* attached to the canons, but at Chalcedon in the following century there are only six. At a local council in Antioch they were told to 'recognize

[124] Mansi, iv. 1432, 1257. For the use of the title 'archimandrite' and the career of Dalmatius, see G. Dagron, 'Les Moines et la ville', *Travaux et mémoires*, 4 (1970), 229–76, 265–70.

[125] *Kyrillos*, 26. 18–19. For the role of *chorepiscops* as bishops in villages, see J. Meyendorff, *Imperial Unity and Christian Division* (New York, 1989), 42. He quotes the remark of Theodore of Mopsuestia that in earlier times 'bishops were ordained not only in cities, but in quite small places where there was really no need of anyone being vested with episcopal authority'.

[126] S. Vailhé, 'Les Premières Monastères de la Palestine', *Bess.* 3 (1897–8), 209–25, 211–12.

[127] Mark the Deacon, *V. Porph.* 10. 1–5, ed. Kugener, 10–11.

[128] *Kyrillos*, 47. 22. Nicephorus Callistus, *HE* 15. 13, PG 147. 40C.

their limitations'.[129] As this position fell into disuse the office of archimandrite emerged to take its place. Passarion, the *chorepiscop*, was also archimandrite. He was the first of a recognizable succession of archimandrites who were the leaders of the large and important monastic population through the later fifth and sixth centuries.[130]

Ecclesiastical organization generally conformed to the already existing structure of the civil administration. It was usual for each city to have its own bishop, even when the church was small in size. Gregory Thaumaturgus, for example, was appointed Bishop of Neocaesarea when there were only nineteen Christians in the congregation.[131] Since, as has been argued, the monasteries were urban-style centres of population in previously undeveloped tracts of land, it was necessary to authorize a proper form of episcopal leadership. A bishop was consecrated for the Saracen communities with the title of Bishop of the Encampments.[132] The archimandrite, although not formally a bishop, had an equivalent authority within the monasteries.

Cyril records the succession of archimandrites after Passarion. They include Elpidius and Gerontius, who were sent by the usurper Theodosius to persuade Euthymius to join the Aposchist party.[133] These were followed by a certain Lazarus and then Anastasius, about whom we have no information. Then unity was lost: 'Anarchy and polyarchy prevailed among the monks.'[134] This situation was improved by the ministry of Marcianus of Bethlehem, who was widely respected. He fulfilled his obligation to support the monastic population by, for example, giving support to Sabas during the building of Castellion.[135] After his death, 'all the monks of the desert gathered in the Patriarch's residence and by a common vote (κατὰ κοινὴν ψῆφον) elected Theodosius and Sabas'.[136] This event shows the monks acting as a unified body and choosing the persons best able to support them in their precarious existence.

The list of archimandrites reveals a slowly shifting focus of power

---

[129] Jones, *Later Roman Empire*, 879.
[130] *Kyrillos*, 114. 27.
[131] Jones, *Later Roman Empire*, 875.
[132] *Kyrillos*, 25. 2–9.
[133] Ibid. 42. 12.
[134] Ibid. 115. 1.
[135] Ibid. 111. 25–112. 9. For Marcianus, see J. Kirchemeyer, 'Le Moine Marcien (de Bethléem)', TU 80 (1962), 341–59; A. van Roey, 'Rémarques sur le moine Marcien', TU 115 (1975), 160–77.
[136] *Kyrillos*, 115. 15–17.

away from the city of Jerusalem into the desert to the east. Passarion and Gerontius both lived in Jerusalem, and were close associates of the Patriarch. Elpidius chose to live at the monastery of Douka, near Jericho.[137] Marcianus resided near Bethlehem, and Sabas and Theodosius in the hills between Bethlehem and the Dead Sea. The cities of the desert were sufficiently established to act as the centre of the monastic movement with the archimandrite presiding over them.

The title of 'archimandrite' was bestowed by the Patriarch. This greater authority bestowed on the leading monks implies a closer working relationship with the Patriarch and with the church in Jerusalem. The growing integration of the monasteries into the Church is shown by a comparison between the attitudes of the two great saints, Euthymius and Sabas.

Once Euthymius had venerated the holy places and left the city to settle in the laura of Pharan in 405, there is no evidence that he ever returned to Jerusalem, even though his monastery was only a few miles distant. He showed a similar reluctance to enter into contact with the Patriarch. This is shown when Anastasius, recently elevated, decided to pay a courtesy call on the old man. In words influenced by his admired Arsenius, Euthymius obligingly declares his willingness to meet the Patriarch but reminds him that, if he does receive the Patriarch, he will have to receive every visitor who comes and his solitude will be lost.[138] The Patriarch cancelled the visit and the two did not meet again until the funeral of Theoctistus.[139]

Euthymius' relationship with Juvenal, the predecessor of Anastasius, had also been slight. In his instructions to Peter, Bishop of the Encampments, when the latter was about to go to the Council of Ephesus in 431, he advised him to follow the lead given by Cyril of Alexandria and Acacius of Melitene, and made no mention of Juvenal, even though his doctrinal views were at that time similar. Several reasons can be given for this choice of mentors, including the contacts between the saint and his Armenian homeland, but the remarks nevertheless demonstrate the weakness of the relationship between Euthymius and his Bishop.[140]

Sabas' attitude to the Patriarchate was completely different. He was closely involved in the life of the Jerusalem church. This was partly a

---

[137] Palladius, *H. Laus.* 48, ed. Butler, 142. 13–14.
[138] *Kyrillos*, 52. 10–17. Cf. *Apoph. Patr.*, Arsenius, 8, PG 65. 89B.
[139] *Kyrillos*, 54. 17–55. 19.
[140] For further analysis of Euthymius' attitude to Juvenal, see Ch. 8.

result of the growing influence of the monasteries on the Patriarchate. Those who held this high office during the lifetime of Sabas included men who shared his background in monasticism. Martyrius (478–86) and Elias (494–516) had both been monks in Euthymius' monastery, as had Sabas. Elias' successor, John, was the son of the priest Marcianus, who had assisted Sabas in the building of the monastery of the Cave.[141]

Sabas maintained a close working relationship with the Patriarch and was a regular visitor to Jerusalem. He was swift to obey a summons from Sallustius, who had received a complaint about Sabas' management of the monastery, and accepted ordination, in spite of having previously been reluctant.[142] Euthymius, in that position, would have kept well away. Later, he purchased property in Jerusalem, a decision motivated in part by a desire to be closer to the new Patriarch Elias.[143] He emerged from his retirement in Nicopolis to be in Jerusalem for the Feast of the Dedication of the Church of the Resurrection.[144] He visited the Patriarch to enlist his support for the building of a new monastery.[145] His friendship with Elias continued after the Patriarch was deposed and he visited him during his exile at Aila, being present at Elias' death before hurrying back to Jerusalem again.[146]

The prominence of Sabas in the church in Jerusalem is shown by his participation in diplomatic missions on behalf of the Patriarch and by his insistence that the new Patriarch John should support the Chalcedonian cause and anathematize Severus.[147]

Some commentators have suggested that Sabas was less important than Cyril claims. Theodore of Petra does not mention Sabas' name in his account of the events of the reign of the Emperor Anastasius, giving the credit to his own hero, Theodosius. F. Loofs thinks that Leontius of Byzantium was the *apocrisarius* of Patriarch Peter in the mission to Constantinople and that Sabas was a subordinate member of the party.[148] The first of these points can be easily disposed of. Theodore's neglect of Sabas is explained by his purpose of giving a eulogy of Theodosius

[141] *Kyrillos*, 127. 4–9; 150. 8.
[142] Ibid. 104. 12–18.
[143] Ibid. 116. 8–24.
[144] Ibid. 121. 14–16. For the Feast of Dedication or 'Encaenia', see E. D. Hunt, *Holy Land Pilgrimage in the Later Roman Empire* (Oxford, 1984), 108–10.
[145] *Kyrillos*, 123. 22.
[146] Ibid. 161. 2–162. 3: 162. 3–4.
[147] Ibid. 139. 20–7; 141. 12–15; 173. 4–9; 151. 18–152. 5.
[148] F. Loofs, *Leontius von Byzanz* (Leipzig, 1887), 261–73.

and by his lack of interest in historical accuracy.[149] Loofs' contention, even if correct, does not affect the significant feature of the participation of Sabas in the embassy to Constantinople, which is that he went at all. Usually monastic leaders, like Euthymius, stayed at home. Antony, for example, made only two brief visits to Alexandria—one in an unsuccessful attempt to achieve martyrdom and the other in order to support the beleaguered Nicene party.[150] Pachomius kept in touch with the capital through visits made by his monks but never went himself.[151] Daniel the Stylite descended from his column and entered Constantinople at a moment of crisis for the Chalcedonian faith and this caused a sensation.[152] Sabas, as a complete contrast to these examples of monastic leadership, showed a readiness to travel and to be involved in diplomacy. Once in Constantinople he showed no longing to return to his monastery but chose to spend the winter in the capital, visited the Empress Ariadne, received visits from the noble ladies of the court, and had three interviews with the Emperor.[153] He is a new phenomenon in the history of desert monasticism.

His unconventional role as ambassador to Constantinople led to a harmonious relationship with the Emperor. The interview with the Emperor Justinian paints an ideal portrait of the mutual respect and complementary responsibilities within the Empire of the Emperor and the Monk. First, Justinian's eyes are miraculously opened and he sees the light of divine glory surrounding Sabas. Then, instead of the customary *proskynesis* offered to the Emperor, Justinian reversed the natural order and reverenced Sabas (προσδραμὼν προσεκύνησεν αὐτῷ). The mutual tasks of the two are then explained. It is Justinian's duty to ensure peace, prosperity, and security for the Church, and to combat heresy. The monks, for their part, pray for the Emperor.[154] The result of these two activities is that God will grant that the Empire is extended. This relationship is summarized in the charming vignette of Sabas reciting the office of Terce while Justinian is making the arrangements for his requests to be granted. Each, says the saint to a companion who rebukes him for not showing a proper respect, is at that moment doing

[149] See above, Ch. 2.
[150] *V. Anton.* 46; 69, PG 26. 909B–C; 941A.
[151] *V. Pach. Bo.* 1. 89; 107.
[152] *V. Dan. Styl.* 71. 19–79. 24.
[153] *Kyrillos*, 141. 24–147. 9.
[154] Ibid. 173. 19–176. 2.

his proper work (ἐκεῖνοι τὸ ἴδιον ποιοῦσιν. ποιήσωμεν καὶ ημεῖς τὸ ἡμέτερον).[155]

It was harder for Cyril to maintain this ideal image in the case of Anastasius, whose tolerance of Monophysitism and support for the heretics led him into conflict with the Patriarch of Jerusalem. In spite of his opposition, he presents personal contacts between Anastasius and Sabas in similar terms to that with Justinian. The divine favour resting on Sabas is revealed to Anastasius, who saw an angelic form preceding the old man (ἀγγελικήν τινα μορφὴν). The requests which Sabas makes were granted. Politely, Sabas offers the traditional *proskynesis* to the Emperor (ἦλθον προσκυνῆσαι τὰ ἴχνη τῆς ὑμετερας εὐσεβείας).[156]

In the passages which describe the Emperor's relationships with Jerusalem, Cyril's portrait is less favourable. He describes the attempts of the Emperor to 'disrupt and overturn the constitution of the Church in Palestine'.[157] He records the resistance by Elias to the depositions of Euphemius and Macedonius, two Patriarchs of Constantinople who offended Anastasius, the Synod of Sidon, and the return to peace in Jerusalem after massive monastic opposition to the Monophysite sympathies of the Emperor.[158]

There are, in Cyril's view, two possible causes of Anastasius' conduct. Either he was misled by bad advisers, like Marinus, who tried to persuade the Emperor not to grant the remission of taxes to Jerusalem on the grounds that it was a city of Nestorians and Jews.[159] Or he was moved by anger, a passion which, as all monks knew, should be attributed to demonic influence. The anger of Anastasius finally provoked the reciprocal anger of God, who punished Anastasius by sending a thunderstorm in which the Emperor died.[160] Since these explanations place the responsibility for the Emperor's evil actions on to somebody or something else, neither requires Cyril to abandon his cherished picture of the God-loving Emperor co-operating with the God-chosen monk.

The emperor plays an important part in Cyril's understanding of Church and Empire. He is more sympathetic to the Emperor than other

---

[155] Ibid. 178. 16–17.
[156] Ibid. 142. 18–143. 1. The interviews are described in 142. 18–147. 9.
[157] Ibid. 139. 25–7.
[158] Ibid. 139. 20–141. 23; 148. 6–150. 11; 150. 11–158. 11. For the relationship between Cyril's account and the parallel passages in Theodore Lector's *Ecclesiastical History* and Theophanes' *Chronography*, see *MH* 60–7.
[159] *Kyrillos*, 142. 20–1; 146. 4–147. 9. Marinus' opposition to Sabas came to a dramatic end when, in accordance with a prophecy of Sabas, he was killed in a fire in his house.
[160] Ibid. 139. 27; 141. 5; 141. 17; 150. 18; 162. 9.

writers of his time. Theodore of Petra, for example, devotes a lengthy passage to a description of the wickedness of the Emperor Anastasius in terms far more critical than any used by Cyril. Even the gift of money to the monasteries is interpreted as a bribe intended to turn the saintly and resolute Theodosius away from his orthodox witness.[161] He seems to assume that the natural relationship of monk and Emperor is one of opposition. John Moschus is also a stern critic of the actions of emperors. He condemns Zeno as deserving punishment for the wrongs done to a woman, although his charity counts in his favour and deflects the vengeance he otherwise deserved.[162] Not only is Cyril more generous in his appraisal of emperors but also more extreme in his condemnation of the Emperor's enemies. He describes, for example, the Arab leader al-Mundhir who attacked Palestine in 529. He was 'enraged with anger ... he pillaged, captured myriads of Romans and ... committed all sorts of crimes'.[163] No specific events are referred to, but an enemy of the Empire is by definition to be reviled.

A comparison of the styles of life of the two saints, Euthymius and Sabas, show the evolution of the monasteries of the desert of Palestine. From a conventional beginning as simple communities of ascetics they became a powerful and unified social institution. This process was characterized by a progressive integration into the life of the Church and Empire. Sabas' achievement was to make the monasteries into a part of society, drawing strength from it and contributing to it. As a result of his work, the monasteries belonged not just to the Judaean desert but to the Church and the Empire, to Jerusalem and Constantinople.

[161] Theodore of Petra, *V. Thds.* 54. 1–56. 19.
[162] *Prat.* 175, PG 87/3. 3014B.
[163] *Kyrillos*, 211. 15–19. See J. S. Trimingham, *Christianity among the Arabs in Pre-Islamic Times* (London, 1979), 115.

8

Witnesses to Truth

HOW PALESTINE BECAME CHALCEDONIAN

The literature of the Palestinian desert was written during a period of controversy. Juvenal visited the newly founded laura of Euthymius to consecrate the church in 428—the year in which Nestorius became Patriarch of Constantinople. The period in which the saint presided over his monastery included the two Councils of Ephesus and the Council of Chalcedon. He died in 473, the year before Zeno become Emperor. Sabas arrived in Jerusalem in 456, three years after Juvenal was restored to the Patriarchate, when the Definition of Chalcedon was viewed with extreme suspicion by the bulk of the monastic population, and lived to see it established in the diptychs by the imperial decree of the Emperor Justin.[1]

Cyril of Scythopolis presents his subjects as playing a central part in this history. They were consistent in their support of Chalcedon and their witness to the truth was vindicated by orthodoxy triumphing in Palestine. In accordance with this scheme, he concludes the *Life of Euthymius*, who was the champion of Chalcedon, with the victory of the Orthodox over the Monophysites. This happened, again according to Cyril, during the reign of Zeno and as a consequence of a reassuring message given by the departed saint in a vision.[2] Such a simple and conclusive end to the dispute does not concur with the historical evidence. Although the final outcome of the conflict in Palestine was the acceptance of Chalcedon, the struggle was long drawn out, the allegiances were more confused, and the resolution less decisive, than Cyril's clear and straightforward account suggests.

Much of the research into the history of the period has examined the reasons why different areas developed different religious allegiances.[3]

---

[1] See *Kyrillos*, 26. 17–23; 59. 12–15; 90. 16–19; 162. 10–13.
[2] Ibid. 63. 9–23; 66. 18–67. 20.
[3] Studies of regional allegiance include the seminal works about Syria, E. Honigmann, *Évêques et évêchés monophysites d'Asie intérieure au 6e siècle*, CSCO subs. 2 (Louvain, 1951), and G. Tchalenko, *Villages antiques de la Syrie du Nord*, 3 vols. (Paris, 1953–8).

This continuing task has produced important findings but has also raised many questions. Frend, in his survey of the state of research at the time when he wrote his history of the *Rise of the Monophysite Movement*, summarized the current situation: 'More ... work will be needed before one will be in a position to say why one area of the Byzantine Empire preferred Monophysitism to Chalcedon and vice versa. For instance, why should the province of Pamphylia in southern Asia be described by John of Ephesus as having been *ex initio* "orthodox" (i.e. Monophysite)? ... Similarly, the island of Chios; why should this island have been singled out as the seat of John, one of James bar Addai's bishops?'[4]

Here, the area in question is Palestine, and the purpose of the discussion is to show why the church in Jerusalem adopted a Chalcedonian Christology while other regions within a hundred miles chose Monophysitism.[5] Reasons for this allegiance are suggested by the historical evidence, and special consideration is given here to three issues—the reason why Euthymius, in opposition to the bulk of the monastic body, decided to accept Chalcedon; the reason why Marcianus and his followers decided to become reconciled to the Patriarch; and the reason why the ordinations performed by Jacob bar Addai did not produce a Monophysite episcopate in Palestine. These moments proved to be of pivotal importance in determining the eventual allegiance of the Palestinian church. The second part of this account discusses the special situation of the Palestinian church which prevented the emergence of a strong Monophysite party in the area. Then there is a brief reminder of the significance of peoples' faith.

When Euthymius arrived in Jerusalem, the church accepted without question the traditional Christological teaching of Cyril of Alexandria. Juvenal, the Archbishop of Jerusalem, played a leading part at the 'Latrocinium' of Ephesus in 449. He helped to bring about the restoration of Eutyches and the deposition of Flavian. According to the Monophysite historian John Rufus, he gave this view of the Tome of Leo before he left for Chalcedon: 'The Tome is Jewish, and the ideas it contains are those of Simon Magus. Anyone who accepts it deserves to remain a Jew.'[6] Euthymius expressed himself less strongly but was in fundamental

---

[4] W. H. C. Frend, *Rise of the Monophysite Movement* (Cambridge, 1972), pp. xv–xvi.

[5] Among the Monophysite areas less than 100 miles distant from Jerusalem were parts of Egypt, Ghassanid Arabia, and Phoenicia Libanensia, as well as pockets of support along the Mediterranean coast of Palestine. See Frend, *Rise*, 250–1.

[6] *Petrus der Iberer*, ed. Raabe (Leipzig, 1895), 53.

agreement: 'He told Peter Bishop of the Saracens ... to follow in every way Archbishop Cyril of Alexandria and Bishop Acacius of Melitene, as being orthodox and opponents of impiety.'[7] The monastic population would have had no hesitation in agreeing.

At Chalcedon Juvenal changed sides. In his dramatic volte-face, he rose from his seat alongside Dioscorus to the right of the imperial commissioners chairing the session and moved to the other side of the church to sit by Patriarch Anatolius of Constantinople. The Monophysite chronicler, Zacharias Rhetor, said that he was motivated by ambition and had been promised, presumably by Anatolius acting on behalf of the Emperor, that a change of sides would be rewarded by the elevation of Jerusalem to the status of a Patriarchate.[8] Modern commentators have often repeated this verdict: 'His conduct was motivated by ambition, and he has been treated by chroniclers with the contempt he deserved.'[9] But at the time there were good reasons to change sides. The circumstances at Chalcedon were very different from those that prevailed at Ephesus two years previously. The Emperor was firmly in control and had arranged that his representatives should preside over the sessions. Much care was taken to demonstrate that the Tome of Leo did not conflict with the theology of Cyril. The Palestinian bishops were ready to follow the lead shown by Juvenal, and along with him Severianus of Scythopolis, Stephen of Jamnia, and John of the Paremboles changed their allegiance and signed the Definition.[10]

In Palestine, the majority of monks greeted the news of the decisions of the Council of Chalcedon with a horror which erupted into violent resistance. For twenty months, from early in 452 until 453, the usurper Theodosius held the throne of the Patriarch of Jerusalem until he was ousted by imperial troops who reinstated Juvenal. Theodosius was supported by the population of Jerusalem and the monks of the desert.[11] Euthymius was one of a small minority who did not accept the new Patriarch. His resistance marks the beginning of a Chalcedonian party among the monks of the desert. In these early months it was small in size and forced to retire into remote areas to avoid reprisals against it by the majority. Among its supporters, Cyril mentions Gerasimus, Peter

---

[7] *Kyrillos*, 33. 2–6.
[8] Zachariah of Mitylene, *HE* 3. 3. 3, ed. Brooks 86. 7.
[9] Frend, *Rise*, 149.
[10] See *ACO* 2. 1. 2, pp. 129–30.
[11] *Kyrillos*, 42. 6–8.

Gournites, Mark, Joullon, and Silvanus.[12] This small but convinced group of supporters of Chalcedon proved to be the basis of a growing body of opinion which came to accept the Council. Its emergence at an early stage in the history of the reception of the Council against the prevailing trend of monastic opinion requires investigation. Various reasons for Euthymius' uncompromising stand can be discerned.

The words with which Euthymius is reported to have defended the Council of Chalcedon are derived in part from the written records of the Council rather than a recollection of the saint's actual speech.[13] Yet in spite of this sign of later reconstruction, Cyril's account is historically plausible. After the 'Latrocinium' of Ephesus in 449, Euthymius is said by Cyril to have been so angry with Auxolaus, Peter's successor as Bishop of the Encampments, for having supported Dioscorus the Patriarch of Alexandria and leader of the party later called Monophysite, that Auxolaus died as a result of the distress that he felt.[14] In the two years which succeeded, the Palestinian bishops, along with those from Egypt and Thrace, continued to support Dioscorus, but those from Pontus, Asia, and Syria declared their support for the memory of Flavian, according to the account of the pro-Chalcedonian Liberatus.[15] If Euthymius was continuing to look towards his homeland in Armenia to the north-east for his theological influence, this could account for his irritation with Auxolaus and an emergent alienation from the Palestinian bishops.

After the Council of Chalcedon, Stephen Bishop of Jamnia and John Bishop of the Paremboles hurried to inform Euthymius of the decisions of Chalcedon.[16] They would have given a first-hand account of the events of the Council, including the decision of the bishops that the teaching of Leo and Flavian was in agreement with that of Cyril. 'Cyril and Leo taught alike' had been one of the acclamations of the Council, and the Definition had been influenced by the theology of Cyril.[17] Euthymius was persuaded that the Council's definition was in harmony with the measure of orthodoxy to be found in the works of Cyril of Alexandria.

---

[12] *Kyrillos*, 44. 19–45. 4.
[13] Cf. ibid. 43. 9–11 with *ACO* 2. 1, p. 325. 31; and 43. 24–5 with *ACO* 2. 1, p. 325. 30. Although Cyril does tell us that Euthymius studied the Chalcedonian Definition before giving his verdict, *Kyrillos*, 41. 13–19.
[14] Ibid. 41. 12–13.
[15] Liberatus, *Breviarium*, 13. 76, *ACO* 2. 5, p. 119.
[16] *Kyrillos*, 41. 12–13.
[17] *ACO* 2. 1. 1, p. 81; 2. 1. 2, p. 124.

But other monks found the alternative account given by the usurper Theodosius, that the Council had betrayed the Christology of Cyril, to be more persuasive, especially as he had the support of Eudocia.[18] The absence of a close relationship between the saint and the Patriarch of Jerusalem makes it more likely that the views of Euthymius might have been out of step with the majority of the church at Jerusalem.[19] Euthymius might also have been encouraged in his opposition to Theodosius through personal dislike. The usurper had visited Alexandria in 448 and accused Domnus, Patriarch of Antioch and a former monk of Euthymius, to Dioscorus of the crime of heresy.[20]

So there are several reasons to account for the decision in favour of Chalcedon which was taken by Euthymius. Arising out of this stand, a tradition of support for Chalcedon entered into the monasteries of Palestine. But the majority of monks remained in determined opposition to the Council. Gerontius, superior of the monastery of Melania on the Mount of Olives, refused to accept the authority of Juvenal. 'God forbid that I should see the face of Judas the traitor,' he exclaimed, and many shared this opinion.[21] Marcianus left the monastery of Elpidius, after the latter's defection, and founded his own coenobium near Bethlehem. This monastery grew in size and importance, so that Marcianus was later appointed archimandrite of the monks of the Judaean desert.[22] Romanus founded a monastery at Thekoa, which became a centre of resistance to Chalcedon. This community numbered 600 monks, according to John Rufus, the Monophysite writer, and was a support to the enemies of Juvenal throughout Palestine and Arabia. Later, Romanus founded a new monastery at Eleutheropolis on land donated by Eudocia, whose reconciliation with Juvenal did not prevent her patronizing Monophysite monks.[23] The size and prestige of these monasteries shows

---

[18] *Kyrillos*, 41. 22–5.

[19] See Ch. 7, under 'Euthymius the Ascetic' and 'Leadership', for Euthymius' relationship with the Patriarch.

[20] J. Flemming (ed.), *Akten der ephesischen Synode vom Jahre 449*, cited in H. Bacht, 'Die Rolle des orientalischen Mönchtums in den Kirchenpolitischen Auseinandersetzungen um Chalkedon (431–519)', in *Das Konzil von Chalkedon*, ed. A. Grillmeier and H. Bacht, vol. ii (Würzburg, 1953), 245.

[21] *Kyrillos*, 49. 8–10; *Petrus der Iberer*, ed. Raabe, 58.

[22] *Kyrillos*, 49. 11–12; 66. 24–6; 115. 12–14.

[23] Ibid. 49. 10–13; John Rufus, *Plerophoriai*, 25, PO 8 (1912), 58. Cyril dated this event to 479, but an alternative account of the move to Eleutheropolis makes it take place well before the death of Juvenal, see *De Obitu Theodosii*, 26. 10–23. Cyril's date has the merit of providing an explanation for a move away from the capital which would otherwise be hard to account for.

that the theology of the monks remained conservative and that Juvenal had little authority over large parts of the Church.

In the half-century after Chalcedon the Patriarchs faithfully carried out imperial policy, reflecting the shifts in the attitude of successive Emperors towards Chalcedon. So the Chalcedonian Juvenal was succeeded in 459 by Anastasius who accepted the Encyclical of Basiliscus, which anathematized Chalcedon. The strength of Monophysite feeling in Palestine led him to oppose the Anti-Encyclical which followed.[24]

He, in turn, was succeeded by Martyrius who successfully sought to unify the monks of the desert on the basis of Zeno's Henoticon. The reconciliation between the Patriarchate and the Monophysite monks is sometimes called the Second Union, the first being between Juvenal and Eudocia.[25]

This episode in the history of the Palestinian church has been misunderstood by historians of the period, among whom were Schwartz and Chitty, as a result of a mistake over dating.[26] It is described by both Cyril and Zacharias in conflicting accounts. Cyril claims that Marcianus, the leader of the Monophysites, persuaded his followers to cast lots and as a result re-entered into communion with the Patriarch, thus implying a divine decision against Monophysitism.[27] Zacharias, on the other hand, attributes the union to a negotiation between the two sides in the course of which Martyrius agreed to anathematize innovations to the faith introduced at 'Arminium, Sardica, Chalcedon or any other place', representing the event as a defeat for Chalcedon.[28] In their accounts of this event, both Schwartz and Chitty accept the statement made by Cyril that the event took place 'a few days after' Fidus' vision of Euthymius which took place in 479. This leads them to date the Second Union to 479, three years before Zeno's Henoticon. As a result, they see Cyril's account of the casting of lots as an unhistorical miracle story told in order to provide divine approval for his favoured viewpoint. Zacharias, according to this view, is correct in presenting the event as the result of negotiations between Monophysites and Chalcedonians, in which Monophysites gained significant concessions. This solution

---

[24] For Anastasius' Monophysite leanings, see Evagrius, *HE* 3. 5, ed. Bidez and Parmentier, 104. 27–31. Perhaps Euthymius' sympathies for Chalcedon were the real reason for his reluctance to meet Anastasius, rather than the excuse of the desire for solitude, *Kyrillos*, 52. 4–18.

[25] For the First Union, see ibid. 47. 5–49. 13.

[26] See *Kyrillos*, 366–72; D. J. Chitty, *The Desert a City* (Oxford, 1966), 102.

[27] *Kyrillos*, 66. 21–67. 20.

[28] Zachariah of Mitylene, *HE* 3. 5, repr. in *Kyrillos*, 367–8.

became—so the argument concludes—the model later to be adopted by Acacius in the framing of Zeno's Henoticon which was issued in 482, three years after the Second Union in Palestine.[29]

An alternative understanding of the event is suggested by the other, admittedly less precise, piece of dating given at the end of Cyril's account, that 'this reunion took place in the region of Zeno', and by the placing of the event in the narrative after the consecration of the rebuilt coenobium of Euthymius in 482.[30] The reference to the 'few days' after the vision then becomes a claim for a connection between the two rather than an exact date. If this suggestion in the text is accepted, then the accounts of Cyril and Zacharias no longer conflict. Both historians are describing the events in Palestine in 482, following the promulgation of the Henoticon. Cyril's casting of lots was a method of deciding whether or not to accept the terms of the Henoticon, which are given by Zacharias and which Martyrius had received from Constantinople and proposed as a basis for union.

Clear support for Chalcedon only developed in Palestine after 490, when the mood in the desert changed. In 492 Sabas and Theodosius became archimandrites, in succession to the Monophysite Marcianus. Their Lives show them to have been supporters of the Chalcedon. Then, in 494, Elias became Patriarch. He had been a monk in Euthymias' monastery and shared his teacher's doctrinal position. At the same time the Monophysite Anastasius was Emperor (491–518). The action by Anastasius in deposing Elias and banishing him to Aila on the Red Sea had the effect of uniting the monks behind their archimandrites. As a result a huge crowd of monks, numbered by Cyril, possibly with some exaggeration, at 10,000, convened at the Church of St Stephen in Jerusalem to ensure that the next Patriarch declared his support for Chalcedon.[31] In 518 the Emperor Justin I acceded to the imperial throne and support of Chalcedon became imperial policy.

Throughout this period, pockets of Monophysite support remained. Determined opponents of the Jerusalem Patriarchate dispersed to the coastal regions. The *Life of Peter the Iberian* describes Peter visiting and encouraging Monophysite communities in his travels between Gaza and Phoenicia. Among these were monasteries and groups of laypeople at Ascalon, Thavatha, Jamnia, Ptolemais, Caesarea, and Afthoria.[32] This

[29] See ibid. 370–1. Also ibid. 66. 21–4.
[30] Ibid. 67. 19–20.
[31] Ibid. 151. 7–152. 6.
[32] *Petrus der Iberer*, ed. Raabe, 96, 111, 112.

solid base in commercial and intellectual centres encouraged a number of educated Greek-speakers who were to become influential authors and leaders of the Monophysite communities, including Severus of Antioch, Zachariah of Mitylene, and John Rufus.[33] Severus, later Patriarch of Antioch,. was superior of the monastery of Romanus. In 512 he gave refuge to 100 Monophysite monks expelled from the monastery of Torgas by Flavian of Antioch. Later, when he was Patriarch of Antioch, he entrusted a priest, John, from Romanus' monastery, with the responsibility of acting on his behalf in Syria.[34] Cyril claims some secessions to the Jerusalem Patriarchate from this group, such as Mamas, a Monophysite archimandrite at Eleutheropolis, through the efforts of Sabas.[35]

Palestine was better known as a haven for Chalcedonians than for Monophysites. Among those who found safety in the desert was Julian, Bishop of Bostra, who was forced into flight by Severus and remained in the monastery of Theodosius from 515 to 518. Peter, Bishop of Damascus, also fled to Palestine to escape Severus.[36]

The survival of Monophysite groups in solidly Chalcedonian areas is seen in other parts of the Empire as well. In the heart of Justinian's Constantinople, the Palace of Hormisdas housed a community of 500 Monophysite monks, so that John of Ephesus spoke of it as 'a vast and admirable desert of solitaries'. Theodosius, the Patriarch of Alexandria who took refuge in the capital until his death in 566, brought with him 300 of his clergy, who found refuge there.[37] The ability of the Emperor, and his Empress, to provide patronage for those opposing the religious policy shows how the two communities could comfortably coexist.

When the ordinations of Monophysite bishops and clergy began in the 540s, Palestine was unaffected. Theodore of Arabia had jurisdiction 'in the regions of the south and the west and in all the desert, in Arabia and in Palestine up to Jerusalem'.[38] He resided, however, in the camp of the Ghassanid Saracens. In contrast to Jacob bar Addai, he performed few ordinations and was content to preside over a Monophysite church in the desert east of the Jordan.

The efforts of the Council of Constantinople to unite the different

[33] See Chitty, *Desert a City*, 103–5.

[34] See Honigmann, *Évêques et évêchés*, 55, 76.

[35] *Kyrillos*, 147. 3.

[36] Honigmann, *Évêques et évêchés*, 158; for the motives of Justinian and Theodora, see Frend, *Rise*, 276; and J. Meyendorff, *Imperial Unity and Christian Divisions* (New York, 1989), 222.

[37] Meyendorff, *Imperial Unity*, 229.

[38] John of Ephesus, *Lives of the Eastern Saints*, PO 19 (Paris, 1925), 150.

parts of the Church were of little relevance to the church in Palestine. For Cyril, the Council was about Origenism, and he mentions four theologians condemned by the Council, of which three are Origenists. He had little interest in its decrees concerning Monophysitism, which, according to his scheme, had been overcome by the witness of Euthymius seventy years previously. By this time Monophysitism was past history in Palestine, and its growing vitality did not penetrate to the Jerusalem desert.

Historical events can explain the gradual withering away of Mono-physite support in Palestine and the corresponding discovery of Chalcedonianism. But the historical events took place in a land with a distinctive geography and distinctive place in the Empire. It is these features that shaped and influenced historical events.

WHY PALESTINE BECAME CHALCEDONIAN

It was not only the nature of the society which made Palestine into an environment favourable for the eventual acceptance of Chalcedon. The geographical make-up of the land itself had an influence on doctrine.

The nature of the desert in which the monks lived has been described above.[39] It was a terrain which encouraged the monks to live in settlements which were dispersed and scattered over a wide area. This tendency towards dispersal was in contrast to conditions in Egypt where the environment encouraged centralization. While Pachomius gathered his monks together within the walls of his coenobitic monasteries along the valley of the Nile, Sabas encouraged his monks to find their own caves or build up their own cells in the neighbourhood of the laura.[40] The search for a suitable shelter led the monk along the ravine away from the monastery. The place chosen was often inaccessible, since many of the most spacious caves were situated in precipitous sections of the wadi. The difficulty in obtaining access deterred contact between monks, as it has also impeded modern researchers.[41] The consequence

---

[39] See Ch. 5.
[40] *V. Pach. G1* 12; 29; 54, trans. Athanassakis, 16. 4–11; 38. 6–23; 80. 4–5. Cf. *Kyrillos*, 99. 27–100. 2.
[41] *Kyrillos*, 15. 13; 16. 7; 98. 7–23. See also the comments of M. Marcoff and D. Chitty, 'Notes on Monastic Research in the Judaean Desert, 1928–1929', *PEFQ St.* (1929), 167–78; O. Meinardus, 'Notes on the Laurae and Monasteries of the Wilderness of Judaea', *SBFLA* 15 (1964–5), 220–50.

of the isolation forced on monks was self-sufficiency within the cell. As
the community grew, so it became more scattered.

These characteristics are clearly shown by the investigation of the
cells of the Great Laura conducted by Virgilio Corbo and, more recently,
Joseph Patrich.[42] A total of 45 cells have been discovered, mostly
constructed in a 2km.-long stretch of the steep wadi. There is a wide
range of style. Some are simple cells in which a cell room was built in
front of a cave. An example is the cell attributed by tradition to
Xenophon, father of Arcadius and John.[43] The cave is built on a large
shelf of rock 20m. above the ground, with approach possible only by a
rope-ladder. The cave is more or less square, over 3m. in length. Its
opening is blocked by a wall with door and window in it. To one side
a room was built, with a cistern and a small garden plot.[44] Nearby is
the cell of Arcadius, his son. This is larger. In front of the cave a tower
was built, supported by a retaining wall reaching down to the foot of
the cliff some 11m. below. The tower is over 8m. in length and 4m. in
width. It is preserved to a height of 10m. and it is approached by a
staircase. This tower formed a large room next to the cave, which was
itself divided into three rooms. The complex includes two cisterns. The
cell, although more extensive, probably only housed one monk, but
others were larger still. Some cells were built in groups. Some are
clusters of caves with a masonry structure built into the cliff to connect
them. Others consist of a small group of buildings constructed on a
section of the slope where the gradient is gentler. Other dwellings are
a number of caves on several levels which are accessible one from
another. Each complex had its own water storage system and chapel.
The variety in size and style is the result of the monks taking advantage
of the natural opportunities of the site and exercising individual choice
in the manner of the building of the cells.

This best known of the monasteries of the desert consisted of about
150 monks living in self-contained units either alone or in groups along
a length of a rocky and inaccessible ravine. The focus of this community
was a group of service buildings, including a bakery and a church. Other

---

[42] See V. Corbo, 'Il cenobio di Zannos e il piccola cenobio della Granda Laura ritrovati
nel wadi el-Nar', *L.T.S.* 34 (1958), 109–10; J. Patrich, 'Hermitages of the Great Laura of
St Sabas', in D. Jacoby and Y. Tsafrir (eds.), *Jews, Samaritans and Christians in Byzantine
Palestine* (Jerusalem, 1988), 131–68.

[43] John the brother of Arcadius has been identified with the author of the *Life of
Chariton*, see Ch. 2.

[44] Y. Hirschfeld, *Judaean Desert Monasteries in the Byzantine Period* (New Haven,
Conn., 1992), 207.

monasteries were smaller and therefore less scattered, and the coenobia had a more strongly developed central community life. Nevertheless the description of the cells of the Great Laura demonstrates the dispersed and fragmented quality of monastic life in the Judaean desert. These isolated dwellings of individuals and groups are the seed-bed in which heresy grew. Within a community of this nature, small groups of monks of different nationality or different doctrinal allegiance could exist alongside each other with little awareness of divergences in lifestyle or belief and with little supervision from the superior residing at the centre of the laura. While fragmentation allowed freedom for heretical and divergent groups to exist within the monastery, it also prevented them developing a strong power-base, because of the obstacles in the way of communication between the cells.[45]

Monophysitism thrived in Syria and Egypt in centralized unified communities. The monasteries tended to be agricultural units. In Syria they were economic centres in an area of dry farming with many olive groves. This resulted not only in a unified monastic body but also in strong links with the surrounding countryside. The combination of economic links with the surrounding villages with a clear doctrinal unity enabled Monophysite communities to develop a strong base in the countryside.[46] Conditions in Palestine were very different.

Into this huge, interdependent, decentralized network of ascetic dwellings streamed an international brotherhood: 'The crowds of pilgrims, the hospices, the monks and the nuns turned Jerusalem into a meeting point of a varied collection of races and imported this "Internationalism" into the laurae and coenobia of the desert from the beginning.'[47] Monastic society was cosmopolitan.

The internationalism of the monasteries affected their reaction to the Council of Chalcedon. During the century which followed the Council, opposition to it came to be concentrated in certain identifiable areas. By 550 Egypt could be considered to be a stronghold of Monophysitism, as could the kingdoms of Ethiopia and Nubia which both had close relationships with the Patriarchate of Alexandria, and Armenia.[48] Syria

---

[45] An exception were the *logioteroi* in the Great Laura, *Kyrillos*, 103. 12–14; 118. 25–7.

[46] See Frend, *Rise*, 333; M. Rodinson, 'De l'archéologie à la sociologie historique: Notes méthodologiques sur le dernier ouvrage de G. Tchalenko', *Syria* 38 (1961), 170–200.

[47] *Kyrillos*, 359; and see above, Ch. 4.

[48] Here decisions of faith were influenced by the kingdom's vulnerable position between the Byzantine and Persian Empires, see Frend, *Rise*, 258–9.

was divided. The provinces of Syria Secunda and Pheonicia Maritima were predominantly Chalcedonian, while other areas, including Isauria, Cilicia Secunda, Syria Prima, Phoenicia Libanensia, and Osrhoene, were centres of Monophysite strength.[49] Monophysitism had become the faith of limited but clearly defined areas of the Christian world.

The relationship between religion and nationalism has been hotly debated. It has been argued by some writers that Monophysite fervour was an expression of the longing of a national group to break free from the oppressive and foreign Byzantine Empire, with doctrinal slogans becoming the identification badge of a political movement.[50] The adoption of Coptic as the language of Monophysitism and the welcome given to Persian and Arab invaders promising freedom from the Byzantine Empire, were pointed to as signs of the political nature of Egyptian Monophysitism. Other studies criticized this approach, in particular the article by A. H. M. Jones, 'Were Ancient Heresies National or Social Movements in Disguise?'[51]

Jones reviewed evidence from several countries to argue that Monophysites also used Greek and that the claim that they welcomed Arab invaders is unproven. He counselled against exaggerating the influence of nationalism on religious movements and recognized the deep religious convictions of heretical groups.[52] The section of his argument which refers to Palestine is weak. Dissenting from the view that the Monophysite movement had a nationalist character, he points to the existence of Syriac-speaking communities within the Palestinian church, a supporter of Chalcedon. He offers two pieces of evidence to support his argument. The first is the description given by Eusebius of Procopius, the Scythopolitan martyr, who translated the Gospels into Aramaic, a language related to Syriac. But Procopius died in 303 and so would have been active in the late third century. His activity can hardly prove the existence of Syriac-speakers in the period after Chalcedon, more than 150 years later.[53] His second piece of evidence comes from the *Life*

---

[49] The distribution of the Syrian dioceses between Chalcedonians and Monophysites is analysed by Honigmann, *Évêques et évêchés*.

[50] e.g. E. L. Woodward, *Christianity and Nationalism in the Later Roman Empire* (London, 1916); elaborated by J. Maspero, *Histoire des patriarches d'Alexandrie* (Paris, 1923); E. R. Hardy, *Christian Egypt* (New York, 1952).

[51] Among the challenges to the 'nationalist' thesis are A. H. M. Jones, 'Were Ancient Heresies National or Social Movements in Disguise?', *J. Th. S.* NS 10 (1950), 280–98; P. Rousseau, *Pachomius* (Berkeley, Calif., 1985).

[52] Jones, 'Were the Heresies?', 280–98.

[53] Jones, 'Were the Heresies?', 291, with reference to Eusebius, *Mart. P.* 1. 1, SC 122.

of Porphyry, where reference is made to a Syriac group in Gaza. But Gaza is in the south-west of Palestine, an area where Egyptian influence was particularly strong and Monophysitism well established.[54] Neither passage supports the contention that there was a significant Syriac-speaking population in the church in Palestine during the period following the Council of Chalcedon.

Such evidence as there is points in the opposite direction. It seems that there was a steady decline in the use of Syriac in the church in Palestine. During her visit to Jerusalem at the end of the fourth century, Egeria listened to the catachesis of the Bishop of Jerusalem. He spoke in Greek but attendant clergy translated his words into Syriac and Latin for the benefit of those who did not understand Greek.[55] Gabrielius, the superior of the Church of St Stephen who died in 492, spoke and wrote in the same three languages, an achievement sufficiently remarkable to be noted by Cyril.[56] But by the start of the sixth century, Sabas and Theodosius were making no provision for Syriac-speakers in the liturgical practice in their monasteries, even though Armenian and Bessan were used.[57] Some time after the death of Sabas the custom became established that no Syrian should be allowed to be the superior in the Sabaite monasteries.[58] At the time when support for Chalcedon was growing in Palestine, there was a simultaneous decline in the use of Syriac and the influence of the Syriac community.

In contrast to the lack of influence of Syriac-speakers in the monasteries, there were two national groupings which were well represented in the monasteries. Both made a distinctive contribution to the continuing debate.

The Bessans, who originated from Thrace, were present in the desert in significant numbers. In addition to the Bessan members of the community of Theodosius, there was a national Bessan centre at a monastery near the Jordan, probably in the region of Calamon.[59] A party of Bessans came to Jerusalem to offer support to the beleaguered monks of the Great Laura when they were suffering from the attacks of the Origenists. Their vigorous intervention is said by Cyril to have ended

---

[54] Jones cites *V. Porph.* 66–8, ed. Kugener 53. 23–55. 22. For Christianity in Gaza, see G. Downey, *Gaza in the Early Sixth Century* (Norman, Okla., 1963), 140–59.

[55] *Itin. Aeth.* 47. 1–4, SC 296 (Paris, 1982), 314.

[56] *Kyrillos*, 56. 15–16.

[57] Theodore of Petra, *V. Thds.* 45. 5–18.

[58] See E. Kurtz, 'Review of A. Dmitrijevskij, *Die Klosterregeln des hl. Sabas* (Kiev, 1890)', *By. Z.* 3 (1894), 167–70.

[59] *Prat.* 157, PG 87/3. 3025B–C.

the violence directed against the Sabaites in the streets of Jerusalem.[60] They are presented as firm allies of Sabas, an association presumably created by their conduct in the Monophysite controversy as well as that over Origenism.

The Armenians, by contrast, tended towards Monophysitism. Their presence in the Great Laura led to the introduction of the Monophysite addition to the Trisagion of the words 'who was crucified for us'.[61] The use of this form of the hymn, which had been introduced into Syria by Patriarch Peter the Fuller of Antioch, had become customary in circles opposed to Chalcedon and had developed into a badge of theological partisanship. As Stein commented, when inserted into the liturgy it 'transformait chaque service divine en manifestation du parti mono-physite et par là donnait constamment occasion aux combats les plus acharnés'.[62] Such a deviation from tradition was quickly suppressed by Sabas, who demanded that the hymn should be sung in Greek to ensure adherence to ancient tradition.[63]

Although the formula 'who was crucified for us' did not enter into liturgical use in Armenia until the mid-sixth century, the Armenian Church had come under the influence of Cyrillian Christology.[64] Among the significant documents in the history of the Armenian Church was a letter from Acacius of Melitene, Euthymius' old teacher, warning against the teachings of Nestorius and Theodore of Mopsuestia, and the Tome of Proclus.[65] There were no representatives from Armenia at the Council of Chalcedon and it was not recognized.

Although contact between Armenia and Palestine led to the intro-duction of Monophysite opinions into the desert, the long-term result was the export of Chalcedonianism to parts of Armenia. Patriarch John of Jerusalem was in close contact with Eastern Armenia and Georgia, and encouraged them to favour the doctrinal statements of Chalcedon.[66]

The close connection between nationalism and Monophysitism has rightly been called into quesiton. However the Monophysite churches developed by building strong regional allegiances, so that they became the national church in clearly defined areas. The peculiarly international

---

[60] *Kyrillos*, 193. 24–194. 12.

[61] Ibid. 118. 1–4. For Trisagion, see Introduction.

[62] E. Stein, *Histoire du Bas-Empire*, i (Bruges, 1959), 355.

[63] *Kyrillos*, 118. 4–5.

[64] See V. Inglisian, 'Chalkedon und die armenische Kirche', in A. Grillmeier and H. Bacht (eds.), *Das Konzil von Chalkedon* (Würzburg, 1951–4), ii. 361–417, 372.

[65] Inglisian, 'Die armenische Kirche', 362; Frend, *Rise*, 311–12.

[66] Inglisian, 'Die armenische Kirche', 373.

composition of the Palestinian monks influenced the course of the conflict in two ways. First, it ensured that the liturgical practices and doctrinal convictions of the nations of origin of the monks would be imported into the desert. Second, the variety of nationalities represented ensured that no one set of practices would prevail. To these general points should be added that the two groups most strongly associated with Monophysitism, the Egyptians and the Syrians, were poorly represented in the monasteries.

A third factor which prevented the emergence of a Palestinian Monophysite church was the presence of Jerusalem. The essential relationship of Jerusalem with the desert monasteries has been discussed above.[67] The whole purpose of being a monk in Palestine was to live in contact with the Holy Places, where the power of God was encountered in physical form. To be true to this central motivation for their monastic vocation the monks, whether Chalcedonian or Monophysite, needed to be a member of the church which worshipped at the Holy Places, and this meant that they needed to be in communion with the Patriarch.

So orthodoxy in Palestine referred to a relationship with the Holy Places and thus to the Patriarch. To call somebody orthodox is to regard him as a member of the true Church rather than to approve his theological opinions. When describing Euthymius' opponents after the Council of Chalcedon, Cyril chooses the term Aposchist (ἀποσχισταί).[68] This means 'cut off from' and points to what is most important to Cyril about their rebellion; not that they held mistaken views but that they were not in communion with the Patriarch. When he describes the joyful scene when the rebels return to the fold of the Church, he makes no reference to accepting a new doctrinal stance. 'Reassured, all entered unanimously into the Holy City, resolved on unity with the Holy Church. The Archbishop welcomed them and ordered lights to be placed in the Church of the Holy Resurrection, and celebrated a public festival with the whole crowd of monks and citizens and there was great gaiety in the streets of Jersulem for the joy of the union.'[69] The stories of John Moschus present a similar approach. They include the experience of a noble lady Cosmiana who finds herself unable to enter the sanctuary of the Church of the Resurrection to venerate the tomb of Christ. She realizes this is because she is a Monophysite and asks the deacon to

---

[67] See above, Ch. 4.
[68] *Kyrillos*, 47. 7; 62. 18; 63. 21; 66. 19. See also 115. 11; 123. 6; 154. 26; 176. 9; 219. 13; 241. 16.
[69] Ibid. 67. 7–13.

bring the chalice. After she had received the Chalcedonian communion
she is able to venerate the Holy Places. Sometimes the reconciled heretic
was required to renounce his error, as in the case of the two Nestorians
who had occupied Eudocia's Tower, but the act of communion remained
the significant act in their regained orthodoxy.[70]

The Monophysites of Palestine recognized the importance of communion with the Holy Places. After Juvenal transferred his support
away from the Monophysites at Chalcedon, the monks quickly consecrated their fellow-monk Theodosius as Patriarch, so that they had
control over the Holy Places. This occupation was short-lived since
Juvenal returned in 453 and then Chalcedonians presided over the
shrines of Jerusalem. By the end of the fifth century the hierarchy began
to act against the Monophysites who were forced to make alternative
responses to the problem of access to the Holy Places.

Sometimes Monophysites managed to share shrines with Chalcedonians. From the shrine of Menas near Alexandria comes an example
of Monophysites taking the communion of the Chalcedonians to their
members outside the church.[71] This makeshift solution indicates the
kind of approach which often prevailed in the region. Another possibility
was the setting up of an alternative sanctuary. At this time devotion to
the Mother of God began on Mount Zion, in addition to that offered
at the Tomb of Mary at Gethsemane. This probably took place at the
initiative of Chalcedonians when Monophysites occupied Gethsemane.[72]
An extreme response was the prohibition of pilgrimage to Jerusalem
made by the Armenian Council of Dvin in 536.[73]

The intractable existence of the Holy Places in Jerusalem ruled out
the option followed in Monophysite areas of establishing a separate
hierarchy. The bishops consecrated in Syria by Jacob Bar Addai were
often monks who continued to reside in monasteries near to their titular
sees. Michael the Syrian tells us, for example, that no Jacobite Patriarch
of Antioch entered the patriarchal city between 518 and 721.[74] A
Patriarch of Jerusalem who did not preside at the liturgy in the Church
of the Resurrection would have had little credibility among either
Monophysites or Chalcedonians as a leader of the Church.

---

[70] *Prat.* 48, PG 87/3, 2904A–B; *Kyrillos*, 128. 14–15.

[71] *Miracles of Cosmas and Damian*, 12. 17; 36. 15.

[72] M. van Esbroeck, 'Les Textes litteraires sur l'Assomption avant le Xe siècle', in *Les actes apocryphes des pères* (Geneva, 1987), 277–82.

[73] P. Maraval, *Lieux saints et pèlerinage d'orient* (Paris, 1985), 75.

[74] Michael the Syrian, *HE* 2, cited in Honigmann, *Évêques et évêchés*, 173.

These three facts of church life—the geography of the desert, the internationalism of the community, and the devotion to the Holy Places—were unique to Palestine and had a decisive influence on the course of the controversy. The claim that they are significant has an implication at first sight surprising. None of them relate to doctrinal conviction and their selection could suggest that the controversy over Monophyitism was not a debate about the nature of orthodoxy and heresy but a stage in the historical evolution of the Church, universal in theory but fragmented in practice.

AN INTERPOLATION ABOUT DOCTRINE

The view that the doctrinal differences were of little significance has sometimes been expressed. The basis of the religious policy of successive emperors was that there was no fundamental disagreement between the two sides, but merely 'matters where you have doubts' which could be resolved with a little goodwill by those concerned.[75] Evagrius Scholasticus shared in this assessment of the situation when he made his irritated statement that the fuss was about one little letter, whether Christ was 'en' (in) or 'ek' (from) two natures.[76] This view is also held by the modern successors of the protagonists who hope for reunion between the churches. Bishop Samuel of the Coptic Church, for example, wrote recently that 'there is no doctrinal division between the Chalcedonian and non-Chalcedonian Churches'.[77]

These mediators might point to the tendency to express theological loyalties through the repetition of slogans rather than through informed debate as a sign that most people did not understand the theological issues involved. The Monophysite version of the Trisagion, used first by Peter the Fuller in Antioch, is a well-known example of a theological formula which developed from being a statement about Christology into being the badge of a party. The cry of Theodosius the archimandrite of the 'four councils like the four gospels' was also a rallying cry for supporters of Chalcedon in Palestine and was sufficiently memorable to

[75] Innocent of Maronea, a city in the province of Rhodope in Thrace, wrote of *quibus ambigitis*, or 'matters where you have doubts', when he described the conference between Chalcedonians and Monophysites in 532. See *ACO* 4. 2, p. 170. 13.

[76] See Frend, *Rise*, *passim*; J. Meyendorff, *Christ in Eastern Christian Thought* (New York, 1975), 13–46.

[77] See M. Fouyas, *The Person of Jesus Christ* (Addis Ababa, 1970), 229.

have been passed down to Cyril who included it in his account.[78] These formulas show theology being used to define a party rather than to articulate a faith. They were war-cries, rather than signs of theological awareness.

Those who shouted out these sentences in the liturgy, the council chamber, or on the streets might not have been aware of the debates being carried out between the bishops in Constantinople or the thought of the theologians expressed in their preaching and correspondence. But they are none the less signs of deeply held convictions about the Christian faith. Some of these preoccupations of popular devotion are clear from the accounts. For example, there are the surprising and often expressed denials of Nestorianism. At the height of the Origenist crisis, Abbot Gelasius of the Great Laura went to Constantinople to try to gain the Emperor's support. His parting words to the community warned them of the dangers of Nestorianism: 'I beg you not to let settle with you any adherent of Theodore of Mopsuestia who was a heretic.'[79] This warning did not arise out of any realistic threat posed by dyophysite Christology but was a response to the popular fear of losing the presence of the divine Son of God from the experience of the Church. Behind the opposition to Chalcedon lay the anxiety that the bishops were declaring that God was no longer the subject of the actions of Christ and so somehow the presence of the holy would evaporate from their churches, leaving a human figure at the centre who would not have the power to bring salvation. Supporters of Chalcedon, such as Gelasius, had to attack Nestorians as a proof to the people that they upheld the historic Christian faith.[80] A similar motivation lay behind the passages in many Monophysite writers which spoke of Christ's human nature in moving and expressive terms. They were responding to another concern of popular faith—that human experience was shared by the incarnate Son of God.[81] The writings of theologians may come from a different milieu than that of the faith of the villages and monasteries, but they give expression to deeply rooted convictions of popular Christianity.

Although the conflict between the different religious groups was carried out in the arena of the society of the time and so was influenced by many geographical, social, and political factors, it remained a conflict

---

[78] *Kyrillos*, 152. 4–5.

[79] Ibid. 194. 19–21.

[80] The anger directed against Nestorius for his attack on the use of the title 'Theotokos' for the Virgin Mary is a sign of the same fear.

[81] Frend, *Rise*, 138.

which concerned the beliefs of the Church and so evoked deep commitments of faith. People were ready to die for what they believed.

ORIGENISM AND INTELLECTUAL STUDY

During the lifetime of Sabas another group of heretics emerged, challenging the orthodoxy of the saint. These were the Origenists. In contrast to the threat posed by the Monophysites which was diffused throughout the East and was, by the start of the sixth century, experienced by Palestinians as an aggressor from outside, the Origenists attacked from within. They came to form a community within the community, challenging the leadership of Sabas and his successors.

Origen had always provoked hostility as well as support. His bishop Demetrius of Alexandria deposed him from the priesthood and caused him to leave Alexandria. Later, in the fourth century, opposition flared with attacks on his teachings from Epiphanius of Salamis and Jerome, and with persecution by Theopilus of Alexandria against the monks who followed his teachings. Alongside these opponents, others were disciples and built on his teaching to produce a developing theological tradition. So by the time of the Council of Constantinople in 553, the name of Origen was indissolubly linked with his interpreters, Didymus and Evagrius of Pontus.[82]

The controversial potential of Origen's ideas is shown by a question addressed to the monks of Gaza, Barsanuphius and John. The questioner has happened upon writings of Origen, Didymus, and Evagrius. In them he has read some of Origen's metaphysical ideas—that souls were created before bodies, that angels and devils were alike pure spirits, some of whom had fallen away from God, and that all will recover their original purity in the final restoration. He is puzzled because these teachings are not encountered in biblical tradition. Barsanuphius' reply is clear and unequivocal. These teachings are harmful to the monk and must be avoided. The other old man, John, does admit, however, that some parts of Evagrius' work can be read with profit.[83]

The passage of the *Questions and Answers* comes from a monastic environment close to the communities of Sabas both in distance and time.

---

[82] Among the many books on the life and writing of Origen is H. Crouzel, *Origen* (Edinburgh, 1989).

[83] Varsanuphius and John, *Questions and Answers*, Letter 60, ed. Regnault, 391–4.

It shows both the availability of Origenist texts and their controversial potential. This potential developed a few years later in the Judaean desert into open and violent conflict which resulted eventually in the anathematization of the Origenists at the Council of Constantinople. This bitter episode in the long history of debate over the nature of the teaching of Origen divided the monasteries of Jerusalem at the time when Cyril was writing. It took place as a response to a specific set of conditions in the monasteries; it grew under the leadership of two influential personalities; it developed a distinctive set of beliefs. These three different themes help to explain the sudden emergence of Origenism from being a subject of debate among monks into an ecclesiastical and even political crisis.

The Origenists who were condemned at Constantinople in 553 emerged from the monasteries of the Judaean desert. The distinctiveness of this environment had impeded the emergence of a Monophysite movement, but nourished and nurtured Origenism. Cyril describes how the movement emerged from within Sabas' Great Laura and how it grew and eventually fell. From his account, it can be seen that the roots of the problem lay in Sabas' style of leadership and in certain weaknesses within his communities.

Sabas' great achievement was the founding of monasteries.[84] A part of the foundation process was always the appointment of leaders, and the list of those who were the superiors of the monastery form a normal conclusion to the description of the foundation. So, at Castellion, Sabas 'appointed an old anchorite Paul, with his disciple Theodore, as steward (διοικητὴν) of the place'. After Paul's death, Theodore succeeded him, followed by his brother Sergius, and his uncle Paul, both of whom had come from Melitene.[85] The accounts of other foundations end on a similar note.[86]

The importance of wise appointments to positions of responsibility is shown by the emphasis given in the more developed organization of the Pachomian communities. The monasteries were divided into groups under the direction of 'housemasters and seconds' (οἰκιάκους καὶ δευτέρους).[87] The elaborate authority structure is shown by the provision

---

[84] *Kyrillos*, 158. 12–159. 3; and see above Ch. 7.
[85] *Kyrillos*, 112. 21–5. Here authority was located in a family group, who no doubt encouraged Armenian traditions.
[86] e.g. ibid. 126. 20–127. 3; 128. 16–22; 130. 19–23.
[87] *V. Pach. G1* 54, trans. Athanassakis, 80. 7–8. But the Bohairic parallel omits reference to stewards, perhaps reflecting older practice, *V. Pach. Bo1.* 49.

made for the monastery of Phbow, where Pachomius 'appointed a steward with some seconds to minister to the brothers, as well as housemasters with seconds according to the rules of the monastery at Tabennisi'.[88] The conclusion of P. Rousseau applies also to Palestine: 'Colonisation was more in evidence than legislation; what mattered most was the appointment of the right kind of leader, rather than the publication of the right kind of rule.'[89]

Cyril attributes the introduction of Origenism into the New Laura to bad leadership. Nonnus and three companions who 'secretly held the dogmas of Origen' were admitted into the laura by the 'simple' Paul who had not been aware of their true allegiance.[90] His successor, Agapetus, arranged for the Origenists' expulsion after discussion with Patriarch Elias, but after Agapetus' death Nonnus and his companions persuaded the new superior, Mamas, to admit them once again.[91] They kept their views to themselves during the lifetime of Sabas, but, after he died, they circulated their opinions around the other monasteries of the desert. They found the most receptive audiences in the monasteries of Martyrius and Firminus, which were also suffering from weak leadership after the deaths of vigorous superiors.[92]

A weak leader gave an opportunity to the Origenists, but the reasons for the spread of Origenism, once established, lay within the monastic society itself. The importance of geography in encouraging a scattered and fragmented style of monastic life has been noted above in the context of the Monophysite conflict. It is equally significant for the growth of Origenism. But to it should be added another feature of desert life: this was the problem of intellectual study.

The early monks were men of action who saw no need for intellectual study. The force which drove them into the desert was the determination to struggle against evil and to prepare themselves for the coming Kingdom of God. The eschatological dimension of monasticism sharpened their commitment to a life of struggle which would purify the flesh. 'La spiritualité est une science pratique. Il faut ajouter: la pratique a precedé la science, au sens technique du mot.'[93] As well as sharing

---

[88] *V. Pach. Bo1.* 60.

[89] P. Rousseau, *Pachomius* (Berkeley, Calif., 1985), 73.

[90] *Kyrillos*, 124. 20–9. Paul's unsuitability for the post of superior was demonstrated by his flight to Arabia only six months after his appointment.

[91] Sozomen, *HE* 6. 28, GCS 277. 7.

[92] *Kyrillos*, 188. 19–22.

[93] I. Hausherr, 'Les Grands Courants de la spiritualité orientale', *Or. Chr. P.* 1 (1935), 114–38, 116.

the peasant's preference for hard work, the monks feared that too much study—or in some cases any study—would lead to the introduction of heretical opinions and the loss of the necessary humility.[94] Of course some monks were highly educated. Hilarion, for example, was said by Jerome to have been famous for his knowledge of Scripture and his grasp of academic studies, although this passage may reflect Jerome's image of himself as the ideal monk rather than the actual abilities of Hilarion.[95] But knowledge tended to be regarded as the result of a divine charism rather than hard work and study. Abba Or had, according to Sozomen, the gift of memory so that 'everything he received with his mind was never afterwards forgotten', and while Cyril of Alexandria was studying the Bible as a monk 'it was enough for him to read a book once for him to know it by heart until at the end of his stay in the desert he knew all the canonical books by memory'.[96] The underlying respect for hard work is shown by the response of Arsenius to the visitor who asked him why he, an educated man, consulted a peasant about his thoughts. 'I have indeed been taught Greek and Latin, but I do not know even the alphabet of this peasant.'[97]

The need for intellectual study grew. First, the communities become more formal as the circles of disciples gathered around a noted ascetic developed into regulated monasteries. Then the initial impetus and insight provided by the founder became diluted and dissolved. Instead of the close contact with the holy man, monks were formed by discussion and regulated by the guidance found in written texts. It has been suggested that the core of the *Life of Pachomius* was committed to writing during the period of Theodore's leadership when memory of the founder was becoming faint. Theodore said to the brothers: 'Pay attention to the words I am speaking to you, because a time is coming when you will not be able to find anyone to recount them to you.'[98] The need of the monasteries for intellectual study is shown by the stories of previously unlearned monks who suddenly became able

[94] For fear of heresy, see I. Hausherr, *Penthos* (Kalamazoo, Mich., 1982), 108–18.

[95] Jerome, *Vita Hilarionis*, 2, in W. A. Oldfather, *Studies in the Text Tradition of St Jerome's Vitae Patrum* (Urbana, Ill., 1943), 313.

[96] Sozomen, *HE* 6. 28, GCS 277. 7; Severus of Ashmunein, *History of the Patriarchs of the Coptic Church of Alexandria*, PO 1. 427–8, cited by F.-M. Abel, 'Saint Cyrille d'Alexandrie dans ses rapports avec la Palestine, in *Kyrilliana* (Cairo, 1947), 203–30, 211–12.

[97] *Apoph. Patr.* Arsenius, 5, PG 65. 89A.

[98] *V. Pach. Bo1.* 196. See also A. Veilleux, *Pachomian Koinonia*, i (Kalamazoo, Mich., 1980), 243, 293.

to read and recite the Scriptures when they were called to lead monasteries.[99]

The Lives of Pachomius provide an illustration of the process whereby study became an important cohesive and formative element in the life of the community. Pachomius sought to free new monks from physical labour so that they could concentrate on learning not only the Psalter but other parts of the Bible as well. He himself worked hard to understand and assimilate the teachings of the Bible and to pass these on to his monks.[100] He arranged for regular periods of instruction. The housemaster was required to give three lessons each week, one on Saturday and two on Sunday, and the second provided instruction on the two fast days.[101] The Life gives a delightful picture of the brothers sitting together under a palm tree at the end of the day's work discussing the meaning of passages of Scripture.[102]

Sabas unfortunately did not share Pachomius' recognition of the importance of study. His own education had taken place entirely within the monastery of Flavianae, which he entered at the age of eight.[103] Here he learnt the Psalter and the rest of the coenobitic rule (τὴν λοιπὴν τοῦ κοινοβιακοῦ κανόνος κατάστασιν).[104] He arranged for the new members of his own monasteries to have similar training. The purpose of the period of noviciate was that 'they should learn the psalter and the canon of psalmody and be educated in monastic discipline'.[105] There is no suggestion here or anywhere else in the Life that Sabas saw any need for knowledge of the whole Bible and certainly not of later theological writing. The monks needed to know enough of the Bible to participate in the week-end worship of the Laura, but no more.

Protest against Sabas' intolerance of intellectual study was immediate, bitter, and persistent. The episode which Cyril places first after the foundation of the Great Laura is the deputation of monks, described as having a 'fleshly judgment' to the Patriarch (τινὲς σαρκικοὶ τῷ φρονήματι). They complained that Sabas was 'unfit to govern the place

---

[99] See Rousseau, *Ascetics, Authority, and the Church* (Oxford, 1978), 68–76.

[100] *V. Pach. G1* 9; 24, trans. Athanassakis, 14. 1–11; 38. 3–4.

[101] *V. Pach. G1* 28, trans. Athanassakis, 34–6.

[102] On the tradition of study in the Pachomian houses, see Rousseau, *Pachomius*, 85–6; P. Ladeuze, *Étude sur le cénobitisme pakhomien pendant le IVe siècle et la première moitié du Ve siècle* (Louvain, 1898; new edn. Frankfurt, 1961), 290–4.

[103] Sabas travelled to Jerusalem when he was 18, having spent ten years in the monastery. See *Kyrillos*, 90. 6, 19.

[104] Ibid. 88. 1.

[105] Ibid. 113. 9–10. Cf. 113. 16–20.

because of his great rusticity' (διὰ τὴν πολλὴν ἀγροικότητα).[106] This grievance seems to have been simmering for a while because the delegation arrived only after Sallustius had been consecrated Patriarch. They presumably hoped that he would be more sympathetic to their cause than his predecessor Martyrius, who had been a member of Euthymius' community.[107] But the response of the new Patriarch was to confirm Sabas' authority by insisting that he was ordained as a priest.[108]

The opposition was not silenced. Twenty years later, when the Church of the Mother of God was dedicated in 501, their number had increased to forty and Sabas became so exasperated that he left the monastery.[109] After a while he returned only to discover that his opponents now numbered sixty, so he went away again and did not come back until Patriarch Elias insisted that he did so and wrote a firm letter confirming his position as superior.[110] The problem was only resolved when the dissidents, after a display of violence, left the Great Laura and, after travelling south, settled in some cells not far from the deserted monastery of Romanus near Thekoa.[111]

At this stage it seems that the dispute was between monks who had a taste for intellectual study and a superior who had little sympathy for this desire. The ideas of Origenism were circulated in the desert and were found to offer an attractive intellectual framework for monasticism. They were, presumably, known by the 'fleshly' monks but had not, at this stage, become the set of beliefs which distinguished the group. The availability of the writings of Origen and his disciples ensured that the intellectual monks became Origenists, and the lack of sympathy shown by Sabas to their aspirations ensured that they became polarized and identifiable.

An identifiable Origenist group was discovered in the New Laura by Agapetus. There were four monks who held 'the myths concerning preexistence related by Origen, Evagrius and Didymus', two of whom were Nonnus and Leontius of Byzantium.[112] Although briefly expelled from the New Laura, they were able slowly to extend their influence

---

[106] *Kyrillos*, 103. 25–6.
[107] Ibid. 51. 3–21.
[108] Ibid. 104. 13–18.
[109] Ibid. 117. 18–19; 118. 24–30.
[110] Ibid. 120. 13–15; 122. 19–20.
[111] Ibid. 122. 21–123. 8. Y. Hirschfeld discovered a coenobium 3 km. to the west of the New Laura, which he suggests is the monastery of Romanus (unpublished).
[112] Ibid. 124. 25; 176. 12–13.

until, after the death of Sabas, they gained the support of 'all the more intellectual monks of the New Laura' (πάντας τοὺς ἐν τῇ Νέᾳ Λαύρᾳ λογιωτέρους).[113] They even managed to infiltrate the Great Laura.[114] Then the leader of the Origenists in the New Laura, Theodore Askidas, sailed to Constantinople with Domitian, the superior of the monastery of Martyrius. There he joined forces with Leontius of Byzantium and, with the help of the court favourite Papas Eusebius, gained access to the Emperor.[115]

Although tension between 'simple' and 'intellectual' monks was often present in monastic society, it was more pronounced in the monasteries of Sabas. The roots of the later Origenist party lay within these tensions.

ORIGENISM AND THE STRUGGLE FOR POWER

From the disgruntled group of frustrated intellectuals emerged the well-organized Origenist group. They formed a community within the community, challenging and opposing the body of monks loyal to Sabas.

It was a struggle for power. The first manifestation of the tension was the delegation of fleshly monks seeking to dislodge Sabas from the leadership of the community, a request which was unsuccessful and which was renewed after several years.[116] In the later stages, the arena of the struggle was broadened and the Origenists sought to influence the appointments of bishops, abbots, and even the patriarch.[117] The fortunes of the Origenists fluctuated in response to the influence of their leaders. The influence of the Origenist leaders, in turn, was only able to increase as that of the Sabaites declined. It followed the shifting balances of power within the monasteries.

During Sabas' lifetime, there was no doubt where it lay. By the popular acclaim of the monks, confirmed by patriarchal appointment, Sabas and Theodosius were recognized as the holders of a joint authority over the monasteries dependent on the Holy City.[118] Their position was based on their close co-operation with the Patriarch and their influence in the imperial court.[119]

---

[113] Ibid. 188. 18–19.
[114] Ibid. 188. 23.
[115] Ibid. 188. 24–189. 3.
[116] Ibid. 103. 16–104. 18; 120. 13–122. 11.
[117] Ibid. 195. 16–17; 198. 10–12.
[118] Ibid. 115. 16–26.
[119] These themes occur throughout the Lives of Cyril and Theodore of Petra's *Life of Theodosius*.

The powerful partnership dissolved when the two leaders died within three years of each other—Theodosius in 529 and Sabas in 532. Sophronius, who became superior of Theodosius' monastery, proved to be a worthy successor. He increased the monastery buildings fourfold, built a new church, tripled the size of the community, and ensured a sufficient annual revenue.[120] But Sabas' successor, Melitas, was less effective. Cyril tells us that he was unable to preserve the unity of the monastery but gives little detail about his failings.[121]

The custom of appointing two archimandrites, one for the coenobia and one for the laurae, was discontinued. Festugière, in his list of the archimandrites of Palestine, includes the names of Sophronius and Gelasius.[122] The inclusion is due to the request of Patriarch Peter that they should direct a *libellus* against Origen to the Emperor, but his choice of them rested not on their status as archimandrites but on the fact that they were not members of the Origenist party.[123] The signature lists of the 536 Synod show a more uncertain situation. Domitian of the Monastery of Martyrius signed himself: πρεσβύτερος καὶ ἀρχιμανδρίτης μονῆς τοῦ μακαρίου Μαρτυρίου; a certain Cyriac was πρεσβύτερος καὶ ἀρχιμανδρίτης λαύρας τῶν Πυργίων; Hesychius was also present representing Sophronius πρεοβυτέρου καὶ ἀρχιμανδρίτου τῆς αὐτῆς μονῆς (of Theodosius).[124] The solidarity of the desert had been fragmented and no one delegate had the authority to speak for the monks. The title of archimandrite was no longer the designation of a recognized leader but was being used in the more general sense of a superior. This led to a reduction in the power of monastic superiors. A sign of this was the appropriation by the Patriarch of money earmarked by Sabas for the building of a fort to protect the monasteries. He distributed it directly to the monasteries, presumably in an attempt to build up his own support.[125]

Into the power vacuum left by the demise of the two archimandrites stepped the two leaders of the Origenists—Nonnus and Leontius of Byzantium. These guided the Origenists into their position of prominence. Nonnus was an organizer and was based in Jerusalem. Leontius settled in Constantinople and gained influence in the capital. From this

---

[120] *Kyrillos*, 240. 20–241. 3.
[121] Ibid. 188. 3–6, 13–15.
[122] *MO* pt. 2, iii. 149.
[123] *Kyrillos*, 191. 25–9. See *MO* pt. 2, iii. 122.
[124] *ACO* 3, p. 133.
[125] *Kyrillos*, 187. 28–188. 3.

double power-base, the Origenists developed into formidable opponents.

Nonnus is said by Cyril to have been responsible for the development of the opposition group from being 'fleshly' and motivated 'by a perverse devil' into the proponents of a distinctively Origenist theology.[126] He is given the credit for being the party organizer. He introduced Origenism into the New Laura, presumably since he was a natural teacher around whom dissident monks grouped themselves.[127] After the death of Sabas, it was the initiative of Nonnus which led to the consolidation and expansion of this group, which gained the support of other monasteries in the desert. From this power-base, the Origenists became a dominant force within the church of Jerusalem. The growth of the power of this group is described by Cyril. They tried to force Patriarch Peter to remove the name of their opponent Ephraem of Antioch from the diptychs, which led the Archbishop to seek the help of the Emperor in condemning Origenism, and for a while the streets of Jerusalem were an unsafe place for the monks of the Great Laura to venture.[128] The Origenists even managed to impose their own candidate as superior of the Great Laura, with the assistance of armed forces.[129]

The other important figure is Leontius of Byzantium. Leontius was a companion of Nonnus and entered the New Laura with him.[130] He accompanied Sabas on his delegation to the court of the Emperor Justinian and remained at Constantinople after his Origenist sympathies were discovered by Sabas who dismissed him.[131] In the capital, he represented the Origenists, gaining the confidence of the Emperor and the Papas Eusebius.[132] Through his influence, leading Origenists— Theodore Askidas of the New Laura and Domitian of the monastery of Martyrius—were appointed to important posts in the Church. Theodore

---

[126] They were σαρκικοὶ and ἔκ τινος σκαιοῦ δαίμονος: ibid. 103. 13; 18. 27.

[127] Ibid. 124. 27–125. 1.

[128] Ibid. 191. 20–5; 193. 19–21. M. van Esbroeck suggests that Peter sympathized with the Protoktist group of the Origenists, but his account does not take into account Cyril's portrayal of Peter as an associate of Sabas and a weak but consistent opponent of Origenism, especially in his appeal to the Emperor against the Origenists which resulted in Justinian's condemnation of Origenism in 543. Van Esbroeck does not offer alternative evidence to Cyril's account, and this part of his argument is not convincing. Cf. M. van Esbroeck, 'L'Homélie de Pierre de Jérusalem et la fin de l'origénisme palestinien en 551', *Or. Chr. P.* 51 (1985), 33–59, esp. 55–7 with *Kyrillos*, 191. 20–192. 3, and also with 173 4–9; 182. 7–12; 184. 4–6; 188. 2–3 (where there is no suggestion that Peter favoured Origenist monasteries).

[129] *Kyrillos*, 195. 16–20.   [130] Ibid. 125. 17–18.

[131] Ibid. 176. 10–15.   [132] Ibid. 189. 1–3; 191. 1–11.

became Metropolitan of Caesarea in Cappadocia and Domitian became Metropolitan of Ancyra.[133] He also participated in the Disputations between Chalcedonians and Monophysites held in Constantinople in 532 and was present at five of the sittings of the 536 Synod of Constantinople.[134] His influence at court ensured that the Origenists in Palestine had strong support from the imperial capital.

Leontius was also a prolific author. Writing under the title Leontius the Hermit, he produced a number of theological and philosophical treatises. These include *Tres Libri contra Nestorianos et Eutychianos*; *Solutio Argumentorum a Severo Objectorum*; *Capita Triginta contra Severum*, and *Adversus Fraudes Apollinistarum*.[135] The importance and influence of these works not only indicate the authority of the Origenist champion in the capital, and so the difficulties the Sabaites were labouring against, but also the creative intellectual environment provided by Origenist groups within the monasteries. Reading the works of Leontius, we cannot but regret the inability of Sabas to integrate a writer of Leontius' stature into his monastic society.

The period of Origenist power was short-lived. Leontius died about the time when Justinian published his Edict against Origen, in 543. The removal of their advocate at court, however, did not prevent the Origenists in Jerusalem continuing to dominate the Church, and four years later an Origenist became superior of the Great Laura.[136] But at this moment of triumph, Nonnus also died. This was more devastating and was, according to Cyril, a sign given by the providence of God.[137] Without his organizing abilities, the party fragmented into opposing factions. Although Nonnus had held no recognized post within the monasteries or the Church and is not given an ecclesiastical title, he was the recognized leader of the party. With his presence removed, the threat of the Origenists disintegrated.

So deaths were significant in the Origenist crisis. Nonnus and Leontius were able to take advantage of the power vacuum left by the deaths of

---

[133] *Kyrillos*, 188. 24–189. 7.

[134] *ACO* 3, pp. 37. 1; 49. 9–11; 50. 30; 145. 34. *ACO* 4. 2, p. 170. 5.

[135] Two other works attributed to a Leontius are *Contra Monophysitas* and *Contra Nestorianos*. They are generally agreed to have been written by another Leontius 'of Jerusalem'. See M. Richard, 'Léonce de Jerusalem et Léonce de Byzance', *MSR* 1 (1944), 35–88. But S. Rees, 'The Literary Activity of Lentius of Byzantium', *J. Th. S.* NS 19 (1968), 229–42, argues for the unity of the Leontian corpus. For a discussion of some of the literary and historical problems surrounding the figure of Leontius, see below, Excursus 2.

[136] *Kyrillos*, 95. 16–17.

[137] Ibid. 195. 25–196. 2.

Sabas and Theodosius, but their attempt lasted only as long as they lived. After they died the alliance between the Great Laura and the Patriarch was reforged with the support of the Emperor. The condemnation of Origenism at the Council of Constantinople and the installation of orthodox monks in the New Laura marked the end of the Origenist bid for power—and concludes Cyril's *Life of Sabas*.[138]

However, although the power-base of the Origenists disintegrated, the Sabaites did not recover their former influence. Sabas had extended his authority by founding new monasteries. After his death, there is no evidence of any new foundations in the high plateau region—the last being the monastery of Jeremias, founded in 531, the year before the saint's death.[139] Instead, new foundations were made in the Jordan valley near Jericho, and it was communities in this area which provided future archimandrites.[140] The focus of power was moving to the east.

THE THEOLOGY OF THE ORIGENISTS

Origen was a prolific writer. Works of biblical exegesis, apologetic, metaphysical speculation, trinitarian theology, and instruction in the spiritual life—all proceeded from his pen. A result of the variety is that the title of Origenism can be used to apply to many different groups and many theological opinions.

The title did not even necessarily imply the conscious acceptance of Origen's opinions. In the usage of the time, Origenism referred not so much to a dogmatic system as to a desire to have an intellectual basis for the ascetic life.[141] Because of the condemnation of Origen's theological views, for example at Alexandria in 400, the name 'Origenist' could be effectively used as an insult to vilify a monk or group of monks who used allegorical methods to expound the Bible. And they, in their turn, might riposte with the epithet 'anthropomorphite'.[142]

But within monastic circles, the writings of Origen exercised a continuing fascination, especially the cosmological ideas set out in the

---

[138] Ibid. 199. 16–200. 3.
[139] Ibid. 179. 23–5.
[140] See above Ch. 2.
[141] For this comment, and an assessment of Origenism, see L. Perrone, *La chiesa di Palestina e le controversie cristologiche* (Brescia, 1980), 204–12; also B. Daley, 'The Origenism of Leontius of Byzantium', *J. Th. S.* NS 27 (1976), 333–69, 362–9.
[142] A. Guillaumont, *Les 'Kephalaia Gnostica'* (Paris, 1962), 83.

First Principles. The themes of the pre-existence of souls, the ultimate destiny of the soul after death, and the nature of the felicity to be enjoyed hereafter provided a possible intellectual framework within which monastic life could be understood. But, although attractive, these ideas resulted in a deviation from the eschatological character of primitive monasticism. In place of the purification of the flesh in order to be ready for the kingdom of God, the Origenist tried to detach himself from the flesh so that his soul could be liberated from the body of sin; and in place of the vigilant labour of the early monks, the Origenist sought to attain the intellectual contemplation which would restore the mind to its original state.

Cyril reports the claims of Origenist monks that speculation about these matters, as permitted by Gregory of Nazianzus, is harmless. Gregory had written: 'In these matters, to find the truth is not without profit, to make a mistake is without danger.'[143] This can be assumed to have been the view of the 'intellectuals' of the New Laura. Their attitude is summed up by A. Guillaumont:

En réalité, il ne faut pas se représenter ces moines comme des hérétiques conscients, cherchant à tenir secrètes leurs opinions par l'effort seulement d'une vulgaire prudence. Leur gnosticisme était bien plutôt un esprit de libre recherche vis-à-vis de certaines questions qui ... restaient un objet d'investigation pour l'intelligence ... Cependant la liberté d'esprit l'audace intellectuale qu'ils estimaient légitimes chez le 'gnostique' étaient certainement associées en eux á un attachement réel à l'écriture, aux dogmes, à l'enseignement ecclésiastique traditionnel et à toutes les exigences d'un christianisme professés.[144]

This loose understanding of the nature of Origenism has been suggested as the background to the writing of Leontius of Byzantium to account for the absence of any clearly recognizable and heterodox Origenist teaching.[145]

Within this generally speculative milieu, Cyril describes the emergence of a self-consciously Origenist group with a clear set of heretical opinions. This development took place after the death of Sabas.[146] The nature of the teachings which they followed are suggested by the names given to the rival groups—the 'Protoktistoi', or Tetradites, and the 'Isochristoi'.[147] The content of the doctrines of some of the Origenists

---

[143] *Kyrillos*, 229. 24–31, referring to Gregory of Nazianzus in PG 36. 25.
[144] Guillaumont, *Les 'Kephalaia Gnostica'*, 161–2.
[145] Daley, 'Origenism of Leontius of Byzantium', 362–9.
[146] *Kyrillos*, 188. 15–24.
[147] Ibid. 197. 10–18.

is revealed in the summary of Origenist teaching given by Cyriac on the occasion of Cyril's visit to him.[148] Whether the reported interview repeats the words of Cyriac, or, as is indicated by the dependence of the text on the anathematisms of 553, whether it is an account constructed subsequently by Cyril, the form of Origenism attacked can be assumed to be that current in the later stages of the Origenist controversy.[149]

The studies of Diekamp and Guillaumont trace a development in Origenist thought between Justinian's 543 Edict against Origen and the 553 anathematisms issued by the Council of Constantinople. Their findings illuminate the course of the conflict in Palestine.

The 543 anathemas are preceded by twenty-four extracts from the writings of Origen, consisting mainly of ideas drawn from *On First Principles*. They refer to the Synodal Letter of the Egyptian Bishops in 400 and describe errors similar to those attacked earlier by Epiphanius. A difference between the 543 anathemas and the comments of Epiphanius is that the subordinationism of Origen is not mentioned in the later document. The anathemas describe how the *logikoi* originally formed a *henad* in union with the One and fell through the satiety of contemplation. The *logikoi* were given bodies with a nature appropriate to the extent of their fall. They also attack false views of the Resurrection.[150] These anathemas resemble previous attacks on Origenism and are directed at commonplaces of Origenist thought. The target had not altered significantly from that which Epiphanius and others discussed in the fourth and early fifth centuries. Its emphasis on the pre-existence of souls suggests that the name *Protoktistoi* could appropriately be given to it. A possible interpretation of the disintegration of the Origenists described by Cyril is that these more conservative elements separated from the more radical *Isochristoi* and joined forces with the orthodox of the Great Laura.[151]

---

[148] Ibid. 230. 2–22. This meeting is said to have taken place when Leontius was still alive (229. 20–1) but this is hardly possible. We have already noted that Leontius died soon after the 543 Edict against Origen (*Kyrillos*, 192. 20–2) and Cyril made this visit after he had entered the monastery of Euthymius in 544 (229. 7). The reference to Leontius should be discounted and the visit dated to some time after 544, when Cyril entered Euthymius' monastery, and 547, when Nonnus died (ibid. 229. 20–2). Probably it took place after the death of Gelasius, when the influence of Origenism was at its zenith.

[149] *MH* 78–83; Guillaumont, *Les 'Kephalaia Gnostica'*, 151.

[150] Guillaumont, *Les 'Kephalaia Gnostica'*, 140.

[151] *Kyrillos*, 197. 24–198. 6 The reason for the alternative name of Tetradites is unclear. A sect which fasted on Easter Day and was condemned by the Council in Trullo (692) was called by this name. It has been suggested that the Origenists had the same practices.

A noticeably different set of opinions was under attack at the 553 Council of Constantinople. Whereas the 543 anathemas referred only to the teachings of Origen, by 553 the names of Didymus and Evagrius were included.[152] The heretical opinions which are proscribed include the ideas that Christ was a *nous* who created the world and became incarnate, and who must be distinguished from the Word of God to which he was united. In the final resurrection or *apokatastasis*, the bodies of human beings will be destroyed, and the *logikoi*, with their spherical resurrection bodies, will be equal to Christ and will reign with him. The emphasis both in the anathemas and in Justinian's Letter to the Council is on the future of souls in the *apokatastasis* and their equality with Christ. These teachings are also encountered in statements of Theodore Ascidas to the 553 Council, in the critical comments of Cyriac, and in some passages of a Christmas homily of Patriarch Peter of Jerusalem, in which he attacks certain Origenist positions.[153] The views are not to be found in the writings of Origen, but can be demonstrated to be derived from Evagrius' *Kephalaia Gnostica*.[154] According to the Letter of Justinian, they are the opinions of 'certain monks of Jerusalem'.[155]

This group of monks are Cyril's *Isochristoi*. The name indicates an interest in the equality of souls with Christ in the Resurrection. The group was based at the New Laura, the traditional pace-setter in Origenist speculation and was led by Theodore Ascidas.[156] After the defection of the *Protoktistoi*, they maintained their opposition to the Sabaites. Their interest in the ideas of Evagrius' *Kephalaia Gnostica* was a new element in the history of Palestinian Origenism. Its contribution was short-lived. It was condemned at the Council of Constantinople and its adherents were driven from the New Laura.[157]

See *MO* pt. 2, iii. 127. A more likely explanation is that it was suspected that Origenist views on the Resurrection introduced a fourth element into the Trinity.

[152] *Kyrillos*, 199. 1–6. Cf. Evagrius, *HE* 4. 38, ed. Bidez and Parmentier, 189. 26–8. See also *Kyrillos*, 186. 26–33; 187. 11–12. F. Diekamp, *Die origenistischen Streitigkeiten* (Münster, 1899), 88–97, and Guillaumont, *Les 'Kephalaia Gnostica'*, 136–9.

[153] *Kyrillos*, 230. 2–17; Evagrius, *HE* 4. 38, ed. Bidez and Parmentier, 189. 26–9. For the anti-Origenist statements in Peter's Christmas homily, see van Esbroeck, 'L'Homélie de Pierre de Jérusalem', 52–5. See also Guillaumont, *Les 'Kephalaia Gnostica'*, 151.

[154] For verbal parallels between the anathemas and the *Kephalaia Gnostica*, see Guillaumont, *Les 'Kephalaia Gnostica'*, 156, 159.

[155] Diekamp, *Origenistischen Streitigkeiten*, 84.

[156] *Kyrillos*, 197. 16–198. 1.

[157] Doubts have sometimes been cast about the condemnation of Origen at the Council of Constantinople in view of the lack of reference in the Acts, with the intention of rehabilitating the memory of Origen. But it has been shown that the Council did condemn

Origenism in sixth-century Palestine arose because of divisions within the monasteries. The origin of the division was the increasing alienation of a group of monks of the Great Laura who valued their intellectual activity. After the death of Sabas, this group became more clearly defined as a result of the leadership given to it by Nonnus and Leontius, and the developing theological opinions based increasingly on the writings of Evagrius. The existence of these three factors—the division in the monasteries, the theological teachings, and the capable leadership—led to the crisis which culminated in the rejection of Origenism in 553.

THE COUNCIL OF CONSTANTINOPLE OF 553

Cyril of Scythopolis wrote his Lives in the aftermath of the Council of Constantinople, which was already, as he wrote, recognized as the Fifth Ecumenical Council. He was conscious of being part of a band of orthodox monks occupying the last bastion of heresy at the New Laura.[158] Within his narrative the Council is the final triumph and the resolution of the problem of heresy. Two issues were dealt with—the Three Chapters and Origenist theology.

For Palestinians, the priority was to resolve the power struggle between the Origenists and their opponents. The death of Nonnus in 547 weakened the party, but the Origenists still had a friend at court in the person of Theodore Askidas, Metropolitan of Caesarea Cappadocia. He helped the extreme *Isochristoi* to fill Palestinian bishoprics with their candidates until an Origenist, Macarius, was consecrated Patriarch of Jerusalem.[159] This election took place without the Emperor's confirmation, a tactical error by the Origenists which angered Justinian. Conon, superior of the Great Laura, quickly proposed an alternative candidate, Eustochius, from Egypt. Eustochius duly became Patriarch and returned to Jerusalem while Justinian convened the Council.[160]

A consequence of the final stages of the battle with the Origenists,

---

Origen (Diekamp, *Origenistischen Streitigkeiten*, 66, 138). A more recent assessment is B. Drewery, 'The Condemnation of Origen, Should it be Reversed?', in R. Hanson and H. Crouzel (eds.), *Origeniana Tertia: The Third International Colloquium for Origen Studies* (Rome, 1985), 271–7.

[158] *Kyrillos*, 199. 1–200. 4.
[159] Ibid. 197. 20–5; 198. 9–12.
[160] Ibid. 198. 12–22; Evagrius, *HE* 4. 37, ed. Bidez and Parmentier, 187.

when Eustochius was engaged in winkling out the last pockets of
Origenist resistance, was that he did not attend the Council. Cyril tells
us that he sent three bishops to represent him, along with Conon,
superior of the Great Laura; Eulogius, superior of the monastery of
Theodosius; Cyriac, of the laura of the Spring; and Pancratius, a
stylite.[161] The account of Evagrius contains no reference to bishops in
the Palestinian delegation and incorrectly substitutes the names of Rufus
for that of Eulogius.[162] However, the lists of the bishops present at the
Council include Palestinian bishops, but only two out of the 150 or so
episcopal delegates. These are Damian, Bishop of Sozusa, representing
Eustochius, and John, Bishop of Caesarea. They were present at all
sessions, but Damian did not sign the decree against the Three Chapters.[163] The presence lists suggest that the Palestinian delegation was
smaller than Cyril claims and as a result that the Palestinian church had
little involvement in the actual meetings of the Council.

The Council acted against two sets of doctrinal teaching. The
expressed reason for the summoning of the Council was to condemn
the Three Chapters, writings of Theodore of Mopsuestia, Theodoret of
Cyrrhus, and Ibas of Edessa. This course of action met with little
enthusiasm in Palestine. The Christological controversy had been
resolved when the Emperor Justin came to the throne in 518. In his
account, Cyril does not even include Theodoret and Ibas in the list of
theologians condemned by the Council.[164]

The bishops also condemned the teaching of Origen, Didymus and
Evagrius. Admirers of the theological achievement of Origen have
questioned whether this condemnation took place at the Council. The
only surviving version of the Acts of the Council omits the anathemas
and includes only a general reference to Origen at the end of a list of
the heretics, Arius, Eunomius, Macedonius, Apollinaris, Nestorius, and
Eutyches. The inappropriateness of listing Origen, who lived before any
of the others, at the end of an otherwise chronological list has aroused
the suspicion that his name was added by a later copyist.[165] So, his

---

[161] This list of monks shows that the two great monasteries of Sabas and Theodosius
were still significant. The Laura of the Spring is a small laura for 15–20 monks in the
wadi Kelt. Pancratius is the only stylite mentioned in the writing of Cyril; he is also
referred to in Evagrius, *HE* 4. 38, ed. Bidez and Parmentier, 188. 25.

[162] Ibid. 188.

[163] *ACO* 4. 1, pp. 3, 32, 39, 137, 225.

[164] *Kyrillos*, 199. 3–5.

[165] See Meyendorff, *Imperial Unity*, 235; Drewery, 'The Condemnation of Origen',
273–5.

defenders seek to establish, the honour of Origen is preserved since he was condemned not by an Ecumenical Council, but by an informal assembly of bishops.

However, the list of witnesses to the condemnation of Origen by the Council does not allow this conclusion. The only version of the Acts which has survived is a Latin translation which is concerned with the conflict between Pope Vigilius and the Emperor Justinian and the eastern bishops, and, from this perspective the Origenist controversy had little interest. F. Diekamp sets out several different accounts of the proceedings of the Council, and these show that Origenism was debated there. Diekamp's sources include not only the contemporary records of Evagrius, Cyril of Scythopolis, and Eulogius, Patriarch of Alexandria (580–607), but also later writers such as Sophronius of Jerusalem, the author of the *Chronicon Paschale*, George the Monk, and Anastasius of Sinai. To these he adds references at the Lateran Council of 649 and the Sixth Ecumenical Council at Constantinople in 680–1.[166] This collection of evidence leaves no room for doubt that the Fifth Ecumenical Council anathematized the teaching of Origen, as well as that of his followers Didymus and Evagrius.

The Fifth Ecumenical Council represented a stage in the task, unsuccessfully undertaken by all emperors from the time of Constantine, of bringing a diverse, multinational Church into unity. It was directed especially at moderate Monophysites who would, it was hoped, share in the condemnation of the Three Chapters and so be seduced into acceptance of a Chalcedonian faith shorn of suspicion of Nestorianism. It also sought to convince Chalcedonians, especially in the west, that this was a development which respected the integrity of Chalcedonian faith. Since the Palestinian church fell into neither category and since it was preoccupied with the damaging disruption caused by the Origenists, the Council seemed of little importance. But they supported its conclusions.[167]

---

[166] Diekamp, *Origenistischen Streitigkeiten*, 66–138. See esp. the Synodika of Sophronius of Jerusalem, in *ACO*, 2nd ser., 2, 470.

[167] The Council, and its failure to arrest the splintering of the Church, is discussed in J. Herrin, *The Formation of Christendom* (Oxford, 1987), esp. 90–127, 250–90; and Meyendorff, *Imperial Unity*, *passim*, esp. 230–50.

Fellow Workers with God

THE PURPOSE OF MIRACLE STORIES

One night a grave robber decided to steal a fine quality shroud from a recently buried corpse. Quietly he opened the grave and began to remove the shroud from the dead body. But suddenly the corpse returned to life and attacked the grave robber tearing out his eyes in punishment for desecrating the sanctity of the tomb.[1]

Admittedly this improving moral tale has a fantastic and bizarre quality which is absent from most of the miracle stories recounted by the hagiographers of Palestine. More usual themes are the discovery of a stream of water by a monk in desperate straits from dehydration in the desert heat, or the joyful conception by a barren woman after the holy man has offered prayers. But the story of the grave robber told by John Moschus shows clearly why some modern critics have been uneasy about the miracle stories and have acted as though the Lives could be expurgated of all such difficult material. There have been two motives for ignoring miracles.

The first is that of the Church, which wanted to ensure that the veneration of the saints rested on scientifically established historical narratives rather than on a compilation of apocryphal and improbable stories.[2] Important representatives of this approach have been the Bollandists with their huge work of editing and evaluating a mass of hagiographical texts.

The second motive is that of historians. Historians have wanted to extract the reliable and relevant pieces of information from those which do not have a proper historical foundation. Edward Schwartz concluded his edition of the work of Cyril of Scythopolis with an essay giving a

---

[1] *Prat.* 77, PG 87/3. 2920D–2922C.

[2] For this approach, see H. Delehaye, *The Legends of the Saints* (London, 1962), 86–9. Delehaye classifies the texts into three categories, the third of which is those stories which describe imaginary figures to whom no historical existence has been imputed. He defines legend as something based on historical fact but distorted by popular imagination.

historical framework within which the texts can be assessed. In this he gave little attention to the miracles, anecdotes, and accounts of ascetic achievement. An essential part of his analysis of the *Life of Euthymius* was to separate the portions which he considered to be historically reliable from the rest, making it clear which sections he was using in his historical survey but at the same time ignoring the rest and so implying that it was of inferior worth.[3] Cyril, because of his historical interests, is well suited to this approach.[4]

Selective approaches such as these may contribute to historical knowledge but they will not assist in understanding the texts. On the contrary, they will set up obstacles because they make no attempt to read the text from the point of view of the author or to appreciate the message he is trying to convey. Study of the saints' Lives in recent years has been altered and shaped by the recognition that these works can only be understood as a whole. Building on insights from anthropology, scholars, of whom the most influential were Evelyne Patlagean and Peter Brown, began to realize that the Lives of the saints are the product of a culture, and must be read on their own terms in their entirety. The need for completeness is expressed in this extract from an essay by Patlagean, in which she criticizes the 'historical' approach: 'On se sent libre de manipuler les textes, d'arracher les renseignements concrets à une trame hagiographique qu'on néglige; on semble n'y voir que l'enchaînement en ordre variable d'un nombre limite de thèmes légendaires, parmi lesquels des auteurs à la fois véridiques et stupides auraient inserés des faits seuls dignes d'être retenus.'[5]

The immediate result of this was a new and serious appreciation of the central place of the miracle stories. They came to be seen as a normal and natural part of life and proper material for inclusion within a historical work. Modern concerns about the nature of the event, its legendary quality or of causality will not find ready answers from the literature of the Byzantine era. Benedicta Ward reminds us on several occasions: 'It is vital to remember ... the question "why", "what for" is always predominant over the question "how", "what are the mechanics of this" in the mind of the ancient world.'[6] The only answer to the

---

[3] *Kyrillos*, 373.

[4] See the assessment of E. Stein, in *Histoire du Bas-Empire*, ii (Paris, 1949), 699, quoted in Ch. 1.

[5] E. Patlagean, 'Ancienne hagiographie byzantine et histoire sociale', *Annales esc.* 23 (1968), 106–26, 107.

[6] See B. Ward, introduction to N. Russell (trans.), *The Lives of the Desert Fathers* (London, 1980), 40; also her *Miracles and the Medieval Mind* (London, 1982), 214–15.

question of whether the miracles really happened is that the writers believed they did. There are no grounds for imputing fraud, deception, or invention to the Palestinian hagiographers. We are offered a record of an event, shaped by the understandings and beliefs of the time. The events themselves are concealed from us.

The understanding that God acts directly, marvelously, and powerfully is not only possible to the Byzantine, but essential. The power of God established order and security within society. In its absence, the chaos of the devils prevailed. Far from a supernatural irruption into an otherwise natural world, miracles were the means by which nature was directed and sustained. ' "Sign" does not connote a violation of natural law, as miracle has been widely understood by man in the post-Enlightenment period, but quite the reverse: it was the establishment of order in what we might call both nature and history that was *the* sign of God's activity.'[7]

So history, for Cyril and the other Palestinian writers, is not the history of human lives but of God working through human lives, the 'gesta Dei per monachos'. In his study of the nature of history and miracle in the writing of Cyril, Bernard Flusin observes,

L'histoire a pour origine et pour objet le miracle, qui est dans cette perspective le véritable événement historique. Le miracle est en effet pour l'histoire sainte ce qu'est l'événement pour l'histoire profane: le fait ponctuel, que l'on peut aisément situer et qui sert donc de repère et de preuve acceptable pour tous, où apparaissent à nu les vraies forces qui guident le cours des choses.[8]

Miracles, as the facts of sacred history, point to the significance of events. They refer to the moments in which the action of God can be clearly discerned, guiding the course of human society. They show that the beneficiaries of the miracles are pleasing to God, since he is active on their behalf. In the context of religious debate they form evidence of truth.[9] Even if miracles are claimed by other rival groups, these are

---

[7] H. C. Kee, *Miracle in the Early Christian World* (New Haven, Conn., 1983), 150.

[8] *MH* 214.

[9] Several miracle stories in the *Spiritual Meadow* make the claim that the Chalcedonian party has been vindicated by God. These 'controversial' miracles involve the proof of the rightness of the Chalcedonians. A typical example is the Monophysite who is unable to enter the Holy Sepulchre until he or she has acknowledged the error of his or her ways by receiving the Chalcedonian eucharist. *Prat.* 48; 49, cf. 29; 36; 178; 213, PG 87/3. 2904A; 2904C; 2867; 2884D–2885C; 3048C; 3105C. Some of the stories in the *Plerophoriai* make the same claim, but from the Monophysite standpoint. *Plerophoriai*, 10; PO 22–7. For a discussion of this type of story, see H. Remus, *Pagan–Christian Conflict over Miracle in the Second Century* (Cambridge, Mass., 1983), 80.

perceived as magic or illusion, serving only to deceive the community concerned.[10] Miracles are perceived, appropriated, and transmitted within a community.

Miracles are an indication of the value and acceptability to God of a person or a community. The barrier between heaven and earth becomes transparent, the love of God becomes available, the order of God prevails. These moments provide hope and reassurance to an uncertain and anxious society. They demonstrate how the holy man drew close to God and how he brought the action of God into the world. The modern concept of spirituality needs reinterpretation in order to be applied to the lives of the Byzantine saints. It is not a personal and interior dimension which can be contrasted to the hard world of the material order. Instead it describes the means by which the saint expressed the purposes of God in the midst of the society of the time.

The miracle stories show in graphic and pictorial language the nature of the relationship between the holy man and God, and his role in bringing the power of God into society. This was his function.

THE NATURE OF THE MIRACLES OF PALESTINE

In modern usage these stories of God's action in his world would be called miracles. In the Byzantine world there were several words which could be used. The richer vocabulary available is a sign of the greater appreciation of the possibility and significance of miracle. Each word drew out different characteristics of the event described. The three most usual words were δύναμις, or act of power; σημεῖον, or sign; and θαῦμα, or wonder. Τέρας, or omen, was used more rarely. In the New Testament it is only used in conjunction with σημεῖον.[11]

Biblical writers tended to use either σημεῖον, or sign, or δύναμις, or power.[12] The first of these two words showed that the event pointed beyond itself to some aspect of God's dealings with humanity. The second testified to the experience of God's power which was made manifest in action. The third possible word, θαῦμα, or wonder, is used

[10] For the sociological implications of miracle and magic, see Remus, *Pagan-Christian Conflict*, 48–72.

[11] *Τέρας* is used especially in the Acts of the Apostles which contains 9 of the 16 occurrences.

[12] For New Testament voacbulary, see C. F. D. Moule, 'The Vocabulary of Miracle', in Moule (ed.), *Miracles* (London, 1965), 235–8.

once only with the meaning of 'admiration', and the verb derived from it, θαυματουργέω, is never used.[13] Other derivatives occur rarely. θαυμασιόν can be found in Matthew 21: 15 referring to a 'wonderful work' and θαυμάστος, or 'wonderful', is used several times.[14]

Monastic writers availed themselves of these options in composing their works. δύναμις σημεῖον, and θαυμα, with their Latin equivalents virtus, signum, and prodigium, are used interchangeably in the Egyptian *Historia Monachorum*.[15] Theodoret, in Syria, used σημεῖον on only three occasions when speaking of the 'sign of the cross' or 'signs of health'. δύναμις and θαυμα are frequent.[16]

The vocabulary of the Palestinian writers was more limited. Their preferred term was always θαυμα. This is used throughout the works to describe the miracles.[17] Exceptions are rare.

Cyril of Scythopolis uses the word τερασρία, derived from τέρας or omen, once. It used alongside θαυματουργήσας in a passage shaped by Theodoret's *Religious History* where τεράτα is also employed with θαυματουργέω.[18] So this isolated use of τερασρία is an example of his capacity to reproduce the material of others rather than his own choice of vocabulary.

His one use of σημεῖον is more significant. The death of Nonnus, the Origenist leader, led to the fragmentation of the Origenist party in the desert. It was seen as a result of God's intervention on the side of the beleaguered Orthodox. Commenting on his demise, Cyril says: 'ὁ θεὸς μέγα σημεῖον πεποίηκεν'.[19] On the basis of this single passage it appears that Cyril used σημεῖον to describe the direct intervention of God with no human involvement, while θαυμα referred to the action of a person which revealed the action of God.

The most likely origin of this feature of Cyril's vocabulary is his own experience. He entered the monastery of Euthymius in 544 at a time when the grave of the founder, who had died 71 years previously, was developing as a place of healing. He describes how he witnessed several of these miracles, which are recorded in a section of the Life.[20] It was

---

[13] Rev. 17: 6.   [14] An example is Matt. 21: 43.

[15] See B. Ward, *Lives of the Desert Fathers*, 39.

[16] *H. Rel.* 1. 5. 2; 9. 7. 16; 9. 14. 22, SC 234 (Paris, 1977), 168; 420; 432.

[17] e.g. Theodore of Petra, *V. Thds.* 10. 13; 23. 8; 73. 4; 73. 12. *V. Char.* 11; 25. 5.

[18] *Kyrillos*, 23. 15, and *H. Rel.* prologue, 10. 11; SC 234, p. 140.

[19] *Kyrillos*, 195. 26.

[20] This set of stories is an early example of a set of shrine miracles. It is a forerunner of the sets of miracles preserved at medieval shrines. For these, see Ward, *Miracles and the Medieval Mind*, 33–109.

the impression made on him by this experience which led him to make enquiries about the events of Euthymius' life.[21]

So his literary career stemmed from a sense of wonder and awe in the face of these amazing happenings. They did not have the purpose behind them to be called 'signs' as did the death of Nonnus, which changed the course of history. They happened through the mediation of a physical object, a grave, which made the reference to divine power, or *dunamis*, less appropriate. But they were clearly, unmistakably, and overwhelmingly wonderful. From that moment the *thaumata*, or wonders, formed an indispensable part of Cyril's records.

Thaumata occur throughout the Lives. A devil is cast out of a young Arab boy and the 'wonder' was reported (τοῦ δὲ θαύματος διαφημισθέντος).[22] Hungry visitors to the monastery were fed with bread from a previously exhausted storehouse and after this 'wonder' the monastery began to be richly blessed.[23] In a moment of insight Euthymius knew that a visiting cleric would become the next Patriarch of Jerusalem.[24] Savage lions became docile when they were met with the prayers of, or even to, the holy man.[25] People find their troubles relieved when they visit the grave of the dead holy man. All are 'wonders'.[26] The sense of trembling amazement and of the glorious unpredictability of God's grace is met again and again in the pages of Cyril's Lives.

The bewildering variety of situations in which the wonder of God's activity is discerned makes it difficult to discuss the place of miracles in the Lives of the saints. Critics have often reacted by seeking out themes and sorting the miracles into categories which can then be analysed. A system of classification can show the kinds of situations in which God's power was discerned and the human experiences for which it was seen as right to ask for the saint's help.

A number of different systems of classification have been used.[27] Benedicta Ward and Pierre Canivet, in their work on the *Historia Monachorum* and the *Religious History* of Theodoret respectively, divided the miracles into various types. For Sister Benedicta these are miracles of clairvoyance; dreams and visions; healings; nature miracles; and

---

[21] *Kyrillos*, 71. 7–9.
[22] Ibid. 22. 19.
[23] Ibid. 28. 9.
[24] Ibid. 35. 17.
[25] Ibid. 71. 7–9.
[26] Ibid. 119. 28.
[27] Moule, in *Miracles*, 239–43, suggests several possible systems of classification.

judgements.[28] Canivet uses similar categories but combines miracles of clairvoyance with dreams and visions, and distinguishes healings from exorcisms.[29] These decisions on the part of Canivet are wise since

TABLE 1. *Classification of miracles*

	Nature	Clairvoyance	Healings	Others	TOTAL
V. Anton.					
No.	2	4	6	0	12
%	17	33	50		
HM					
No.	23	19	18	2	62
%	37	31	29	3	
Theodoret, H. Rel.					
No.	12	6	23	7	48
%	25	12	48	15	
Cyril					
No.	25	25	25	4	79
%	32	32	32	4	
Leim					
No.	24	20	7	20	71
%	34	28	10	28	
V. Thg.					
No.	5	1	4		10
%	50	10	40		
V. Thds.					
No.	8	7	2		17
%	47	41	12		
V. Geor. Choz.					
No.	4	4	5	1	14
%	29	29	35	7	
V. Char.					
No.	1	1			2
%	50	50			

clairvoyance is often the result of a dream or a vision, and exorcisms are not necessarily miracles of healing but can be carried out on a place.

[28] Ward, *Lives of the Desert Fathers*, 40.

[29] P. Canivet, *Le Monachisme syrien selon Théodoret de Cyr*, Théologie Historique, 42 (Paris, 1977), 120–44; and, with A. Adnes, 'Guérisons miraculeuses et exorcismes dans l'Histoire Philothée de Théodoret de Cyr', *RHR* 171 (1967), 53–82, 149–79, esp. 60–7, 149–79.

Below are my own classification tables. They use four categories. Clairvoyance, including dreams and visions; nature miracles, including exorcisms of places; healings, including exorcisms of persons; and others, since several miracles contain a quality of the bizarre and unusual which makes them impossible to classify satisfactorily. The placing of miracle stories in these categories is the result of personal judgement and so the resulting distribution has a rough-and-ready quality. Other critics would produce different results. In consequence, references are not given and the purpose is limited to the indication of general trends. The works which I have used are the main Palestinian sources, of which the *Spiritual Meadow* presents particular problems since almost every story has miraculous elements and many stories have a colourful and popular quality which can result in strange tales. For comparative purposes I include the Life of Antony, as the paradigm saint's life; the *Historia Monachorum*, describing Egyptian monasticism and with a lively interest in miracles; and the *Religious History*, as the main source for Syrian monasticism.

Table 1 shows that the three main categories chosen here are all significant in the understanding which these authors have of the ways in which God acts in the lives of his holy ones.

These categories will form the basis for the remaining discussion. Further study of these forms show the directions in which the ascetic disciplines led the saints and the situations in which they exercised their charismatic powers. These are the basis of a spirituality of the desert.

NATURE MIRACLES

The nature miracles describe the monk's relationship with his environment. This environment was the dangerous world of the desert, in which survival depended on the power of God. The monk approached his desert dwelling-place with a mixture of excited anticipation, because it was the place of God, and nervous anxiety, because it was the home of devils, wild beasts, and Saracens.

One monk who set out for the desert was the 30-year-old Sabas, who had completed a lengthy period of preparation in the coenobium, and persuaded his superior to allow him to live the solitary life. He spent the next fifteen years alone. Cyril recounts four anecdotes from that period, which have the common theme of survival.[30] They describe how the saint overcomes the difficulties of desert life. First, there is thirst. He faints from the lack of water while in the company of Euthymius. Euthymius prays and then digs, to find a spring of flowing water which revives his young disciple. Then there are the temptations and fantasies of the devils. These, as is customary in the lives of the monks, take the appearance of animals—snakes, scorpions, and a lion. Again the saint has recourse to prayer and, at the authoritative words, the devils vanish. The third trial comes from Saracens, or Arabs, who are the subject of two stories. In the first of these Sabas gives food from his slender stock to four Arabs who are faint from hunger, who in return seek him out to bring him food in gratitude. In the second, the earth opens at the prayers of the saint and swallows up six Arabs, 'barbarous in character and mischievous in intent'. After the saint has survived these trials he is ready to found a community and, after a further five years, disciples begin to arrive.

These five episodes are an initiation into desert life, which the saint has to pass through. Each is followed by an editorial comment which points out this theme. After drinking the water supplied by Euthymius' prayer Sabas 'received power from God ($\delta \acute{u}\nu a\mu\iota\nu\ \theta\epsilon\acute{\iota}a\nu$) to bear the trials of life in the desert'.[31] After he had dispelled the demonic temptations, 'God made every poisonous and carnivorous beast subject to him and he received no hurt from living with them in the desert.'[32] Then the swallowing up of the Arabs had the result that 'our father Sabas received the divine grace (charisma) of never being in fear of barbarian plots'.[33] After all this is over, he can move on to the next stage of his monastic life:

Now in the forty-fifth year of his life, he was entrusted by God with the charge of souls; he was persuaded by the word of God not to devote time pointlessly to enemies who had been defeated but to transfer his spiritual energies from a warlike disposition to husbanding those who had grown rank with evil thoughts ... so he began to receive all those who came to him.[34]

This long fifteen-year initiation into the desert life is marked by the signs of divine grace which indicate both God's election of the saint and also the suitability of the saint for his calling.

[30] *Kyrillos*, 97. 8; 94. 27–95. 2; 95. 18–96. 11; 96. 12–97. 2; 97. 2–97. 21.
[31] Ibid. 94. 30–95. 2.
[32] Ibid. 96. 9–11.
[33] Ibid. 97. 17–18.
[34] Ibid. 99. 10–18.

The initiation of Chariton into the monastic life is more dramatic but is also brought about through a nature miracle. He is captured by robbers while he is on the way to Jerusalem and left tied up in their cave. A devil tempts him to despair but Chariton resolutely turns to prayer upon which a snake slithers into the cave and, rather than harming the saint, drinks from the robbers' drinking pots and leaves his venom in the drink. The robbers return, drink and die, leaving the saint, who is automatically loosed (αὐτομάτως λυθεὶς) from his bonds, to benefit from the treasure in the cave. The cave then became the church of the laura of Pharan.[35] The same ingredients are present in this dramatic and far-fetched story as in the more sober account of Sabas' initiation into desert life. Chariton, through divine help, is unharmed by devil, wild beast, and robbers, and, as a consequence of surviving these trials, enters into the period of his life in which he founds a community and receives disciples.

Nature miracles were also experienced in the early days of the monastic communities as the monks together went through the same sorts of experience as befell their founders in the years of solitude. There was the discovery of a spring at the site of the Great Laura, gifts of food brought to Theodosius and his community which arrived fortuitously at moments of great need, store-cupboards miraculously replenished when an unexpectedly large number of guests arrived.[36]

The nature miracles have the purpose of showing how God's power enabled the holy man to survive. Within this general classification there are smaller groups which make it clearer how the power of God is given and with what purpose.

Several miracles describe the provision of rain after a period of drought. Among these was the intervention of Sabas during a five-year period without rain. The monks of the monastery of the Cave sought Sabas' permission to desert their monastery since they had no water and the rainy season had finished without relieving their necessity. At the prayer of Sabas a local storm suddenly raged in the area of the monastery and their cisterns were filled, provoking complaints from the monks of other neighbouring monasteries who did not benefit from the

---

[35] *V. Char.* 10–13; ed. Garitte, 23. 11–26. 9. *V. Char.* 25. 19 for αὐτομάτως λυθεὶς.

[36] *Kyrillos*, 101. 6–19 for the spring; Theodore of Petra, *V. Thds.* 24. 21–7. 7 for the gift of food; ibid, 27. 5–28. 8 for the multiplication of food, with a lesson about the need for hospitality; ibid. 36. 15–30; 38. 11–39. 2 for further examples.

late downpour.[37] During this same drought, the saint's help was asked for by the Patriarch for the city of Jerusalem. He had organized a huge programme of ditch-digging using a mass of workmen who dug down 200 feet in the hope of discovering water. All to no avail. In desperation the Patriarch requested Sabas' prayers. The next day 'there was thunder and lightning, and rain cascaded down, so that before dawn the conduits were filled to the brim and torrents poured from all sides. The mounds of earth raised with such expenditure of time, labour and money were swept in one moment into the ditch, covering ladders, tools and baskets.'[38]

This miracle, and another similar rain miracle worked by Euthymius on behalf of the people of Jerusalem, extend the theme of survival to new and wider dimensions. The gift of water to the thirsty through the prayer of the saint is given to a whole city rather than just to a solitary monk or a struggling community. But the discovery of the desert dweller applies here too. In times of need the sufferer turns to God in prayer.

Bernard Flusin, in an important study of the miracles of Cyril of Scythopolis, associated the power to work miracles with the position held in the monastic hierarchy. He compared various rain miracles and argued that the geographical extent of the rainfall widened as the authority of the saint grew: 'Le cercle des bénéficiaires de leurs miracles coïncide strictement avec leurs attributions institutionelles: Cyriaque, simple anachorète, fait pleuvoir sur sa cellule; Sabas, comme abbé, remplit les cisternes d'un de ses monastères dans le besoin; comme archimandrite, il fait pleuvoir sur Jérusalem; et Euthyme, qui le préfigure, sur la Palestine.'[39] Flusin is undoubtedly correct to point to the popular expectation that the saint is somebody with the power to intercede with God and that those under his jurisdiction will turn to him for help, but too close a correspondence between the miracles and the hierarchical position cannot be maintained. In the case of the examples he gives, Euthymius did not have authority over Jerusalem when he prayed for rain and there is no indication in the text that this miracle is seen as prefiguring the work of Sabas. Further, Sabas' two miracles are performed during the same drought and the more extensive miracle is not the sign of an ecclesiastical promotion.

The set of miracles which describe the provision of food and drink

---

[37] *Kyrillos*, 167. 4–24.
[38] Ibid. 167. 25–169. 24, with the citation from 169. 13–20. Cf. ibid. 38. 1–39. 17.
[39] *MH* 199, where Flusin refers to *Kyrillos*, 232. 19–233. 3; 167. 4–24; 167. 25–169. 24; 38. 1–39. 17.

concern the means by which the monks receive the necessities of life. The giver of these gifts is recognized to be God and the occasions of their provision are 'wonders' since they are examples of God's providing care. The hand of God is perceived in everyday events, such as gifts of food. After four Saracens bring a feast of loaves, cheeses, and dates to Sabas as he lives alone in the desert, the saint breaks out into a hymn of praise to God who bestows such 'divine graces and favours'. A similar event in the *Life of Antony*, by contrast, is seen as a happy, but natural, experience of desert life, with no suggestion that it should be interpreted as a miracle.[40]

Alongside these timely but essentially 'natural' events are feeding miracles of a different nature, as when Theodosius visits Marcianus and is given lentils to eat but no bread. On being told there is no grain in the monastery, Theodosius finds a single grain in Marcianus' huge beard. This is placed in the storehouse which becomes so full of wheat that the door cannot be opened until Theodosius comes to give his blessing.[41] The monks were not interested in whether the event took place in accordance or in defiance of the normal course of natural processes, but in whether they could discern the action of God in caring for his creatures.

A number of nature miracles describe the encounter of the monks with lions. The lion stories are a distinctive feature of the Palestinian literature and reflect the conditions in which the monks lived. Lions were common in the Palestinian desert in this period and were a hazard which confronted any monk who set off to discover greater solitude than was possible in the monastery. Equivalent stories from other countries involved other animals. In Egypt the monks met hippopotamuses, hyenas, and asps.[42] In Syria there were dragons, which were probably venomous snakes, although here too a lion is encountered by Symeon the Old.[43]

[40] Ibid. 96. 17–27; 210. 5–211. 14. For *Life of Antony*, see *V. Anton.* 50, PG 26. 916B.

[41] Theodore of Petra, *V. Thds.* 73. 17–77. 12. Flusin, at *MH* 205, suggests that the monks of Theodosius' monastery developed a tradition of miracles to rival the stories produced at the Sabaite monasteries. Against this is the fact that Theodore's life predated Cyril's writings.

[42] See *V. Anton.* 15; PG 26. 865C, and *H. Mon.* 12. 6–9, SHG 94–5, for crocodiles; *H. Mon.* 4. 3, SHG 53, for hippopotamuses; Palladius, *H. Laus.* 18. 27–8, ed. Butler, 57. 4–58. 2, for hyenas; *H. Laus.* 2. 4; 8. 10, Butler 18. 2–22; 51. 5–9, for asps.

[43] Theodoret, *H. Rel.* 2. 6. 15; 3. 7. 2, SC 234 (Paris 1977), 208; 256, for dragons. Canivet, in *Monachisme syrien*, 209, comments that the dragon is 'un animal qui symbolise les forces du mal'. For Symeon and the lion, see *H. Rel.* 6. 2. 19–24, SC 234 (Paris, 1977) 348–50.

The meetings between the lion and the monk took place in the deep wadis which provided water, vegetation, and shelter from the hot sun. Here there were also caves, and several stories describe the monk competing with the lion for the same cave in which to live. The unfortunate lion always came off worst and either retired before the superior power of the monk's holiness or remained to become a friend and servant to the monk.[44] John Moschus tells the popular story of Gerasimus, who removed a thorn from the foot of a lion and thus forged a close friendship with the lion who became his inseparable companion and performed various tasks for him, including looking after his donkey.[45] The story is a paradigm for the harmonious coexistence of man and beast in the Palestinian desert.

The presence of lions in the miracle stories reminds the reader of other stories in which lions are familiar characters. These are the stories of the martyrs. Here again the holy man, or woman, confronts the savage beast in the arena of combat. So the appearance of the lion is a reminder that the vocation of the monk arose out of that of the martyr. The opening pages of the writings of Cyril compare the combats of the monk with those of the martyrs.[46] This experience of confronting evil shared by the martyr and the monk links the two halves of the *Life of Chariton*, when, after being denied the opportunity to die for Christ, the saint sets off to live as a monk. Similarly Antony longed to die and, during the persecution under Maximin Daia in 311–13, set off eagerly for Alexandria and glory. His lack of success in this endeavour led him to a renewed understanding of monastic endurance in terms of martyrdom. He 'was daily being martyred by his conscience, and doing battle in the combats of the faith'.[47]

The stories of the submission of lions to monks would remind the readers of the stories of the power of the martyrs over the wild beasts which were intended to tear them to pieces. Cyril was familiar with the *Life of Thecla*, one of his favourite source books. He would have known the passage which spoke of Thecla's martyrdom when 'the fiercest of lions, denying his natural instincts' attached himself to Thecla and caressed her.[48] Another episode contains the phrase, παρὰ τῶν τὰ θηρία

---

[44] *Kyrillos*, 118. 32–119. 9.
[45] *Prat.* 107, PG 87/3. 2965C–2969B, cf. *Kyrillos*, 138. 19–139. 13.
[46] *Kyrillos*, 7. 28–8. 2.
[47] *V. Anton.* 47, PG 26. 912B. For further discussion, see E. Malone, 'The Monk and the Martyr', *St. Ans.* 38 (1956), 201–28.
[48] *V. Thecl.* 16. 26–32, SHG 234–6.

διεγειρόντων ἐκ τῆς των μαστίγων πληγης καὶ ἤχης.[49] This idea lies behind the thought, borrowed immediately by Cyril from the *Life of Antony* and used twice in his stories about lions, when lions are chased away by the prayers of the saint.[50] The literary connection with the *Life of Thecla* shows that the origin of this striking phrase lies in the accounts of martyrdom.

The struggle of the monks with the devils has a greater streak of seriousness than that with the wild beasts. Although the desert was an arena in which the ascetic challenged the forces of evil, it was by no means the only habitat in which devils thrived. The men and women of late Antiquity had a vivid sense of the impending force of evil which continually threatened their well-being. 'The sharp sense of an invisible battle hung over the religious and intellectual life of late Antique man. To sin was no longer merely to err; it was to allow oneself to be overcome by unseen forces.'[51]

The methods of combating evil are the same whether it is encountered in a person or a place. The cleansing of the hill of Castellion from demonic occupation contains details reminiscent of exorcism of persons. 'This hill was terrifying and unfrequented because of the large number of devils who lurked there ... as a man subject to fear he would have wished to withdraw.'[52] So evil evoked fear. Then, second, 'through ceaseless prayers and divine praises the place was tamed'.[53] Prayer is the weapon which is most effective. Third, in addition to praying Sabas sprinkled the place with oil from the Holy Cross, and took courage from the power of the Cross, a feature also of exorcisms of persons.[54] Fourth, 'they departed from the place shouting in human speech the words, "What violence from you, Sabas . . . see, we withdraw from our own territory. We cannot resist you." '[55] Other examples of devils shouting as they leave what they have occupied are encountered in the Lives of the saints.[56] Wherever they are found the devils are attacked and receive the same treatment.

A familiar saying of the Egyptian fathers was 'stay in your cell and

[49] *V. Thecl.* 19. 3, SHG 244.
[50] *Kyrillos*, 107. 15, cf. 215. 19–20; *V. Anton.* 52, PG 26. 920A.
[51] P. R. L. Brown, *The World of Late Antiquity* (London, 1971) 53.
[52] *Kyrillos*, 110. 7–8; 110. 15.
[53] Ibid. 110. 12–13. Cf. 22. 22; 76. 18–20; 218. 6.
[54] Ibid. 110. 11, 17. Cf. 20. 23; 164. 15–18; 218. 7.
[55] Ibid. 110. 26–111. 1.
[56] Ibid. 77. 17–18.

your cell will teach you everything'.[57] For the monks of Palestine this saying could be applied to the experience of being in the desert. When the saint had developed sufficient maturity and toughness through the training given in the coenobium, he could leave for the desert. In the harsh terrain he grew to know God. He learnt the virtue of trust, so that he could live in confidence and without fear. 'God supplied every need bountifully, so that there was more need among those who counted on their own riches and revenues than among the monasteries that he (Sabas) cared for.'[58] He fought against evil, continuing here the great and constant engagement of the monks against the fantasies and the temptations of the evil one. He learnt to live at peace with creation. John Moschus reminds his reader that the monk rediscovered the state of innocence: 'All this took place not because it was necessary to attribute to the lion a reasonable soul, but because God wished to glorify those who glorify him ... and to show how the beasts were subjected to Adam before he had transgressed the commandment and was chased out of Paradise.'[59]

The attitude to the desert was changing by the start of the seventh century. The possibility of a harmonious ordered relationship with the desert in which food was provided, animals tamed, and devils kept at bay receded with the lack of security. The increasing danger from Persian troops and deteriorating relationships between the Empire and the Arab tribes made it dangerous for the monk to live alone in the desert, and this insecurity affected the total relationship with the environment. Antony of Choziba wrote of this change: 'From the time of the Persians the wadi was infested by wild beasts and unclean spirits.' He also noted that the yield from the capparis plants declined dramatically: 'Men who are evildoers and murderers turn the world upside down.'[60] The result of this disorder in the desert is a new emphasis on community living. The process of purgation and growth towards God now took place within the coenobium. In the *Life of George of Choziba* an asceticism based on love, humility, and gentleness within the community replaces the disciplines of solitude and persistence which were more appropriate to desert living.[61]

[57] R. D. Williams, *The Wound of Knowledge* (London, 1979), 94.
[58] *Kyrillos*, 159. 2–23.
[59] *Prat.* 107, PG 87/3. 2969 A–B.
[60] *V. Geor. Choz.* 42, *An. Boll.* (1888), 143. 13–144. 2.
[61] An example of this is the early miracle of George in which a harsh monk is taught to be gentle with his novice, *V. Geor. Choz.* 4–5, *An. Boll.* (1888), 99. 1–101. 7.

The nature miracles present in simple and pictorial form a rigorous and prolonged process of growth in the spiritual life. Through it the holy man leaves the world behind and enters into the society of God. This is achieved by the unrelenting practice of the ascetical life, the fruits of which are evidence enough of the growing purity of heart and closeness to God. Occasionally a comment points to the interior dimension of this process of purgation: 'He spent five years alone by himself in solitude, conversing with God and purifying the eye of his thought so as "with unveiled face to behold as in a mirror the glory of the Lord", since the evil spirits had already been conquered by his ceaseless prayers and nearness to God.'[62]

CLAIRVOYANCE

There came a moment in the Lives of the saints when they began to receive disciples. This step was taken with reluctance and after clear evidence that it was in accordance with the will of God. When three Cappadocian brothers came to Euthymius, he was reluctant to accept them but he heard a voice in a vision commanding him to 'accept these brothers, since God has sent them'.[63] So from the outset the life of the community was shaped and guided by God. The saint undertook his responsibilities only in obedience to this call. It was an attitude which governed all the holy man's dealings with his community.

The miracles of clairvoyance occur mostly in the section of the Lives which deal with the ministry of the saint within the Church. They describe occasions when the saint is given miraculous knowledge. This gift is the result of the long period of ascetic preparation and is exercised by the saint so that he can order the life of the community.

Through his gift of clairvoyance, the holy man knew the interior disposition of the soul: 'The inspired Euthymius had received this charism too from God, that from seeing the appearance of the body he beheld the movements of the soul and knew which thoughts each person was wrestling with, and also which he prevailed over and which he was mastered by.'[64] Faults could be corrected harshly as is seen in the group of miracles which administer punishment. An example of these is the

---

[62] *Kyrillos*, 99. 5–9.
[63] Ibid. 25. 25.
[64] Ibid. 45. 28–46. 3.

cautionary tale of Maron and Clematius, two monks who decided to leave the monastery without telling Euthymius. Their plan was revealed to him in his solitude; and he summoned them. Clematius remained obstinate and as a result of his defiance he fell to the ground trembling and shuddering. This condition remained until he was restored to health by the saint, after which they remained in peace.[65] Through the gift of clairvoyance the saint is enabled to act as judge and lawgiver in cases involving discipline and direction of souls.

An important stage in the life of the community was the death of the founder. The saints are given warning of their forthcoming death by God. The only miracle of clairvoyance in the *Life of Chariton* is his foreseeing of his death.[66] The inclusion of this story in a Life written so long after the life of the subject is an indication of its importance. It was an opportunity for the holy man to gather the brethren around him, give a final edifying address and arrange for the appointment of a successor. Sabas used these final moments to commit to writing the rules governing the life of the community and to formally hand this document over to his successor.[67] The securing of the monastery's future was the final task of the saint in his earthly life and was enabled through this aspect of the gift of clairvoyance.

The gift of clairvoyance enabled the holy man to be involved in the life of Church and Empire. Euthymius knew in advance who would become Patriarch. Anastasius, a priest who visited Euthymius, was surprised to be spoken to as though he was the Patriarch but in due course this took place.[68] He also knew that Martyrius and Elias, two refugees from the Monophysite conflicts in Egypt whom he received into his community, would become Patriarchs.[69]

Further occurrences of these miracles reveal the divine blessing bestowed on Sabas' visits to the Emperors in Constantinople. Both Anastasius and Justinian are given evidence of the holiness of the old

---

[65] *Kyrillos*, 30. 7–32. 5.

[66] *V. Char.* 25, ed. Garitte, 35. 3–11; cf. *Kyrillos*, 57. 12–14; 58. 22–5; 182. 12–14; *Prat.* 42; 57, PG 87/3. 2896C; 2912A.

[67] *Kyrillos*, 182. 21–3. A 12th-c. MS purports to be this document. See E. Kurtz, 'Review of A. Dmitrijevskij, *Die Klosterregeln des hl. Sabas* (Kiev, 1890)', *By. Z.* 3 (1894), 167–70; S. Vailhé, 'Les Écrivains de Mar Saba', *E. Or.* 2 (1899), 1–11; 33–47.

[68] *Kyrillos*, 35. 13–25. This episode provides the information, not found elsewhere, that the Patriarch can be recognized by his white clothing. See P. Devos, 'Cyrille de Scythopolis, Influences littéraires: Vêtement de l'évêque de Jérusalem—Passarion et Pierre l'Ibère', *An. Boll.* 98 (1980), 25–38.

[69] *Kyrillos*, 51. 7–9. Gregory, the future Patriarch of Antioch, is seen in a vision wearing the Patriarchal omophorion, *Prat.* 139, PG 87/3. 3001C.

man. Anastasius sees him being led in by an angelic form and Justinian saw Sabas' head blazing with radiance. Immediately both Emperors offer the obeisance to the holy man which was normally offered to them.[70] On these occasions Sabas was given further gifts of foresight. He knew that those who opposed him at the court of Anastasius would meet untimely and violent ends and that Justinian's military campaigns would be blessed with success so that the Empire would be expanded to reach the boundaries it had had under Honorius.[71]

The supernatural gift of clairvoyance was exercised within the community. Through the practice of asceticism and prayer it became a frequent experience to enable the holy man to act according to God's will. Sabas expected God to keep him properly informed. When he discovered that there was an event in the former life of John the Hesychast which prevented him being ordained priest, he was most put out that God had kept this from him. He complained bitterly in his prayers until eventually an angel came to inform him of the true situation, that John was in fact already not only a priest but also a bishop. The appearance of the angel caused him no surprise since he was 'used to theophanies and angelic visions'.[72]

The miracles of clairvoyance show that the work of the saint is an aspect of his relationship with God. The labour of setting up and guiding the monasteries, and the church, arises naturally and inevitably out of the saint's discovery of intimacy with God. God acts through the saint to build up his church and to regulate his society on earth.

HEALINGS

Through the healing miracles the saint becomes public property. With very few exceptions, monks did not benefit from the healing powers of the holy man. When the saint's power to heal is exercised within the community it is usually in the context of clairvoyance. Devils which afflict the monks are recognized and exorcised, as happened, for example in the case of Euthymius' monk Aemilianus from whom the demon of luxury was cast out after the saint entered the church and, sniffing the air, recognized the unmistakable odour of demonic activity.[73] On other

---

[70] *Kyrillos*, 142. 17–20; 173. 21–6.
[71] Ibid. 146. 11–18; 163. 8–13; 175. 19–22.
[72] Ibid. 208. 15–16.
[73] Ibid. 36. 13–37. 29.

occasions, the demonic influence or the physical symptoms of trembling or paralysis was induced by the saint only in order to be relieved, so that the monk received a salutary warning that a change of life was called for.

In cases of illness the monk was more likely to have recourse to practical medical advice.[74] Theognius suffered from two illnesses. The first was an inflamed and bleeding finger, which was cured through the practical advice to move to a more favourable climate. The second was a broken bone in the foot, caused by falling from a donkey. A doctor was summoned from Jerusalem and only after he failed to cure the limb did an angel appear to Theognius and grant immediate relief.[75]

The healing ministry of the holy man took place in the third and latest stage of his ministry. It arose after his time of solitude and his formation of the community, when he began to have contact with the shepherds, villagers, and citizens of the neighbourhood. It developed as his reputation spread. As long as he remained in the monastery, the circle of beneficiaries was limited to the few people whom he encountered in the desert or who, through persistence or divine guidance, sought out the saint. The early healing by Euthymius of Terebon, so decisive for the evangelization of the Arabs, was an exceptional event which took place after the tribe travelled from Arabia across the Jordan to discover the person who had been shown to the chief in a dream.[76] But when Sabas travelled around the country on behalf of the Patriarch or when Theognius became Bishop of Betelia, then they became available to a wider circle and the number of healings grew. After the saint died he was no longer able to restrain the crowds. His body became a public facility maintained by the monks of the monastery in which the tomb was located. The sick came freely to him. This development is particularly striking in the case of Euthymius who is recorded by Cyril as working one cure before he died but nine cures after his death through his relics.

Most of the healing miracles in the writings of Cyril of Scythopolis come from a later period than the nature miracles and clairvoyance. While these are found in the strands of the monastic oral traditions which describe events that took place before the birth of Cyril in 525, the healings tend to take place during his lifetime, and are often part of his own experience. They happened at a time when miracles were

[74] *Kyrillos*, 131. 26–7.
[75] *V. Thg.* 7 and 15, *An. Boll.* (1891), 85. 4–10 and 96. 18–97. 9.
[76] *Kyrillos*, 19. 10–15.

becoming more popular and the expectation of the extraordinary greater. So while earlier 'monastic' miracles often describe the action of God within everyday events, such as the arrival of a visitor with a food parcel, healings are, by definition, dramatic. So it was remembered at Scythopolis how a woman who had a haemorrhage used to lie in the street. She had been ill for many years and smelled so disgusting that nobody would go near her. Sabas allowed her to place his hand on the afflicted place and immediately the flow of blood ceased. The story is told with relish, dwelling on the seriousness of the affliction and the immediacy of the cure, and referring freely to biblical miracles to remind the reader of the conformity of the ministry of the saint with biblical models.[77]

Some of the posthumous miracles, not always healings, are more remarkable. On one occasion a thief has stolen a large sum of money from Euthymius' monastery. He hid the money but when he went to retrieve it he was prevented first by a terrifying snake which pursued him and then by a spirit from the air which knocked him senseless.[78] The *Spiritual Meadow*, written in the course of the succeeding half century, is full of fantastic stories, as, to take an extreme example, the improving tale of the grave robber whose eyes are torn out referred to at the start of this chapter.[79] With the healings and the posthumous miracles of other kinds the narrative changes, leaving the sober milieu of the monk and entering the world of popular religion.

The people of the province wanted somewhere to turn to in their poverty, uncertainty, and sickness. The evocative summaries of the mood of the age presented by Peter Brown have emphasized the search for power and protection in an uncertain and changing world: 'Much of the contrasting developments of Western Europe and Byzantium in the Middle Ages can be summed up as a prolonged debate on the precise locus of spiritual power ... In Byzantium, the locus of spiritual power wavered as paradoxically as did the fluid society in which it was exercised.'[80] For the people of Palestine, the question of power received a simple and clear answer. Power was concentrated in the Holy Places, where Christ died, was buried, and rose again. This power was tangible and could be parcelled up and carried away. It drew pilgrims to Jerusalem

[77] *Kyrillos*, 163. 23–164. 10. Cf. Acts 3: 6; Luke 8: 44.
[78] *Kyrillos*, 69. 25–70. 20.
[79] *Prat.* 77, PG 87/3. 2929D.
[80] P. R. L. Brown, 'Rise and Function of the Holy Man in Late Antiquity', *JRS* 61 (1971), 80–101, 95.

and developed to satisfy their demand. 'In the place where the Lord's body was laid, at its head, has been placed a bronze lamp. It burns there day and night, and we took a blessing from it, and then put it back. Earth is brought up to the tomb and put inside, and those who go in take some as a blessing.' The Piacenza pilgrim, who visited the city at the time of Cyril, was among those who received God's power in the form of earth from the Sepulchre or, best of all, oil taken from the lamps. 'They offer oil to be blessed in little flasks. When the mouth of one of these little flasks touches the wood of the Cross, the oil instantly bubbles over and, unless it is closed very quickly, it spills out.'[81] Such oil was frequently used by Sabas and the others in their struggles against the demons. An alternative weapon was the sign of the Cross.[82]

In a society in which a Tomb lay at the spiritual and economic heart, it was natural for the tombs of holy men to be valued and venerated as foci of power. It was a period in which relics were becoming prominent. The discovery of the bodies of Gervasius and Protasius at Milan, of Vitalis and Agricola at Bologna, and of Nazarinus also at Milan have been described as a turning point in the attitude of the western Church to miracles.[83] In the Holy Land, with its plentiful supply of biblical characters whose mortal remains, it was evident, must be located somewhere awaiting discovery, interest in relics was strong. There was a growing appetite for holy bones, for which the departed desert saints provided nourishment.

Cyril witnessed the steady stream of visitors to the tomb of Euthymius. The tomb was in a small building to the north of the church, which can be visited today. It is now surrounded by tombs of other leading monks but would then have been a single tomb, covered with a stone slab with oil lamps burning over it. To this room came the sick. If they could not walk they were carried by friends and laid down next to the tomb until the power of the saint worked the healing.[84] The custom of incubation, or sleeping in the sanctuary, developed from pagan practices

---

[81] Antoninus Placentinus, *Itinerarium*, 18 and 20, CCL 175 (Turnhout, 1965), 138 and 139. Collections of these little flasks or *ampullae* dating from the time of Cyril have been found at Bobbio and Monza. See E. D. Hunt, *Holy Land Pilgrimage in the Later Roman Empire* (Oxford, 1984), 130–1.

[82] *Kyrillos*, 110. 11; 136. 16–17; 164. 15. For a similar miracle, see *Life of Peter the Iberian*, 29–39, ed. Raabe, 34–5. See also *Kyrillos*, 20. 22–3; 171. 4–5.

[83] See J. Petersen, *Dialogues of Gregory the Great in their Late Antique Cultural Setting* (Toronto, 1984), 58.

[84] *Kyrillos*, 75. 24–5; 76. 10.

at Epidauros and elsewhere, and became a part of popular devotion.[85] The sick might be anointed with the oil taken from the lamps, especially in the case of women, who were discouraged from entering the monastery.[86] On one occasion a desperate sufferer drank the oil.[87] The twin beliefs of the reality of spiritual power and its localization in objects ensured the success of the tombs of the saints as centres of popular devotion. The result was that the death of the saint led to the intensification of his healing activity rather than its conclusion.

The healing miracles demonstrate a further dimension of the spirituality of the desert. The saint was a man of compassion. His power had an immediate and popular impact. He was claimed by the people, and, in spite of a preference for solitude, was ultimately available to them.

FRIENDS OF GOD

Desert spirituality has at its root movement. It involves a physical journey from the city to the desert, even if, for many of the saints, this is by way of the intermediate stage of the coenobium. This movement is mirrored in the interior life of the soul as the saint becomes closer to God, more sensitive to his leading, and more able to approach him. He leaves earth and enters heaven through his asceticism. As a result the moment of death, for the saint, loses its abrupt quality of discontinuity and, instead becomes a deepening of an already achieved status. This perception of the saints' change of spiritual place has been summarized by Peter Brown. They 'played in the heavenly sphere a role analogous to that played on earth by the great men of the court, through whom petitions could be more efficaciously brought to the Emperor's notice than if they were directly addressed to him; in the language of the day the same terms were applied to both heavenly and earthly patrons whose *suffragia* were sought.'[88]

To describe this state of intimacy with God, the Palestinian authors use the term '*parresia* (or παρρησία). Since *parresia* describes the goal

---

[85] See P. Maraval, *Lieux saints et pèlerinages d'orient* (Paris, 1985), 223–7. Flusin, in *MH* 280–1, suggests that the haemorrhagic woman cured by Sabas had been hoping to be cured by incubation.

[86] *Kyrillos*, 68. 14–15; 76. 2.

[87] Ibid. 76. 20–1. Cf. the medieval custom of mixing dust from the tomb of the saint with water which was then drunk by the sufferer. See Ward, *Miracles and the Medieval Mind*, 93; 94; 101.

[88] A. H. M. Jones, *Later Roman Empire* i. (Oxford, 1964), iii. 958.

of the ascetic life, the concept strongly influences the spiritual teaching of the Lives. Earlier uses of the term are developed in fresh directions and the concept is given an original prominence by them.[89] This is in contrast to much of the other parts of Palestinian ascetic teaching which contents itself with repeating well-tried formulas such as the need for humility and obedience as the foundation of the ascetic life.[90]

In classical Greek, *parresia* was a political term which described the privilege, much prized in the city-state, of speaking openly. It could refer to the right to speak, or to the quality of truth within the speech, or to the courage required to state convictions honestly.[91] It could have a negative connotation when used to describe speech which was scandalous or immoral, misusing the right to free expression. This negative use, especially by Cynic philosophers who were known for the unrestrained quality of their behaviour, led to the word falling into disrepute and disuse.[92]

In the New Testament, *parresia* describes the confidence with which the Gospel is proclaimed by the Apostles. They speak without fear of persecution, rejection, or any human obstacle. So, after Peter and John had been released from prison, the congregation prayed together and 'all were filled with the Holy Spirit and spoke the word of God with *parresia*'.[93] The concept was suitable for references to the virtue of boldness required to witness during times of persecution. So *parresia* became a quality of the witness of the martyrs. Eusebius tells how the martyrs of Palestine would speak out boldly exhorting their persecutors to turn to God.[94] Even after the periods of official repression ceased, *parresia* was still required to challenge impious or overbearing behaviour by those in positions of power. The holy men were among those who did not hesitate to speak frankly, openly, and boldly to the emperors or their officials. They looked back to the example of John the Baptist who

[89] Festugière notes, in *MO* i. 59, that 'le mot παρρησία dans les Vies des Moines mériterait une étude'. These pages provide some preliminary notes to this end.

[90] D. J. Chitty, in *The Desert a City* (Oxford, 1966), 131, comments: 'We have little impression of originality in Cyril's personal religion.' For references to the virtues, see *Kyrillos*, 17. 13–14; 89. 13–14; 92. 4; 120. 22 for humility; ibid. 29. 22–4; 122. 22 for obedience.

[91] See article by H. Schlier in G. Kittel (ed.), *Theologisches Wörterbuch zum Neues Testament* (Tübingen, 1933), 871–6.

[92] See W. C. van Unnik, 'The Christian's Freedom of Speech in the New Testament', *BJRL* 44 (1961/2), 466–88, 471.

[93] Acts 4: 31. Among many other examples see Acts 2: 29; 4: 13; 9: 27; 13: 46. Eph. 6: 19; 1 Thess. 2: 2.

[94] Eusebius, *Mart. P.* 4. 9, SC 73 (Paris, 1960), 132. 14.

combined his desert asceticism with opposition to a corrupt authority—
an opposition which cost him his life.

Evagrius relates that Symeon Stylites wrote to the Emperor with
parresia, and Palladius includes the story of the Galatian priest Phi-
loromus who was tortured for speaking to the pagan Emperor Julian
with *parresia*.[95] This meaning of *parresia* is found in the Palestinian
writer Theodore of Petra in his *Life of Theodosius*. Theodosius spoke
boldly (ἐπαρρησιάσατο) before emperors and also used *parresia* in his
witness to orthodoxy before the Monophysite Emperor Anastasius.[96]
Cyril, perhaps shaping his vocabulary on his source Theodoret, avoids
this meaning of the term *parresia*.

The negative use of free speech also occurs in monastic writings. In
the literature of Egypt it usually implies that the speaker is immodest
and speaks with excessive licence. Under the influence of Egyptian texts
this use is found in the *Instructions* of Dorotheus of Gaza.[97] There is a
single and uncharacteristic use of this negative *parresia* in a passage
of Euthymius' ascetical teaching which is derived from one of the
Apophthegmata: 'Know that it is folly for a monk to speak or to be
moved against what is fitting or to speak boldly (παρρησιάζεσθαι). The
Fathers say that *parresia* is dangerous and gives rise to passions.'[98] This
saying is also the inspiration behind a homily delivered by Antiochus,
a monk of the Great Laura in the seventh century.[99]

The capacity to speak freely lay behind the development of the
meaning of the word which is found in certain strands of the biblical
literature. The word came to be used to describe the nature of the
relationship which makes freedom of speech possible as well as the
speech itself. It spoke of the intimacy of the relationship between God
and the believer.

The earliest example of the this use is in the Septuagint version of
Job 22: 26 which reads, παρρησιασθήσῃ ἐναντίον κυρίου, a meaning
developed by Philo and Josephus.[100] The most significant texts in this
context are in the First Epistle of John, where the use is noticeably
different from other documents of the New Testament. It becomes an

---

[95] Evagrius, *HE* I. 13, ed. Bidez and Parmentier, 22. 15; Palladius, *H. Laus.* 45, ed.
Butler 132. 22.

[96] Theodore of Petra, *V. Thds.* 18. 8; 62. 2.

[97] Dorotheus of Gaza, *Instructions*, 4. 53, SC 92 (Paris, 1963), 233.

[98] *Kyrillos*, 31. 13–15. Cf. *Apoph. Patr.*, Agathon 1, PG 65. 109A. See the comments
in I. Hausherr, *Penthos* (Kalamazoo, Mich., 1982), 94–5.

[99] Antiochus Monachos, *Homilies*, 16 (περὶ παρρησίας), PG 89. 1476D–1477D.

[100] Van Unnik, 'Christian's Freedom of Speech', 471.

eschatological gift, belonging to the age to come, while in other parts it is used in the spread of the Gospel in this age. It also comes to be used towards God, whereas it had previously been used towards men. It becomes available to all, whereas before it was reserved to the Apostles. It becomes dislocated from its function of describing a quality of speech and comes to encompass the trust, conviction of salvation, overcoming of sin, and the power to pray. For example, 'this is the *parresia* which we have towards him, that if we ask anything according to his will, he hears us'.[101]

The Johannine traditions are associated with the Church in Asia Minor and this concept of *parresia* was developed here. According to Gregory of Nyssa, Adam before the Fall was 'being filled with *parresia*, enjoying the divine manifestation itself face to face'.[102] This lost *parresia* is rediscovered through baptism. 'Those who yesterday were captives are now free and citizens of the Church, those who previously were in the place of shame are now in *parresia* and justice'.[103]

Parresia is received at baptism and grows to fullness through ascetic discipline. Theodoret describes the spiritual progress of James of Nisibis: 'Thus his *parresia* towards God increased each day and, asking from God what it was necessary to ask, he immediately received it.'[104] *Parresia* was often translated by the Syriac phrase *galyut 'afe*, which literally means 'the unveiling of the face', so linking the idea with the familiar ascetic text of St Paul: 'We with our unveiled faces reflecting like mirrors the brightness of the Lord, all are changed from glory to glory as we are turned into the image which we reflect.'[105]

The use of *parresia* in the context of the ascetic life was faithfully reproduced by Cyril. He has used the passage about James of Nisibis as a source for his descriptions of the ascetic growth of both Euthymius and Sabas. Of Sabas he wrote: 'Sabas remained in the ravine alone for five years speaking to God in the silence and cleansing the mirror of his mind.'[106] Their experience of solitude in the desert established their *parresia* before God.

The *parresia* of the saint is shown by his power to perform miracles.

---

[101]   1 John 5: 14. For other examples, see 1 John 2: 28; 3. 21; 4. 17; 5. 14. Also Hebrews 4: 16.

[102]   Gregory of Nyssa, *Oratio Catachetica*, 6. 10, discussed in R. G. Coquin, 'La thème de la thélogie de la παρρησία et ses expressions symboliques dans les rites d'initiation à Antioche', *POC* 20 (1970), 3–19.

[103]   John Chrysostom in *Huit Catechèses Baptismales*, SC 50 (Paris, 1957), 153.

[104]   Theodoret, *H. Rel.* 1. 3. 8, SC 234 (Paris, 1971), 164.

[105]   Coquin, 'La thème de la παρρεία', 12. 2 Cor. 3: 18.

[106]   *Kyrillos* 99. 5–6.

This shows that he has sufficient intimacy with God both to know the mind of God and also to approach God confidently on behalf of others. Euthymius, for example, is approached by a crowd desperate for rain. He hesitates to pray on their behalf. 'On account of my sins, I do not have the *parresia* to pray about this.' But he agrees to do so, and, since he is humble, his prayer is granted.[107] *Parresia* is also associated with the power to work miracles in the writing of Theodore of Petra and George of Choziba.[108]

The moment of death has special significance. Cyril shows the importance he attaches to the death of the saints by dating the dying of Euthymius and Sabas with a precision not given to other events.[109] All that the saint has achieved comes to fulfilment when the course of his life is completed. It is only after the death that the saint's conflict against heresy is finally won, that miracles flow from the tomb so attracting visitors, that the community is secure due to the patronage of one who is now a citizen of heaven. His intercession becomes more effective and his protection more powerful once he has been welcomed into the closer presence of God.[110]

So death leads to a deeper intimacy with God, or *parresia*, which is again demonstrated by an outflowing of miracles after the holy man has died. Euthymius' makes a final promise to his disciples: 'If I find *parresia* towards God, I will ask this first request of him, that I may be in spirit with you and with those who come after you until eternity.'[111] Sabas' *parresia* is made manifest by a succession of appearances which he makes in the form of visions to those who pray to him asking for his protection. One vision is to a certain Romulus who is puzzled as to why St Theodore has delayed giving him an answer to a prayer. Theodore appears to him two days later, apologizing for the delay and saying that had been otherwise occupied in escorting Sabas into the presence of God.[112] Theodosius, Sophronius, and Heraclides also receive *parresia* at death.[113]

---

[107] Ibid. 38. 15–16; 220. 14–15.

[108] Theodore of Petra, *V. Thds.* 32. 5; Antony of Choziba, *Miracles of the Blessed Virgin*, 6, *An. Boll.* (1888), 368. 9.

[109] *Kyrillos*, 59. 22–60. 8; 183. 5–13.

[110] Further indications of the importance of the moment of death is provided by stories in which a holy man sees the soul of a dying monk being carried to heaven. See ibid. 214. 21–215. 7. *V. Anton.* 60; 65, PG 26. 929A; 933C–936A; Palladius, *H. Laus.* 7, ed. Butler, 26. 16–17.

[111] *Kyrillos*, 59. 9–11.

[112] Ibid. 185. 10–13.

[113] Ibid. 241. 4–7; Theodore of Petra, *V. Thds.* 91. 22; 92. 11; 95. 5. *V. Geor. Choz.* 9, *An. Boll.* (1888), 105. 9.

The concept of *parresia* was developed in literature from Asia Minor, and was adapted by Cyril of Scythopolis and other Palestinian authors to apply to the spiritual development of the saints. It spoke of the inner relationship with God given in baptism and developed through a life of ascetic struggle until it reaches final fulfilment in death. It is a relationship which is expressed in outward behaviour rooted in knowing God's will, speaking out fearlessly, and working miracles. The study of the use of the concept provides a theological commentary on the miracle stories.

AT PRAYER

Through their ascetic disciplines the holy men grow close to God. A part of this process is prayer. Generally the Lives maintain a discreet silence about the details of the intimate relationship between God and the saint expressed in prayer. One anecdote in the *Life of George of Choziba* suggests the intensity and ecstatic quality of the prayer of the holy man. George asked his disciple Antony to spread out his mat in a corner of the coenobium and then to leave him undisturbed. He lay down on the mat and covered himself with a piece of cloth. After he had not moved for three days the brothers assumed that he had died and prepared for his burial, but Antony touched his feet and found that they were still warm. Eventually George sat up groaning and saying, 'Glory to you, our God, glory to you,' his face trembling at the vision of the glory of God.[114]

[114] *V. Geor. Choz.* 36, *An. Boll.* (1888), 135. 6–136. 7.

CONCLUSION

The dates chosen to form the temporal boundaries of this study are 314 and 631. In 314 Macarius became Patriarch of Jerusalem. In the previous year the Emperors Constantine and Licinius had met at Milan and agreed that the Church should be granted legal personality and that the persecutions should cease, and so a new era of toleration was beginning. A few miles to the east, Chariton was living the ascetic life in his cave at Pharan and companions were beginning to join him. During his episcopate Macarius visited the infant community to consecrate the robbers' cave so that it became the church of the first monastery in the desert. So it can reasonably be claimed that the history of the monasteries of the Judaean desert began in 314.

Three centuries later the Holy City of Jerusalem fell to the Persians. The lurid descriptions of hardship described by Antony of Choziba, referred to in the Introduction, seem tame when compared with the catalogue of destruction which took place when the Persians entered Jerusalem, recorded by Strategius, the monk of the Great Laura. When Nicomedes, the superior of the Great Laura, returned from Arabia after the Persian conquest, he was so horrified at the sight of the unburied dead bodies littering the monastery that he collapsed in a faint.[1] The destruction, which claimed between 55,000 and 65,000 Christian lives, seemed to herald the end of the monastic movement.

Between those years, the group of settlements which we have examined was established in the dry and empty lands to the east of Jerusalem. People arrived from all parts of the Empire to populate these new centres. Lines of communication were developed with Jerusalem and with Constantinople beyond. The monasteries were more than places of prayer, they were an integral component of Byzantine society. It follows that with the passing of Byzantine Palestine, the monasteries could no longer fulfil the same social role. The fall of Jerusalem in 614 was an ending.

But the last source considered here was written in 631, the year in which Heraclius restored the True Cross to Jerusalem. The *Life of*

---

[1] See above, Introduction. Also Antiochus Monachos, *Epistle*, PG 89. 1424C–1425C.

George of Choziba is a witness to the continuing life of the monasteries of the desert. This continuity was also maintained after the arrival of the Arabs. As part of the terms negotiated by Patriarch Sophronius with the Arabs, the Christians were permitted to retain their churches and the monks were allowed to stay in the monasteries. The Great Laura, in particular, developed a vibrant and effective tradition of scholarship and liturgy which has had a lasting influence on the tradition of the Orthodox Church. Liturgical practice, enshrined in the *Typicon* of Mar Saba, contributed to the evolution of the worship of the Church, and some of the best-loved hymns and poems were written by the Sabaite monks, including the *Great Canon* of St Andrew of Crete, recited as an essential part of Lenten devotion in the Christian East. John of Damascus was the great systematic theologian of the Christian East, and struggled to preserve the veneration of the icons in the Iconoclast controversy. The monastery of Mar Saba also contributed to the monastic revivals on Mount Athos and in Russia. This list of achievements could be extended. It leaves no doubt that the arrival of the Arabs might have signalled a change in the nature of life in the monasteries but certainly did not lead to its extinction.[2]

One of the strangest sights of the desert today is the remains of the monastery of Euthymius. The ruins, which include the grave of the founder, stand among modern factories, since Khan el Ahmar is now an industrial estate. Although the juxtaposition of different standards and civilizations jars on the visitor, the place still conveys a sense of the grandeur and simplicity of the monasteries, and many visitors have admired the walls and gateways, usually identified as the Byzantine buildings. But the recent excavations of Yizhar Hirschfeld have discovered coins which date from the eighth to the twelfth centuries underneath the floor of the so-called Byzantine residential quarters.[3] This building, which has captivated many with its evocation of the early monks, was in fact built under the Arabs. It is a reminder of the continuing and indestructible spirit of the institution founded by Euthymius and his disciples which persisted through the medieval centuries and continues to witness to different standards and possibilities of living, among the activity of modern industrial society.

[2] For the literature of Mar Saba, see S. Vailhé, 'Les Écrivains de Mar Saba', *E. Or.* 2 (1899), 1–11, 33–47.

[3] For an account of the excavations at the monastery of Euthymius, see Y. Hirschfeld, 'List of the Byzantine Monasteries in the Judaean Desert', in G. C. Bottini *et al.* (eds.), *Christian Archeology in the Holy Land: New Discoveries* (Jerusalem, 1990), 1–90, 14–18.

EXCURSUS I

John of Scythopolis

There is no information in contemporary sources about when John was Bishop of Scythopolis. We know that Theodosius was Bishop in 518, when Sabas made his first visit to the city, and in 536, when he was present at the Council of Jerusalem.[1] We also know that Theodore, the Origenist superior of the New Laura, was made Bishop about 548 as part of Theodore Ascidas' campaign to advance as many of his supporters as possible to high positions in the church, and that he was still in post in 553.[2] So there are three possible times when John could have been Bishop; either before 518, the latest date for Theodosius' consecration; or between 536, the earliest date for Theodosius' death, and 548, when Theodore became Bishop; or after 553, the earliest date for Theodore's death.

As a result of the work of F. Loofs, L. Perrone, and B. Flusin, it has become accepted that John was Bishop between Theodosius and Theodore.[3]

This dating is proposed on the basis of indications in contemporary or near-contemporary literature. The early date, before 518, is ruled unlikely since John himself refers to the quarrel between Severus and Julian of Halicarnassus, which took place *after* 518.[4]

The late date, after 553, seems to be ruled out by two pieces of evidence. First, there is a reference to John as Bishop of Scythopolis in the *Contra Monophysitas* of Leontius of Jerusalem, a work dated by M. Richard to a time before the affair of the Three Chapters in 553, since Leontius writes of these three authors with no apparent awareness of their heretical status.[5] Second, Photius writes of a debate between John and Basileios, a presbyter in Antioch at the time of the Emperor Anastasius. Since Anastasius died in 518, it seems unlikely that one of the protagonists, John, could have lived long enough to be Bishop after 553.[6]

---

[1] *Kyrillos*, 162. 26–7; ACO 3, p. 188. 8 for the list of signatories to the Acts of the Jerusalem Council.

[2] *Kyrillos*, 197. 19–198. 1.

[3] F. Loofs, *Leontius of Byzantium* (Leipzig, 1887), 269–72; L. Perrone, *La chiesa di Palestina e le controversie Cristologiche* (Brescia, 1980), 240–9; *MH* 20–1.

[4] Mansi, xi, col. 437D.

[5] Leontius of Jerusalem, *Contra Monophysitas*, PG 86/2. 1865B–C. See also M. Richard, 'Léonce de Jérusalem et Léonce de Byzance', *MSR* 1 (1944), 35–88.

[6] Photius, *Bibliotheca*, cod. 107, ed. R. Henry, (*Bibliothèque*), ii (Paris, 1960), 48.

The middle date is suggested by a remark in the *Scholia*, in which John writes of the Origenists as his contemporaries: καὶ νῦν δὲ οἱ ἀπὸ τῶν Ὠριγένους προσερχόμενοι μύθων.[7] This would apply most naturally to the period before 548 when the Origenists were at the height of their influence.

But this conclusion is put in doubt by the silence of Cyril. It supposes that this glittering theological scholar was Bishop of Cyril's home town at a time when Cyril was living either in Scythopolis or in monasteries about fifty miles distant, and that Cyril made no mention of him at any point in the Lives.

Cyril's narrative makes it likely that Theodosius lived some time after 536, when he was at the Council of Jerusalem. Theodosius presided over Cyril's education, often enquired after him, and administered the tonsure to him.[8] Although, as Flusin points out, the tonsuring took place before Cyril actually entered the monastery in 543, it would be surprising if Cyril was tonsured as a young boy.[9] It should be assumed that there was a considerable lapse of time between Sabas' second visit to Scythopolis in 532 when he 'called' Cyril and Theodosius' ordination and tonsuring of Cyril. It is probable, in the absence of any reference to another bishop, that Theodosius was still Bishop of Scythopolis in 543 when Cyril left the city to travel to Jerusalem.

On the basis of Cyril's account, it seems that John was Bishop after 553. The pieces of evidence suggesting an earlier date are not conclusive. The reference to the Origenists as contemporary in the *Scholia* is either an attempt to add vividness to the account or a sign that Origenism was still rife after 553. The lack of condemnation by Leontius of Jerusalem of the authors condemned at the Council of Constantinople in 553 is an indication that he did not wish to associate himself with the decision. The reference to the debate with Basileios is found in a ninth-century work, and is not corroborated. These three references cannot be held to be conclusive when placed alongside the historical account of Cyril.

The most likely date for John's episcopate is the third and latest of the three possibilities: he succeeded Theodore some time after 553.

---

[7] *Scholia*, PG 4. 176A.
[8] *Kyrillos*, 181. 15–18.
[9] *MH* 16.

Leontius of Byzantium

A number of historical problems surround the figure of Leontius of Byzantium. For many of the events and personalities in the Origenist controversy, Cyril is the only contemporary source, but for Leontius there is a mass of confusing evidence. These sources present us with no fewer than four different people called Leontius. There is, first, the Leontius of Byzantium, the Origenist and opponent of Sabas, whose career, described by Cyril, has been briefly outlined. There is also a monk called Leontius who took part in the disputations between Monophysites and Chalcedonians in 532 and was present at five sittings of the 536 Synod at Constantinople. Then there is Leontius the Hermit, author of a number of philosophical and theological treatises. Then, finally, one of the Scythian monks of John Maxentius was called Leontius. The question to be considered here is whether there are four different Leontiuses or whether these figures are one Leontius ubiquitously appearing in several different contexts.

The fourth figure can be dismissed most quickly. The Scythian monk called Leontius has been identified with both Cyril's Leontius the Origenist and with the author Leontius the Hermit.[1] The identification of the Scythian monk with Cyril's Leontius was made by R. V. Sellers on the misunderstanding that the 'Scytharum monachi' of John Maxentius are monks of Scythopolis and include both Leontius and Cyril of Scythopolis. This view is rendered quite impossible by Cyril's account. It is also impossible that a monk holding the views of John Maxentius would have written the works of Leontius the Hermit which were strongly hostile to Monophysitism. This group sought rather to find common ground between Chalcedonians and Monophysites. The works of the Scythian monks would also have been more likely to have been in Latin. The Scythian monk can be disposed of.

The third Leontius in our list is the author, Leontius the Hermit. An extensive corpus of works is attributed to him. These include *Tres Libri contra Nestorianos et Eutychianos*; *Solutio Argumentorum a Severo Objectorum*; *Capita Triginta contra Severum*; *Adversus Fraudes Apollinistarum*; *Contra Monophysitas*, and *Contra Nestorianos*. It is generally agreed that the last two of these should be assigned to a different Leontius on the grounds of literary style, dogmatic

---

[1] For the identification of this Leontius with Cyril's Leontius, see R. V. Sellers, *The Coucil of Chalcedon* (London, 1961), 305; and with Leontius the Hermit, see E. R. Hardy, *Christology of the Later Fathers* (London, 1964), 375.

content, and historical reference.[2] The Leontius who wrote these two works is known as Leontius of Jerusalem, and need not concern us in this discussion.

The identification of Leontius the Hermit with Cyril's Leontius is supported by an autobiographical reference in *Contra Nestorianos et Eutychianos*, in which the author writes of his youthful flirtation with the school of Antioch and his subsequent salvation in Palestine 'at the hands of wise and pious men'.[3] He also says that the book contains the substance of several lectures which he had frequently delivered. The disputations with the Monophysites which are described by Cyril as taking place during Sabas' second visit to Constantinople provide an occasion on which these lectures could have been delivered.[4]

Against this circumstantial evidence is the unfortunate fact that not only do Leontius' writings uphold a consistent Chalcedonian Christology, but they also include an attack on Origen. Leontius wrote: 'they do not admire Origen, because the well-named and admirable Gregory, collecting together numberless objections, has directed a book against him'.[5]

Recent studies have examined the problem of Leontius' Origenism.[6] Two preliminary suggestions favour the possibility that he might have been Origenist. First, the passage apparently attacking Origen could be construed as an ironical question and, if so, far from indicating disapproval of Origen's teaching, might be a sign of sympathy.[7] Secondly, marginal notes have been inserted by an unknown scholiast into the codex of Leontius' works. In a section attacking Eutyches, Leontius wrote: 'a pious and devout man has said these things well', and the scholiast noted: περὶ τοῦ αββὰ Νόννου. Alongside a remark about 'a certain man who went before us with wisdom from God' the commentator has added: περὶ 'Ευαγρίου.[8] These marginal notes suggest that Leontius was known as an Origenist sympathizer.

The strange absence of clear Origenist content to the works of Leontius can be explained by the complex theological and ecclesiastical environment of the capital. M. Richard has pointed out that an Origenist in Justinian's Constantinople might well wish to conceal his sympathies with Origenist speculation.[9]

---

[2] See M. Richard, 'Léonce de Byzance, était-il Origéniste?', *RE Byz.* 5 (1947), 31–66; and 'Léonce de Jérusalem et Léonce de Byzance', *MSR* 1 (1944), 35–88. The same author argues that the treatise De Sectis cannot be attributed to Leontius in 'Le traité De Sectis et Léonce de Byzance', *RHE* 35 (1939), 695–723. Some scholars have championed the unity of authorship of the whole Leontian corpus, including S. Rees, 'The Literary Activity of Leontius of Byzantium', *J. Th. S.* NS 19 (1968), 229–42.

[3] *Contra Nestorianos et Eutychianos*, 3, prol. PG 86. 1357C–1360B.

[4] Ibid. 1, prol. PG 86. 1268C; *Kyrillos* 176. 8–9.

[5] *Contra Nestorianos et Eutychianos*, PG 86. 1377B–C.

[6] These include D. B. Evans, *Leontius of Byzantium: an Origenist Christology* (Washington, 1970), and B. Daley, 'The Origenism of Leontius of Byzantium', *J. Th. S.* NS 27 (1976), 333–69.

[7] See F. Loofs, *Leontius von Byzanz* (Leipzig, 1887), 294.

[8] See PG 86. 1273C, 1285A–B. The codex is Vat. Gr. 2195.

[9] Richard, 'Léonce de Byzance, était-il Origéniste?', 63.

He shows that Leontius is decidedly opposed both to Monophysitism and Nestorianism, and directs his work to Chalcedonians who incline to error.[10] Richard describes Leontius' position as that of 'un chalcedonisme très stricte interprété à la lumière de la théologie cappadocienne et d'une philosophie originale'.[11] An approach such as this could accommodate Origenism. As a context for this work, Richard suggests the period following Justinian's 543 Edict against Origen.[12] This edict was a set-back for the Origenists, who participated in the attack on the Three Chapters in an attempt to draw attention away from themselves and to regain the Emperor's favour. According to Cyril, Leontius died at about the time of the 543 Edict, so the historical context proposed by Richard would argue against identifying Cyril's Leontius with Leontius the author. But there could have been times other than 543 when imperial opinion swung against Origenism and when a judicious Origenist might wish to conceal some of his views.

D. B. Evans sought to provide a stronger argument for Leontius' Origenism by demonstrating that Leontius develops his theology in an Origenist framework.[13] He makes a detailed examination of two chapters of Book One of the *Contra Nestorianos et Eutychianos*, which discuss the author's classification of beings, the nature of the soul, and the use of the soul/body paradigm of the word/flesh union in Christ. He then considers Evagrius' theology and concludes that Leontius' soul occupies the same place in his anthropological scheme as does the nous in that of Evagrius. It can be concluded that Leontius' Christology depends on the Origenist idea of an Evagrian sinless nous uniting to both word and flesh.[14]

Evans cannot be said to have established his case. B. Daley sets out other passages in which Leontius contradicts important Origenist views. These include references to a creation which takes place in history; the Fall as a historical rather than cosmic event; and the Logos uniting directly to the flesh in the Incarnation.[15] He concludes:

> All the similarities Prof. Evans adduces between their conceptions of the spirit of man—the tripartite soul, the distinction between form and matter and of the four elements, the contrast between οὐσία and ποιότης, even the notion that soul and body are different natures—are all too much a part of the mixed heritage of any sixth century Greek philosopher to be by themselves

---

[10] See PG 86. 1277. Leontius can only just accept the standard Cyrillian formula of μια φύσις τοῦ θεοῦ λόγου σεσσαρκωμένη.

[11] Richard, 'Léonce de Byzance, était-il Origéniste?', 46.

[12] Ibid. 48–9.

[13] This is argued in Evans, *Leontius of Byzantium*, also in J. Meyendorff, *Christ in Eastern Christian Thought* (New York, 1975), 47–68.

[14] Evans, *Leontius of Byzantium*, 84–131.

[15] Daley, 'Origenism of Leontius of Byzantium', refers to passages where Leontius contradicts Origenist positions at PG 86. 1284C; 1384B–D; 1369C.

evidence of dependence of one writer on another ... The real drift of Evans' book ... is to say: the Evagrian myth *could* be expressed without contradiction in Leontian terms.[16]

The conclusion that must be drawn from an examination of Leontius' works is that it is possible, but not proven, that an Origenist from Nonnus' circle was the author. The identification of Leontius the Hermit and Cyril's Leontius is not ruled out, but nor is it established beyond doubt. In view of the improbability of there being two theologians and leaders in Constantinople at the same time, the possibility that the two are to be identified is a more likely conclusion.

There is another Leontius, the second of the four mentioned earlier. This is Leontius the Monk who took part in doctrinal discussions in Constantinople in 532 and in the Synod of 536. In the records of the meeting of 532 he is described as 'Leontius a venerable monk and apocrisarius of the fathers assembled in the holy city' (*Leontio viro venerabili monacho atque apocrisario patrum in sancto civitate constitutorum*).[17] In the lists of the participants at the five sittings of the 536 Synod, he is: Λεόντιος ἐλέει θεοῦ μοναχὸς καὶ ἡγούμενος καὶ τοποτηρητὴς πάσης τῆς ἐρήμου; as Λεόντιος ἐλέει θεοῦ μοναχὸς (to which the Latin translation adds *et prior proprii monasterii*); ποιούμενος τὸν λόγον ὑπὲρ τῶν κατὰ τὴν ἔρημον ἁγίων πατέρων; and as Λεόντιος ἡγούμενος καὶ μοναχὸς ἰδίου μοναστηρίου καὶ ὑπὲρ πάντων τῶν ἐν τῇ ἐρήμῳ καὶ Ἰορδάνῃ ἁγίων πατέρων.[18]

The objections to identifying this Leontius with Leontius the Origenist are that, although Cyril describes his Leontius as being in Constantinople during the discussions, he also records that he had been dismissed from the delegation by Sabas. If this is so, he could not have been accurately described as *apocrisarius* or τοποτηρητής, since he was no longer anybody's representative; nor as a superior, since he had left his own monastery.

Various answers to these problems can be given. The puzzle of how Leontius could be referred to as an *apocrisarius* has two possible solutions. Schwartz suggests that he had been appointed by the Emperor Justinian.[19] In support of this there are the statements of Cyril that Leontius was influential at court. An alternative possibility is that Leontius remained the representative of the Patriarch of Jerusalem. According to this understanding Cyril has exaggerated the importance of Sabas in the delegation. Leontius was at least as important as Sabas, if not more so. Far from being dismissed by Sabas, he remained in Constantinople to continue to represent the interests of the Patriarchate—as well as those of his own Origenist party.[20]

The second objection to the identification is the description of him as 'superior' or ἡγούμενος in the presence lists. Leontius the Origenist was a monk

---

[16] Daley, 'Origenism of Leontius of Byzantium', 354–5.
[17] *ACO* 4. 2, p. 170. 5.
[18] *ACO* 3, pp. 37. 1, 50. 30, 145. 34, and also *Kyrillos*, 130. 34, 158. 56, 165. 30.
[19] *Kyrillos*, 391.
[20] Loofs, *Leontius von Byzanz*, 261–73. See also *Kyrillos*, 173. 5–11; 176. 7–20.

who, before his departure from Palestine, had been a member, but not the superior, of the New Laura. He might have been described as a superior since he was living as a solitary at Constantinople. At the same Synod of 536 a hermit, Isidore, signed himself as ἡγουμένος μονῆς ἰδίας, in a context which makes it clear that his monastery was a single cell.[21] A similar usage is to be found in the jocular remark of Sabas to Theodosius that he was a ἡγουμένων . . . ἡγούμενος, since he was responsible for hermits.[22] This explanation is further supported by the possible, or, as is argued above, probable, identification of Leontius the Monk with Leontius the Hermit, the author. It is also likely that a monk of his reputation, representing an influential group of Palestinian monks, would have been asked to preside over one of the numerous monasteries in the capital, in which he may have lived alone or with others.

In the presence lists of the 536 Synod, Leontius' name is included with those of the Palestinian monks. In addition to him, there are four monks from the Monastery of Theodosius, four from the Monastery of Martyrius, two from the Great Laura, three from the Laura of the Towers, four from the New Laura, and one from the Laura of Firminus.[23] Leontius is the only monk of this group whose name is not associated with a monastery. Instead he is described as τοποτηρητὴς τῆς ἐρήμου πασῆς.[24] This description fits Cyril's Leontius, a monk who came from the Palestinian desert, who had been part of a delegation to Constantinople, who had been in the capital too long to retain membership of a specific monastery, and whose authority was accepted by the monks present in 536.

There are, therefore, no significant objections to the identification of Leontius the representative of the Origenists of Palestine, Leontius who participated in the disputation and synod, and Leontius the author of numerous theological works. The Origenists could look to a formidable leader to present their case in the capital.

---

[21] *ACO* 3, p. 49. 9–11.
[22] *Kyrillos*, 166. 25.
[23] See lists referred to in n. 18.
[24] *ACO* 3, p. 158. 29.

BIBLIOGRAPHY

PRIMARY SOURCES

Acta Conciliorum Oecumenicorum, ed. E. Schwartz, cont. J. Straub, 4 pts. in 13 vols. (Strasburg, Berlin, Leipzig, 1914–40), 2nd ser. ed. R. Reidinger (Berlin, 1984–92).

AMMIANUS MARCELLINUS, *Rerum Gestarum Libri qui Supersunt*, ed. R. J. C. Rolf, LCL, 3 vols. (London, 1952–6).

ANTIOCHUS MONACHOS, *Homilies*, PG 89. 1428–1849.

ANTONINUS PLACENTINUS, *Itinerarium*, ed. P. Geyer, 'Itineraria et alia geographica', CCL 175 (Turnhout, 1965).

ANTONY OF CHOZIBA, *Life of George of Choziba* and *Miracles of the Blessed Virgin Mary*, *An. Boll.* 7 (1888), 97–114, 336–70.

Apophthegmata Patrum, alphabetical collection, PG 65. 71–442. ET, B. Ward, *The Sayings of the Desert Fathers* (London, 1975).

Apophthegmata Patrum, anon. collection, *Histoires des solitaires égyptiens*, ed. F. Nau, *ROC* 12 (1907), 48–69, 171–81, 393–404; 13 (1908), 47–57, 266–83; 14 (1909), 357–79; 17 (1912), 204–11, 294–301; 18 (1913), 137–46.

ATHANASIUS, *Life of Antony*, PG 26. 835–978. Eng. trans., R. Gregg (London, 1982).

BASIL, *Regulae Fusius Tractatae et Regulae Brevius Tractatae*, PG 31. 889–1305. Eng. trans., *The Ascetic Works of St Basil*, ed. and trans. W. Lowther Clarke (London, 1925). Fr. trans., *Saint Basile: Les Règles monastiques*, ed. and trans. L. Lébé (Maredsous, 1969).

Chronicon Paschale, PG 92. 67–1028. ET, M. and M. Whitby (Liverpool, 1989).

Codex Theodosianus, ed T. Mommsen and P. Meyer (Berlin, 1905).

Collectio Avellana, Epistulae Imperatorum Pontificium aliorum, CSEL 35 (Vienna, 1901).

CYRIL OF ALEXANDRIA, *Letters*, PG 77. 9–390.

CYRIL OF JERUSALEM, *Catachetical Lectures. Catachèses Mystagogiques*, trans. P. Paris, SC 126 (Paris, 1966).

CYRIL OF SCYTHOPOLIS, *Lives. Kyrillos von Skythopolis*, ed. E. Schwartz, TU 49/2 (Leipzig, 1939). FT, A.-J. Festugière, *Les Moines d'Orient*, 4 pts. in 7 vols. (Paris, 1961–5), pt. 3 (1963). ET, R. M. Price and J. Binns (eds.), *Cyril of Scythopolis: Lives of the Monks of Palestine*, CS 114 (Kalamazoo, Mich., 1991).

de Obitu Theodosii Hierosolymorum et Romani Monachi, in E. W. Brooks, *Vitae Virorum apud Monophysitas Celeberrimorum*, CSCO.S 3/25 (1907), 15–27.

De Syncletica in Deserto Jordanis, ed. B. Flusin and J. Paramelle, *An. Boll.* 100 (1982), 305–17.

Diocletian's Price Edict [Diokletian's Preisedikt], ed. S. Lauffer (Berlin, 1971).

DOROTHEUS OF GAZA, *Works*, *Dorothée de Gaza, Œuvres Spirituelles*, ed. L. Regnault and J. Préville, SC 92 (Paris, 1963).

EPIPHANIUS, *Panarion*, ed. K. Holl, GCS 25 (Leipzig, 1915).

EUSEBIUS OF CAESAREA, *Ecclesiastical History*, [*Eusèbe de Cesareé, Histoire Ecclésiastique*], ed. G. Bardy, SC 31, 41, 55, 73 (Paris, 1952–60).

—— *Life of Constantine. Uber das Leben des Kaisers Konstantin*, ed. F. Winkelmann, GCS Eusebius 1/1 (Berlin, 1975).

EVAGRIUS SCHOLASTICUS, *Ecclesiastical History*, ed. J. Bidez and L. Parmentier (London, 1898).

Expositio Totius Mundi et Gentium, ed. J. Rougé, SC 124 (Paris, 1966).

FLEMMING, J. (ed.), *Akten der ephesischen Synode vom Jahre 449*, Abhandlungen den Kgl. Gesellschaft der Wissenschaften zu Göttingen, NS 15/1 (Berlin, 1917).

GEORGE THE MONK, *De Haeresibus ad Epiphanium. Le Traité de Georges Hiéromoine sur les Hérésies*, ed. M. Richard, *RE Byz.* 28 (1970), 239–69.

GREGORY THE GREAT, *Dialogues. Grégoire le Grand: Dialogues*, ed. and trans. A. de Vögue and P. Antin, SC 251, 260, 265 (Paris, 1978–80).

GREGORY OF NAZIANZUS *Theological Orations*, PG 36. 11–172, ET in *Christology of the Later Fathers*, ed. E. R. Hardy (Philadelphia, 1954).

—— *Funeral Discourses. Grégoire de Nazianze: Discours funèbre en l'honneur de son frère Césaire et de Basile de Cesarée*, ed. F. Boulenger (Paris, 1905).

GREGORY OF NYSSA, *Letters. Gregorii Nysseni Opera*, 8/2, ed. G. Pasquali (Leiden, 1959).

GREGORY THAUMATURGUS, *Panegyric on Origen. Grégoire le thaumaturge: Remérciement à Origène*, ed. H. Crouzel, SC 148 (Paris, 1969).

HIPPOLYTUS, *Chronography*, ed. R. Helm, GCS Hippolytus, 4 (Berlin, 1955).

Historia Monachorum in Aegypto, ed. A.-J. Festugière, SHG 34 (Brussels, 1961). Latin text: *Tyrannius Rufius: Historia Monachorum sive de Vita Sanctorum Patrum*, ed E. Schulz-Flugel, PTS 34 (Berlin, 1990). ET, N. Russell (ed.), *The Lives of the Desert Fathers* (London, 1980).

Inscriptiones Latinae Selectae, ed. H. Dessau (Berlin, 1892–1916).

Itinerarium Aetheriae, Étherie: Journal de voyage, ed. P. Maraval, SC 296 (Paris, 1982). ET, J. Wilkinson, *Egeria's Travels to the Holy Land*, 2nd edn. (Warminster, 1981).

Itinerarium Burdigalense, ed. P. Geyer, 'Itineraria et alia geographica', CCL 175 (Turnhout, 1965).

JEROME, *Commentaries on Ezekiel*, ed. F. Glorie, CCL 75 (Turnhout, 1964).

—— *Life of Hilarion. Studies in the Text Tradition of St Jerome's* Vitae Patrum, ed. W. A. Oldfather (Urbana, Ill., 1943).

JOHN CASSIAN, *Conferences. Jean Cassien: Conférences*, ed. F. Pichéry, SC 42, 54, 64 (Paris, 1955–9).
—— *Institutes. Jean Cassien: Institutions Cénobitiques*, ed. J. C. Guy, SC 109 (Paris, 1965).
JOHN CHRYSOSTOM, *Baptismal Lectures. Jean Chrysostome: Huit Catachèses baptismales inédites*, SC 50 (Paris, 1957).
JOHN OF DAMASCUS, *Homilies. Die Schriften des Johannes von Damaskos V*, ed. B. Kotter, PTS 29 (Berlin, 1988); PG 96. 545–815.
JOHN OF EPHESUS, *Ecclesiastical History*, pt. 3, ed. E. W. Brooks, CSCO.S 3/3 (Paris, 1935–6).
—— *Lives of the Eastern Saints*, ed. and trans. E. W. Brooks, PO 17–19 (Paris, 1923–5).
JOHN MALALAS, *Chronography*, PG 97. 65–718. ET, *The Chronicle*, trans. E. Jeffreys *et al.* (Melbourne, 1986).
JOHN MOSCHUS, *Spiritual Meadow*, PG 87/3. 2951–3112. FT, M. Roüet de Journal (ed.), *Jean Mosche: Le Pré Spirituel*, SC 12 (Paris, 1946).
JOHN OF NIKIU, *Chronicle*, trans. R. H. Charles (London, 1916).
JOHN RUFUS, Bishop of Maiuma, *Plerophoriai*, ed. F. Nau, PO 8 (1912), 11–183.
JOSEPHUS, *On The Jewish War*, ed. H. St J. Thackeray, LCL Josephus, ii–iii (London, 1927–8).
JUSTINIAN, *Nouvellae*, ed. R. Schoell and W. Kroll (Berlin, 1928).
LEONTIUS OF BYZANTIUM, *Works*, PG 86. 1–2.
LEONTIUS OF JERUSALEM, *Contra Monophysitas*, PG 86/2. 1769–1902.
LIBERATUS, *Breviarium Causarum Nestorianorum et Eutychianorum*, ACO 2. 5, pp. 98–141.
Life of Chariton, ed. G. Garitte, *BIHBR* (1941), 5–50.
Life of Daniel the Stylite, in R. P. Delehaye, *Les Saints stylites*, SHG 14 (Brussels, 1923), 1–94.
Life of Hypatius, ed. G. J. M. Bartelink, SC 177 (Paris, 1971). FT, A.-J. Festugière, *Les Moines d'Orient*, 4 pts. in 7 vols. (Paris, 1961–5), pt. 2, 13–82.
Life of Melania. Vie de Sainte Melanie, ed. D. Gorce, SC 90 (Paris, 1962).
Life of Pachomius, First Greek Life. Sancti Pachomii Vitae Graecae, ed. F. Halkin, SHG 19 (Brussels, 1932). ET, A. N. Athanassakis (Missoula, Mont., 1975).
Life of Pachomius, Coptic Lives. S. Pachomii Vita Bohairice Scripta, ed. L. T. Lefort, CSCO 89 (Louvain, 1925). ET, A. Veilleux, *Pachomian Koinonia*, i, CS 45 (Kalamazoo, Mich., 1980).
Life of Peter the Iberian, R. Raabe, *Petrus der Iberer: Ein Charakterbild zur Kirchen- und Sittengeschichte des 5. Jahrhunderts* (Leipzig, 1895).
Life of Porphyry. Marc le Diacre: Vie de Porphyre, ed. H. Grégoire and M. A. Kugener (Paris, 1930).
Life of Stephen the Sabaite, 'Le début de la vie de S. Étienne le Sabaite retrouvé

en Arabe au Sinai', ed. G. Garitte, *An. Boll.* 77 (1959), 332–69.

Life of Symeon the Fool. Das Leben des heiligen Narren Symeon von Neapolis, ed. L. Ryden (Uppsala, 1963).

Life of Thecla. Vie et Miracles de Sainte Thècle, ed. G. Dagron, SHG 62 (Brussels, 1978).

Life of Theodore of Sykeon. Vie de Theodore de Sykeon, ed. A.-J. Festugière, SHG 48 (Brussels, 1970). Partial ET, E. Dawes and N. Baynes, *Three Byzantine Saints* (Oxford, 1948).

MICHAEL THE SYRIAN, *Chronicle*, ed. J. B. Chabot, 3 vols. (Paris, 1899–1905).

Midrash Rabbah, i. *Genesis (Bereshith)*, trans. H. Freedman and M. Simon (London, 1939).

Miracles of Cosmas and Damian, ed. A.-J. Festugière, *Collections greques de miracles: Sainte Thècle, Saints Côme et Damien, Saint Georges* (Paris, 1971).

Mishnah, trans. H. Danby, (Oxford, 1933).

Narratio de Obitu Theodosii Hierosolymorum et Romani Monachi, in E. W. Brooks, *Vitae Virorum apud Monophysitas celeberrimorum*, CSCO.S 3/25 (1907), 15–27.

NICEPHORUS CALLISTUS, *Ecclesiastical History*, PG 146–7.

NILUS OF ANCYRA, *Liber de Monastica Exercitatione*, PG 79. 720–809.

ORIGEN, *On First Principles. Origène: Traité des principes*, ed. H. Crouzel and M. Simonetti, 5 vols., SC 252, 268, 312 (Paris, 1978–84). ET, G. Butterworth (London, 1936).

—— *Homilies on Luke. Die Homilien Zu Lukas*, ed. M. Rauer, GCS 35 (Leipzig, 1930).

PALLADIUS, *Lausiac History*, ed. C. Butler, Texts and Studies 6, vol. ii (Cambridge, 1904). ET, R. Meyer (New York, 1964).

PAUL OF ELOUSA, *Life of Theognius*, ed. P. van den Gheyn, *An. Boll.* 10 (1891), 78–113.

PAULINUS OF NOLA, *Letters*, ed. G. de Hartel, CSEL 29 (Vienna, 1894). ET, P. Walsh, Ancient Christian Writers, 35/63 (Westminster, 1966–7).

PHOTIUS, *Bibliotheca. Bibliothèque*, ed. R. Henry, 9 vols. (Paris, 1960–77).

POLYBIUS, *Histories*, ed. W. Paton, LCL 6 vols. (London 1922–7).

PROCOPIUS, *Buildings*, ed. H. B. Dewing, LCL Procopius, vii (London, 1914).

—— *Secret History. Anecdota*, ed. H. B. Dewing, LCL Procopius, vi (London, 1935).

SEVERUS, *Liber Contra Impium Grammaticum*, trans. J. Lebon, CSCO.S 94 (Louvain, 1930).

SEVERUS OF ASHMUNEIN, *History of the Patriarchs of the Coptic Church*, ed. B. T. A. Evetts, PO 1 (1907), 5 (1910).

SOCRATES SCHOLASTICUS, *Ecclesiastical History*, PG 67. 53–842. ET in Library of Nicene and Post-Nicene Fathers, ser. 2, vol. ii (Grand Rapids, Mich., 1979).

SOZOMEN, *Ecclesiastical History*, ed. J. Bidez, GCS (Berlin, 1960). ET in

Library of Nicene and Post-Nicene Fathers, ser. 2, vol. ii (Grand Rapids, Mich., 1979).

STRATEGIUS, *Capture of Jerusalem. La Prise de Jerusalem par les Perses en 615*, ed. G. Garitte, CSCO.Ib. 11–12 (1960).

SULPICIUS SEVERUS, *Dialogues*, PL 20. 183–247.

—— *Letters*, PL 20. 175–82.

—— *Life of Martin. Sulpice Sevère: Vie de s. Martin*, ed. J. Fontaine, SC 133, 134, 135 (Paris, 1967–9).

Supplementum Epigraphicum Graecum (Leiden, 1923–60), viii, Palestine (1937).

Talmud. Babylonian Talmud, ed. I. Epstein, 35 vols. (London, 1935–62).

THEODORE LECTOR, *Ecclesiastical History*, ed. G. C. Hansen, GCS (Berlin, 1971).

THEODORE OF PETRA, *Life of Theodosius*. H. Usener, *Der heilige Theodosius* (Leipzig, 1890, repr. Hildesheim, 1975).

THEODORET, *Ecclesiastical History*, ed. L. Parmentier, GCS (Berlin, 1954).

—— *Graecarum Affectionum Curatio. Therapeutique des maladies helléniques*, ed. P. Canivet, SC 57 (Paris, 1938).

—— *Religious History. Histoire Philothée*, ed. P. Canivet and A. Leroy-Molinghen, SC 234, 257 (Paris, 1977–9). ET, R. M. Price, *A History of the Monks of Syria*, CS 88 (Kalamazoo, Mich., 1985).

THEOPHANES, *Chronography*, ed. C. de Boor, 2 vols. (Lipsiae, 1883–5). Partial ET, H. Turtledove, *Chronicle* (Philadelphia, 1982).

VARSANUPHIUS and JOHN, *Questions and Answers*, ed. S. N. Schoinas (Volos, 1960); FT, L. Regnault, P. Lemaire, and B. Outtier, *Correspondance* (Solesme, 1972).

ZACHARIAH OF MITYLENE, *Ecclesiastical History*, ed. E. W. Brooks, CSCO.S 3/5–6 (Louvain, 1924). ET, R. Hamilton and E. W. Brooks, *Syriac Chronicle Known as that of Zachariah of Mitylene* (London, 1899).

SECONDARY WORKS

ABEL, F.-M., 'Beisan', *RB* 9 (1912), 409–23.

—— *Géographie de la Palestine* 3rd edn. (Paris, 1967).

—— *Histoire de la Palestine* (Paris, 1952).

—— 'Saint Cyrille d'Alexandrie dans ses rapports avec la Palestine', in *Kyrilliana, Spicilegia edita Sancti Cyrilli Alexandrini XV recurrente saeculo* (Cairo, 1947), 203–30.

ADNES, A., and CANIVET, P., 'Guérisons miraculeuses et exorcismes dans l'Histoire Philothée de Théodoret de Cyr', *RHR* 171 (1967), 53–82, 149–79.

AHARONI, Y., EVENARI, M., SHANAN, L., and TADMOR, N. H., 'The Ancient Desert Agriculture of the Negev', *IEJ* 10 (1960), 23–36, 97–111.

ALEXANDER, P. J., *The Oracle of Baalbek: The Tiburtine Sibyl in Greek Dress*, Dumbarton Oaks Studies, 10 (Washington, 1967).

AMÉLINEAU, A., 'Samuel de Kalamoun', *RHR* 30 (1894), 1–47.

APPLEBAUM, S., 'The Theatre at Scythopolis', *IEJ* 10 (1960), 126–7, 263–7.

ARMSTRONG, G., 'Fifth- and Sixth-Century Church Building in the Holy Land', *GOTR* 14 (1969), 17–30.

ATLAS OF ISRAEL, 3rd edn. (Tel Aviv, 1985).

AUGUSTINOVIC, A., *Gerico e dintorni* (Jerusalem, 1951).

AVI-YONAH, M., 'The Bath of the Lepers at Scythopolis', *IEJ* 13 (1963), 325–6.

—— 'The Development of the Roman Road System in Palestine', *IEJ* 1 (1950–1), 54–60.

—— 'The Economics of Byzantine Palestine', *IEJ* 8 (1958), 39–51.

—— (ed.) *Encyclopedia of Archeological Excavations in the Holy Land*, 3 vols. (London, 1975–8).

—— *Gazetteer of Roman Palestine*, Qedem, 5 (Jerusalem, 1976).

—— 'Mosaic Pavements in Palestine', *QDAP* 2 (1932), 70–82.

—— *The Madaba Mosaic Map* (Jerusalem, 1954).

—— 'Scythopolis', *IEJ* 12 (1962), 123–34.

BACHT, H., 'Die Rolle des orientalischen Mönchtums in der Kirchenpolitischen Auseinandersetzungen um Chalkedon (431–519)', in *Das Konzil von Chalkedon*, ed. A. Grillmeier and H. Bacht, 3 vols. (Würzburg, 1951–4), ii. 193–314.

BAHAT, D., 'A Synagogue at Beth-Shean', in ed. L. Levine, *Ancient Synagogues Revealed* (Jerusalem, 1982), 82–5.

BALTHASAR, H. U. VON, 'Das Scholienwerk des Johannes von Skythopolis', *Sch* 15 (1940), 16–38.

BAR-ADON, P., 'A Possible Fortified Synagogue at Beth Yerah', in *Roman Frontier Studies 1967*, Proceedings of the 7th International Congress held at Tel Aviv (Tel Aviv, 1971), 185.

BARTELINK, G. J. M., 'Quelques observations sur παρρησία dans la littérature paléo-chrétienne', in *Graecitas et Latinitas Christianorum Primaeva*, suppl. fasc. 3 (Nijmegen, 1970), 7–57.

BEAUVERY, R., 'La Route romaine de Jérusalem à Jéricho', *RB* 64 (1957), 72–101.

BET SHEAN PROJECT', contributed by the excavators Y. Tsafrir, G. Foerster, G. Mazor, *et al.*, *Excavations and Surveys in Israel*, 6 (1987–8), 7–45, 7–8 (1988–9), 15–32.

BINNS, J., 'The Distinctiveness of Palestinian Monasticism, 450–550 AD', in *Monastic Studies*, ed. J. Loades (Bangor, 1990), 11–20.

—— 'The Early Monasteries', *Medieval History*, 1/2 (1991), 12–22.

—— 'The Miracle Stories of Cyril of Scythopolis', in *Studia Patristica*, 23, Papers presented at the 10th International Conference of Patristic Studies in

Oxford 1987, ed. E. A. Livingstone (Louvain, 1989), 3–7.

BOUSSET, W., *Apophthegmata, Textüberlieferung und Charakter der Apophthegmata Patrum* (Tübingen, 1923).

BROCK, S., 'The Thrice-Holy Hymn in the Liturgy', *Sobornost* 7/2 (1985), 24–34.

BROOKS, C. E. P., *Climate Through the Ages*, 2nd edn. (London, 1949).

BROSHI, M., 'The Population of Western Palestine in the Roman Byzantine Period', *BASOR*, 23 (1980), 1–10.

BROWN, P. R. L., *The Cult of the Saints* (London, 1981).

—— 'The Rise and Function of the Holy Man in Late Antiquity', *JRS* 61 (1971), 80–101.

—— *The World of Late Antiquity* (London, 1971).

BROWNING, R., *Justinian and Theodora* (New York, 1981).

—— 'The "Low Level" Saint's Life in the early Byzantine World', in S. Hackel (ed.), *The Byzantine Saint*, University of Birmingham 14th Spring Symposium of Byzantine Studies (London, 1981), 117–27.

BUCK, D. F., 'The Structure of the Lausiac History', *Byz.* 46 (1976), 292–307.

CAMERON, AVERIL, 'Cyril of Scythopolis: Vita Sabae 53: A Note on Kata in Late Greek', *Glotta*, 66 (1978), 87–94.

—— 'The Early Religious Policies of Justin II', in D. Baker (ed.), *The Orthodox Churches and the West*, SCH 13 (1976), 51–67.

—— 'Eusebius of Caearea and the Re-thinking of History; in *Tria Corda: Scritti in onore di Arnaldo Momigliano* (Como, 1983), 71–88.

—— 'Eustratius' Life of Eutychius and the Fifth Ecumenical Council', in J. Chrysostomides (ed.) *Kathegetria: Essays Presented to Joan Hussey for her 80th Birthday* (Camberley, 1988), 225–47.

—— *Procopius and the Sixth Century* (London, 1985).

CANIVET, P., *Le Monachisme Syrien Selon Théodoret de Cyr*, Théologie Historique, 42 (Paris, 1977).

CHADWICK, H., 'John Moschus and his Friend Sophronius the Sophist', *J. Th. S.* NS 25 (1974), 41–74.

—— 'Pachomios and the Idea of Sanctity', in S. Hackel (ed.), *The Byzantine Saint*, University of Birmingham 14th Spring Symposium of Byzantine Studies (London, 1981), 11–24.

CHARANIS, P., *Church and State in the Later Roman Empire: The Religious Policy of Anastasius I, 491–518*, 2nd edn. (Thessalonika, 1974).

CHESNUT, G. F., *The First Christian Histories*. Théologie Historique, 46 (Paris, 1977).

CHESNUT, R., *Three Monophysite Christologies* (Oxford, 1976).

CHITTY, D. J., *The Desert a City* (Oxford, 1966).

—— 'The Monastery of St Euthymius', *PEFQ St.* (1931), 188–203.

—— 'Two Monasteries in the Wilderness of Judaea', *PEFQ St.* (1928), 134–52.

—— and JONES, A. H. M., 'The Church of St Euthymius at Khan ed Ahmar near Jerusalem', *PEFQ St.* (1928), 175–8.

CLAUDE, D., *Die byzantinische Stadt im sechsten Jahrhundert* (Munich, 1969).

CLAUS, A., ὅ σχολαστίκος, dissertation, University of Cologne, 1965.

CLUGNET, L., 'Vies et récits d'anachoretes', *ROC* 10 (1905), 39–50.

CONDER, C. R., and KITCHENER, R. E., *Survey of Western Palestine*, 3 vols. (London, 1881–3).

COQUIN, R. G., 'Le thème de la théologie de la παρρησία et ses expressions symboliques dans les rites d'initiation à Antioche', *POC* 20 (1970), 3–19.

CORBO, V., 'L'ambiente materiale della Vita dei Monaci di Palestina nel periodo Bizantino', *Or. Chr. A.* 153 (1958), 235–57.

—— 'Il Cenobio di Zannos e il piccolo cenobio della Granda Laura ritrovati nel wadi el-Nar', *TS (I)* 34 (1958), 109–10.

—— *Gli scavi di Kh. Siyar el-Ghanam (Campo dei Pastori) e i monasteri dei dintorni* (Jerusalem, 1955).

—— 'Il romitorio egumeno Gabriele', *TS (I)* (July–Aug. 1951), 202–7.

COURET, A., *La Palestine sous les empéreurs grecs 326–636* (Grenoble, 1869).

COX, P., *Biography in Late Antiquity: A Quest for the Holy Man* (Berkeley, Calif., 1983).

CROUZEL, H., *Origen* (Edinburgh, 1989).

CROWFOOT, J. W., *Early Churches in Palestine* (London, 1941).

DAGRON, G., 'Les Moines et la ville: La monachisme à Constantinople jusqu'au Concile de Chalcédoine (451)', *Travaux et mémoires*, 4 (1970), 229–76.

DALEY, B., 'The Origenism of Leontius of Byzantium', *J. Th. S.* NS 27 (1976), 333–69.

DECHOW, J. F., 'The Heresy Charges against Origen', in L. Lies (ed.), *Origeniana Quarta*, Die Referate des 4. Internationalen Origeneskongresses (Innsbruck, 2–6 Sept. 1985) (Innsbruck, 1985), 112–22.

DELEHAYE, H., *The Legends of the Saints*, 3rd edn. (London, 1962).

—— *Les Origines du culte des martyres*, SHG 20, 2nd edn. (Brussels, 1933).

—— *Les Saints stylites*, SHG 14 (Brussels, 1923).

DEVOS, P., 'Cyrille de Scythopolis: Influences littéraires—vêtement de l'Évêque de Jérusalem—Passarion et Pierre l'Ibère', *An. Boll.* 98 (1980), 25–38.

—— 'Quand Pierre l'Ibère vient-il à Jérusalem?', *An. Boll.* 86 (1968), 327–50.

DIEKAMP, F., *Die origenistischen Streitigkeiten im sechsten Jahrhundert und das fünfte allgemeine Konzil* (Münster, 1899).

DOLGER, F., 'E. Schwartz: Kyrillos von Skythopolis', *By. Z.* 40 (1940), 474–84.

DOWNEY, G., *Gaza in the Early Sixth Century* (Norman, Okla., 1963).

—— 'Imperial Records in Malalas', *Byz.* 38 (1938), 299–311.

—— 'The Perspective of the Early Church Historians', *GRBS* 6 (1965), 57–70.

DRAGUET, R., 'L'Histoire lausïaque, une œuvre écrite dans l'esprit d'Évagre', *RHE* 41 (1946), 321–64.

DRAGUET, R., 'Réminiscences de Pallade chez Cyrille de Scythopolis', *RAM* 98–100 (1948), 213–18.

DREWERY, B., 'The Condemnation of Origen: Should It be Reversed?', in R. Hanson and H. Crouzel (eds.), *Oriegeniana Tertia: The Third International Colloquium for Origen Studies*, University of Manchester, 7–11 Sept. 1981 (Rome, 1985), 271–7.

EBIED, R. Y., and WICKHAM, L. R., 'Timothy Aelurus: Against the Definition of the Council of Chalcedon', in C. Laga, J. Munitiz, and L. van Rompay (eds.), *After Chalcedon: Studies in Theology and Church History* (Louvain 1985), 115–66.

ESBROECK, M. van, 'L'Homélie de Pierre de Jérusalem et la fin de l'origénisme palestinien en 551', *Or. Chr. P.* 51 (1955), 33–59.

—— 'Les Textes littéraires sur l'Assomption avant le Xe siècle', in *Les Actes apocryphes des pères* (Geneva, 1987).

EVANS, D. B., *Leontius of Byzantium: An Origenist Christology*, DOS 13 (Washington, 1970).

FEDERLIN, J. L., 'Recherches sur les laures et monastères de la plaine de Jourdain et du désert de Jérusalem', *La Terre Sainte*, 19 (1902), 129–32, 152–6, 166–8, 181–4; 20 (1903), 117–29, 132–4, 148–50, 168–71, 180–2, 196–9, 215–18, 232–4, 263–6, 278–9, 299–301, 309–11, 328–31, 342–6, 360–2, 372–5; 21 (1904), 7–10.

FESTUGIÈRE, A.-J. *Antioch païenne et chrétienne* (Paris, 1959).

—— 'Lieux communs littéraires et thèmes de folk-lore dans l'hagiographie primitive', *W. St.* 73 (1960), 123–52.

—— *Les Moines d'orient*, 3 pts. in 7 vols. (Paris, 1961–3).

—— 'La Vie de Sabas et les tours de Syrie-Palestine', *RB* 70 (1963) 82–92.

FITZERGERALD, G. M., *Beth-Shan Excavations of 1921–1923: The Arab and Byzantine Levels*, Publications of the Palestine Section of the University of Pennsylvania (Phildaelphia, 1931).

—— *A Sixth-Century Monastery in Beth-Shan (Scythopolis)* (Philadelphia, 1939).

FLUSIN, B., *Miracle et histoire dans l'œuvre de Cyrille de Scythopolis* (Paris, 1983).

FOERSTER, G., and TSAFRIR, Y., 'Nysa-Scythopolis: A New Inscription and Titles of the City on Its Coins', *Israel Numismatic Journal* 9 (1986–7), 53–60.

FOUYAS, M., *The Person of Christ* (Addis Ababa, 1970).

FREND, W. H. C., *The Rise of the Monophysite Movement* (Cambridge, 1972).

GARITTE, G., 'La Mort de S. Jean l'Hésychaste d'après un texte géorgien inédit', *An. Boll.* 72 (1954), 75–84.

—— 'Réminiscences de la Vie d'Antoine dans Cyrille de Scythopolis', in *Silloge bizantina in onore de Silvio Giuseppe Mercati* (Rome, 1957), 117–22.

—— 'La Version géorgienne de la Vie de S. Cyriaque par Cyrille de Scythopolis', *Muséon* 75 (1962), 399–440.

—— 'La Vie géorgienne de Saint Cyriaque et son modèle arabe', *Bedi-Kartlissa* 28 (1971), 92–105.

—— 'La Vie prémetaphrastique de S. Chariton', *BIHB* 21 (1940), 5–50.

GENIER, R. P., *La Vie de S. Euthyme le Grand* (Paris, 1909).

GHEYN, J. VAN DEN, 'St Théognius, Évêque de Bételie en Palestine', *RQH* 50 (1891), 559–76.

GILL, J., 'The Life of St Stephen the Younger by Stephen the Deacon', *Or. Chr. P.* 6 (1940), 114–39.

'Glorious Beth Shean' (report prepared in consultation with the excavators), *Biblical Archeology Review* 16 (July–Aug. 1990), 17–32.

GOEMAN, M., 'Chalkedon als "Allgemeines Konzil"', in *Das Konzil von Chalkedon*, ed. A. Grillmeier and H. Bacht, 3 vols. (Würzburg, 1951–4), i. 251–89.

GOLOMB, B., and KEDAR, Y., 'Ancient Agriculture in the Galilee Mountains', *IEJ* 21 (1971), 136–40.

GOUILLARD, J., 'L'Herésie dans l'Empire Byzantin des origines au XIIe siècle', *Travaux et memoires*, 1 (1965), 299–324.

GRANT, R. M., *Eusebius as Church Historian* (Oxford, 1980).

GRAY, P. T. R., *The Defense of Chalcedon in the East* (Leiden, 1979).

GREGOIRE, H., 'La Vie anonyme de S. Gerasime', *By. Z.* 13 (1904), 114–35.

GRIFFITH, S., 'Greek into Arabic; Life and Letters in the Monasteries of Palestine in the Ninth Century: The Example of the Summa Theologiae Arabica', *Byz.* 56 (1986), 119–38.

GRILLMEIER, A., *Christ in Christian Tradition*, i. and ii. pt. 1 (London, 1965, 1987).

—— 'Eine Flucht des Eutyches nach Jerusalem', in G. Wirth (ed.), *Romanitas-Christianitas*, Untersuchungen zur Geschichte und Literatur des Romischen Kaiserzeit (Berlin, 1982), 645–53.

—— and BACHT, H. (eds.), *Das Konzil von Chalkedon*, 3 vols. (Würzburg, 1951–4).

GRUMEL, V., 'L'Auteur et la date de composition du Tropaire o monogenes', *E. Or.* 22 (1923), 398–418.

GUILLAUMONT, A., *Les 'Kephalaia Gnostica' d'Évagre le Pontique et l'histoire de l'origénisme chez les grecs et chez les syriens*, Patristica Sorbonensia, 5 (Paris, 1962).

—— *Aux origines du monachisme chrétien*, Spiritualité Orientale, 30 (Begrolle-en-Mauges, 1979).

HALKIN, F., *Bibliotheca Hagiographica Graeca* (Brussels, 1957).

HALLEUX, A. DE, *Philoxène de Mabbug* (Louvain, 1963).

HARDY, E. R., *Christian Egypt: Church and People* (New York, 1952).

—— *Christology of the Later Fathers* (London, 1964).

HARVEY, S. A., *Asceticism and Society in Crisis: John of Ephesus and the Lives of the Eastern Saints* (Berkeley, Calif., 1990).

—— 'Remembering Pain: Syriac Historiography and the Separation of the Churches', *Byz.* 58 (1988), 295–308.

HAUSHERR, I., 'Les Grands Courants de la spiritualité orientale', *Or. Chr. P.* 1 (1935), 114–38.

—— *Penthos: The Doctrine of Compunction in the Christian East*, Cistercian Studies, 53 (Kalamazoo, Mich., 1982).

HERMANN, T., 'Zur Chronologie des Kyrill von Skythopolis', *ZKG* (1926), 318–39.

HERRIN, J., *The Formation of Christendom* (Oxford, 1987).

HESSE, M., 'Miracles and the Laws of Nature', in C. F. D. Moule (eds.), *Miracles* (London, 1965), 33–42.

HEUSSI, K., *Der Ursprung des Mönchtums* (Tübingen, 1936).

HEYDOCK, G., *Der heilige Sabas und seine Reliquien* (Geisenheim, 1970).

HIRSCHFELD, Y., *Archeological Survey of Israel: Maps of Herodium Talpiot and Mar Saba* (108/2), 17–11 (Jerusalem, 1985).

—— 'Edible Wild Plants: The Secret Diet of Monks in the Judaean Desert', *Israel, Land and Nature* 16 (1990), 25–8.

—— *The Judaean Desert Monasteries in the Byzantine Period* (New Haven, Conn., 1992).

—— 'List of the Byzantine Monasteries in the Judaean Desert', in G. C. Bottini, L. Di Segni, and E. Allata (eds.), *Christian Archeology in the Holy Land: New Discoveries*, Studium Biblicum Fransciscanum Collection Maior, 36 (Jerusalem, 1990), 1–90.

—— 'Masada during the Byzantine Period: The Monastery of Marda', *Eretz Israel*, 20, 'Yadin Volume' (forthcoming).

—— 'Monastery of St Euthymius: Survey and Excavations', *ESI* 3 (1984), 80–2.

HOHLFELDER, R. L., 'A Twilight of Paganism in the Holy Land', in Hohlfelder (ed.), *City, Town and Countryside in the Early Byzantine Era* (New York, 1982), 75–113.

HOLL, K., *Enthusiasmus und Bussgewalt beim griechischen Mönchtums* (Leipzig, 1898; new edn. Hildesheim, 1969).

HOLUM, K. G., 'Caesarea and the Samaritans', in R. L. Hohlfelder (ed.), *City, Town and Countryside in the Early Byzantine Era* (New York, 1982), 65–73.

HONIGMANN, E., *Évêques et évêchés monophysites d'Asie antérieure au VIe Siècle*, CSCO Subs. 2 (Louvain, 1951).

—— 'Juvenal of Jerusalem', *DOP* 5 (1950), 211–79.

HUNT, E. D., *Holy Land Pilgrimage in the Later Roman Empire, AD 312–460* (Oxford, 1984).

INGLISIAN, V., 'Chalkedon und die armenische Kirche', in A. Grillmeier and H. Bacht (eds.), *Das Konzil von Chalkedon*, 3 vols. (Würzburg, 1951–4) ii. 361–417.

'Israel Exploration Society; 17th Annual Convention: The Valley of Beth-Shan', *IEJ* 10 (1960), 126–7, 263–4; 11 (1961), 198–201.

JAMES, F., 'Beth-Shean', in M. Avi-Yonah (ed.), *Encyclopedia of Archeological Excavations in the Holy Land*, 3 vols. (London, 1975–8), i. 207–25.

JONES, A. H. M., *The Later Roman Empire*, 4 vols. (Oxford, 1964).

—— 'Were Ancient Heresies National or Social Movements in Disguise?', *J. Th. S.* NS 10 (1959), 280–98.

KEDAR, Y., 'Ancient Agriculture at Shivtah in the Negev', *IEJ* 7 (1957), 178–9.

KEE, H. C., *Miracle in the Early Christian World* (New Haven, Conn., 1983).

KELLY, J. N. D., *Jerome: His Life, Writings and Controversies* (London, 1975).

KHITROVO, B. DE *Itinéraires russes en orient* (Geneva, 1889).

KIRCHEMEYER, J., 'Le Moine Marcien (de Bethléem)', TU 80 (1962), 341–59.

KIRK, G. E., 'The Negev or the Southern Desert of Palestine', *PEFQ St.* (1941), 57–71.

KURTZ, E., 'Review of A. Dmitrijevskij, *Die Klosterregeln des hl. Sabas* (Kiev, 1890)' *By. Z.* 3 (1894), 167–70.

LADEUZE, P., *Étude sur le cénobitisme pakhomien pendant le IVe siècle et la première moitié du Ve siècle* (Louvain, 1898; new edn. Frankfurt, 1961).

LAMPE, G. W. H., 'Miracles and Early Christian Apologetic', in C. F. D. Moule (ed.), *Miracles* (London, 1965), 203–18.

LANG, D. M., 'Peter the Iberian and his Biographers', *JEH* 2 (1951), 158–68.

LASSUS, J., *Sanctuaires chrétiens de Syrie* (Paris, 1947).

LEBON, J., 'La Christologie du monophysisme syrien', in A. Grillmeier and H. Bacht (eds.), *Das Konzil von Chalkedon*, 3 vols. (Würzburg, 1951–4), i. 425–580.

LEVINE, L., *Caesarea under Roman Rule*, Studies in Judaism and Late Antiquity, 7 (Leiden, 1975).

LEVI-STRAUSS, C., *Anthropologie structurale*, 2nd edn. (Paris, 1974).

LEVY, S., 'The Ancient Synagogue at Ma'on', in *Roman Frontier Studies*, Proceedings of the 7th International Congress, Tel Aviv (Tel Aviv, 1971).

LIETZMANN, H., *A History of the Early Church* (London, 1937–51).

LIFSHITZ, B., *Donateurs et fondateurs dans les synagogues juives* (Paris, 1967).

—— 'Scythopolis, l'histoire, les institutions et les cultes de la ville à l'époque hellénistique et imperiale', in *ANRW* 2/8 (Berlin, 1977), 262–94.

LOOFS. F., *Leontius von Byzanz und die gleichnamigen Schriftsteller der griechischen Kirche*, TU 3, (Leipzig, 1887).

MAGOULIAS, H. J., 'The Lives of the Saints as Sources of Data for the History of Byzantine Medicine in the Sixth and Seventh Centuries', *By. Z.* 57 (1964), 127–50.

MALONE, E. E., 'The Monk and the Martyr', *St. Ans.* 38 (1956), 201–28.

MARAVAL, P., *Lieux saints et pèlerinages d'orient* (Paris, 1985).

MARCOFF, M., and CHITTY, D. J., 'Notes on Monastic Research in the Judaean Wilderness', *PEFQ St.* (1929), 167–78.

MARKUS, R. A., 'Church History and the Early Church Historians', in D. H. Baker (ed.), *The Materials, Sources and Methods of Ecclesiastical History*, SCH 11 (Oxford, 1975).

MARROU, H.-I., *Histoire de l'éducation dans l'antiquité*, 2nd edn. (Paris, 1948).

MASPERO, J., *Histoire des Patriarches d'Alexandrie depuis la mort de l'Empereur Anastase jusqu'à la reconciliation des églises jacobites* (Paris, 1923).

MEINARDUS, O., 'Notes on the laurae and monasteries of the Wilderness of Judaea', *SBFLA* 15 (1964–5), 220–50; 16 (1965–6), 328–56; 19 (1969), 305–27.

MERCENIER, E., 'Le Monastère de Mar Saba', *Iren.* 20 (1947), 283–97.

MEYENDORFF, J., *Christ in Eastern Christian Thought*, 2nd edn. (New York, 1975).

—— *Imperial Unity and Christian Divisions* (New York, 1989).

MILIK, J., 'The Monastery of Castellion', *RB* 42 (1961), 21–7.

—— 'Notes d'épigraphie et de topographie Palestiniennes', *RB* 66 (1959), 550–75.

—— 'La Topographie de Jérusalem vers la fin de l'époque Byzantine', *MUSJ* 37 (1960–1), 127–89.

MOELLER, C., 'Le Chalcédonisme et le néo-chalcédonisme en Orient de 451 à la fin du VIe siècle', in A. Grillmeier and H. Bacht (eds.), *Das Konzil von Chalkedon*, 3 vols. (Würzburg, 1951–4), i. 637–720.

MOMIGLIANO, A., 'Pagan and Christian Historiography in the Fourth Century AD', in A. Momigliano (ed.), *Paganism and Christianity in the Fourth Century* (Oxford, 1963).

MOSSHAMMER, A. A., *The Chronicle of Eusebius and Greek Chronographical Tradition* (Lewisburg, NJ, 1979).

MURPHY-O'CONNOR, J., *The Holy Land* (Oxford, 1980).

NAU, F., 'Deux épisodes de l'histoire juive sous Théodose II', *REJ* 83/4 (1927), 184–206.

NESBITT, J. W., 'A Geographical and Chronological Guide to Greek Saints' Lives', *Or. Chr. P.* 35 (1969), 443.

NOONAN, F., 'Political Thought in Byzantine Palestinian Hagiography', dissertation, University of Chicago, 1975.

OAKESHOTT, W. F., *The Mosaics of Rome* (London, 1967).

OSTROGORSKY, G., *History of the Byzantine State*, 2nd edn. (New Brunswick, 1960).

OVADIAH, A., *A Corpus of the Byzantine Churches in the Holy Land*, Theophaneia, 22 (Bonn, 1970).

—— 'Greek Cults in Beth-Shan/Skythopolis in the Hellenistic and Roman Periods', *Eretz Israel*, 12 (1975), 116–24, in Hebrew with English summary in *SEG* 26 (1976), 1906.

—— and DE SILVA, G., 'Supplementum to the Corpus of Byzantine Churches in the Holy Land, 1. Newly Discovered Churches; 2. Updated Material of Churches Discussed in the Corpus', *Levant* 13 (1981), 200–61; 14 (1982), 122–70.

PATLAGEAN, E., 'Ancienne hagiographie byzantine et histoire sociale', *Annales esc.* 1 (1968), 106–26.

—— 'L'Histoire de la femme deguisée en moine et l'évolution de la sainteté feminine à Byzance', *St. M.* 3rd ser. 17 (1976), 597–623.

—— 'La Pauvreté à Byzance au temps de Justinien: Les Origines d'un modèle politique', in *Études sur l'histoire de la pauvreté, Moyen-Age–XVI siècle*, i. *Sous la direction de Michel Mollat* (Paris, 1974), 59–81.

—— *Pauvreté économique et pauvreté sociale à Byzance, 4e–7e siècles* (Paris, 1977).

PATRICH, J., 'Hermitages of the Great Laura of St Sabas', in D. Jacoby and Y. Tsafrir (eds.), *Jews, Samaritans, and Christians in Byzantine Palestine* (Jerusalem, 1988), 131–68 (in Hebrew).

PATTENDEN, P., 'The Text of the Pratum Spirituale', *J. Th. S.* NS 26 (1975), 38–54.

PEETERS, P., *Le Tréfonds oriental de l'hagiographie byzantine* (Brussels, 1950).

PERRONE, L., *La chiesa di Palestina e le controversie cristologiche* (Brescia, 1980).

PETERSEN, J. M., *The Dialogues of Gregory the Great in their Late Antique Cultural Background* (Toronto, 1984).

PHILIPSBORN, A., 'Der Fortschritt in der Entwicklung des Byzantinischen Krankenhauswesens', *By. Z.* 54 (1961), 338–65.

REES, S., 'The Literary Activity of Leontius of Byzantium', *J. Th. S.* NS 19 (1968), 229–42.

REGNAULT, L., 'Les Apotegmes des pères en Palestine aux Ve–VIe siècles', *Iren.* 54 (1981), 320–30.

REMUS, H., *Pagan–Christian Conflict over Miracle in the Second Century*, Patristic Monograph Series, 10 (Cambridge, Mass., 1983).

RICHARD, M., 'Léonce de Byzance, était-il Origéniste?', *RE Byz.* 5 (1947), 31–66.

—— 'Léonce de Jérusalem et Léonce de Byzance', *MSR* 1 (1944), 35–88.

—— 'Le Traité *De Sectis* et Léonce de Byzance', *RHE* 35 (1939), 695–723.

RIESS, R. DE, *Atlas Scripturae Sacrae*, 2nd edn. (Freiburg-im-Breisgau, 1906).

RINGEL, J., *Césarée de Palestine* (Paris, 1975).

RODINSON, M., 'De l'archéologie à la sociologie historique: Notes méthodologiques sur le dernier ouvrage de G. Tchalenko', *Syria*, 38 (1961), 170–200.

ROEY, A. VAN, 'Remarques sur le moine Marcien', *TU* 115 (1975), 160–77.

Roman Frontier Studies, 1967, Proceedings of the 7th International Congress, Tel Aviv (Tel Aviv, 1971).

ROUSSEAU, P., *Ascetics, Authority, and the Church in the Age of Jerome* (Oxford, 1978).

—— *Pachomius: The Making of a Community in Fourth-Century Egypt* (Berkeley, Calif., 1985).

ROWE, A., *Beth-Shan; Topography and History* (Philadelphia, 1930).

RYDEN, L., 'The Holy Fool', in S. Hackel (ed.), *The Byzantine Saint*, University of Birmingham, 14th Spring Symposium of Byzantine Studies (London, 1981), 106–13.

SAINTE-CROIX, G. E. B. DE, *The Class Struggle in the Ancient World* (London, 1981).

SAUVAGET, J., 'Les Ghassanides et Sergiopolis', *Byz.* 14 (1939), 11–130.

SCHNEIDER, A.-M., 'Das Kloster der Theotokos zu Choziba im Wadi el Kelt', *RQ* 39 (1931), 297–332.

SCHONBORN, C. VON, *Sophrone de Jérusalem*, Théologie Historique, 20 (Paris, 1972).

SCHWARTZ, E., *Codex Vaticanus Gr.* 1431 (Munich, 1927).

—— *Kyrillos von Skythopolis*, TU 49/2 (Leipzig, 1939).

—— *Publizistische Sammlungen zum acacianischen Schisma*, Abhandlungen der Bayerischen Akademie der Wissenschaften, Philosophisch-historische Abteilung, NS 10 (Munich, 1934).

SELLERS, R. V., *The Council of Chalcedon* (London, 1961).

SHAHID, I., *Byzantium and the Arabs in the Fifth Century* (Washington, DC, 1989).

SPERBER, D., *Roman Palestine, 200–400: The Land* (Ramat-Gan, 1978).

STANCLIFFE, C., *St Martin and his Hagiographer: History and Miracle in Sulpicius Severus* (Oxford, 1983).

STEIN, E., 'Cyrille de Scythopolis à propos de la nouvelle édition de ses œuvres', *An. Boll.* 62 (1944), 169–86.

—— *L'Histoire du Bas-Empire*, 2 vols. (Paris, 1949–59).

SUCHLA, B. R., 'Die sogenannten Maximus-Scholien des Corpus Dionysiacum Areopagiticum', *NAWG* (1980), 3.

SUSSMANN, J., 'The Inscription in the Synagogue at Rehob', in L. Levine (ed.), *Ancient Synagogues Revealed* (Jerusalem, 1982), 146–53.

TCHALENKO, G., *Villages antiques de la Syrie du Nord (le Massif de Belus) à l'époque romaine*, 3 vols. (Paris, 1953–8).

Theologisches Wörterbuch zum Neuen Testament, ed. G. Kittel, 9 vols. (Stuttgart, 1933).

THOMSEN, P., 'Kyrillos von Skythopolis', *OLZ* 43 (1940), 457–63.

—— 'Die römischen Meilensteine der Provinzen Syria, Arabia und Palästina', *ZDPV* 40 (1917), 1–103.

TRIMINGHAM, J. S., *Christianity among the Arabs in Pre-Islamic Times* (London, 1979).

TSAFERIS, V., 'The Synagogue at Ma'oz Hayim', in L. Levine (ed.), *Ancient Synagogues Revealed* (Jerusalem, 1982), 86–9.

TSAFRIR, Y., 'Further Evidence of the Cult of Zeus Akraios at Beth Shean (Scythopolis)', *IEJ* 39 (1989), 76–8.

TSATSOS, J., *The Empress Athenais: Eudokia* (Brookline, Mass., 1977).

UNNIK, W. C. VAN, 'The Christian's Freedom of Speech in the New Testament', *BJRL* 44 (1961–2), 466–88.

USENER, H., *Der heilige Theodosius* (Leipzig, 1890).

—— *Der heilige Tychon* (Leipzig, 1907).

VAILHÉ, S, 'Les Écrivains de Mar Saba', *E. Or.* 2 (1899), 1–11, 33–47.

—— 'Jean Mosch', *E. Or.* 5 (1902), 108.

—— 'Les Laures de saint Gérasime et de Calamon', *E. Or.* 2 (1899), 106–19.

—— 'Le Monastère de saint Théoctiste (411) et l'évêché des Paremboles (425)', *ROC* 1st ser., 3 (1898), 58.

—— 'Les Premières Monastères de la Palestine', *BESS* 3 (1897–8), 39–58, 209–25, 334–56; 4 (1898–9), 193–211.

—— 'Répertoire alphabétique des monastères de la Palestine', *ROC* 1st ser., 4 (1899), 512–42; 5 (1900), 19–48, 272–92.

—— 'Les Saints Kozibites', *E. Or.* 1 (1897–8), 228–33.

VASILIEV, A., *Justin I* (Cambridge, Mass., 1950).

VEILLEUX, A., *Pachomian Koinonia* i, Cistercian Studies, 45 (Kalamazoo, Mich., 1980).

VITTO, F., 'The Synagogue at Rehob', in L. Levine (ed.), *Ancient Synagogues Revealed* (Jerusalem, 1982), 90–4.

VÖÖBUS, A., *A History of Asceticism in the Syrian Orient*, CSCO 184, subs. 14, 17, 2 vols. (Louvain, 1958, 1960).

WALKER, P. W. L., *Holy City, Holy Places?* (Oxford, 1990).

WARD, B., *Harlots of the Desert* (Oxford, 1987).

—— Introduction to N. Russell (trans.), *The Lives of the Desert Fathers* (London, 1980), 3–46.

—— *Miracles and the Medieval Mind* (London, 1982).

—— 'Signs and Wonders: Miracles in the Desert Tradition', in E. A. Livingstone (ed.), *Studia Patristica* (Oxford, 1982), 539–42.

WHITBY, M., *The Emperor Maurice and his Historian* (Oxford, 1988).

WILES, M. F., 'Miracles in the Early Church', in C. F. D. Moule (ed.), *Miracles* (London, 1965), 219–34.

WILKINSON, J., with HILL, J., and RYAN, W. F., *Jerusalem Pilgrimage 1099–1185* (London, 1988).

WILLIAMS, R., *The Wound of Knowledge* (London, 1979).

WOODWARD, E. L., *Christianity and Nationalism in the Later Roman Empire* (London, 1916).

WRIGHT, G. E. H., 'The Archeological Remains of el-Mird in the Wilderness of Judaea', *RB* 42 (1961), 1–21.

ZOHARY, N., *Plants of the Bible* (Cambridge, 1982).

ZORI, N., 'The House of Kyrios Leontis at Beth-Shan', *IEJ* 16 (1966), 123–34.

INDEX